Advertising on Trial

THE HISTORY OF COMMUNICATION

Robert W. McChesney and
John C. Nerone, Editors

*A list of books in the series appears
at the end of this book.*

Advertising on Trial

CONSUMER ACTIVISM AND
CORPORATE PUBLIC RELATIONS
IN THE 1930S

INGER L. STOLE

UNIVERSITY OF ILLINOIS PRESS

Urbana and Chicago

Library of Congress Cataloging-in-Publication Data
Stole, Inger L.
Advertising on trial : consumer activism and corporate
public relations in the 1930s / Inger L. Stole.
p.   cm. — (The history of communication)
Includes bibliographical references and index.
ISBN-13: 978-0-252-03059-8 (cloth : alk. paper)
ISBN-10: 0-252-03059-1 (cloth : alk. paper)
ISBN-13: 978-0-252-07299-4 (paper : alk. paper)
ISBN-10: 0-252-07299-5 (paper : alk. paper)
1. Advertising—United States—History.
2. Corporations—Public relations—United States.
I. Title. II. Series.
HF5813.U6S77   2006
659.1'0973'09043—dc22   2005017226

Contents

Preface   vii

1. The Rise of a Corporate Culture:
   Early Consumer Response   1

2. Advertising Challenged: The Creation
   of Consumers' Research Inc. and the
   Rise of the 1930s Consumer Movement   21

3. The Drive for Federal Advertising
   Regulation, 1933–35   49

4. A Consumer Movement Divided:
   The Birth of Consumers Union
   of the United States Inc.   80

5. Defining the Consumer Agenda:
   The Business Community Joins the Fray   106

6. Legislative Closure: The Wheeler-Lea Amendment   138

7. Red-Baiting the Consumer Movement   159

   Epilogue   185

   Appendix A: Key Players   199

   Appendix B: Legislative Developments, 1933–38   205

   Notes   209

   Index   279

Preface

From its inception in the mid-nineteenth century, national advertising has evolved into a massive enterprise. In 2003, U.S. advertisers spent an estimated $236 billion, and today some scholars conclude that each day the average American is exposed to several thousand advertisements. By all accounts, advertising has saturated every nook and cranny of our lived experiences, bringing enormous social, cultural, and economic implications for this republic. Our media system is drenched in advertising and commercialism, yet these profit-driven enterprises are problematic for the democratic functioning of society and, some argue, for human happiness.[1]

And some Americans are unhappy. A 2004 study commissioned by the American Association of Advertising Agencies revealed a significant level of public dissatisfaction with advertising. Sixty-five percent of the respondents thought they were "constantly bombarded with too much advertising," 61 percent believed that advertising and marketing levels were "out of control," and 60 percent of those interviewed said they currently held a more negative opinion of advertising than they had a few years ago. Nearly half the respondents reported that the excess advertising and marketing detracted from "the experience of everyday life," and 33 percent would be willing to settle for a slightly lower standard of living if this meant having a society devoid of marketing and advertising.[2]

In view of this apparent public antipathy, one might expect advertising to be scrutinized and debated just like our other major institutions are examined. This is rarely the case, however. To the extent that advertising is analyzed, discussions tend to focus on its excesses (its ability to project a certain set of images and values) and not on its shortcomings (its inability, for example, to provide consumers with facts and information or, despite all its flag-waving patriotism, to serve as a truly democratizing force). Although advertisers countenance certain forms of symbolic criticism of their methods, such as the "inappropriateness" or anticipated ill effects of a particular ad or campaign, they will rarely, if ever, encourage a dialogue about advertising's role in the economy or its power to influence cultural and social institutions. Interestingly enough, at the same time that advertising has increased its social and cultural impact, legitimate discussions regarding its exact function and overall merit have dwindled to the point to which they are virtually nonexistent.

In this environment most Americans logically assume that advertising is a given, that it is a natural institution built into the American experience, much like free enterprise and its governing institutions. Nothing of the sort is true. Modern advertising is a relatively recent phenomenon resulting from dramatic changes in capitalism that crystallized approximately one century ago, and extensive government policies were initiated to protect and promote it. When it matured in the early twentieth century, advertising was met with ferocious political opposition, mostly in the form of a militant consumer movement arguing that advertising was business propaganda that undermined consumers' ability to make wise choices in the market and citizens' ability to live in a healthy industrial and civic environment. In the 1930s these consumer activists organized popular support for their campaign to significantly regulate and radically transform advertising into a medium that provided legitimate product information. The advertising industry responded as if its survival was in jeopardy and deployed a wide range of strategies aimed at removing criticism from the public agenda. Indeed, the advertising industry helped establish many techniques that would become staples of public relations.

In this book I chronicle the struggle between consumer activists and the advertising industry over the role advertising would play in our economy and culture. This is a book, then, not really about advertising as a cultural phenomenon so much as it is about the political debate surrounding advertising as an institution in U.S. society. In the 1930s, for the only time in U.S. history, a public debate erupted and persisted over how best to craft federal regulation to control advertising. At this moment activists had a real chance to reroute advertising and commercialism from their well-established course, a course that has led at least one observer to characterize twentieth-century U.S. life as "the age of advertising."[3] When consumers lost that legislative battle with the passage of the Wheeler-Lea Amendment in 1938, advertising never again faced a direct challenge to its legitimacy. Soon thereafter, with tremendous encouragement by the advertising industry's public relations campaigns, advertising was regarded as a natural American institution. Once that status was reached, the threat of a popular political revolt against it weakened and such a move became almost unthinkable. Dissatisfaction with advertising's excesses remained, but lost was any sense that an informed and aroused citizenry could change this institution's character.

This story strongly resembles the struggle over U.S. broadcasting regulation in the early 1930s and its eventual outcome. The media scholar Robert W. McChesney has chronicled how educators and nonprofit groups fought a losing battle against powerful commercial interests that were determined to turn radio into a purely commercial medium. Although public dissatisfaction with the resulting Communications Act of 1934 clearly existed, broadcasters and other commercial interests managed, until very recently, to marginalize such dissent and prevent it from reaching the legislative level.[4]

Although these related conflicts may seem like ancient history, they are every bit as important today as they were in the 1930s; arguably they have increased in importance. Moreover, these consumer advocates understood something we have since forgotten: In our self-governing society the role and nature of advertising and commercialism should be determined by the citizenry. To remove these issues from legitimate political debate diminishes the range and quality of democratic self-governance; indeed, it undermines it. So I write this book to provide a better understanding of why the battle over advertising's role in the 1930s assumed the form it did and what lessons we can draw from it as we face similar questions in our own times. In the process, I draw on scholarly work from several different disciplines, including accounts from advertising and public relations historians and the works of scholars who have documented the history of U.S. consumer activism and regulatory strategies. What sets this book apart is that it explores the 1930s consumer movement through the lens of its demand for advertising reform—a challenge with radical ramifications for the advertising industry and the capitalist economy it supported.

By highlighting this issue, I combine the interdisciplinary accounts of advertising, public relations, consumer activism, and regulatory history with the consumer movement's key demand. My story exposes the advertising industry's view of consumer activism and shows the role corporate public relations played in securing a victory over consumers.

Modern corporate advertising has existed since the American Civil War, and initially, at least, it seemed like a benign way to help local manufacturers reach a national audience and spread the word about their products. Useful in this regard was an increasingly commercial mass media industry that catered to advertisers' needs. Before long a large segment of U.S. newspapers and magazines depended on advertising revenue to stay in business. Some advertisers, in turn, used this as an opportunity to pressure mass media into compliance with agendas that benefited business. The development was gradual, but by the early 1920s commercial values had permeated most aspects of society. The mass media, leisure activities, and even to some extent education all were becoming dependent upon, and influenced by, advertising. For the average person, advertising soon became the most important link to the many consumer products on the market. Because advertising was an unregulated industry, however, manufacturers were allowed to make wild promises and exaggerated claims about their products.

If such advertising practices had been limited to small, obscure manufacturers, the public on the whole may not have been affected. Unfortunately, most advertisers, including the largest companies, engaged in such practices. By the 1930s most national advertisers participated in what are commonly referred to as oligopolistic markets. In such markets a handful of advertisers make largely interchangeable products and sell them for approximately the same price. What sets the competitors apart is their advertising and the images they create for their products through this promotional device. This context breeds advertising of trivial or dubious content because telling the truth would be commercially counterproductive. This conflict between truth in advertising and financial viability explains why advertising has always been, and will always be, a controversial undertaking.

But with a healthy consumer movement in place, the advertising industry is vulnerable. Such a movement opens up a dialogue on advertising's questionable practices and politicizes the laws that make advertising possible. Because the consumer movement is charged with linking political concerns about advertising with broader and complementary social and political problems, any study of the advertising debate is invariably a study of the consumer movement's relationship with advertising. During the twentieth century Americans witnessed the rise of four distinct, but by no means unrelated, consumer movements and the demise of three of them. Each expressed a different stance toward advertising, but all had related concerns. The first wave arose at the turn of the twentieth century, during what is commonly referred to as the Progressive Era; the second emerged in reaction to increased commercialization in the late 1920s and the 1930s; the third erupted as a demand for corporate accountability in the 1960s; and the fourth evolved in the late

1990s and linked its concerns to a set of global issues. The Progressive Era consumer activists primarily concerned themselves with production and labeling issues, and the second wave of consumer activism expanded on these issues but also articulated its own set of demands in reaction to increased commercialization and advertising's shortcomings.

Although the consumer movement of the 1930s has been at the center of some scholarly studies, few have discussed the movement in terms of an economic, and ultimately political, threat to the capitalist system. This was a far more radical consumer movement than what would evolve in later decades. Its most militant wing attempted to link middle-class and working-class concerns and tie consumers to producers. For mainstream business interests and political conservatives, this consumer movement was arguably as much of a threat to their interests as was the labor movement. Advertising was the number one concern of the 1930s consumer movement. Insisting that advertising should provide consumers with more facts and information, consumer advocates told advertisers that unless they complied, strict federal regulation would be on the agenda.

Concerned that the consumer movement would be able to build substantial support for its demands, the advertising industry adopted a wide range of public relations strategies. The first goal was to make sure that any legislative measures were as gentle on advertising as possible. The second was to marginalize the consumer movement's influence and thereby minimize the chance of similar future attacks. These PR approaches, some based on techniques developed by press agents and masterminded by Edward L. Bernays, helped the industry develop its own strategy and turn a problematic situation to its own advantage.[5]

Third-party techniques emerged as a popular solution. These practices included creating and funding neutral-sounding groups to further a political agenda. For example, to diminish the public influence of grassroots consumer groups, representatives from the advertising industry started, and financially supported, similar-sounding organizations to sway the public to its own interpretation of the issues. The rise of *industry front groups,* staffed with publicly known or highly accomplished individuals ready to advocate on the side of business, added to the growing PR arsenal, as did *lobbying,* the practice of having a third party make contacts with key lawmakers to sway the legislative process. Yet another technique was *divide and conquer.* This strategy played on conflicts or differences within an opposing group, and advertisers looked for ways to split it by trying to form coalitions with elements posing the least threat. The advertising industry's attempts to align with mainstream consumer groups to marginalize the more militant segments of the movement demonstrate this strategy.[6] The advertising industry's PR apparatus also included supplying schools and institutions of higher learning with commercially sponsored educational material, creating bureaus to disseminate information, and furnishing public speakers to interested groups. To influence the public's perception of the consumer movement and its demands, the industry also did not shy away from using the mass media's dependence on advertising as leverage to gain favorable treatment in the press.

Although the advertising industry did its best to fight radical advertising reform, what transpired was not simply a battle of good consumer advocates versus evil and greedy advertisers. Ideological differences and professional jealousy among activists created a situation that somewhat unexpectedly played into the advertising industry's hands. The end results of the 1930s quest to reform advertising were a severely fractured consumer movement, a reaffirmed advertising industry, and an advertising regulatory law that basically sanctioned the very practices it was initially designed to prevent.

The central focus in this book is on the range of negotiations between what I loosely refer to as the consumer movement and the advertising industry. Both terms deserve more accurate definitions. With the consumer movement, I refer to a host of liberal, even radical, groups influenced by consumer advocacy books and the formation of Consumers' Research in the late 1920s. It includes the many professional women's organizations with an interest in consumer issues as well as Consumers Union, the pro-union society born of a labor strike at Consumers' Research in 1935. Although varied in their approach, these groups were unified in their self-declared intention to advocate on consumers' behalf.[7] Among the many consumer organizations, however, Consumers' Research and Consumers Union led the attack on advertising, headed the fight for federal regulation, and, naturally, most often felt the advertising industry's wrath. More than any of the many other consumer groups, they were instrumental in putting advertising on trial.

With the advertising industry or community, I refer not to advertisements or advertising copywriters. Although the advertising industry consists of three major components—advertisers, advertising agencies, and the major media that carry advertising—my main focus is on the first two groups because the advertising-supported mass media tend to have their own distinct agenda and their own PR or regulatory issues with which to contend. The major national advertisers—also referred to as business or the business community throughout the book—and advertising agencies—organized in the form of a few national trade organizations, such as the Association of National Advertisers, the American Federation of Advertisers, and the American Association of Advertising Agencies—were left to articulate and deploy a political strategy that dealt directly with protecting and promoting advertising's role in the political economy.

Although I examine the PR activities of the advertising industry, it should be noted that advertising and public relations are very distinct enterprises. Both do tend to serve large corporate clients, but whereas advertising agents create and place advertising to improve sales of their clients' products, PR agents seek free and favorable publicity for their clients. In sharp contrast to advertising, which is public and highly visible, the best PR strategies are invisible to the public, even though these campaigns sometimes employ flashy techniques. Unlike advertising, which is meant to cause a direct, immediate response (e.g., the purchase of a particular soap, cereal, or shampoo) and therefore protect the client's monetary fortunes, PR is designed to protect the client's political fortunes. Successful PR must first move public opinion in a direction more favorable to the client and then (using roused public opinion if necessary or if possible) exert pressure on lawmakers and regulators to better serve and acknowledge the client's needs. In this sense, PR is closely related to what is traditionally called political lobbying.

The basic problem facing the advertising industry in the 1930s was that it had no valid response to the consumer movement's criticism. After all, by its very nature advertising did not need or even want to convey reliable information; in oligopolistic markets such information was usually counterproductive, a point Thorstein Veblen had established by the 1920s. Most economists of the time, to the extent that they studied the matter, regarded advertising at best as a noncompetitive institution and at worst one that promoted monopoly.[8] The industry's lack of a ready-made defense for advertising's existence encouraged, even necessitated, the use of public relations. The industry had to eliminate or corrupt any possibility of public or congressional debate about advertising's actual role in the political economy, replacing it instead with a highly sanitized vision of advertising that was carefully cloaked in the mythology of competitive free market capitalism, political democracy, and Americanism.

The industry's ability to wage such a counterattack resulted from the growth of a powerful corporate culture in the latter part of the nineteenth century. In chapter 1 I explore some of the major social and cultural implications of this trend and chronicle the rise of national advertising, the birth of corporate public relations, and the subsequent shift in people's buying habits. Products that only a few years earlier had been made by hand were being produced in factories where individual consumers had little influence over production. Not surprisingly, then, the rallying point for what is frequently referred to as the first wave of consumer activism in the United States during the Progressive Era was for regulation of corporate conduct, improved sanitation, and better factory working conditions.

By the late 1920s advertising had become the key means of communication between manufacturers and their consumers, but oligopolistic markets encouraged ads that stressed images and slogans over information. The consumer movement demanded advertising that guided consumers in the marketplace rather than confused or defrauded them. In chapter 2 I review the emergence of the second wave of consumer activism during this period with Consumers' Research at its forefront. I also explore the somewhat complex relationships between organized consumers, the Franklin Delano Roosevelt administration's interest in consumer issues, and the advertising industry's reaction to the new burst of consumer activism.

In response, the industry initially renewed efforts at self-regulation. Because it failed to address the consumer movement's concerns, however, considerable momentum had built to revise the Federal Food and Drugs Act of 1906 and include advertising regulation. Chapter 3 chronicles the debate over proposed legislative measures and demonstrates how the advertising industry, the consumer movement, and various politicians and government officials negotiated a series of amendments and changes between 1933 and 1935. Realizing that its fate depended on securing a favorable outcome, the advertising industry devoted its maximum resources and attention to defeating—or at least hobbling—this legislation.

In chapter 4 I explore the consumer movement in more detail, focusing on the strike over labor conditions at Consumers' Research and a split that resulted in the creation of Consumers Union. The rupture not only suggested that the consumer movement was less than unified; it also provided the advertising industry with an opportunity to develop its own form of consumer education designed to overwhelm and eventually undermine the original grassroots efforts.

Chapter 5 elaborates on the advertising industry's plan to undermine the public's confidence in the consumer movement through third-party or industry front groups. Few strategies were off-limits as advertisers, fighting the consumer movement's presence in schools and institutions of higher learning, devised educational tools to secure a pro-advertising presence in the nation's classrooms.

In chapter 6 I chart the end of the legislative debate over federal regulation of advertising that resulted in the 1938 Wheeler-Lea Amendment to the Federal Trade Commission Act and some of its practical implications. Largely because of corporate pressure, each new proposed bill typically provided less consumer protection than the previous one had. This chapter outlines some of the late-stage negotiations and illustrates how most demands for consumer protection drawn up in the original legislation were stricken from the Wheeler-Lea Amendment.

The utmost test of the advertising industry's ability to disarm the most dangerous threats from the consumer movement came in late 1939 when right-wing political forces accused a host of consumer groups of engaging in un-American behavior. In chapter 7 I probe the Dies Committee—a forerunner of the House Un-American Activities Committee—and the motivation behind its attack on left-leaning consumer groups, including Consumers Union. Although this strategy for discrediting the movement did not succeed, this outcome suggests how mainstream consumer issues had become and attests to how handily the advertising industry had dominated the consumer agenda. And although even most critics did not believe that the consumer movement was Communist-inspired, the newly subdued activists also could not have much impact on the status quo.

As the battle over advertising's federal regulation was lost to business interests and the country moved toward war, further legislative control of the industry appeared off-limits. Although the third wave of consumer advocacy sweeping the country in the 1960s posed some radical demands for corporate accountability to the public, advertising reform was not among them. But, as the epilogue suggests, the story of failed consumer activism is not without a silver lining. Bombarded with advertising from all angles, people are slowly realizing the costs of living in a hypercommercial society and are once again eyeing systemic change as a possible option. Thus, the aim of this book is not only to reopen a forgotten chapter in U.S. history but also to connect a past struggle with modern concerns and possibilities.

Acknowledgments

I could not have written *Advertising on Trial* without support from a long list of people. My first thanks goes to my dissertation committee at the University of Wisconsin–Madison where my advisor James L. Baughman and committee members Ivan Preston and Stephen Vaughn provided help, guidance, and encouragement. In Madison I also benefited from working with Paul S. Boyer, Julie D'Acci, and Lewis A. Friedland. I owe a world of thanks to Rima Apple, who took an early interest in my work. Her encouragement meant more than she might imagine.

Among my colleagues at the University of Illinois, I would particularly like to thank like to thank Susan G. Davis and Dan Schiller for their continuous support and Daniel Thomas Cook for his willingness to listen and provide help where needed. I am also indebted to Vivek Chibber who read a very early version of this manuscript and offered excellent advice. Thanks also to Mark Crispin Miller, Chris Hoofnagle at the Electronic Privacy Information Center (EPIC) and Carrie McLaren (of *Stay Free!* fame).

At the University of Illinois Press I have had the great fortune of working with Kerry Callahan and Rebecca Crist. Their professionalism has made the process of preparing the book manuscript for publication much easier than it might otherwise have been.

While writing *Advertising on Trial* I have had the good fortune of working with dedicated archivists across the country. In particular, I would like to thank David Kuzma and Erica Gardner at the Rutgers State University Archives and Special Collections for their help with the Consumer's Research collection and for obtaining many of the illustrations included in this book. Edythe Rosenblatt at the Brooklyn College Library Archives and Special Collections and the staff and archivists at Consumers Union were also helpful indeed.

I would also like to thank Stuart Calderwood, Paul Haas, Rebecca Livesay, Molly C. Niesen and Becky Standard for their help in bringing the manuscript to completion. Thanks also to Anne Mork, Pat Dibiase, Liv Hege Stole, Sandra Hammond and Tracy L. Bovee for their help, support and friendship and to my wonderful daughters Amy and Lucy for being who they are and for inspiring me in ways they may not think possible.

Without Bob McChesney's encouragement, patience and willingness to read and comment upon endless drafts, it would have taken me much longer to write this book and the end result would have suffered. It is with all my love and gratitude that I dedicate this book to Bob.

1

The Rise of a Corporate Culture: Early Consumer Response

The end of the Civil War heralded a new industrial era in the United States. By the mid-nineteenth century the Industrial Revolution, already a century in the making, was gaining strength and momentum. Some technological innovations spurred more efficient factory production whereas others, such as the railroad, steamboat, and telegraph, allowed for easier transportation and communication that, in turn, facilitated changes with large social, cultural, and economic ramifications. As the number of factories increased, immigrants and native-born Americans flocked to industrial centers in search of work. U.S. cities grew in direct proportion. Between 1880 and 1890, for example, Chicago's population doubled. Other cities experienced tremendous growth as well. Detroit, Milwaukee, and Cleveland were among the cities to witness a population increase of more than 60 percent, and Minneapolis–St. Paul saw its population triple.[1]

Technological innovations, combined with the massive influx of immigrant workers to America's burgeoning industrial centers, contributed to a record production of goods in the years immediately following the American Civil War. Increasingly sophisticated machinery enabled large factories to mass-produce items that only a few years earlier had required labor-intensive processes at home. The result was a torrent of well-made, lower-priced goods flowing into shops, stores, and, eventually, the homes of people. By the turn of the century men and women alike came to rely on mass production to fill their product needs, and Americans began to think of themselves as consumers. Commercialization had so infiltrated U.S. life that corporate influence had grown quite significant.

This power, however, was not absolute or ironclad, and by the early twentieth century a sizable group within the middle-class population attempted to lessen corporations' might. Commonly referred to as the Progressive movement, these reformers did not want to do away with big business altogether but rather sought to pass laws and regulations that would make it more accountable to the citizenry. As people adjusted to their new role as consumers, one large legislative battle during the first decade of the twentieth century raged over the extent to which the public was entitled to information about the food and drugs they bought and consumed.

If corporate power assumed many faces during this time, its most visible one was advertising. After the Civil War national advertising crystallized into its modern form, and within a few decades national advertising media, advertising agencies, and advertising trade groups emerged. In a relatively few years, as advertising veered from mere price and product information to an emphasis on image-based, emotional, even deceptive appeals, it became both an influential and a controversial business practice. To the public a less visible development within the corporate political economy was public relations. In addition to becoming a vital weapon for business in the marketplace of ideas, public relations would become an essential component of the advertising industry's campaigns to protect itself from public criticism throughout the twentieth century.

The Rise of National Advertising and a Modern Consumer Culture

The starting point for understanding advertising is asking why it exists. Advertising must be understood, first and foremost, as a business expense. But this is far from sufficient; the United States has had a private-enterprise economy throughout its history, but national advertising emerged as a dominant institution only in the twentieth century. Advertising was in use before, of course, but most ads were akin to what today is called classified advertising, that is, dry factual reports informing costumers about products and their availability. A merchant might place a notice in the local paper informing customers about a new shipment of lace, calico, or French milled soaps, for example. Following the Civil War advertising began its climb to prominence. By around 1890 the market situation had changed from one in which many local manufacturers produced a variety of consumer products for local consumption to one dominated by a few large companies. It did not take long, however, before these large producers were faced with a problem. Limited outlets hampered the distribution of their goods, and this, in turn, threatened capital investment in machinery, labor, and products. Manufacturers realized that they needed to seek national markets—in effect to cast a wider net. They turned to national advertising.[2]

This explanation is good as far as it goes, but it fails to convey exactly why some industries featured a great deal of advertising and others showed less interest. It also fails to explain why advertising became a mandatory business expense for firms in so many industries. To get to the bottom of the issue we need to understand the transition from an economy dominated by relatively competitive markets to one dominated by what economists refer to as oligopolistic markets. Competitive markets offer little incentive to advertise, nor are they especially attractive to the firms in them. Firms can sell all they produce at the market price, over which they have no control. Think, for example, of a farmer going to market with corn or wheat. Why would the farmer advertise such a product when he or she could sell it all at the market price but not a penny over it? If the industry becomes especially profitable, new firms will enter the market, increase the supply, lower the market price, and reduce the profits. More farmers would come to market with their corn and wheat and prices would fall. This is not a very desirable type of market for a capitalist. In contrast to competitive markets, their oligopolistic counterparts tend to be dominated by a small handful of firms that provide the vast majority of an industry's output. These firms are not *price takers,* as are firms in competitive markets, but they are *price makers* with considerable control over industry output and pricing. Capitalistic firms prefer to be in an oligopolistic rather than a competitive industry. The former tend to be more profitable, with pricing and output levels closer to those in a pure monopoly than to those in a purely competitive market. The key to having a stable oligopolistic market is creating barriers that make it difficult for new firms to enter it. Because of their size, large firms are in a position to win any price war with newcomers trying to enter the market. Most rational entrepreneurs would therefore not try to crash the party but instead hope that their enterprises would appear so attractive to one of the big companies already in the oligopoly that they would be bought up.

Facilitating the trend toward such markets was an unprecedented wave of mergers and acquisitions at the turn of the twentieth century that helped solidify large corporations' economic dominance.[3] Three large industrial consolidations took place in 1895, four followed the next year, and six took place in 1897. In 1898 the number of new mergers reached sixteen, and in 1899 there were a total of sixty-three. After twenty-one consolidations in 1901 and seventeen in 1902, the surge tapered off. The year 1904 witnessed only three such mergers.[4] The predominant process among the turn-of-the-century mergers was horizontal consolidation: the simultaneous merger of many or all competitors into an industrial structure comparable to a single giant enterprise. More than half the consolidations formed between 1885 and 1904 absorbed more than 40 percent of their industries, and close to one-third absorbed in excess of 70 percent of their competitors.[5] By the early 1900s firms such as the California Fruit Canners Association, Royal Baking Powder, National Biscuits, and National Candy dominated between 40 and 70 percent of their individual industries, and American Can, Du Pont, and Eastman Kodak controlled more than 70 percent of the markets in their categories. Historians consider this consolidation the greatest wave of mergers in U.S. business history.[6]

The rise of oligopoly is the gasoline that fuels the flames of modern advertising. In oligopolistic markets the dominant firms are hesitant to engage in cutthroat price competition. Each firm is large enough to survive a price war, so price competition would only reduce the size of the revenue pie that they are fighting over. Firms instead tend to gravitate toward a pricing structure that maximizes the total revenue coming into the industry. Understood this way, advertising becomes a mandatory business expense for all firms in an oligopolistic market to protect their market shares from attack. To large corporations advertising represents a competitive weapon superior to cutthroat price competition in the battle to expand and protect market shares.

In the early twentieth century advertising became not merely an adjunct to the "real business" of manufacturing; it became as vital as the steel, the workers, and the machinery because it created its own by-product: the loyal consumer. Instead of representing a competitive selling of goods and services, advertising came to represent the competitive creation of consumer habits—and of consumers. Because the products offered by these oligopolistic firms tended to vary little in terms of price and quality—one facial soap, shaving cream, or toothpaste was pretty much like another—they did not necessarily "sell themselves." Merely stating a product's physical attributes and price did not provide a potential consumer with a reason to purchase a particular product over its competitors. This form of marketing is commonly referred to as *parity advertising*. The task for advertising copywriters was to come up with ways to make consumers prefer one brand over another. This led to advertising strategies that attempted to capture and exploit consumers' emotions.[7] The role of advertising, then, was twofold. First, it served to establish an aura of prestige or desirability around a given product or service, thereby making it less susceptible to price competition. Second, advertising permitted firms to increase their sales without cutting prices, thereby maintaining healthy profit margins.

Advertising as a percentage of the gross domestic product rose in direct proportion to the increase in giant corporations operating in oligopolistic markets. It went from less than 0.3 percent in 1865 to more than 3 percent of the gross domestic product by 1920.[8] Between 1880 and 1900, for example, the annual amount spent on advertising ballooned from $200 million to $542 million and helped lay the foundation for the growth and success of well-known companies such as Coca-Cola, Campbell Soup, Carnation, Quaker Oats, Heinz, Pillsbury, Colgate-Palmolive, Libby, and Procter and Gamble.[9] Since the 1920s advertising expenditures as a percentage of the gross domestic product have remained in the 2 percent to 3 percent range.[10]

Contributing to, and profiting mightily from, the growth in national advertising was an increasingly commercial mass media. Fundamental changes within the newspaper and magazine industries helped develop a media system that simultaneously served publishers' need for revenues and advertisers' desire to reach a broader public. In contrast to the pre–Civil War era when most newspapers functioned as partisan organs to gain support for a political viewpoint, most newspapers in the 1870s and 1880s had become business enterprises. As start-up costs and daily expenses increased, publishers no longer viewed their primary mission as that of rousing readers to support political causes. Their new objective was to offer advertisers a large audience at low cost and generate the largest possible profits. By the early twentieth century this had become the dominant model as an increasing number of newspapers accepted or actively sought advertising revenues to offset their production costs and came to view their readers as a commodity that could be exchanged for advertising patronage.[11] In 1880, for example, 44 percent of all newspaper revenue came from advertising. Ten years later the figure approached 50 percent, and by 1919 U.S. newspapers depended on advertising for two-thirds of their income.[12]

No medium was more affected by advertising than the magazine industry. In the late nineteenth century publishers produced a flood of national magazines for popular consumption. Although differing in their editorial approach, *McClure's, Ladies' Home Journal, Munsey's, Cosmopolitan, Century, Delineator,* and *Scribner's* quickly gained favor with the large middle-class and mainly female readership—the group that purchased the most products and that advertisers were eager to reach. Unlike most newspapers, which tended to reach people in a limited geographical area, the new generation of magazines offered individual copies for sale at newsstands and therefore found a national market.[13] Between 1882 and 1885 the average October issue of *Harper's* devoted 7 pages to product advertising. Ten years later the average had climbed to an astonishing 85 pages. And whereas the November 1880 issue of *Atlantic Monthly* carried only 13 pages of advertising, the December 1904 issue boasted 121 pages filled with advertising. Other publications could point to similar changes. By the turn of the twentieth century magazine publishers were relying increasingly on brand-name advertising for their income.[14]

Large and impressive advertising campaigns were not the only way to create brand loyalty, however. Manufacturers also gained local merchants' trust in the hope that they would recommend branded products to their customers. This strategy was tricky because it involved persuading local merchants to rely less on generic products from wholesalers and more on brand-name goods. To make the process easier, manufacturers offered fully developed marketing campaigns that included displays, product demonstrations, free posters, and window decorations to participating merchants. This way, merchants could not only meet the increasing consumer demand for advertised products but also spur its growth.[15] Some promotional strategies designed to create consumer loyalty were predicated on active consumer involvement. In exchange for repeat purchase of a particular brand, customers were awarded premiums and prizes, including trading cards, wall hangings, games, and handkerchiefs. Some manufacturers carried the practice to an extreme. By 1905, for example, loyal buyers of Larkin soap could choose from 116 different premiums ranging from soaps, jellies, coffee, and teas to perfume in exchange for their saved labels. Thirteen years later, Larkin customers who had saved enough soap wrappers could outfit an entire household with the soap maker's premiums.[16] Manufacturers' goal, Susan Strasser argues, was to replace consumers' faith in generic products with trust in brand-name versions. It did not take long before customers began to ask for Ivory Soap, which could be obtained only from Procter and Gamble, and for Uneeda Biscuit, another heavily advertised brand. Although these products were more expensive than their generic counterparts, advertisers argued that they were worth the price due to the quality assurance that came with the brand.[17]

Consider what a dramatic change this constituted. Prior to the Industrial Revolution little manufacturing was undertaken solely to build up inventories. Production was typically based on daily orders. Consumers were close to manufacturers and often visited those who made household products. During the nineteenth century, when industry after industry grew larger and the expanded economy allowed retail stores to be flooded with cheap merchandise, the close interactions between manufacturers and consumers gradually eroded.[18] As the twentieth century proceeded Americans became dependent on mass-produced goods for their everyday needs. Although these products were cheap and readily available, they also represented a trade-off. Consumers, who only a generation earlier had been able to monitor the raw materials' quality and the conditions under which the final products were made, were suddenly at the manufacturers' mercy. Goods came from distant sources. People knew less about how they were made, how they worked, and how they could be fixed. As factories supplanted home production and as food stores became more distant from food sources, people lost touch with the means of production.[19] As time went by, household routines involved fewer homemade items, and consumption, as opposed to production, came to play a central role.[20]

Although some might have mourned a rapidly diminishing way of life, others welcomed the changes. Mass production of products that previously had required hours of work by skilled artisans enabled many people, including the poor and recent immigrants, to dress nicely and buy objects that only a few decades earlier had been reserved for the well-to-do. In her study of working-class immigrant women at the turn of the century, Kathy Peiss documents how participation in consumer culture provided a coveted ticket to social acceptance and freedom from patriarchal dominance. Andrew Heinze chronicles how turn-of-the-century Jewish immigrants used consumer products to buy social assimilation and acceptance. Other notable scholars have reached similar conclusions about the liberating aspects of consumer culture.[21]

Despite its positive aspects, egalitarianism through consumption, or what the advertising historian Roland Marchand describes as democratization through goods, had its limitations. Although new and better merchandise could improve the material aspect of people's lives, it was less suited to fulfill other functions. Consumer society, because it emphasized individual solutions to collective problems, helped articulate a new form of citizen sovereignty. Gradually winning acceptance was the view that it was in the marketplace, and not at the polls, where the public should cast its vote.[22] Within this new society, argues the historian Charles McGovern, consumption was becoming a cornerstone, and this new version of democracy equated, even replaced, participation in civic life with spending dollars in the marketplace: "Consumption was the foundation of a distinctly American way of life; this was the new order of the ages."[23] In this setup, advertising was the dominant lingo.

Consumer Activism in the Progressive Era

Many Americans did not fully accept the social and political alterations brought on by the accelerated commercialization that had taken place since the Civil War. Among members of the middle class, the period immediately after the war was characterized by anxiety that could be attributed to cultural, social, and economic changes.[24]

Organizing around progressive ideas and forming what would later be called the Progressive movement, a group of middle-class individuals dismissed radical political changes as a solution to this economic situation. The answer, they argued, would come in the form of laws and regulations. With the citizenry in control, corporations would have to reform, and the resulting modifications would improve society.[25] Aiding the Progressive cause was a group of socially conscious writers commonly referred to as *muckrakers.* Writing for popular magazines such as *McClure's, Cosmopolitan,* and *Everybody's,* muckraking journalists investigated corporate misconduct and reported their findings to their mostly middle-class readers. Much to the dismay of conservative business interests, muckrakers demanded that government use its regulative powers to protect citizens against business abuse and exploitation. In contrast to later consumer activists, who placed advertising regulation high on their agenda, the most pressing issue among Progressive Era consumer advocates was not product promotion but labeling practices.

The work toward what would eventually result in the Federal Food and Drugs Act of 1906 had started as early as 1892 when a concerned group led by Dr. Harvey W. Wiley began its crusade against adulterated foods. The cause caught the attention of other reform-minded individuals and soon included a demand for regulation of drugs as well. It should come as no surprise that manufacturers put up a fight.[26]

Newspapers and magazines did not rush to the consumers' aid. A large part of mass media depended on patent-medicine advertising for income and therefore had no desire to see it outlawed or restricted. A few, most notably the powerful magazine publisher Cyrus H. K. Curtis, begged to differ. In a move that diverged dramatically from those of his competitors, Curtis forbade proprietary ads in his widely read *Ladies' Home Journal.* Curtis did not stop there, however. In 1904 the magazine's editor, Edward Bok, started a string of editorial columns calling for a boycott of patent medicines. Reaching out to temperance and religious groups, Bok equated taking patent medicines, which had a high alcohol content, with drinking alcoholic beverages. Deploring religious publications for accepting nostrum advertising, Bok went so far as to warn that the practice might undermine people's trust in churches.[27] Much to the patent-medicine industry's dismay, other journalistic jabs followed. In 1904, for example, *Collier's* assigned the successful muckraker Samuel Hopkins Adams to conduct a thorough investigation of the nostrum industries.[28]

Not surprisingly, groups such as the National Wholesale Liquor Dealers Association and the Proprietary Medicine Association opposed all regulation. Their deep coffers and organizational skill in enlisting powerful representatives in Congress helped them trip up legislation they found inimical. In spite of several revealing exposés, their business muscle ensured that legislation was not forthcoming.[29] The situation appeared at a standstill when *The Jungle* was published in 1906.[30] Upton Sinclair's best-seller unveiled the extent to which the meatpacking industry was willing to accept unsafe and exploitative labor conditions to maximize profits. The result was rotten and contaminated meat on (middle-class) consumers' tables. Although much of Sinclair's call for labor reform fell on deaf ears, his plea for stricter regulation of the meat industry gained massive support. In the months following Sinclair's exposé meat sales dropped drastically. President Theodore Roosevelt finally threw his support behind the passage of a meat-inspection bill, which was written into law in 1906.[31] The momentum created by Sinclair's work and the subsequent meat-inspection bill lent new support to Wiley's crusade. The proposal for federal regulation of food and drugs, however, involved a complex set of manufacturers and public-interest groups. In addition to their old accusations, patent-medicine makers spent vast amounts of time and energy arguing that regulation amounted to a plot by physicians to make money for themselves by outlawing self-prescribed remedies. Using their considerable influence over the press, drug manufacturers warned that the proposed law might result in drastically reduced advertising incomes. More direct tactics designed to influence press coverage of what had evolved into a growing demand for food and drug regulation included loyalty clauses in some advertising contracts that newspapers signed with their advertisers. In exchange for advertisers' patronage, newspapers had to commit to fighting on the advertisers' side should hostile legislation arise.[32] In the case of newspapers, business leaders did not shy away from pressuring and trying to bribe reporters to have favorable stories about themselves and their businesses highlighted and any not-so-favorable stories suppressed. It did not take long before newspapers realized that, in a competitive business environment, refusal to comply with advertisers' wishes could cause economic hardship, even ruin.[33]

This experience pointed to an ongoing tension between commercial journalism and its coverage of issues that affected its advertisers. It was one reason why reformers such as Sinclair launched ferocious attacks on the commercial press as being pawns of business interests.[34] It also meant that proconsumer muckraking held a tenuous position within journalism; the relationship between commercial magazines and social reformers made for strange bedfellows. Whereas muckrakers craved national attention for their exposés of corporate wrongdoings, their access to national magazines was predicated on their ability to attract a large audience of predominantly female readers, which corporate advertisers had determined to be significant if not essential to their survival and prosperity. In a somewhat ironic turn of events, then, to sell their products national advertisers came to rely on the popularity of writers with a critical view of business. According to Louis Filler, "the big circulation of the muckraking magazines attracted the financially necessary advertisers who, although they suffered from the exposures, nevertheless wanted to use such popular organs."[35] Aside from their ability to deliver a national market, however, corporate America was neither enthusiastic about nor amused by muckraking exposés. The ultimate fear from a business perspective, of course, was that middle-class voters, duly influenced by muckrakers' work, would press for even stricter business regulation. This, maintains Filler, is why muckraking journalism disappeared from view around 1912–13.[36]

In 1906 muckraking was alive and well, however, and public support for federal regulation of the food industry was growing significantly. Many manufacturers gave nominal support to the Food and Drugs Act but opposed the specific stipulations that applied to their own industries. Some, such as the National Association of Manufacturers (NAM), a group established in 1895 to protect business interests, experienced internal disagreement over the issue. Although its Pure Food Committee lobbied in favor of the legislation and received overwhelming support for this stand during its 1906 convention, the NAM's leadership, protecting the interests of some influential members, worked to weaken it. The American Medical Association and many women's groups, in contrast, supported the measure. The end result was a 1906 law that made all forms of misbranding, including falsification of drug labels, illegal.[37] One scholar notes that the passage of the Food and Drugs Act in 1906 represented "a substantial victory for consumers. It showed that consumer interests finally counted, at least in politics, and it did a great deal to dissolve the old nineteenth-century American habit of viewing political issues solely from the standpoint of the producer."[38]

The creation of the National Consumers' League (NCL) represents one of the most successful examples of organized consumer activism during this period. Formed in 1899, the NCL devoted itself to the conditions under which products were made and worked relentlessly to improve working conditions in factories. Only garments produced in factories that refused to employ children, paid its workers fair wages, and treated workers well were allowed to display the NCL's white label. Operating in many states, the NCL conducted regular factory inspections and worked diligently to pass local and federal laws to improve conditions. "The first step toward political power for NCL members lay in their recognition of the economic significance as consumers," Kathryn Kish Sklar insists. "The league's use of the term 'consumers' rather than 'buyers' emphasized purchasers' dynamic relationship with producers."[39]

The NCL was not alone in its effort to organize consumers. The Cooperative League of the United States, formed in 1915, gained support from a cross section of Americans. Its strategy was to reconstruct the economics of consumption by establishing a system in which distributors were left out and the resulting savings were passed on to cooperative members. This model also eliminated the need for advertising. These consumer cooperatives were based on the fundamental tenet that production should be responsive to society's consumption needs and should not generate profits regardless of the social implications. Enjoying steady growth for decades, the Cooperative League by 1934 consisted of 1,498 consumer societies with more than five hundred thousand members.[40]

The Rise of Public Relations and Commercial Propaganda

In the cauldron of controversy surrounding corporate power and behavior, another major institution was created in the Progressive Era: public relations. As Alex Carey observes, three major developments characterize twentieth-century society. The first is the rise of democracy and the trend toward universal adult suffrage. The second is the rise of corporate power. The third is the rise of public relations—a strategy designed to protect corporate power from universal adult suffrage or, as Carey puts it, to take the risk out of democracy for corporate interests. Because the masses, in the views of corporate interests, could not be trusted to accept the importance of maintaining the social and economic status quo, it was up to business to influence the information on which voters formed their decisions. It was in this capacity that newly developed theories of persuasion and the evolving field of public relations came to the corporations' rescue. Specifically, during these early years, PR came to be used by industries to ensure that they were not subject to government regulation that might interfere with their profitability.[41]

Muckraking journalism is sometimes credited with spawning a PR industry to protect business from journalistic exposés. This simplistic explanation,
however, does not account for how PR responded to broader social forces
that evolved over several decades before crystallizing in the first decade of
the twentieth century.[42]

Muckraking, and journalism more broadly, plays an important role in
the story. Before muckraking came to a somewhat abrupt halt, it created
several important legacies that the emerging PR industry was quick to adopt
or address. Progressive ideas had suggested a potential coalition between
working- and middle-class interests against corporate dominance, and this
caused concern in business circles, where it was believed that such a union
would be dangerous. Set into motion before and after World War I, PR efforts
utilized the momentum and methods popularized by muckraking journalists to sway middle-class opinion toward U.S. business's needs and interests. Taking advantage of people's reliance on news and information from
secondhand sources, PR practitioners viewed the commercial mass media
as an excellent forum for promoting business interests.[43] In practice, public
relations often meant having a newspaper publish material surreptitiously
planted by a company's PR agent. The client would look good, and the public would assume that the article was the product of legitimate journalism.
This underhanded aspect of PR makes it even more controversial in many
respects than advertising is.

It is fitting, therefore, that Ivy Lee, a former journalist, pioneered the craft.
Lee launched his PR career when he was hired by the Citizens' Union to
serve as a "press representative" for the Fusion Ticket candidate in the New
York City municipal election in 1903. After the election Lee continued to
handle publicity for several clients, including the Democratic Party. In 1904
he teamed up with George F. Parker, an older and more experienced journalist and publicity operator, and together they offered to help prominent
businesses and organizations.[44] As a press representative for groups such as
the General Asphalt Company, the Anthracite Coal Operators' Committee,
and International Harvester, the two men used articles and press releases to
gain positive publicity for their clients. Lee's most important PR intervention
came in response to a series of muckraking articles that alleged fraudulent
dealings on the part of Mutual Life, Equitable Life, and New York Life, three
of the largest insurance companies. Fearing that these exposés might lead to
demands for government-sponsored health insurance, the three companies
hired Parker and Lee to make sure that their version of the issue reached
the public. In response to the insurance probe, Parker and Lee arranged for

hundreds of letters, all with the president of Equitable Life's signature and an explanation of the company's position, to be sent to newspaper editors across the country. Not only did the publicity firm succeed in getting them printed but it also managed to put the text in conspicuous places without any direct payment or undue influence by Equitable.[45]

Although scholars may disagree on the exact time when early forms of PR began to manifest themselves, few disagree that the field grew and changed dramatically in the first two decades of the twentieth century. Instrumental in transforming the profession from the publicity function that Lee had pioneered into one that claimed to be able to mold public opinion was Edward L. Bernays. The goal for a PR practitioner, according to Bernays, was no longer simply to disseminate news after a crisis had occurred. To secure a favorable social environment for business, public relations counsels—as Bernays preferred to call PR practitioners—should manipulate social environments, including the press.[46] Truth, in the hands of a skilled PR agent, could be manipulated to fit a client's needs—an approach to the standards of factual evidence that stood in stark contrast to Enlightenment ideals. "If Enlightenment faith had held that facts were instruments of knowledge by which informed citizens would rule their own destiny," Stuart Ewen comments, "now the 'fact' was being marshaled, from both sides of the aisle, as a dramatic device, a conscious play to the balcony. The presumed connection between 'the fact' and objective measures of evaluation was vanishing. The *fact* had surfaced as the *factoid*."[47]

The successful use of PR—or propaganda, as it was called then—by the U.S. government during World War I was not only instrumental in elevating PR's prestige but also helped legitimize advertising. In 1917 President Woodrow Wilson created the Committee on Public Information (CPI), also known as the Creel Commission after its leader, George Creel. CPI's purpose was to organize an extensive propaganda effort to mobilize U.S. support for the war. This involved a wide variety of informative techniques and persuasive methods, and both Edward L. Bernays and Ivy Lee served the war administration in an advisory capacity. The government's ability to develop massive war support and hysteria toward the "barbaric Huns" in a short time through aggressive propaganda revealed PR's potency in shaping the minds of the masses.

World War I, with its great outpouring of patriotic fervor and the government's attempts at propaganda, presented the advertising industry with an excellent chance to prove itself, to improve its public image, and to firmly establish its place in the larger business process. The war enhanced the prestige of advertising executives, demonstrated "the dignity of the profession," and helped legitimize advertising as an industry.[48] Advertising practitioners had been aiding the CPI almost from the beginning of the war, and in early 1918 Creel established a separate division of advertising. This unit became a clearinghouse for distribution of space and services donated by the advertising industry to the CPI. The division acted much like a national advertising agency, assisting the government just as an advertising agency would help a client. The advertising division determined how donated space could be put to the most effective use and was credited with the successful outcome of campaigns to sell Liberty Bonds and encourage Red Cross membership. "If advertising techniques could sell soap or face cream or biscuits, [Creel] reasoned, why not a war?"[49] The CPI advertising division became a crossroads for everyone who worked in advertising during World War I. Scholars argue that it not only knit "widely scattered and decentralized groups and individual practitioners into an occupational community" but also helped formalize advertising as an industry, served as PR for advertising, and succeeded in educating Washington about advertising's value.[50]

By most accounts the advertising industry's assistance, estimated at $5 million, really did help to win the war. But this substantial contribution paled in comparison with the dividends reaped by the industry.[51] "Not only did the [last] war not hurt advertising—it ushered advertising into a larger usefulness and a greater importance," reflected the advertising executive Raymond Rubicam.[52] Throughout most of the 1920s the business of advertising gained increased respect and social standing. Advertising and its practitioners were seen as instrumental to war victories and just as important in securing the success of private industry.[53] "Even war needs [the advertising executive], to say nothing of Swift and Company," mused a writer for *New Republic*.[54]

In addition to laurels won, a renewed faith in its persuasive methods, and close association with the war effort, the advertising community emerged from the war with an impressive financial record. The estimated advertising volume rose from $682 million to $1.41 billion between 1914 and 1919.[55] Much of this increase is apparently attributable to a wartime tax rule that exempted advertising as a business expense. This loophole encouraged many businesses and industries to experiment with new and enlarged advertising budgets. Further, many advertisers with no actual goods to sell also benefited by turning from product advertising to "institutional" or "goodwill" advertising as a means of keeping their brand names in the public eye while evading government taxes.[56]

A variety of organizations representing various aspects of the advertising industry also emerged around the war years. In addition to providing help and support for their members, they also suggested that advertising was an integral part of U.S. business and was therefore deserving of professional respect.[57] The Associated Advertising Clubs of the World (AACW) was formed in 1914 from a loose federation of local advertising groups. It was financed by national advertisers who hoped to promote the spread of national brands and establish fair trade rules on a national scale. Many of its members, however, rejected the group's turn toward a national focus and remained more interested in an organization that would provide social prestige and fulfillment for their local aims. A split occurred, and national advertisers soon established a collection of trade associations distinct from the AACW. The new organization, which superseded the AACW in 1929, called itself the Advertising Federation of America (AFA). Its overarching goal was to formulate general business policies that national advertising associations and major advertising clubs across the country could agree upon. In addition, to help standardize advertising rates and contracting practices, the AFA took an interest in advertising research. The association also kept in close touch with developments in Washington and worked through affiliated local organizations on state bills affecting advertising.[58] The American Association of Advertising Agencies was founded in 1917 to protect the interests of the large advertising agencies most closely connected with national advertising. The Association of National Advertisers broke away from the AACW in 1915 and became the official group for national advertising interests.[59] These organizational developments signaled that the advertising industry was playing a larger and increasingly important role in U.S. society.

The Advertising Industry Post–World War I

In addition to the immense value of being recognized as a contributor to the war victory, the advertising industry used its war-related experiences to fine-tune its persuasive strategies. Just as PR content assumed an opportunistic relationship with truth, so, too, did advertising content change considerably as the institution solidified in the early twentieth century. The type of content used by advertisers to successfully sell their wares increasingly became a form of commercial propaganda.[60] And just as PR was predicated on a dim view of people's capacity to think rationally, so was modern advertising's content.

Although advertisers had typically veered away from copy that provided consumers with information, statistics, and the ability to comparison shop, this avoidance became far more prominent after World War I. Many advertising executives learned from the successful use of wartime propaganda that powerful images and slogans provided a key to controlling the public's actions, including their consumer choices.[61] Advertisers' use of trademark or brand names helped serve this purpose, as did advertisements that stressed glossy illustrations over information. The emotional attributes associated with a trademark, and the corollary idea that the consumer could best be reached by an appeal to irrational thinking and unconscious desire, fit manufacturers' purpose perfectly. That scientific opinion buttressed this view legitimized, even justified, the intensified focus of business and industry on the "irrational" consumer.[62]

This view of consumers as largely irrationally motivated had begun to win acceptance in the advertising community as early as the 1890s, when a growing minority argued that advertising's function was to persuade and create desires in potential consumers. For advertisers eagerly searching for national exposure, these findings were tantalizing. Before long, new knowledge concerning human behavior, especially Sigmund Freud's theories of the human mind as irrational, easily manipulated, and driven by unconscious (mainly sexual) instincts and desires, lent great justification to advertisers' persuasive methods.[63] Other academic research bolstered this approach. In 1903 Walter Dill Scott, a professor of advertising at the Northwestern School of Business, began work on what would turn into several decades of advertising research based on psychological theories. Scott used laboratory experiments in attempts to measure sensations and was especially interested in the role of instincts as motivational forces in consumer behavior.[64] By the 1920s Scott's theories had won general acceptance in the advertising community. The strategy of gearing advertisements to appeal to consumers' emotions as opposed to their intellect made more sense if advertisers could assume that consumers' actions were motivated by impulses and instincts rather than rational thinking.[65]

Advertising practitioners increasingly subscribed to the notion that most consumers were of low intelligence and that advertising copy, in order to have appeal, needed to address consumers' emotions rather than their intellect. "Convincing arguments don't always convince because 'the average mind either cannot or will not follow [the advertiser's] arguments to their logical conclusion,'" a 1911 *Printers' Ink* article concluded. "Let the reason-whyer study the census reports and see how many people work at jobs a monkey could do; let him stand on a street corner before dawn any morning—he'll see plenty of people who won't respond to reason-why!"[66] Psychological tests conducted during World War I provided further evidence for the view that the masses were dull, complacent, and easily led. When a U.S. Army test revealed that a large percentage of prospective soldiers were unfit for military service because of their low IQs, advertising copywriters were quick to infer that the average U.S. consumer had the mental ability of a child between nine and sixteen years of age. Thereafter they tailored their advertising copy accordingly.[67]

By the 1920s the advertising profession was generally accepted as an important part of the larger business process. Its patriotism had been established during the war, its practitioners were well on their way to achieving professional status, and advertising expenditures were at an all-time high in a booming economy. The decade truly belonged to the advertising industry. It was during this period that advertisers took it upon themselves to serve as what advertising historian Roland Marchand has described as "apostles of modernity."[68] This mission involved fusing new products with real or created consumer needs. Marchand shows how advertisements of the time, by playing a dual role as both coach and confidant, "guided" consumers through the task of choosing the "right" products. The same advertisements also played on people's fears and insecurities, frequently magnifying minor problems to the point that they appeared crucial to important life decisions. Potential consumers were told that bad breath or old-fashioned furnishings or sagging socks prevented professional and social success and that failure to use certain products for health, hygiene, or attire would hinder their ability to keep up with modern society, much less get ahead. As Marchand observes, "in the service of modernity, they [advertisers] could console, befriend, and reassure the public as well as stimulate and guide it."[69]

The view that some people might be more receptive to persuasive copy than others gained credence in the 1920s. Contemporary survey research had revealed the possibility that intervening variables such as demographic background, selective perception, and other mental and social states could possibly affect how audiences were influenced by advertised messages. Advertisers believed that most consumers, because they lacked the intelligence and cultural tastes of the elite, were best reached through advertising that played on their emotions.[70] Not only the "lower classes" were viewed as less intelligent and more susceptible to emotional advertising copy than other consumers; promotional experts speculated that successful advertising depended upon gender-specific targeting. Advertising addressed to men, it was argued, should be short and to the point, whereas advertising aimed at women should take into consideration that women's minds were "vats of frothy pink irrationality."[71]

Women as a consumer group had greatly interested advertisers since the late nineteenth century, when those in business concluded that women were far more susceptible to others' control and suggestions than were men and that they were more likely to follow direct commands from advertisements. Moreover, the prevailing notion was that women did not want detailed selling points or technical specifications and that it was far easier to reach them by an emotional appeal than by an intellectual one.[72] By the early twentieth century the conventional wisdom held that 85 percent of consumer purchases were made by women, and the trend toward perceiving advertisements' readers as female, emotional, and irrational continued. Drawing on a long tradition that considered women as fickle and debased consumers, advertising leaders of the 1920s and 1930s concluded that women possessed a "well-authenticated greater emotionality," a "natural inferiority complex," and "inarticulate longings." Advertisements reflected and reinforced such beliefs by playing on emotions and portraying "idealized visions" rather than "prosaic realities." Advertising copy tended to be intimate and succinct because business leaders believed that women were unwilling to read anything that was not pitched to them personally and broken into short paragraphs. Illustrations—though not necessarily of the product—were considered especially important in advertisements geared toward women.[73]

Whereas the advertising community considered consumers to be irrational and easily manipulated, advertising executives and copywriters did not think that this characterization fit themselves, their peers, or their business associates. The upper and upper-middle classes, most of whom were university educated, were regarded as less susceptible to propaganda than were other members of society. It was "the masses," represented by immigrants, women, and the uneducated, who were seen as targets for advertising's emotional lure. T. J. Jackson Lears comments that executives and copywriters claimed to be among the relatively small number of persons who understood the masses' mental processes.[74] In addition to the political problem this arrogance posed for advertising as a social institution, it also revealed an internal dilemma for the advertising industry and its effectiveness.

Advertising executive Wallace Boren of the J. Walter Thompson Company worried in 1936 that the writer of advertisements talked down to readers and addressed them "from a false position, a position of superiority which has been determined by his own limited circle of friends whose views are assumed to be the same as the views of the much larger audience to whom he should be talking."[75] Just how much did the average copywriter differ from the rest of the population? In 1936 not one copywriter at J. Walter Thompson's New York office belonged to a fraternal lodge or civic club, only one in twenty-five ever attended political meetings, and only one in five attended church. Half the writers had never visited Coney Island or similar resorts, whereas the other half went only rarely. "This," snorted Boren, "in a nation that can almost be described by such experiences."[76] Considerably more than half of J. Walter Thompson's copywriters had never lived within the average national income, and half could not even recall any relatives or friends who did. Although only 5 percent of all U.S. homes had servants, 66 percent of the agency's copywriters employed such help. Only one in eight did his or her own grocery shopping, only half bought their own drug supplies, and a little more than half shopped in department stores. As Boren declared poignantly, "The men writers are virtually unanimous in their agreement that shopping is something to avoid entirely. All this in an agency that depends on the retail sale of staple consumer goods to the masses for its principal income!"[77] When one executive argued that she was fed up with advertising men's habit of showing copy to their wives for approval, another replied soberly, "Yes, they'd do better if they showed it to their sweeties."[78]

The advertising industry's newfound boldness in talking down to consumers and playing upon their fears and insecurities did not escape criticism. Liberal pundits and intellectuals accurately diagnosed the problem. Advertisers "hold that the 'common people' (of whom the Lord providentially made so many) never think, they merely feel," argued one critic. "To sell them, you must appeal not to reason, but emotion; preferably vest your product with a golden aura of romance, outlined against a backdrop of fear."[79]

Although the advertising community viewed the average consumer with a certain amount of contempt, it also realized that public recognition of the field was important to its status and survival, so it tried to be sensitive to consumers' views of advertising and its practitioners. In the early part of the twentieth century, then, the advertising industry was faced with two closely related tasks. One was to convince the public that advertising deserved professional respect (even when it failed to extend this to consumers in return); the other was to prove to the larger business community that advertising performed a necessary, if not an invaluable, service.[80]

The industry struggled to gain acceptance in both quarters. Local advertising clubs worked hard to impress upon business and the consuming public that advertising was a legitimate enterprise and that its practitioners were professionals who performed an important business function. Professional advertising organizations, in their attempts at improving the field's social acceptability, went so far as to have advertising executives give guest lectures from the pulpits of some of the wealthiest churches. The purpose was to let the congregation members "see for themselves what an advertising man actually looked like."[81]

These efforts were parts of the advertising industry's attempt to improve its relations with the public and facilitate a general acceptance of this business practice in consumers' minds. As such, the industry's endeavors were closely linked to the larger PR effort, on behalf of all business, that was taking place simultaneously.

Conclusion

By the 1920s, advertising had gone from being a peripheral business activity to a dominant force in U.S. life. It was not without cause that the industry trade publication launched in those days named itself *Advertising Age*. When the sociologists Helen Merrell Lynd and Robert S. Lynd conducted their work on what would become the first comprehensive studies of modern consumer society, they found a society in rapid transition. In their widely read books, based on participant observer studies of people in Middletown, a fictitious name for Muncie, Indiana, the Lynds concluded that social institutions and democratic ideas were eroding and that advertising—persuasive and seductive—was everywhere.[82]

Far from everyone had the same adverse reaction to advertising and commercialization as the Lynds did, but discontent and uneasiness were unquestionably brewing in some camps. Despite its challenges in connecting with consumers, the advertising community did not anticipate the negative public reaction it would receive in the late 1920s. Quite suddenly the industry was forced to contend with a full-fledged consumer movement that challenged the industry's view of consumers as helpless and irrational and called for a discontinuation of advertising that played too heavily on emotions. After three decades that included unprecedented business growth, massive population upheaval due to immigration and migration, a war, and the development of national markets and advertising, many Americans in the mid- to late 1920s appeared ready for a critical look at advertising. Slowly, the advertising community came to realize that despite its exalted status within business, it did not know consumers very well after all.

2

Advertising Challenged: The Creation of Consumers' Research Inc. and the Rise of the 1930s Consumer Movement

After the first wave of consumer activism in the early twentieth century, organized consumer activity tapered off by the end of World War I. No longer pushing for major federal regulation, consumer organizations largely concerned themselves with retail prices and sanitary issues. The National Consumers' League (NCL) remained active. In addition to working on its white-label campaign, the organization also harnessed its political power to promote fair minimum wage and labor standards.[1] Scholars note how the surviving strands of progressive thought influenced social and political thinking as the Roaring Twenties came to an end and the Great Depression approached.[2] By the end of the decade a new surge of consumer activism, similar in many respects to its Progressive Era predecessor, was emerging. This consumer movement consisted of several loose-knit organizations with somewhat different strategies.

Much like Progressive Era consumer activists, who had focused their efforts on food safety and the passage of the Federal Food and Drugs Act of 1906, the new consumer movement pushed for legislation. Unlike those in the previous movement, however, the newcomers directed their attention to advertising. In the early twentieth century advertising had been a relatively new phenomenon and few could have predicted its immense growth. By the late 1920s, however, advertising had become the key means of communication between manufacturers and consumers. This link, according to the budding consumer movement, was not without problems. Because most advertising failed to provide much product information, consumers were ignorant about products. Leading a crusade to educate consumers about advertising's pitfalls was Consumers' Research Inc., a group that quickly gained support from other organizations and from consumer advocates who had been appointed to the Consumer Advisory Board in Franklin D. Roosevelt's National Recovery Administration. In this advertising age the contours of the modern consumer movement were shaped.

Advertising and the Second Wave of Consumer Activism

During the first three decades of the twentieth century Americans witnessed a massive increase in branded goods. By 1930, for example, consumers in Milwaukee, Wisconsin, could chose among 87 brands of breakfast foods, 93 brands of butter, 101 brands of packaged coffee, 256 brands of toothbrushes, 73 brands of shaving cream, and 76 brands of toothpaste.[3] The task of differentiating each product from its many competitors was left to advertising, and between 1900 and 1930 advertising expenditures increased fivefold from $542 million in 1900 to $2.6 billion in 1930.[4]

As national companies grew and operated in more oligopolistic markets, consumers could barely discern tangible differences between products. In a whole range of categories, and especially among the small-ticket items that consumers used daily, manufacturers were hard-pressed to point out substantial differences that set their products apart from those of their competitors. The particular quality of a soap, perfume, mouthwash, or toothpaste no longer distinguished a brand but rather the emotional attributes that consumers associated with it. The irony of modern advertising was that the more alike products in a certain category were, the more manufacturers had to increase their advertising to convince consumers that there were differences. Small and cheap commodities were virtually indistinguishable from one another, so their advertising had to be distinct. "The number and variety of these small articles and the makers of them are so numerous, the competition among them so intense," remarked one observer, "that the sponsor of any new but similar product must find some novel peculiarity to exploit rather than any inherent qualities which his products may possess."[5]

By the 1920s the trend swung toward image-driven ads that played on people's fears and insecurities.[6] "People rarely buy 'things,'" advised a J. Walter Thompson memo directed at copywriters. "They put down their money for what things will *do* for them; sell the 'complexion' not the soap." The most active human virtue, reminded the advertising executive, is hope: "That's why the 'promise' is the most important thing in advertising."[7] According to one study, advertisements based on logical appeal shrank from 62 percent in the 1900s to 35.5 percent in the 1930s, whereas advertising appealing to emotions increased from 27 percent of all product advertisements in the 1900s to 42 percent of the total in 1930.[8] An industry-sponsored study conducted in 1931 confirmed ads' general lack of factual product information. Only one-third of the total advertising space was devoted to product information, and a large proportion of the descriptive terms referred to style and appearance. Clear, definite statements about specific qualities were few and far between.[9] Some ads implied spectacular personal transformations from the use of particular products; sometimes the products not only failed to deliver but also caused severe health problems, even death.[10] "It seems probable," concluded Middletown books' coauthor Robert S. Lynd, "that under the pressures of modern business development, the consumer is becoming confused and illiterate as a buyer more rapidly than the combined positive factors of education, standardization, and so on are succeeding in making him literate as a buyer."[11]

Against this backdrop Stuart Chase and Frederick J. Schlink rose to prominence. Chase, a Harvard graduate and accountant, had spent some time in Washington, D.C., before turning to professional writing. His first book, the 1925 *Tragedy of Waste*, was a strong critique of advertising, an enterprise he called a squanderer of resources. His follow-up book, *Men and Machines*, provided a critical view of industrialization's effect on society. Schlink was a 1912 graduate of the University of Illinois Engineering Department whose employers had included the National Bureau of Standards and Bell Telephone Laboratories. In the late 1920s Schlink was employed by the American Engineering Standards Committee, which changed its name to the American Standards Association in 1928. After meeting at a New York University get-together at a Greenwich Village speakeasy in the mid-1920s, the pair discovered their similar interests and came up with the idea of collaborating on a book. Chase would do the writing while Schlink would provide the factual information for a blistering attack on U.S. business practices.[12]

The result was *Your Money's Worth: A Study in the Waste of the Consumer's Dollars*, a 1927 book that some supporters have referred to as "the *Uncle Tom's Cabin* of the consumer movement."[13] The authors exposed frauds and manipulations by U.S. manufacturers and argued that most advertisements failed to give consumers sufficient product information. This led to people wasting money on products that they would never have bought had they been given sufficient and accurate information. Inefficiency in buying, Chase and Schlink contended, thrived in inverse proportion to consumers' knowledge. Whereas industrial and government buyers bought efficiently because they possessed the necessary knowledge to deflate and disregard advertising, the average consumer was forced to rely on advertising propaganda that provided him or her with almost no factual information. Urging consumers to educate themselves against the perils of such marketing devices, the two authors also called for increased consumer protection against these practices.

Explaining much of the ultimate success of the book was Schlink's experience as a member of a Methodist men's club in White Plains, New York. Utilizing his technical knowledge, Schlink had started to interview his fellow club members about their product experiences and, based on their reports, developed a series of mimeographed sheets for distribution. The left-hand column of the newsletter was devoted to products deemed superior by their users, whereas the opposite side of the page was reserved for products they had found inferior. At times the newsletter also listed products that had been tested in government and business laboratories. Readers of *Your Money's Worth* were invited to send in one dollar to Chase's New York address for a copy of the list.[14] Encouraged by the strong response, the authors decided to expand their initial Consumers' Club in White Plains into a national organization known as Consumers' Research Inc. (CR) in 1929. The new organization received financial support from several liberal magazine patrons and a generous grant from Dorothy Elmhirst, whose first husband had been a partner in J. P. Morgan and Company. Many of Schlink's friends contributed editorial and technical assistance, and Schlink worked doggedly. His superior in the American Standards Association accommodated his need for time off. "What had been a hobby," reflected Schlink some years later, "was taking all my spare hours, at week ends and holidays."[15]

Within a couple of years Schlink quit his job and became the full-time director for CR, which employed technical experts and its own laboratory to test consumer products. The test results were published in the confidential *Consumers' Club Commodity List,* later renamed the *Consumers' Research General Bulletin* (and later yet simply the *Consumers' Research Bulletin*). Whereas the original 1927 bulletin had 565 subscribers, five years later the total soared to about 42,000.[16] Because of the bulletin's critical content, CR's leaders lived in constant fear of being sued by businesses and took great care to prevent this from happening. The organization published two versions of its bulletin. One was intended for general circulation, whereas subscribers to the confidential—and more libel-prone—version were required to sign pledges in which they promised not to share the information with persons outside their immediate household.[17]

Of the two authors, Chase proved to be the less aggressive. He contended

The chemistry set in Consumers' Research's earliest laboratory. Reprinted with permission from the Consumers' Research Collection, Special Collections and University Archives, Rutgers University Libraries.

F. J. Schlink at Consumers' Research in the 1930s. Reprinted with permission from the Consumers' Research Collection, Special Collections and University Archives, Rutgers University Libraries.

that he had no quarrel with advertising as long as advertisements gave him all the necessary information and treated him as an adult. He castigated advertising for defrauding the public but believed that the problem could and should be corrected through the existing economic structure. In contrast, Schlink was, at least in the late 1920s and early 1930s, less comfortable with capitalism and took a much more confrontational stance.[18]

In 1932 Chase resigned from his post as CR's president to devote more time to his own writing, but Schlink was left far from stranded. Prominent individuals such as Rexford G. Tugwell, a Columbia University economics professor who was soon to become the assistant secretary of agriculture, and the well-known sociologist Robert S. Lynd came out in strong support of CR.[19] Many women's clubs and professional organizations climbed on board as well.[20] Appointed as CR's secretary was Arthur Kallet, a fellow engineer from the American Standards Association.

From the laboratory at Consumers' Research before the 1935 labor strike. (Arthur Kallet is seated and F. J. Schlink is standing second from the right.) Reprinted with permission from the Consumers' Research Collection, Special Collections and University Archives, Rutgers University Libraries.

Together, Schlink and Kallet wrote *100,000,000 Guinea Pigs,* which rapidly became a best seller, providing more fuel for the budding consumer movement's fire.[21] In their book the authors exposed inadequacies and laxities in consumer-goods production and pointed to fraudulent advertising practices and the general absence of laws to protect consumers. "Case after case," argued the two authors, "demonstrates only too well that the average manufacturer will resist to the end any interference with his business, any attempt to deprive him of his vested interest, even when it has been proved beyond doubt that his product is a menace to health and life."[22]

Skin Deep by M. C. Phillips, another CR associate and who was married to Schlink, was published in 1934 and did for cosmetics what *100,000,000 Guinea Pigs* had done for food and drugs. The drug and cosmetics trade, argued the author, was so fraudulent that cosmetics manufacturers and copywriters did not even believe their own advertisements. Phillips scorched the advertising practices of *Ladies' Home Journal, McCall's, Women's Home Companion, Delineator, Pictorial Review,* and even the venerable *Good Housekeeping* and its institute for product testing.[23] Much to advertisers' dismay, these consumer advocacy books found a large group of readers and became frequently requested library books.[24]

CR focused on gathering facts to support a drive to supplement the inadequate consumer protection under the existing food and drug legislation. It also illuminated the scant consumer information presented in advertising. This strategy, of course, did not sit well with the advertising industry. Advertisers argued that average consumers were incapable of understanding product specifications and that information about composition, construction, and performance of goods was lost on them. Consumers, they concluded, did not wish to be bothered with intricate product details. Consumer advocates, in contrast, denounced these arguments as smoke screens invented by manufacturers to prevent consumers from knowing the truth about advertised products.[25] "Basically, however, he [the advertiser] cannot be neutral, else his copy will be called ineffective and his income lessened," claimed the economics professor and CR advisor Colston E. Warne. "He must mix truth and falsehood, fear and flattery in the attempt to break sales resistance. He may appeal to the emotions, he may introduce testimonials, or he may employ convincing scientific or pseudo-scientific arguments. Basically, however, he can never be impartial. Whatever pretenses of public service he may make, his sponsorship of a superior product ordinarily depends more upon chance than upon design." According to Warne, the advertising industry's deliberate practice of inducing consumers to rely on trademarks and slogans instead of

M. C. Phillips, 1930s. Reprinted with permission from the Consumers' Research Collection, Special Collections and University Archives, Rutgers University Libraries.

Arthur Kallet, 1930s. Reprinted with permission from the Consumers' Research Collection, Special Collections and University Archives, Rutgers University Libraries.

providing them with product information revealed advertising's true function in an oligopolistic economy.[26]

By the early 1930s advertising had come under scrutiny by more than just consumer groups. Organizations with less radical views were beginning to criticize the institution as well. Although both left-leaning and middle-of-the-road groups argued that advertising's emotional appeals made the entire practice a waste of time and money, the moderate critique focused largely on advertisers' tendency to address consumers in a disrespectful and condescending manner, often suggesting that consumers were like children. Individuals subscribing to this view were highly critical of advertising copy that offended decency and good taste but did not, as did the more radical group of advertising critics, attack or question advertising's economic role or function. This distinction provided little comfort to the advertising industry, which viewed most criticism of its marketing strategies and their practical consequences as a direct threat to its legitimacy.

By all accounts, a negative view of advertising seemed to be spreading. The use of advertising testimonials, a technique that had increased in popularity during the 1920s,[27] irked large segments of the public, who also found the excessive use of pseudoscientific jargon, unwarranted superlatives, tabloid-like appeals to fear, and advertisements that touted sex objectionable.[28] Jested one observer:

> By reading or listening to really advanced advertising, we find that the up-to-date maiden does not buy toilet soaps, dentifrices and antiseptic solutions for the sordid purpose of coping with dirt and germs. She employs them to ward off the host of dread menaces—all bearing horrific names—which stand between her and her coveted goal, the altar. Once she has "got her man" she buys certain foods, not for their flavor or nutritive value, but to cajole her sulking mate by the well-known stomach-to-heart route. Of course his ill temper is due to his having to endure that torturing masculine ordeal, shaving; and any of the certain aids to "starting the day with a smile" will solve the problem. In the remote event that happiness still eludes them, the fine ecstasy of the honeymoon can always be recaptured by the use of a (of course not habit forming) laxative. And should there be a "blessed event," the heir is certain to become an athletic champion if he eats glowingly endorsed cereals.[29]

Another gauge of the growing public skepticism toward advertising was the popularity of *Ballyhoo.* Launched as a humor magazine, *Ballyhoo* lampooned notorious and well-known advertisements, much as *Mad* magazine and *Adbusters* would do in subsequent generations. Only five months after its first issue in August 1931, circulation had reached an astonishing million and a half copies. In the words of Roland Marchand, *Ballyhoo* became "one of the most sensational new business enterprises to defy the depression."[30] Consumer dissatisfaction with advertising expressed itself in other ways as well. Groups and individuals produced screenplays that spoofed advertising and highlighted the need for consumer education. A play called *Consumers in Wonderland,* for example, offered a dramatization of themes in *100,000,000 Guinea Pigs* and received a strong endorsement as well as a production-related contribution from CR.[31]

The emergence of radio broadcasting in the 1930s as an explicitly advertising-based medium also fanned the flames of public discontent with advertising. Although some listeners accepted the notion that advertising made broadcasting of their favorite programming possible, others found radio ads in their living rooms offensive.[32] Moreover, radio advertising, with no written record to which consumers could refer, was regarded as potentially far more fraudulent than print copy. Whereas a print ad addressed its readers one at a time and in comparative privacy, acknowledged the trade publication *Printers' Ink,* "radio blares forth a three-minute essay on some subject that generally is confined to the boudoir or whispered into the ear of a physician."[33] In 1932 a report by the Federal Radio Commission revealed that more than one-sixth of the average commercial program devoted itself to sales pitches. Pressure from advertisers, claimed critics, had turned radio "from a valuable social resource into an instrument of torture."[34] This discontent escalated into large-scale debates and public hearings on the merits of commercial radio broadcasts in the early 1930s. Letters from concerned listeners poured in to the commission. Listeners demanded a stop to, or at least a drastic reduction in the amount of, radio advertising. Some wished for a noncommercial radio system like the British Broadcasting Corporation or at least a day of commercial-free broadcasting each week.[35] Commercial radio broadcasters' concern that public antipathy toward advertising might cause the establishment of noncommercial radio in the United States ended with the passage of the Communications Act of 1934. The law effectively sanctioned commercial broadcasting and ensured that the government would oversee it. At the same time, the Federal Radio Commission was renamed the Federal Communications Commission.[36]

In these early years of the consumer movement the advertising industry made few attempts at meeting the movement halfway or even bothering to listen to its claims. On the contrary, the industry responded indignantly and defensively. Instead of attacking advertising, industry representatives argued, consumers should be grateful for the modern conveniences it showcased. "Advertising in its essence is simply telling a great many people about something in the quickest possible time at the lowest possible cost," declared Roy S. Durstine, vice president and general manager of the advertising firm Batten, Barton, Durstine, and Osborn. "There's nothing mysterious about it." Much like other defenders, he accused the consumer movement of picking out the worst excesses and applying broad generalizations to make all advertising look bad. Some of the consumer movement's findings, he contended, would be laughable if "sincere and intelligent women" did not take them seriously.[37] Advertising's benefits, according to the American Association of Advertising Agencies president John Benson, were not only that it prevented economic stagnation but also that it lowered prices and spurred people to work harder to afford advertised products.[38] When asked to explain why emotional appeals were considered necessary in advertising, however, Benson could not hide his true view of consumers:

> Advertising does not offer a woman a cake of soap as a bare means of washing off the dirt. It surrounds that purely physical function with an imaginative appeal to her love of beauty, of personal charm. There is no doubt that keeping clean is a factor in being attractive. There is no illusion about that. But there is an illusion about personal charm in a woman. When advertising invests a prosaic article like soap with the sentiment of feminine attraction, it adds color and perfume to a menial thing. It also stirs in women the renewed desire to be comely, [and] appeals to a deep-seated hope. It is an illusion, of course. No sane woman is going to seriously believe that soap can keep or restore youthful charm. Still it is a means to that end and its proper use [is] a very desirable practice.[39]

The advertising community argued that most people liked advertising and that the real problem appeared to be a small percentage of questionable ads that gave the entire industry a bad reputation.[40] It offered evidence for its case: One publication had decided to reject advertising in favor of a 200 percent increase in subscription prices. The resulting (and disastrous) renewal rate of 40 percent proved, according to *Advertising Age,* that the public liked advertising's price-subsidizing effect and that it desired and relied on advertising as a form of information. "The conveniences of life and the high standard of living known in America have resulted primarily because of advertising," contended the journal's editors.[41] Others stressed advertising's role in making an almost endless list of commodities and services within most people's reach. Oranges, which only a few years earlier had been a rare treat, had, thanks to advertising, become a staple item in most U.S. homes. Heavy advertising of other items ranging from radios and cameras to canned soup and tires were credited with improving product quality and offering lower prices to consumers.[42]

Instead of listening to consumer advocates, businesses urged consumers to trust the most reputable manufacturers when making product selections. Because of their investments in product development and marketing, so the reasoning went, such manufacturers could not risk selling products that were of inferior quality.[43] Brand-name products therefore represented a reliable and adequate information source for consumers.[44]

These claims failed to answer some of the consumer movement's most damaging accusations. Demands from organized consumers not only directly contradicted the advertising industry's low opinion of the average consumer but also challenged advertising's privileged, and arguably elevated, role in an economy typified by oligopolistic markets. (As consumer advocates maintained, it was precisely advertising's ability to add glamour and prestige to a product and remove it from price competition that manufacturers considered valuable.) In a sense, the consumer movement and its demands exposed some of the industry's limitations and contradictions. The advertising industry's claims to serve consumers rang hollow when advertisers refused to take the consumer movement's advice to heart. How could the same people be content as consumers but angered as citizens? The consumer movement's demands seriously challenged the advertising community's concept of consumer sovereignty and demonstrated the parameters of citizens' power.[45]

The Advertising Industry Responds to the Consumer Movement

From the standpoint of the advertising industry, the consumer movement could hardly have arrived at a more inopportune time. Like most other business enterprises, advertising had been devastated by the Great Depression. By 1933 the amount of advertising had plummeted more than 50 percent from its 1929 level of $2 billion.[46] "The Golden Bowl of advertising is not broken, but it has been badly cracked, and through that crack has leaked about half of the 1929 personnel of the profession and, probably, a bit more than half of the profession's 1929 income," reflected the left-wing advertising critic and sometimes copywriter James Rorty in 1933.[47] After a prosperous decade advertising writers and executives in the 1930s found themselves joining the ranks of the unemployed. The industry viewed the future with insecurity. At first, contends T. J. Jackson Lears, there was a lot of brave talk about reasserting managerial ideals and claims that older production values had acquired new luster in the harsher economic climate. But two years into the Depression anxiety and despair grew inside advertising agencies as clients cut back on their ad expenditures.[48] Hard times hit everyone, but advertisers had only recently arrived at the top, and many fell a long way. Salaries of $150 a week for good copywriters and as much as $50,000 a year for advertising executives were suddenly a thing of the past.[49] Several national advertising organizations held meetings to discuss shrinking billings and help members obtain employment. *Advertising Age* offered to print "position wanted" advertisements for unemployed members of the advertising community free of charge and wholeheartedly supported the Advertising Federation of America's (AFA's) efforts to establish an employment service for out-of-work practitioners.[50]

Although the advertising community's first response had been to ignore consumer discontent and critics such as Chase, Schlink, and Kallet, its PR nightmare was not going away.[51] On the contrary, an increasing number of people—predominantly middle-class women—voiced their concerns. That these energized, educated women, who spoke "dignified and correct English," pronounced themselves skeptics of advertising set off alarm bells throughout the advertising industry.[52] "There is one thing that every manufacturer in the country can paste in his hat and that is the fact that this consumer movement cannot be met by evasion or by shrill cries of 'Bolshevik,'" commented the editor of *Printers' Ink,* C. B. Larrabee. He urged the advertising community to face the oncoming middle-class consumer revolt.[53] Much of the industry's uneasiness centered on CR's "highbrow" and highly educated group of followers.[54] The problem was not Schlink himself, argued a writer in *Printers' Ink.* "If I were seriously interested in the advertising business, I don't think I'd devote much time to the height of Mr. Schlink's forehead or the hang of his tweeds. He isn't important at all—just an old troublemaker and if he doesn't like our country, he ought to go back where he came from. What I'd do is tackle the problem of getting those 40,000 high-brows to have as much faith in advertising as they have in Mr. Schlink."[55]

As it gradually recognized that the consumer movement deserved serious consideration, the advertising industry continued to assert that much of the criticism against advertising was unjust. Although admitting that a few advertisers tended toward exaggerated, loud, and offensive advertising and that such practices needed to be discouraged, the general consensus was that it was unfair to punish the entire industry for the sins of a small minority.[56] The industry accused CR and consumer-interest book authors of abusing the public's confidence and contributing to advertising's weakening influence.[57] Although representatives for the advertising industry acknowledged that CR had made thousands of people more conscious of their role as consumers, they accused the growing consumer organization of employing unscientific research methods and of disseminating anti-advertising propaganda.[58] Coming to the industry's defense was Raymond Pearl, the director of the Institute of Biological Research at Johns Hopkins University. He declared that *100,000,000 Guinea Pigs* gave the false impression that food and drug manufacturers were engaged in a massive conspiracy with the dual goal of conducting toxicological experiments and amassing vast wealth. The professor, although acknowledging that some food and drug manufacturers had engaged in questionable practices, accused Kallet and Schlink of overgeneralizing and exaggerating. The pair's conduct, he claimed, demonstrated all too well that they were prone to the same chicanery that they accused the advertising industry of employing.[59]

Public criticism of advertising did not emanate only from CR. In 1934 James Rorty published what was arguably the most devastating critique of advertising penned to that date. In *Our Master's Voice: Advertising,* Rorty portrayed the industry as a fundamentally antidemocratic institution that helped cement corporate domination of both the economy and the polity. Both directly, by selling useless products that appealed to people's vanities, and indirectly, by influencing the editorial content of the mass media it supported, advertising had demonstrated its limits as a useful economic force and social influence, argued Rorty. Few kind words were offered to his former colleagues in the advertising industry whom he accused of addressing the consuming public as if their minds were frozen at the fourteen-year-old stage. Neither did the lobbying efforts employed by major advertisers to prevent federal regulation of its practices escape his scorching criticism.[60]

Although critics characterized some of Rorty's arguments as "balderdash" and some of his conclusions as "obviously silly," Rorty's considerable personal success as a copywriter and firsthand knowledge of the profession lent a certain degree of credence to his work.[61] This may also help explain why the management of *Printers' Ink,* which harbored a great dislike for CR and its leaders, appeared to enjoy a more cordial relationship with Rorty than with Schlink. Never one to bury a hatchet or forget a cross word, Schlink carried a grudge against the trade journal because of the many critical, even insulting, articles it had printed about CR. In fact, the entire executive and technical staff at CR was so burnt by their experiences with the trade press that they made a point of interacting with business and advertising executives by written correspondence only. This way, they reasoned, the ambiguity and misunderstandings that frequently arose from oral communication could be kept to a minimum. Schlink's contempt for *Printers' Ink* did not extend to the entire trade press, however. He held trade publications such as *Advertising and Selling* and *Tide,* which provided a more welcoming platform for the consumer movement, in higher regard.[62] Conciliatory attempts by Roy Dickinson, the president of *Printers' Ink,* were met with a great deal of skepticism that bordered on hostility.[63]

Schlink's dislike for *Printers' Ink* extended to Rorty, who occasionally wrote for the publication. A self-declared Marxist, Rorty had made it clear that he was involved with the consumer movement primarily because it provided a basis for propaganda and agitation against the capitalist system. His attitude and commitment to consumer issues did not impress Schlink and his fellow CR leaders, who viewed the fight for consumers' rights as one of the most important battles of the time. Although Schlink's anti-Communist stance was not pronounced in the early 1930s, it is quite possible that Schlink realized that any association with Rorty might hurt CR and scare away potential supporters.[64] Although he turned down a request to review *Our Master's Voice,* Schlink had to admit that parts of the book were "very well done."[65] Schlink was also upset with Rorty's involvement in an organization called Cooperative Distributors. Like CR, Cooperative Distributors tested products and published a bulletin. Unlike CR, however, Rorty's group bought the approved products and sold them wholesale and by mail order to the public. Claiming that its testing was substandard, Schlink did not approve of the outfit at all. Although the cooperative movement as a whole increased in popularity during the 1930s, Cooperative Distributors was short-lived, folding within a few years.[66]

Segments of the publishing industry, which relied to varying degrees on advertising for revenue, were so threatened by the consumer movement's potential that in some cases they tried to prevent consumer advocacy books from being published. This became particularly evident when John Day Publishers changed its decision to print M. C. Phillips's *Skin Deep.* Contending that the book's accusations about cosmetics testing were bitter and vindictive, John Day refused to publish the book unless Phillips agreed to leave out the most damaging sections. Phillips then accused Richard Walsh, who in addition to being a John Day editor wrote for the *Women's Home Companion,* of wanting to protect his employer. In spite of Walsh's protests, Phillips' suspicion was confirmed when it was revealed that Stanley Latshaw, who served as the president of *Delineator,* another popular women's magazine that relied heavily on cosmetics advertising, also served on John Day's board of directors.[67] Upset over Phillips's accusation that he was trying to hamper the consumer movement, Walsh argued that his role in helping *Our Master's Voice* get published had once and for all proved any lack of bias. Ultimately Phillips found a more sympathetic publisher in Vanguard, which agreed to publish *Skin Deep* late in 1934.[68]

Women's magazines were not alone in wanting to prevent CR and its leaders from gaining more influence. Several advertising-supported publications refused to accept ads for CR's services. Although the *Nation* and the *New York Times* agreed to carry CR's ads, *Time, Newsweek,* and *Harper's* declined.[69]

Whereas the advertising industry was uncomfortable with the consumer movement's criticism and the attention it received, it was even more concerned that a consumer critique would be taken as a true indicator of public opinion and actually influence lawmakers in their capacity as guardians of the public interest. Adding to the industry's uneasiness was that the Roosevelt administration, unlike its predecessor, seemed to have taken a strong interest in consumer issues.[70]

Roosevelt, the National Recovery Administration, and Consumer Issues

By the early 1930s the Great Depression that had started with the 1929 stock market crash was taking its toll. Before the Depression more than 40 percent of the population had existed at a subsistence or a poverty level. By 1935–36 more than 60 percent of the population fit into this category. Consumers were not simply paying more attention to their spending habits; they were also starting to ask questions about the overall economy.[71] Whereas Herbert Hoover's strategy for dealing with the Depression had been based on the assumption that overproduction was the key problem, Roosevelt gradually came to assess the source as one of underconsumption. In his opinion, the key to lifting Americans out of the Depression was by increasing spending and putting money into motion.[72]

The initial challenge for the new administration as it came to power in 1933 was how to start the chain of events. Weak purchasing power among large groups of the public represented a real obstacle to the plan. The solution, in Roosevelt's opinion, was to give workers shorter hours and increase their wages. This, he reasoned, would enable consumers to buy and thus start the upward spiral of business recovery.[73] The president's Reemployment Agreement stipulated a work week no longer than forty hours, a minimum wage of twelve dollars a week, and no child labor. To increase workers' purchasing power Roosevelt asked that prices not be increased beyond what they were on July 1, 1933. With the expected boost in purchasing power due to higher wages, however, merchants anticipated increased sales.[74] Formalizing this plan was the 1933 National Recovery Administration (NRA), which would promote the organization of industry to eliminate unfair competitive practices, establish fair practices, reduce unemployment, improve labor standards, raise or maintain wages and working hours, and otherwise rehabilitate industry. Through a suspension of antitrust laws, and in an effort that involved nineteen thousand trade groups from all fields, each industry was required to develop its own set of codes on issues such as minimum prices, competitive practices, maximum work hours, minimum wages, and possible curtailment of output and present them to the NRA for approval.[75] Complementing the overall plan was the Agricultural Adjustment Act, which Congress passed in 1933. The act provided acreage and production control, restricted marketing agreements, and authorized new lending. It also regulated the licensing of processors and dealers and awarded farmers who cut back on production. In addition to these considerations, Roosevelt's New Deal administration also recognized the consuming public as a special-interest group in need of official representation.[76]

One of the most challenging tasks facing the NRA during summer 1933 was to negotiate code agreements with all the industries.[77] Many within the advertising industry initially opposed the NRA, arguing (as did many other members of the business community) that it represented an unwarranted intrusion into private enterprise. That belief notwithstanding, Roosevelt's solution to economic recovery, at least initially, did not drastically differ from that of Hoover. Although Democrats paid lip service to giving consumers a real voice, their strategies ultimately perpetuated the Republican tendency to give power to major industries. "The New Dealers," argues Lizabeth Cohen, "may have articulated different commitments than their Republican predecessors, but in Roosevelt's first administration they still functioned within a classical economic paradigm where attention focused on achieving recovery through more efficient production, with the assumption that increased consumption would automatically follow. Underconsumption may have been a root of depression, according to the Democrats, but the route to improving consumer fortunes—and hence the economy—still lay with assisting business, not its customers."[78]

After an industry submitted a code of "fair competition" to the NRA, the proposal went through the gamut of public hearings before the president signed it into law. The NRA had the advice of three official advisory boards: the Industrial Advisory Board, the Labor Advisory Board, and the Consumers' Advisory Board (CAB). The CAB, with its focus on consumers as an interest group, was a novel concept. To some, it proved that the government had finally recognized consumers' stake in U.S. industry's organization and regulation.[79] For consumer advocates who had claimed that government had been lax and indifferent toward consumers' rights and interests, the CAB offered a strong ray of hope. "We have often heard that the consumer is helpless, because [he is] unorganized," observed an enthusiastic Lynd, who had been selected as a CAB member. "The reason the consumer is helpless is not that he has no organization but that as a matter of course, through traditions long accepted he takes it for granted that the officers he selects to manage his organization will represent the opposing interest instead of his. For the first time in the history of the country," he continued, "those officers have 'heard their master's voice.' They have recognized that they are helpless unless their policies are approved and enforced by the *consuming* public."[80] Schlink, who at this point had not developed a dislike for the government's strategy, also offered encouragement. "The government service," he asserted, "is by no means a safe basket to put our eggs in, but it is one of the places where focusing on interest and attention can be achieved, at least, and that is a necessary first step toward any effective change."[81]

The task of protecting consumers' interests was not without challenges, however. Because the codes were voluntary, they were drawn up and presented by industry and so naturally reflected industry's viewpoint. This huge advantage given to companies and big business concerned the CAB a great deal.[82] But because the NRA's Advisory Council was supposed to reach a consensus among the Industrial Advisory Board, the Labor Advisory Board, and the CAB on particular issues, the CAB used this need for unanimity as a way to modify original NRA policies to consumers' advantage.

This was not particularly popular with some NRA leaders, who viewed the CAB's opposition to industry codes as "obstructionist" tactics by a "left-wing brain trust." And CAB officials did not necessarily object to this characterization.[83] Also along these lines, Gen. Hugh S. Johnson, the head of the NRA, and other leaders had scant sympathy for the consumer program particularly because the fair competition codes being framed by various industries were repeatedly challenged by the CAB on the grounds that they involved output restriction, price pegging, and the absence of quality guarantees.

Some business leaders assumed that consumer representatives lacked popular support to back up their demands and lend them legitimacy. "What is a Consumer?" asked a *Printers' Ink* writer. "Even the most vociferous of the self-appointed champions of the consumer [has] failed to make clear the nature and identity of this suffering class."[84] Whereas numerous trade organizations backed the Industrial Advisory Board, and the Labor Advisory Board held the support of many labor unions, the CAB could not count on a strong and organized consumer movement. Although industry and labor representatives could, if necessary, be financed by their business or labor unions, the CAB was never able to make attractive offers in either tenure or salary. The weak and uncoordinated nature of consumer organizations at the time represented yet another problem. Few individuals emerged as obvious leaders to be included in the CAB. Members were recruited from academia, from what existed of mainstream consumer organizations, and from an assortment of technical experts on consumer goods.[85]

In addition to these problems, the CAB had a limited budget that made it impossible to hire enough staff or bring the same number of representatives to code hearings as did labor and industry. The situation was helped somewhat when the Federal Trade Commission loaned the board some of its advisors.[86] Despite this assistance, during the NRA's early stages few officials could understand consumers' role in the program. Even Lynd began to realize that the CAB was just "a gesture to the women of the country that was never intended by General Johnson to work."[87] Making the CAB's situation more difficult was the official stipulation that it could not openly criticize NRA policy. All CAB publicity had to be approved by the NRA publicity division before it was released.[88]

The Roosevelt administration's interest in consumer issues was not limited to its CAB activities. Under the leadership of Frederick C. Howe, the Agricultural Adjustment Administration established local consumer councils. The initial plan called for the establishment of a consumer council in each of the more than three thousand counties in the United States. Each local council would have between five and seven members, and the administrative leadership of the entire program was left to Paul H. Douglas, a professor of economics at the University of Chicago who would later become a Democratic U.S. senator from Illinois. Each consumer council was made up of representatives from a variety of fields and professions. Their purpose, states the historian Meg Jacobs, was to tie the councils to labor and cooperative movements, do away with any notion that their functions belonged to women's social clubs or teachers' clubs, and foster an alliance between farmers and labor. Although he fell far short of realizing his goal of establishing twenty thousand local councils, Douglas had, by early 1934, managed to create several local councils in forty states. Approximately 150 of the councils survived the downfall of the NRA in 1935 and continued in an unofficial capacity for some time afterward.[89]

These consumer councils were charged with acting as government watchdogs and ensuring that industry adhered to the fair trade codes submitted to the NRA. It goes without saying that their actions were poorly received in advertising circles. A *Printers' Ink* editorial, for example, found a striking resemblance between consumer councils and "what the keyhole peepers were to Prohibition." Consumer councils, the editorial concluded, was yet another part of a New Deal scheme to impose a Socialist order upon U.S. industry.[90] Others questioned how well the average consumer was equipped for the job. "Consumers," argued the editors of the liberal trade journal *Tide,* "don't know the ins and outs of business, the meaning of quantity discounts, hidden price increases and the like. In any man to man struggle with business their lack of technical business knowledge makes them ineffectual. Their only weapon is the buyers' strike and no one believes that the Administration through Consumer Councils, or any other kind of an organization, would foster a buyers' strike when the political future of the Democratic party depends so absolutely on a lusty business revival."[91] The Agricultural Adjustment Administration also published a newsletter called *The Consumers' Guide.* Although it was primarily concerned with the agricultural production program, it also served a more general group of consumers. The guide and its attempts to point consumers toward more "intelligent purchasing" did not escape the attention of advertisers, who questioned the necessity of both the administration and the consumer councils. Most business interests were not impressed. "The notion appears to have been accepted by some of these new dealers that the consumer should be given information about how and what to buy by the United States government, instead of being forced to rely on what she is told by the manufacturer or merchant," asserted one representative from the advertising community.[92] One advertising executive went so far as to call this educational effort an act that bordered on "actual government control."[93] Although business and powerful leaders inside the NRA criticized the government for doing too much to accommodate consumers, advocates—especially CR—castigated the government's unwillingness to aid them.[94]

Advertising under the NRA

The advertising community's initial reaction to the code-building effort was one of suspicion. Some feared that codes might undermine direct competition and that advertising would be seen by business as an extravagance. Others, however, were more optimistic, suggesting that code agreements might translate into an improved economy and increased advertising.[95] Regardless of individual attitudes, the advertising industry on the whole did not assume an entirely adversarial stance toward the NRA.[96]

Between June 1933 and May 1935 the Advertising Federation of America (AFA) and the National Better Business Bureau (NBBB) aided the NRA in the advertising-related aspects of code building. The AFA maintained representatives in Washington, D.C., who ensured that provisions against false and misleading advertising were incorporated into each set of NRA trade practices.[97]

As an industry, according to Roosevelt, advertising itself could serve the useful function of informing people about the various government programs. "If ever one thing needed advertising publicity," he stated, "it is government—national, state, county and city. Our citizens are often in abysmal ignorance as to how government functions or how it is intended to function."[98]

This was the kind of assurance that the industry was longing to hear. "Advertising," concluded the editor of *Printers' Ink*, C. B. Larrabee, "has nothing to fear from the National Industrial Recovery Act."[99] Some of the most optimistic representatives from the advertising industry speculated that advertising, by creating consumer confidence and increasing buying, could alleviate the economic Depression. Thus, some hoped, advertising would no longer be viewed as a problem but rather as a helpful tool.[100] In September 1933 the AFA accepted a formal invitation from the NRA to establish a national advisory committee of advertising men and women to act as advisors on advertising and publicity matters. Its task, as it turned out, was to design a campaign to "sell" the NRA to the U.S. public and to promote the importance of consumer spending (called *money in motion*) as a means of "carry[ing] the battle against the depression into every city and hamlet."[101] In addition to increasing consumer buying and directing consumers to businesses that operated under the NRA, the committee worked to attract more firms to the NRA program and stimulate sales activity among businesses that had products to sell. To achieve its goals the NRA accepted the help of the AFA's Bureau of Research and Education.[102] Combining its efforts with newspapers, magazines, and other forms of mass media, the advertising industry helped spread information about the NRA's Blue Eagle program and also aided its "buy now" campaign. The Blue Eagle was intended as a goodwill trademark; only businesses affiliated with organizations that had signed code agreements with the NRA were allowed to display the emblem, and the government relied on advertising to get this message across. The motivating force behind this effort was the NRA's desire to encourage consumer spending.[103] It did not take long before a pleased Hugh S. Johnson congratulated the advertising industry on a job well done. "You pick up a newspaper and glance through the advertising columns and you find a small cut of a blue eagle in that advertising," reflected the NRA head. "Over the radio you hear the announcer state the fact [that] 'this product is manufactured under the NRA.' All this is advertising and it has been through advertising that the country has been rallied behind the 'Blue Eagle and the NRA.'"[104]

Much as they had during World War I, advertising agencies served the government by preparing and placing advertisements free of charge. Newspapers and magazines did their part by donating space. The "buy now" campaign tried to convince consumers that they should buy products immediately because prices would soon increase. It reassured them that their anxiety about spending money was unfounded. It also explained the reasons for upcoming price increases and why these eventually would work in everyone's best interest. The administration contended that both the advertising and the publishing industries would harvest their rewards from the increased consumer spending spurred by the campaign.[105] These ads went pretty far to convince people to part with their money. One advertisement, for example, told of little Mary Anne, unable to attend a birthday party because her clothes were old and patchy:

> Mary [Anne] can't go because her clothes aren't fit. Her little dresses are clean, yes—but frayed and pale from many washings. Her shoes are scuffed and battered. Other children in the neighborhood will be gayly and neatly dressed. And Mary Anne would be cruelly out of place. So Mary [Anne]'s mother sends regrets. How sharply the little tragedies of our own childhood stand out—even today! They are not lightly brushed aside. Child authorities tell us that such incidents are, all too often, the deep-rooted cause of shyness and a lack of confidence that lasts through life. Mary Anne must have new things. And now is the time to buy them—*while prices are lower than they are ever likely to be again. Read the advertisements in this newspaper. They bring you news of many fine clothing bargains which you can obtain by acting immediately. Supply your present and future needs at these low prices!*[106]

"Government-sponsored advertising," contended a writer for *Printers' Ink* proudly, "recognizes that good advertising is not propaganda or ballyhoo."[107] The Roosevelt administration's relationship with business in general and the advertising industry in particular did not exactly impress CR. Schlink soon developed a great deal of hostility toward the CAB and its feeble efforts to aid consumers.[108] Although Schlink at least initially kept a somewhat open mind about the CAB's potential, he quickly expressed great disappointment with its work and even went so far as to describe the NRA as an example of "industrial fascism."[109] One of Schlink's major complaints was the CAB's inability to represent the average consumer. Its members, he argued, were highly respectable, although terribly dull, social workers, women's magazine editors, and commercial purchasing agents who neither understood nor shared the interests of "the factory-product-making-buying-and-using class of workers, farmers, and other consumers" that CR wanted to reach.[110] Because of their social traditions and viewpoints, he argued, CAB members were not equipped to fight consumers' struggle against powerful business interests.[111] Particular contempt was bestowed upon CAB chair Mary Harriman Rumsey, a wealthy socialite who, according to Schlink, had no business intervening in the consumption and income problems that 120 million Americans were facing. "I have yet to meet anyone who knows a single economic idea that Mrs. Rumsey, the Consumer's Defender, has had, or holds to, or who has been able to understand or find an element of the public interest in anything that she has said publicly or privately," Schlink smirked.[112]

Far from everyone at CR shared Schlink's militant views. Frank L. Palmer, the head of the American Civil Liberties Union in Chicago and a close friend of Arthur Kallet, suggested that Schlink become an NRA member. Palmer speculated that this would help influence code building and bring it more in line with CR's goals and objectives. "You would go into the organization," suggested Palmer, "with the utter willingness to get thrown out if that were necessary to expose some of the crookedness and worse in manufacturing and distribution."[113] Although pretending not to show much enthusiasm for this idea, Schlink became quite interested when it was rumored that he had been considered, but quickly rejected, for an advisory position. Palmer speculated that the NRA feared that Schlink would impose CR's agenda on the board.[114] Schlink did not admit to being disappointed. "Participation in government," he remarked, "is dirty work, and if it doesn't start that way it will end that way."[115] Acting on Schlink's motion in fall 1933, CR passed a resolution that prohibited any member of the organization's board or corporation from accepting state or national governmental positions. Not only did the new stipulation prevent the possibility of compromised loyalties but it also served as a convenient shield against any public humiliation associated with CR's absence from the NRA's inner chambers.[116]

As time went by Schlink became increasingly outraged over what he perceived as the NRA's inability to protect consumers. He argued that business had not only bilked consumers in nearly every code that had been established but it had received the government's blessing in doing so. Consumers, he warned, should not fool themselves into thinking that the government was looking out for their interests. In his opinion the New Deal had boiled down to a partnership between business and government.[117] "It is bad enough to have the consumer sunk by the operations of the NRA," Schlink concluded. "It is intolerable and cries out for correction that a board nominally set up to provide consumer protections and guard their interests on every point of the NRA program is actually by the connivance of its membership spurned and disregarded in all the operations of NRA executives."[118] Many CAB members considered themselves strong supporters of CR and noted, not without regret, that CR had taken "a hostile attitude to the Board."[119] The Blue Eagle of the NRA, warned the *Consumers' Research General Bulletin*, "is, appropriately, a bird of prey, symbolizing the way in which business plunders consumers."[120] Because consumers did not have the same power as labor or more influence than business, Schlink could not see how the recovery plan could be successful or bring prosperity.[121]

By September 1933 a group of consumer activists had assembled to organize the Emergency Council on Consumer Organizations. The group, which counted Rorty, Howe, Lynd, Tugwell, Kallet, and Schlink as members, protested the CAB's marginal position and lack of power within the NRA and asked Roosevelt to establish the Department of the Consumer, a plan that Schlink was quick to embrace and promote.[122] Just as the Department of Commerce represented business and the Department of Labor presented its constituents' views, the Department of the Consumer would guard and represent the consumer. Included in the proposal, which received support from a range of organizations including CR, the Co-operative League of the United States, Cooperative Distributors, the Consolidated Home Owners Mortgage Committee, the Committee for the Defense of Schools, and Consumer Co-operative Services, was a demand for transferring the Food and Drug Administration, which functioned as a bureau in the Department of Agriculture, to the proposed department.[123] This, it was argued, would relieve the Food and Drug Administration of political pressure from special-interest groups and help it to better serve consumers. Schlink also proposed incorporating the Bureau of Standards, which was a subdivision of the Department of Commerce, into the new department.[124] "If consumers are to have any authoritative spokesperson for their interest, we are convinced that this is the only means by which their rights to well-made goods at low prices, [to] a food supply free from poisonous spray residues and other dangerous adulterants, and to protection from harmful cosmetics and useless or dangerous and misrepresented patent medicines will secure any recognition."[125] This proposal strongly resembled CR's goals and objectives. By moving the Food and Drug Administration as well as the Bureau of Standards to the new department, much of the work started by CR could be adopted on a larger scale by the government.[126]

The Mandatory Grading Controversy

One idea CR popularized was product grading. Consumers, as CR had pointed out, were unable to monitor product quality, and because advertisements failed to provide much useful information, they had no way to protect themselves against marketplace disappointment. In an attempt to institutionalize consumer protection against this practice the CAB suggested grading requirements as part of the code-building process. This proposal did not sit well with the advertising industry, which considered the plan fundamentally at odds with sound business practices. The CAB soon developed its own plan for making the many industry codes serve their interests. Supported by the American Standards Association, the CAB demanded that grading and standard requirements be written into industry codes. Based on a simple system of identification, this grading scheme would enable consumers to determine the quality and durability of goods. In addition to textile labeling, the plan included mandatory labeling of canned goods so that consumers would know their size, ingredients, and relative quality. In contrast to advertising superlatives and claims that frequently left consumers disillusioned, grading, it was claimed, would increase consumer confidence and, consequently, increase sales.[127] "I have no patience with the calamity howlers who say that if we have quality standards we'll take all the color and variety out of life," asserted Lynd in defense of the plan. "Do you want to have to dull the color of living and to blunt the edge of your wants by spending energy fumbling over whether the silk in a necktie you buy will stand up or will acquire permanent wrinkles after three tyings? Or whether a cotton broadcloth shirt is a good broadcloth or not?"[128]

The advertising community, however, was quick to counter the CAB's arguments. It claimed that the public did not demand grading, that government had no business interfering with consumers' sovereignty, and that consumers should have the opportunity to judge products based on their own standards rather than those of a third party whose criteria might differ. For example, advertisers claimed that a practice of labeling canned goods solely as either A, B, or C quality was flawed. Because flavor depended to a certain degree on individual preference, this quality was particularly difficult to grade and would therefore affect a product's overall rating. Consumers, according to industry representatives, were better served by advertising than by paternalistic government information. The CAB, in contrast, argued that advertisements consistently failed to provide consumers with information about advertised commodities. "If the buyer takes [the advertiser's] words at their face value," contended the board members, "he is frequently misled into believing the goods to be one or two grades higher in quality than they are in fact."[129] Even if such standards were in place, countered a representative from the advertising industry, "the average consumer would not understand a Government standard if he saw one."[130] The real fear for advertisers, of course, was that quality standards would go far toward reducing advertising's significance and effectiveness.[131] It might make the institution of advertising irrelevant, even counterproductive, in consumers' eyes.

Discussions such as these brought one of the advertising industry's most obvious contradictions into focus. Although advertising practitioners perceived consumers as being easily influenced and manipulated—childlike—and rarely shied away from discussing them as such in front of clients and other members of the managerial elite, when confronted by consumer advocates wielding arguments on behalf of labeling, however, they primly maintained that consumers were sovereign.[132] This contradiction was not lost on CAB members. As Lynd complained, "I am fed up with this bland complacency of pandering to natural human desires—exploiting them deliberately to the limits that the traffic will bear, and then retreating sanctimoniously behind the excuse 'But milady wants it.'" Lynd concluded that advertisers' opposition to quality standards and grading undermined the notion of consumer sovereignty, a concept the industry had been known to flaunt.[133] In fact, concurred CR, the advertising industry's opposition to the labeling program bordered on hypocrisy: "Industry itself uses quality standards freely in its own purchasing; its most ably administered plants will defend to the death their right to buy soap and paper and typewriter ribbons on a basis which assures a grade and quality neither too high nor too low, precisely adapted to their needs, at a price level their purposes and finances permit or incline them to pay." Why then, asked Schlink, was the same courtesy not extended to consumers?[134]

Another industry worry was that the mandatory labeling program would have a "'deflationary' effect on the advertising of all canned goods."[135] According to the CAB, however, the only advertisers who needed to fear the plan were those making false or misleading claims about their products. Honest advertisers would benefit because grading would help eliminate false and misleading advertising, a goal that the advertising industry itself was on record as supporting. "Consumer distrust of the advertising ethics which permit all products to be advertised as of highest quality could be dissipated were a series of grade names to become part of the advertising vocabulary," concluded the CAB. "An accurate identification of grade is not incompatible with a colorful description of the many qualities incapable of standardization. Brands will always differ."[136]

To head off this argument advertising industry representatives tried to channel the discussion into more familiar territory. This strategy included a condescending and at times confrontational attitude toward the government and the CAB. Industry insiders argued that the government lacked knowledge of economics and of advertising's role in the marketplace. They strongly attacked those who viewed advertising as a competitive weapon and persistently denied that the sole purpose of advertising was to push people into purchasing one product or another for which they had no desire. "Let us carry the reasoning further," sputtered a frustrated and sarcastic Alfred T. Falk, director of education for the AFA. "Besides advertising, there are other influences that lead the consumer from one product to another. Of these, one is superior quality. Hence quality must be wrong. Wrong, too, is better value. Wrong, also, is easier accessibility. And wrong, finally, is some thing whose elimination will call for something drastic. Often, that which leads the consumer from product to product is consumer taste. In the economists' Utopia—although to the fellow trying to sell a few orders of honest goods the place will seem far from perfect—consumers, no doubt, will have to be abolished."[137] The government's inability to recognize advertising's vital role in the overall distribution scheme was viewed by the advertising industry as part of a punishing strategy. Argued one industry defender, "It is up to all of us to combat intelligently, this rather definite and certainly unfortunate attitude on the part of certain officials in the Administration toward advertising. I believe that they are quite wrong in their beliefs. I am willing to go so far as to say I believe that they have been misled into that belief by extremists against advertising."[138]

Much to the advertising industry's concern and dismay, a 1934 survey by *Sales Management* concluded that a majority of respondents believed that the federal government was the most convincing authority regarding the quality and performance of consumer goods. Testing laboratories maintained by associations or colleges ranked second, whereas the manufacturer and testimonials by famous people ranked at the bottom of the list. Half the respondents believed that advertisements were based on exaggerated claims and identified their failure to provide consumers with price information as a major problem.[139] In the end, however, despite all its efforts, the CAB did not succeed in imposing quality standards and grade labeling. The CAB's weak position vis-à-vis business in the code-making process combined with the CAB's lack of a well-defined constituency to back it proved to be a real handicap.[140]

Conclusion

The emergence of CR and the second wave of consumer activism in the late 1920s and early 1930s triggered changes for business and consumers, but not necessarily for advertising. Consumer advocates did raise serious questions about advertising practices, however. If the marketplace, as many industry defenders had come to claim, represented a new democratic forum in which each dollar counted as a vote, a big piece of the democratic model, namely a forum in which the free flow of information could take place, was missing. Advertising, because it failed to provide consumers with information, was not just flawed, according to consumer advocates, it was antidemocratic.

The seemingly innocent demands from the consumer movement for less emotional hype and more product information in advertisements ultimately cast advertising in a harsh light. For one thing, the consumer movement's claims and demands debunked the prevailing view of consumers as irrational and emotionally driven. This, in turn, challenged advertising's newly attained position of strength in industry and commerce. Advertising's function as an oligopolistic marketing tool hinged on its ability to deemphasize price and product comparisons and to assist producers of goods and services in building brand loyalties. If consumers were not as stupid and as docile as sheep, this marketing strategy was built on a flimsy foundation. The advertising industry's initial reaction was to deny that the consumer movement's demands had merit. Unfortunately, this position patently contradicted the industry's claims about "consumer sovereignty," exposed its hypocrisy, and contributed little to the industry's credibility. Matters worsened for the advertising industry in 1933 when the government established the CAB and staffed it with several individuals who held strong loyalties to CR and its objectives. Although the CAB was mostly ineffective and unable to change the status quo, the advertising industry could by no means ignore its pronouncements and recommendations. The consumer movement stood its ground. If the advertising industry refused to cooperate with its demands, consumer advocates were ready to seek federal regulation of advertising.

3

The Drive for Federal Advertising Regulation, 1933–35

Until the 1930s the few existing advertising regulations were passed and enforced at the state and local levels. In 1906 when the Federal Food and Drugs Act was passed, advertising played only a minor role in food and drug sales. Thus, it did not occur to Congress to outlaw false and misleading advertising along with misbranded foods and drugs.[1] With the emergence of national advertising in the twentieth century, some lawmakers introduced bills to outlaw misleading advertising in interstate commerce, to levy a national tax on advertising, or to extend the act's powers. The first federal attempt at regulating advertising came in 1914 when the Federal Trade Commission (FTC) was established. Its founding amounted to weak consumer legislation because the FTC held limited powers to intervene on consumers' behalf. Legally the FTC was allowed to regulate advertising only when it was used by a business to gain an unfair advantage over another. By the early 1930s advertising had greatly increased its presence, and most people's purchases were more likely to have been inspired by advertising than by product labels.[2] Given these circumstances and a growing problem with fraudulent and misleading advertising, the demand for federal regulation of advertising would soon dominate the budding consumer movement's agenda.

By the time of Franklin D. Roosevelt's inauguration in 1933, considerable momentum had built to revise the food and drug law to include advertising regulation. In June Senator Royal S. Copeland of New York introduced a bill, drafted under the supervision of the Food and Drug Administration (FDA) and supported by Assistant Secretary of Agriculture Rexford G. Tugwell, to amend the act. Commonly referred to as the Tugwell bill, the proposed law met with a storm of protests not only from business interests, who viewed it as too stringent and intrusive, but also from consumer activists, who argued that it provided insufficient protection for consumers.

The Road to the Tugwell Bill

Although the Food and Drugs Act of 1906 had made misbranding of foods and drugs illegal, it applied only to labeling and not to general advertising of such products. Adding to this flaw was the law's definition of *misbranding.* Only when brands and labels bore information that was misleading, fraudulent, or deceptive could the FTC investigate. The commission could not regulate manufacturers who deliberately omitted key ingredients on their packages and labels or promised consumers unrealistic rewards from their products' use.[3] Another drawback from consumers' perspective was that the government could not proceed against a misbranded product until after a long judicial procedure had concluded. Consequently, before the FTC could force a manufacturer to withdraw a misbranded or mislabeled product from the market, numerous consumers might be adversely affected, or even dead.[4]

Although the FTC held the power to address misleading advertising, it could only do so to regulate unfair methods of business competition. The FTC could not intervene directly on consumers' behalf. A U.S. Supreme Court decision in 1930 delineated the limits of the FTC's authority quite clearly. The case involved a diet product called Marmola produced by the Raladam Company. The diet cure contained a tissue-burning chemical that caused several users' deaths. Acting promptly in response to this health crisis, the FTC issued a cease-and-desist order against Raladam's advertising of Marmola on the grounds that the diet cure was a dangerous remedy.

The Supreme Court, however, overturned this decision, stating that Raladam had not violated any law that regulated business competition and that the FTC, therefore, held no jurisdiction in the matter.[5] This ruling illuminated the serious lack of consumer-protective legislation and helped spread the perception that strong federal measures were required to curb deceptive and untruthful advertising.[6] The public's growing dependency on advertising to provide information made updated federal regulation vital. Supporting this demand was a growing consumer movement led by Consumers' Research Inc. (CR).

In fact, the first version of proposed legislation to replace the Food and Drugs Act of 1906 was heavily influenced by Frederick J. Schlink and Arthur Kallet's best-selling *100,000,000 Guinea Pigs.* During the early months of 1933

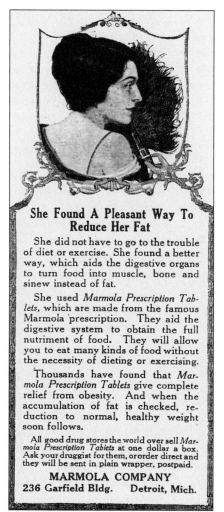

She Found A Pleasant Way To Reduce Her Fat

She did not have to go to the trouble of diet or exercise. She found a better way, which aids the digestive organs to turn food into muscle, bone and sinew instead of fat.

She used *Marmola Prescription Tablets*, which are made from the famous Marmola prescription. They aid the digestive system to obtain the full nutriment of food. They will allow you to eat many kinds of food without the necessity of dieting or exercising.

Thousands have found that *Marmola Prescription Tablets* give complete relief from obesity. And when the accumulation of fat is checked, reduction to normal, healthy weight soon follows.

All good drug stores the world over sell *Marmola Prescription Tablets* at one dollar a box. Ask your druggist for them, or order direct and they will be sent in plain wrapper, postpaid.

MARMOLA COMPANY
236 Garfield Bldg.   Detroit, Mich.

Marmola, a dangerous diet cure that helped illustrate the need for advertising regulation to protect consumers. Reprinted from the D'Arcy Collection at the Communications Library at the University of Illinois at Urbana-Champaign.

the two consumer activists worked closely with Milton Handler, a Columbia law professor who had been instrumental in drafting the 1906 law. This cooperation was not without snags, however. Throughout their collaboration Schlink stressed the need for a brave proposal that would give consumers the best protection possible and pointed to the tremendous public response to *100,000,000 Guinea Pigs* as a sign of broad support for change.[7] The public, according to Schlink, was demanding a new and powerful food and drug law. "I think," he wrote to Handler, "that lawyers in general tend to under-estimate the extent to which radical revisions can be gotten away with."[8] Acknowledging Schlink's frustration, Handler was quick to assure that consumer protection was his first priority as well. "My job primarily," he promised an anxious Schlink, "will be to translate into statutory language the ideas and desires of those who have given thought to the problem of consumer protection and food and drug regulation."[9]

In addition to asking Schlink and Kallet to share their research findings with the government, Handler also solicited their help in determining whether certain members of his staff could be entrusted with drafting important consumer legislation. Schlink did not miss this opportunity to weigh in on legislative matters. "You will be defeated from the start if you do not have around you, in key positions, persons who *want* to do something pretty clear and positive about reform of the administrative practices, and who at the same time have made no past commitments which would make it absurd or impossible for them suddenly to discover that arsenic and sulfur dioxide are poisons, and that steady and long-continued ingestion of lead is a bad thing for the people of the United States," he warned. Outlining this exchange in a letter to Tugwell, Schlink also recalled Handler's plea for advice on "men whose services for the Department of Agriculture are thought not to have been in the public interest."[10]

Although obviously finding the attention and respect bestowed upon them quite flattering, CR members sagged under the extra responsibilities. Working as the government's extended arm represented a financial strain on the organization and diminished its ability to function as a consumer watchdog. "We shall be glad to help the little that we can, on a volunteer basis, but the amount of what we can do and keep our present jobs running is very limited," Schlink cautioned Tugwell. "We don't think we should be asked to do the government's detail work in preparation of . . . additional . . . material, when the government is the one agency in the present highly complex and swirling situation which has resources of men and money at its command."[11] The consumer group was nevertheless reluctant to leave the proposal's faith in the hands of lawyers and bureaucrats. It stressed that scientists and technicians with enough knowledge to assess adulteration and dangerous levels of poison needed to be consulted as the proposed law took shape.[12] As momentum for legislation swelled, David F. Carver, a law professor from Duke University, joined the team of legal experts.[13]

To write a prospective law was one thing, but hoping for a congressional hearing, let alone a measure that Congress would pass, was another matter.

Congressional and administrative support had to be obtained. Enter Rexford G. Tugwell, a professor at Columbia University until 1932, when he became part of FDR's brain trust, the president's inner circle of advisors. Through his scholarly work, Tugwell had won a reputation as an ardent defender of consumers' rights and someone who bore little patience for corporate greed. He supported advertising only to the point that it helped consumers make educated choices between different products, and he considered advertising, designed with the single purpose of shifting consumer loyalties from one brand to another, as wasteful. Tugwell's theories of planned capitalism and his strong critique of classical economics won him few sympathizers in business circles, and his political views were compared to Socialism, even to Communism.

When Tugwell accepted the position as assistant secretary of agriculture in 1933, he assumed direct responsibility for the Department of Agriculture's consumer protection program. Tugwell believed that the outdated 1906 Food and Drugs Act provided loopholes for dishonest advertisers to take advantage of consumers. He was irked that the law provided no means of punishing advertisers who promised health and beauty but delivered illness, even death, to unsuspecting consumers.[14] "One thing seems perfectly obvious," he argued. "In a consumer economy, the interest of the consumer must come first in all our planning. Merciless profit-taking and unscrupulous adulteration are an unacknowledged sales-tax which reduce his purchasing power and nullif[ies] all of the Government's efforts to see that industry and agriculture are so organized as to give him the purchasing power with which to buy their products."[15] No wonder, then, that Handler considered Tugwell's support to be of utmost importance.[16]

The Tugwell Bill

The outcome of these deliberations resulted in S 1944, most commonly referred to as the Tugwell bill. The final version had been prepared by Walter G. Campbell, director of regulatory work for the Department of Agriculture, and was introduced into the Senate in June 1933 by Royal S. Copeland. At the same time William I. Sirovich, a Democrat from New York, introduced a companion bill in the House of Representatives. The Tugwell bill's stated purpose was to strengthen the government's power to combat public deception in the sale of food, drugs, and cosmetics. In addition to new stipulations to regulate product labeling and adulteration, the bill contained several provisions to oversee advertising. It designated an advertisement as "all representations of fact or opinion disseminated in any manner or by any means other than by labeling," it defined any advertisement as false if it by "ambiguity or inference" created a false or misleading impression, and it entrusted the FDA with the power to prohibit "false advertising" of any food, drug, or cosmetic. The truth or falsity of food, drug, and cosmetics advertising, according to the Tugwell bill, should be measured by the same standards as those that determined the truth or falsity of label statements. Falsely advertised products, in other words, should be treated as misbranded products that were thus subject to seizure by the Department of Agriculture. According to the bill, a food or drug advertisement should be considered false if any part of it was untrue or if it, by ambiguity or inference, created a misleading impression of the product. Any advertiser engaging in such practices was to be prosecuted.

The Tugwell bill also prohibited advertisements of purported or actual remedies for a long list of specific diseases for which self-medication was known to be dangerous. It specifically prohibited manufacturers from advertising a product as a cure when the remedy represented a palliative, and it barred advertising claims that ran contrary to the medical profession's general opinion. Authorization to initiate probes into false and misleading advertising practices was handed to the secretary of agriculture. Although the bill placed severe restrictions upon drug advertisements intended for the general public, it was more lenient toward drug advertisements appearing in medical journals and thus intended for the medical profession.[17] The bill also contained provisions aimed specifically at food, drug, and cosmetic manufacturing and labeling. It permitted government inspection of factories and seizure of adulterated goods and included a provision that made grade labeling mandatory.[18] The primary purpose behind the Tugwell bill, claimed its supporters, was to protect the public against injurious advertising.[19] Although conceding that the terms *ambiguity* and *inference* were rather vague, the framers maintained that the broad wording was necessary to make the law effective.[20]

The Tugwell bill generated a powerful reaction within the advertising community even before its introduction into Congress. Food and drug manufacturers expressed profound reservations about it. They wanted to protect their right to advertise, but at the same time they also worried about coming out too strongly against a bill that might receive massive public support.[21] In addition, CR, which still boasted strong membership numbers, was widely regarded as the driving force behind the proposed law.[22] The Advertising Review Committee, an industry-appointed group speaking on behalf of national advertisers, advertising agencies, publishers, and broad-casters, viewed the bill as a response to the advertising industry's failure at self-regulation. Fearing that the Tugwell bill represented the start of a trend in which all advertising activities would be "supervised and dictated to by bureaucratic authority," the advertising community did its best to fight the measure.[23] Even before its first congressional hearing the proposed revi-sion of the Food and Drugs Act of 1906 came face-to-face with some strong opposition. In fall 1933, for example, the patent-medicine producers devoted an entire three-day conference to designing strategies for defeating a mea-sure that might "spell the doom of the industry" if it was passed into law.[24] By October 1933 drug interests had drafted seventeen plans, all designed to thwart the Tugwell bill. Some suggested that they use strategies they had developed during passage of the Food and Drugs Act of 1906 and proposed that advertisers use their patronage as leverage for securing newspaper pub-licity against the bill. Others recommended that groups with a direct inter-est in defeating the bill solicit elected officials in Washington, D.C., for their help. Radio, mail, and personal contacts were seen as integral to the overall strategy.[25]

The advertising community also responded with an alternative piece of legislation. The Capper bill (S 1592) was introduced into the Senate in May 1933, just a few weeks before the formal introduction of the Tugwell bill. The former was largely a modified version of the Printers' Ink Model Statute, a set of guidelines propounded by the industry for self-regulation in 1911 that by 1933 had become accepted as advertising law in twenty-five states. Unlike the Tugwell bill, which proposed to regulate advertising of food, drugs, and cosmetics only, the Capper bill sought regulation of all forms of advertising and punishment of untrue, misleading, or deceptive advertising claims as misdemeanors through fines, imprisonment, or both.[26]

The main, but quite considerable, difference between the two bills was their widely divergent criteria for identifying false and misleading advertising. The Tugwell bill proposed "inference" and "ambiguity" as standards of judg-ment, opening the door for the subjective element of opinion; the Capper bill banned only misstatements of facts.[27] This distinction was quite significant because much of advertising relied heavily on emotional appeals.[28] Playing on ambiguity, ads invited consumers to make inferences about products. When their expectations went unfulfilled, consumers were frequently left disappointed. Exactly this practice had caught the consumer movement's attention, and the Tugwell bill now wanted to outlaw it. Consumer activists considered the Capper bill's intention to crack down on misstatements of facts in advertisements to be of limited value because so many advertisements provided consumers with so little factual information in the first place. What consumers needed was a bill that protected them against ambiguous inferences and forced advertisers to provide more factual information. This was part of the Tugwell bill's goal—and one that the Capper bill tried to evade. The Capper bill was intended to deter quacks yet leave honest advertisers leeway for "puffery." This meant that under the Capper bill advertisers would not be punished for omitting important facts and, consequently, for creating ambiguity and misleading consumers. This important loophole would become one of the most debated points during the ensuing legislative struggle.

The Capper bill, however, was not universally hailed in the advertising industry. Lee Bristol, the vice president of the Bristol-Myers Company, for example, worried that the bill's call for punishment of deceptive and misleading statements would prevent a manufacturer from using a "colorful and different story to dramatize its selling points."[29] A stop to such practices, he warned, would rob advertising of much of its value as an economic force. "I am fearful," announced the drug manufacturer who, like his colleagues, preferred that no bill be passed, "of entrusting to low-salaried, Governmental employees the opportunity of weighing in censorship scales, important decisions regarding advertising policy and advertising copy that might have serious reactions on advertising as a whole and upon advertising as an economic force in selling."[30] Elements of the advertising community that supported the Capper bill, in contrast, emphasized that the Printers' Ink Model Statute—the blueprint for the Capper bill—had led to few convictions. The general consensus was that convictions under the proposed Capper bill would follow the same pattern. Publishers, advertising groups, and the National Better Business Bureau (NBBB) were enthusiastic in their endorsement of the measure.[31] The Capper bill was sent to the Senate Committee on Interstate Commerce in May 1933, but it did not garner enough support and was soon shelved in favor of the Tugwell bill.[32]

To say that the advertising industry reacted adversely to the Tugwell bill would be an understatement. Industry group after industry group scrutinized its many provisions and developed strategies to attack the bill. "Large publishing, advertising, and broadcasting interests have been demanding a clean-up of shady advertising habits," observed a *Business Week* writer in an apt summary of reactions to the proposed law. "But they [became] somewhat breathless after a look inside the mouth of the Tugwell bill. They wanted a measure with teeth in it, but nobody expected a crocodile."[33] The

major objection concerned the bill's criteria for determining false and misleading advertising. The industry found the Tugwell bill's wording too vague
and objected to the government's role in identifying such advertising. That
broad powers were given to the secretary of agriculture—Tugwell's boss—was
seen as problematic as well. "After all," argued the editor of *Printers' Ink,*
"how many Government employees are intelligent enough to decide what
'ambiguity' and 'inference' in advertising mean? Just how far can these terms
be carried?"[34] "And who is to say whether such [an] impression has been
created?" questioned another detractor. "The censor in the Department of
Agriculture, of course. He is the sole judge."[35] Also highly contested was
a Tugwell bill provision that gave the secretary of agriculture the right to
publicize proceedings and judgments against manufacturers.[36] Echoing Lee
Bristol's concerns about the Capper bill, critics of the Tugwell bill worried
that advertising puffery would come to be interpreted as false or misleading
advertising and therefore prohibited under the proposed law. To most of
the advertising community's members, this was completely unacceptable.
Advertising, according to the American Association of Advertising Agencies (AAAA) president, could in no way be restricted to a "cold statement
of facts." "Advertising is a special plea," John Benson claimed. "It is not a
judicial analysis; it is salesmanship in print."[37]

Tugwell, in an attempt to smooth advertisers' ruffled feathers, was quick
to promise that the bill would allow for a certain amount of "trade puffing,"
although the right to "a little prideful boasting" should not be read as a sign
of a more lenient government attitude toward false and misleading advertising. "Abundant evidence" demonstrated all too clearly that the public wanted
fraudulent and misleading advertising cleaned out of the press.[38] Tugwell and
his boss, Secretary of Agriculture Henry A. Wallace, both tried to calm Madison Avenue. Advertisers' claim that the Tugwell bill would destroy advertising
was "not only absurd and wholly unwarranted," argued Wallace, "but logically proceeded from the amazing assumption that honest advertising does
not pay."[39] In fact, concurred Tugwell, instead of destroying advertising, the
bill sought to improve its character and restore public confidence in it. As
such, the end result would be a boost to honest advertisers and possibly an
overall increase in advertising.[40]

Advertising Age remained unconvinced. The trade journal's editors urged
the entire advertising field to organize in opposition to the bill "as to leave
no room for Congress to mistake the informed opinion of advertising interests."[41] "No fair-minded advertiser," argued Paul W. West, general manager
of the Association of National Advertisers, "quarrels with an honest attempt

to stop false and misleading advertising, the result of which is harmful to all consumers, but they are concerned with the writing of any laws the terms of which are so broad as to be subject to future administration and interpretation by bureaucratic officeholders."[42] Industry leaders called for a united front against the measure, otherwise the bill could pass and those engaged in the ongoing campaign to cripple legitimate advertisers' work would win the battle.[43]

The Problem of Industry Self-Regulation

As the issue of advertising's federal regulation burst onto the scene in the early days of the New Deal, it drew increased attention to the industry's attempts at self-regulation. Although the advertising industry viewed the consumer movement with skepticism, it also worried about the movement's growing popularity. One of its worst fears was that public opinion would pressure elected officials into legislating federal regulation and supervision of advertising.[44] Advertising wanted to keep those jobs for itself.

One of advertising's earliest attempts at improving relations with the public began in 1911, when the AACW launched a movement to encourage "truth in advertising." This effort was first and foremost intended as a rallying point for advertising clubs and associations in their struggle to secure advertising's respectability. But merely to denounce dishonest advertising and hold it up to scorn was no way to cure evil. The trade magazine *Printers' Ink* quickly hired a well-known corporate attorney named Harry D. Nims to draft guidelines based on the truth in advertising movement's principles. The Printers' Ink Model Statute, unveiled in November 1911, declared that advertisers who intentionally or unintentionally disseminated false advertising violated its principles. That no consumer had been hurt by such advertising did not serve as an acceptable excuse.[45]

By 1913 the statute, or at least parts of it, had been written into law in fifteen states. Most state regulations, however, were watered-down versions of the original. In most cases intent to defraud the public had to be proved before the states would prosecute. Because of its heavy burden of proof, the law was largely ineffective in protecting consumers against false and misleading advertising.[46]

Inspired by the Printers' Ink Model Statute, the truth-in-advertising movement also used local advertising clubs across the country to broadcast its mission. In addition to handling consumer complaints, the clubs organized vigilance committees to initiate their own probes into questionable advertising practices. The local clubs realized that the job of enforcing national advertising standards was more than they could handle, so in 1925 the newly formed NBBB took over this function.[47]

The NBBB, however, could issue only "verbal slaps," which severely limited its ability to halt abuses, and lacking power to impose meaningful sanctions and prevent future violations would prove to be a recurring problem in all of the advertising industry's self-regulatory attempts. It made it that much more difficult for self-regulation to fulfill its mission of undermining the growing popularity of the consumer movement's critique of advertising as a dubious undertaking.[48]

Other industry groups joined the effort to improve advertising's image. Failed attempts to solve the field's credibility crisis had prompted the AAAA to create its own Code of Ethics and Practice in 1924, and in 1932 the Advertising Federation of America (AFA) launched its "Declaration of Ideals and Principles." The latter committed members to principles of truth, honesty, and integrity in business transactions; discouraged them from "misrepresentation, indecent or misleading advertising," and "deceptive methods"; and dissuaded them from making promises that could not "reasonably be fulfilled."[49] These efforts, it was argued, would not only make advertising more beneficial to consumers and business alike but would also "tend to lessen the misuse of advertising by the few and make it more profitable to the great majority of advertisers who use[d] it fairly."[50] These efforts supported a national truth-in-advertising campaign to educate the public about advertising's economic value that the AFA had launched a few years prior. "The value of work of this kind in making the public more friendly to advertising, as a force in this modern world, and in anticipating attacks on advertising by those unfamiliar with its operations, seems to be evident," concluded an *Advertising Age* writer.[51] The general hope was that the combined effort would protect honest advertisers from the less honest ones and also increase consumers' confidence in advertising.[52]

In 1933, as the need for regulation was growing in urgency for the advertising industry, *Printers' Ink* teamed up with the NBBB to launch a more extensive drive for self-regulation. The result was a set of copy codes that denounced the "seven sins" of competitive advertising and a review committee to monitor adherence to them.[53] The committee consisted of representatives from the Association of National Advertisers, the AAAA, publishers, and members of the public. Enforcement of alleged code violations was left to the NBBB's national and local chapters, who were supposed to investigate violations and notify advertisers of the outcome. Accused advertisers could appeal to the review committee and request a hearing. In line with the common pattern, however, the major shortcoming of this elaborate organizational setup was a dearth of real sanctions. Neither the NBBB nor the review committee could impose penalties on code-violating advertisers. After deciding that a claim against an advertiser was justified, the NBBB could not issue enforceable decrees but only recommend that the advertiser abandon the code-violating statements or practices. The committee could report code violators to national advertisers, advertising agencies, and publishers, but this was as far as it could go in imposing sanctions.[54]

Many offenders found it objectionable that the NBBB acted as both judge and jury, so they often defied it on the ground that it did not reflect other business leaders' judgment. The programs failed from the public's perspective as well. False, misleading, and deceptive advertising still flourished, whereas public confidence in advertising's ability to regulate itself had not improved. "The advertising business," observed the advertising executive Lawrence Valenstein in 1933, "has probably gone on record more frequently, and in more flowery language, with regard to the importance of a code of ethics than any of the hundreds of industries in this country. . . . Yet the advertising business is as guilty of unfair and misleading practice as almost any industry to which one may point. Its codes of ethics have been little more than scraps of paper."[55]

Nor were matters improved by advertising agencies' failure to submit an acceptable fair trade code to the NRA that stipulated agency compensation, a minimum salary for advertising employees, and copywriting guidelines. In September 1933 a proposal from twelve of the nation's most prominent advertising agencies suggested incorporating a set of copy rules (designed by the advertising community and the NBBB back in 1931) into the overall NRA program. Under the advertisers' plan the power to notify the federal government of violations was granted to the industry-appointed Committee on Planning and Fair Practice.[56] The suggestion was greeted with ire by smaller agencies, who complained that clients would pressure them to violate the stipulations. Most agencies, the advertising historian Otis Pease confirms, knew that it was not possible to both obey the copy code and survive in business.[57] Large segments of the advertising community were disappointed, however, when the proposal failed to be adopted. They had hoped that its effectiveness would improve the public's perception of advertising and deflect pressure for federal regulation.[58]

These miserable attempts at self-regulation led to several industry debates. A significant sector of the industry always refused to acknowledge (much less accede to) some of the consumer movement's most pressing demands. It hoped that repeated promises to clean up questionable copy practices would mollify the consumer movement and the general public.[59]

Much of the advertising industry claimed that advertising, due to its "peculiar nature," was incapable of providing consumers with the kind of information they desired. "Advertising is of the marketplace and can never be literally truthful to the degree now urged by many reformers," insisted a J. Walter Thompson executive. "It must by the very nature of its job be partisan. Advertising, like politics, belongs to the persuasive arts and will live in proportion as it is successfully persuasive."[60] John Benson acknowledged that advertisements tended to underestimate consumers' abilities and talked down to them, but he maintained that these practices were justified given advertising's need to "appeal to the basic emotions" and keep "the level of intelligence of the audience" in mind.[61] Industry representatives admitted, however, that some advertising practices were questionable. Frederic R. Gamble, the executive secretary of the AAAA, agreed, for example, that celebrity testimonials and "the ridiculous predominance of sex appeal" in advertising was objectionable. Yet he claimed, as did other advertising executives, that questionable copy practices were limited to a mere 5 percent of all advertising.[62]

William C. D'Arcy of the D'Arcy Advertising Company in St. Louis was one of many advertisers upset that the industry as a whole was being penalized for the sins of a few. How to stop unethical practices was an open question, however. The limited number of manufacturers who did not worry about advertising's future and reputation and who profited from the use of questionable practices troubled D'Arcy.[63] Others countered that misleading and distinctly unethical advertising practices had a way of spreading because they were connected so closely with business competition. As long as questionable advertising produced sales for a particular manufacturer, others were forced to follow suit or suffer. "I don't like this dirty business any more than you do," assured an industry observer, "but we've both got to keep our jobs and that means we've got to produce profitable sales. As long as Blank & Co. sell by using that sort of stuff, we *must* follow suit. . . . It isn't the individual, it is the system."[64]

Most advertisers wanted to eliminate questionable advertising, but few knew how to control "a small amount of objectionable advertising" without imposing a heavy burden on the large volume of "sound and legitimate advertising."[65] It was a widely recognized framing of the problem. "Let us go out into the highways and by-ways and defend advertising for the fine, powerful business force that it is," urged C. B. Larrabee of *Printers' Ink.* "In doing so, let us realize that one of the strongest defenses we can make is to do everything we can to eliminate those shabby, shoddy, unethical gentlemen who do more by their unethical tactics to destroy advertising than Jim Rorty and the entire Communist party."[66] The industry readily admitted that most of its self-regulatory measures had faltered, so it needed new strategies to prevent offensive and indecent advertising. "The inequities of crooked advertisers," confirmed a writer for *Printers' Ink,* "are so universally known and are so openly and brazenly practiced as to constitute a scandal. The great need, therefore, is not another re-telling of this old, old story. The whole root of the trouble, instead of being the absence of evidence of which there is more than plenty, is rather the fact that nothing really useful and constructive has been done about it."[67]

The AFA's Plan to Make Commercial Media Responsible for Advertising Self-Regulation

The AFA, which represented a wide range of industry interests, emerged as a leader in a renewed attempt at industry self-regulation in 1934. Its strategy involved strengthening the Advertising Review Committee's function. The AFA also urged its members to closely monitor their advertising copy.[68] Many industry observers regarded this undertaking as one of the industry's last chances to prove that it could regulate itself. "At the risk of being a bit tiresome," counseled the board of *Printers' Ink,* "we say here as we have said many times before that if advertising—meaning advertisers, publishers and agents—had done a real job of self-cleansing, when it should have been done, there would now be no organized enmity on the part of consumers"—and no attempt to federally regulate advertising. The trade journal urged the advertising industry to start "a real cleansing process."[69]

The AFA's plan envisioned an especially prominent role for media owners and publishers. The argument was that the media were in a crucial position to monitor self-regulatory attempts and effectively prevent questionable advertising from reaching the public. *Advertising Age* was wholeheartedly in support of the proposal. If the mass media could monitor its own editorial material, it could do the same for advertisements. The editors of *Advertising Age* advised publishers to assume a larger degree of responsibility for the elimination of objectionable advertising.[70]

In their eagerness to transfer the task of monitoring advertisements, manufacturers and advertising agencies claimed that the media were in a better position to recognize questionable copy as well as monitor ads' accuracy and desirability from the standpoint of public welfare.[71] "Those who attack advertising because of the publication of the wrong kind of copy," urged agency interests, "must remember that the advertisers alone are not involved; no advertiser can publish copy without the cooperation of the publisher, and, in most cases, of the agency."[72] The proposal appealed to Roy S. Durstine, owner of one of the largest advertising agencies in the country. He believed that the media industries carried their share of responsibility for questionable advertising practices. Durstine claimed that many advertising abuses resulted from the Great Depression; publishers, for economic reasons, had been forced to admit advertising copy of questionable value to generate revenue. Examples included advertisements that contained blatantly false claims, descriptions of bodily functions, vulgarities, sex, and unfounded promises. These ads never would have been published had the business cycle been better. "Advertising is too fine and useful and valuable a tool to be blunted by misuse," stressed Durstine. "It has too great a task ahead of it. For without the truthful, believable spreading of information this country just hadn't any way to get itself back on the track and forge ahead into the exciting and useful future which coming generations are going to enjoy."[73] "The neck of the bottle is the media and the people who control that neck are media owners," concurred another advertising defender. "There is where your censorship must come. As long as media owners accept false advertising, just so long will it come to them."[74]

Attempts at involving the media in the advertising industry's self-regulatory plans were not new. For example, the 1911 Printers' Ink Model Statute contained a clause asking media owners to prevent questionable advertising from being published. By the early 1930s, however, the media industries' role in monitoring questionable advertising had taken center stage in the debate over advertising self-regulation. This obviously was far from popular with media owners, and they were not the only ones to sniff the scent of opportunism in the air. By 1934, critics argued, the advertising industry wanted to emphasize the media industries' obligation to monitor advertising content so that they could pass the buck to someone else.[75]

Advocating on behalf of media owners, C. B. Larrabee argued that advertisers' need for a new PR strategy did not justify an attempt to push the problem onto others. "The fact remains that no advertising agent submits to publishers copy that has not been O.K.'d by the client and no publisher prints advertising that is not paid for by an advertiser. . . . Whether they like it or not, the problem belongs to advertisers themselves."[76]

The plan fed other trepidations as well. One fear among advertisers was that the proposal would give publishers and media owners too much power. "Suppose, for instance," worried a writer for *Printers' Ink,* "that the magazine publishers should get together and decide that they would not admit to their columns any advertisement that did not measure up to definite specifications. Suppose that the leading newspapers should do likewise. And then to make the thing complete, suppose that the great radio broadcasting systems should apply a similar censorship." This insider suggested the appointment of an "advertising czar" who could eliminate bad advertising copy before it reached the public.[77] Another trade publication's editors concurred that this position could provide the advertising industry with another chance at self-regulation and demonstrate that federal regulation was unnecessary.[78]

No czar was ever appointed, however. The advertising industry may have set itself the next-to-impossible task of finding a person well suited for the job. One industry representative's speculations about "the ideal czar" illustrate some problems with the plan:

> This czar should not be taken from the ranks of advertising managers, sales managers, or distribution directors. Such a man, if he were big enough for the job would naturally be somewhat lopsided in his judgment. He would know soap or shoes or sealing wax too well. He would certainly have too-well-ingrained prejudices in the field in which he had worked to judge fairly and he would be at sea in judging the advertising of other products. This czar should not be an ex-advertising agent. Such a man could hardly help being prejudiced in favor of his ex-clients, try as he might to live down that prejudice. And he would be most certainly accused of favoritism, rightly or wrongly. This czar should not be a media man. That same criticism would hold true here. Advertisers would charge he was favoring former accounts. Who, then, would be the ideal man? You pick him. All I recommend is that he be a man of unquestioned integrity, a man who knows advertising, a man who is not working for nor holds stock in any company which advertises or in any agency or in any publication or station or plant. There must be such a one, one who has the confidence of *all* of the elements of advertising.[79]

The "czar" proposal was quickly dropped.

By the mid-1930s, after several decades of aborted self-regulatory campaigns and constant external pressure to follow stricter guidelines, the advertising industry gradually conceded that its attempts at self-regulation were useless: They never produced action or results. "The advertising arena is littered with the dead and decaying bodies of self-regulatory commissions, of control boards, of 'Truth in Advertising' crusades, clean-up campaigns and the like," summarized a critic. "These brave projects tend to have several common denominators: They are customarily effective only on the rim; they seldom set up actual penalties or, if they do, the penalties are seldom applied; they are regularly ignored by the major malefactors. They don't work (ask the walls of any convention hotel)."[80] Public pressure was mounting, however, and the advertising industry realized the pressing need for solutions. Instead of enacting new measures, however, it moved a reevaluation of its PR strategies to the top of its agenda.

The Battle over the Tugwell Bill

Some commentators reminded the advertising community that the Tugwell bill only tried to accomplish what advertising self-regulation had failed to achieve. "In urging support of the truth in advertising section of the new Food and Drugs Act," confirmed Consumers' Advisory Board (CAB) member Robert S. Lynd, "the consumer is simply bringing back to you business men and to advertising men the thing that for 20 years you have been talking so proudly about in printers' ink [*sic*] and elsewhere, the simple, plain fact of truth in advertising."[81] Although acknowledging it had some problems, the Advertising Review Committee did not view the Tugwell bill as a better alternative for regulation. "In view of the small amount of questionable advertising published, inviting Federal intervention look[ed] like using a shot-gun, instead of a swatter, as a means of eliminating houseflies," argued the committee members.[82] The advertising community fretted over the bill's wording and considered it ironic that consumer advocates had drafted an ambiguously worded bill to regulate ambiguous advertising. "What is meant by 'ambiguity' and 'inference'?" questioned one industry representative. "Shall ad writers be held responsible for somebody's—anybody's—inference?"[83]

Exactly how the proposed law would treat advertising claims and how ambiguity and inference should be interpreted turned out to be one of the bill's largest stumbling blocks, but there were other objections to it as well. Each industry potentially affected by the Tugwell bill had a separate set of concerns. The American Newspaper Publishers Association, for example, was particularly disturbed by the bill's provision that made newspapers and other mass media partly responsible for the dissemination of false advertisements. Fixed penalties, including imprisonment, were proposed under the bill, which some believed offered only ambiguous guidelines to determine whether an advertisement was false.[84] Publishers feared that the bill, if passed into law, would frighten honest advertisers to the extent that publishing revenues would be affected.[85] The trade association of the fledgling commercial broadcasting industry, the National Association of Broadcasters, also opposed the bill on similar grounds.[86]

Not surprisingly, some of the bill's stiffest resistance came from the ultraconservative Proprietary Association, a group that represented approximately 80 percent of all U.S. drug manufacturers. The organization contended that the Tugwell bill's criteria for false and misleading advertising were so strict that only 10 percent of all advertising would be able to meet the bill's proofs. Less advertising would lead to less demand and lower production. Moreover, warned the New York Board of Trade, if the contested bill became law, hundreds of manufacturing plants and stores might be forced to close and nearly 1.8 million jobs could be lost.[87]

Proprietary interests also accused the American Medical Association, characterized as "the most abominably vicious and un-American legislature lobbying machinery for corrupt politics, the human brain ever designed," of being a driving force behind the Tugwell bill.[88] Twisting the medical group's opposition to sales of dangerous and ineffective over-the-counter drugs into a desire for money and patients, drug makers not only cast themselves in a populist role but also hoped to deflect attention from the profit motive underlying their own opposition to the law. "Will the U.S. Congress stoop to sign for such enslaving debasement? Will those Lawmakers sell their souls to please a batch of unscientific charlatans? Will the President Of the United States of America place his signature to such an absurd document?" asked a writer for the conservative trade journal *Spectro-Chrome*. "What on Earth is our Constitutional Liberty worth anything, if our right to choose our own healer is snatched away?"[89] All in all, the advertising community presented a more or less united front with the patent-medicine interests, although the rough tactics of the patent-medicine lobby sometimes embarrassed the more respectable advertisers.[90] Bill supporters were becoming increasingly convinced that "commercial interests which gain[ed] through tricky advertising or misrepresentation, or who market[ed] dangerous cosmetics, drugs and patent medicines [would] fight the bill bitterly."[91]

The Tugwell bill's opponents held the advantage of having easy press access. In newspaper and magazine offices, advertising managers were flooded with letters and analyses that predicted large business losses should the bill slip through Congress. Most publishers were opposed to the bill and freely expressed their opinions.[92] Bill opponents were also supported by the general trade press and benefited from its up-to-the-minute reports on legislative developments.[93] The uneven playing field greatly concerned consumer advocates, who recognized that commercial interests were well prepared for the fight. "The manufacturers are fully informed thru their trade press and thru private channels of information, lobbyists in Washington, lawyers etc. what is going on and what general direction it is likely to take. Consumers are practically not being reached with respect to the intended changes because the newspapers and popular magazines ignore the story or play it down for reasons you know as well as I," worried Schlink. He urged the government to sponsor a campaign to educate consumers about the Tugwell bill and its merits.[94]

Schlink had grounds for concern. The bill's opponents, in general, and the Proprietary Association, in particular, were equipped with sizable war chests for their PR and lobbying campaigns. Groups such as the Drug Institute, the Proprietary Association, and the United Medicine Manufacturers of America contacted retail stores, newspapers, and magazines to scare them into believing that the Tugwell bill would drastically reduce their business revenues. Drug interests were also behind the Joint Committee for Sound and Democratic Consumer Legislation, a 1934 group founded to fight the proposed law that counted among its members industry leaders such as Lee Bristol, S. B. Colgate of the Colgate Palmolive Company, and K. F. MacLellan of the United Biscuit Company of America.[95] Disguising its statements against the bill as regular news reports and claiming the support of several hundred health officers who unbeknownst to the public were on the group's payroll, the committee used all means in its power to defeat the proposed legislation.[96] Bill supporters, in contrast, had far fewer funds and resources. Government attempts at speaking up in favor of the bill were often met with accusations that the government "played favorites." Tugwell-bill opponents interpreted Eleanor Roosevelt's interest in the issue as a sign of presidential support for the measure. They complained that her scrutiny helped create free—and therefore unfair—publicity for the Department of Agriculture.[97]

But the mass media were quite obedient to their advertising interests. In early 1934, for example, when the First Lady publicly expressed her support for some provisions outlined in the Tugwell bill, all major newspapers ignored her statement.[98] "Advertising," concluded an exasperated James Rorty, "is the Sacred and Contented Cow of American journalism. Any irresponsible naturalist who attempts to lead that cow into the editorial office of any advertising-sustained American publication is greeted by hoots of derision."[99]

To reach the public, Tugwell and FDA officials had to rely on the support of a handful of liberal and radical publications that carried little or no advertising, on the desultory and unorganized support of the medical profession, and on the intermittent and poorly financed help of a few women's and consumer organizations. Although the FDA had no publicity budget, it did manage to stage an educational exhibit at the 1933 Chicago World's Fair on the dangers of unregulated drug advertising that later traveled to women's clubs and other organizations upon request.[100] The American Medical Association, the *Nation,* the *New Republic, Good Housekeeping,* and also, to a certain degree, *Advertising and Selling* were among the publications that helped endorse the bill.[101]

These modest attempts were greeted with massive opposition from the patent-medicine lobby. The Joint Committee for Sound and Democratic Consumer Legislation, for example, was outraged when NBC gave bill supporters time to present their views over its Red Network.[102] The committee claimed that radio, due to the many adverse public reactions to its advertising practices, was more responsible for the Tugwell bill's existence than were other media: "It is a well known thought in the industry that at the present time statements over radio are far more extreme than the printed statements in the press. If such be the case, would not the passage of the Tugwell bill tend to seriously hamper the volume of radio advertising?"[103] Such scare tactics, although not entirely fair, did not fall on deaf ears because broadcasters were already seriously concerned that the bill would hurt advertising revenues.[104] In an attempt to exploit these fears, the Joint Committee provided NBC with a set of prepared speeches against the bill and urged the network to air them. Defeating the Tugwell bill was not just in the network's self-interest, argued the committee members, but also represented a chance to defend the public. Instead of keeping control of food, drugs, and cosmetics in the industry's experienced hands, they warned, Tugwell and his supporters wanted to give this responsibility to the secretary of agriculture. "For the free choice of the consumer, based on a truthful label," stated one of the radio scripts, "is substituted the bureaucratic principle that people are to have not what they want, but only such things as the Secretary of Agriculture believes is good for them."[105] Speaking in Philadelphia in spring 1934, AFA president Edgar Kobak promised the audience that manufacturers sponsoring the fight against the Tugwell bill had launched a nationwide campaign to "heap ridicule" on consumer organizations in general and on CR in particular. "We were just waiting for Schlink to stick his head out before we hit him," confirmed Kobak when he was unaware that he was speaking on the record. "And to put this over right, we are getting the backing of the American Legion." Although all reporters present turned in the story, no newspaper had the courage to anger its advertisers by printing Kobak's indiscreet comments.[106] "The AFA," observed a critic, "constitutes a very powerful national influence in manufacturing public opinion."[107]

Advertisers were not alone in rejecting what they perceived as an aggressive move by the FDA to regulate advertising. The FTC, which had been entrusted with this power, was far from willing to let go of it. The commission did not consider its lack of laboratories or experts to determine the validity of medical, mechanical, and scientific claims to be a weakness. On the contrary, because it was a judicial body with access to all the government's testing facilities and information from major hospitals and private laboratories across the United States, it claimed to be in a unique position to protect the public yet also make sure that advertisers received a fair deal. "Most People," argued an FTC member, "prefer to have their troubles judged by a fair-minded judicial commission without traditions to uphold or theories to serve."[108]

1933–34 Hearings on S 1944 and Its Successors

The first hearing on S 1944 was held in early December 1933. Although its strongest opponents, drug and cosmetics manufacturers, were intent on killing the bill, other interested parties, such as newspapers, magazines, and most major organizations representing the advertising community, desired substantial revisions. The American Medical Association and most large women's organizations, in contrast, supported the bill and wanted it passed in its current form.[109] More radical consumer advocates, represented by CR, were less enthusiastic because they did not think that the Tugwell bill provided consumers with sufficient protection. Only if no hope existed for a more efficient law would the organization lend its support to the measure.[110] In fact, the months between the June introduction of the bill and the December hearing had been a difficult period for the organization's leaders. As new revisions were added, the bill held fewer and fewer similarities to the blueprint for consumer protection that Kallet and Schlink had provided in *100,000,000 Guinea Pigs*.[111] During the two-day hearing, witness after witness representing manufacturing interests was called to testify, but consumer advocates were given only a limited time to be heard. Speaking on behalf of consumers were people from various women's groups as well as Robert S. Lynd, who in this instance did not represent the CAB. Representing CR, Kallet used the hearing to call for a law that provided maximum consumer protection but pointed to the difficulty in reaching this goal because of commercial interests' preferential treatment.

Kallet was particularly troubled by the prominent role played by Copeland, who had introduced the bill in the Senate and presided over the December hearing.[112] A tall and sturdy man with wavy graying hair, bushy black eyebrows, and silver-rimmed bifocals, Copeland was easily recognizable. His habit of garnishing the lapel of his coat with a fresh red carnation every morning also set him apart from the crowd. After receiving his M.D. from the University of Michigan in 1889, Copeland spent ten years practicing medicine in the state. He was elected mayor of Ann Arbor in 1901 and later became dean of the Flower Hospital in New York City. Copeland's big political break came when the Democrats drew up their 1922 ticket and Alfred E. Smith, the Democratic candidate for governor, refused to accept William Randolph Hearst as the candidate for U.S. senator. Copeland, a Republican on friendly terms with both men, was brought in as a compromise candidate and ended up winning the Senate seat. His conservative bent, combined with a rural and Methodist background, helped him attract many votes that normally would have gone to Republican contenders. Although a somewhat controversial figure, Copeland was reelected in 1928 in spite of persistent rumors linking him to political corruption.[113]

In the advertising debate Copeland became the target of criticism from consumer advocates besides Kallet. Many found it rather curious that the Senator, an avowed and sincere conservative who frequently opposed Roosevelt and his New Deal, was asked to introduce a measure calling for radical government regulation of business. A troubling aspect of Copeland's behavior, according to critics, was his tendency to exploit his medical background for commercial purposes. "No man who ever held that exalted position [U.S. senator] has consistently and constantly appeared so cheap, so transparent, so out of place, as has Senator Copeland," concluded a Poughkeepsie, New York, columnist. "He has peddled his official name to the newspapers like a cheap quack doctor while sitting in the highest legislative chair in the world. His syndicated bellyache medicines have been advertised in every nook and corner of the land. In many newspapers alongside of the 'Advice to the Lovelorn' [has] appeared the senatorial doctor's advice upon the treatment of bodily ailments."[114] That Copeland endorsed Eno's Fruit Salts on the Rudy Vallee radio show did not exactly improve this image. Particularly troubling was his role as a shill for Fleischmann's Yeast, whose ads made rather far-fetched claims about the health benefits of eating yeast daily.[115]

It was Kallet who took the opportunity of the December 1933 hearing to launch a full-scale attack on Copeland's integrity. Consumers, according to

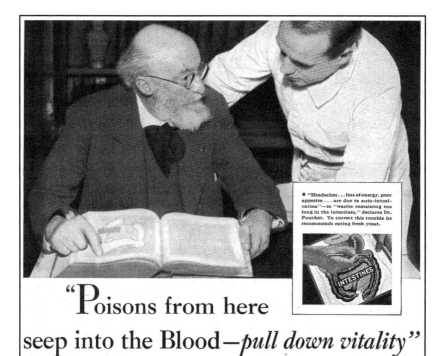

A print version of the advertising campaign for Fleischmann's Yeast that Senator Royal S. Copeland promoted on radio. (Fleischmann's long ago discontinued recommending human consumption of active yeast.) Printed with permission from Fleischmann's Yeast Co.

Kallet, could not expect to receive fair play from a person who received pay for advertisements that, under the terms of the pending legislation, would be considered false or misleading. Aggravating the situation, he argued, was the fact that Copeland's broadcasts on behalf of Fleischmann's Yeast started after the Tugwell bill's introduction. Copeland's fourth broadcast in the series, in which the senator advised the American public that clogged-up intestines were the source of many health troubles, took place following the close of the hearing's first day. Kallet argued that not only were the senator's advertising statements gross exaggerations but they were also unsupported by reputable physicians. On behalf of CR, Kallet demanded the hearing be reconvened under a new committee and an impartial chair.[116]

CR even considered initiating criminal proceedings against Standard Brands, the maker of Fleischmann's Yeast, for bribing the senator and against Copeland for accepting the bribe.[117] This strategy was soon shelved, however, when the organization realized that it lacked the necessary evidence to prove intent.[118] Even if criminal charges could not be filed, CR argued, Copeland should at least be barred from any further connection with food and drug legislation. "His conscious efforts to make the hearings appear fair, though actually they were far from fair, made the disclosure of his connections all the more urgent," insisted one CR member. "In a society not governed by business ethics, not only would Copeland be ejected from the committee but he would also, and quite rightfully, be booted out of public life."[119] During his testimony, Kallet accused the Senator of siding with the bill's opponents, noting that Copeland had allowed ample time for corporate interests but barely allowed consumer interests a chance to testify.[120]

Conservative proprietary interests also found Copeland and William I. Sirovich, who had introduced the bill into the House, troubling figures to lead this battle. The drug manufacturers claimed that the senator and the representative, who both were medical doctors, wanted to protect their own turf and thus supported a bill that would prohibit many forms of self-medication.[121]

The one conclusion that almost everybody seemed to draw from the S 1944 hearing was that the measure, unless revised, had no chance of being written into law. The combined advertising community lobbied vigorously against the Tugwell bill, and consumer advocates, holding out for legislation that, in their opinion, would provide better consumer protection, were not too eager to see it pass either.[122] A mad scramble for a revised version ensued. Although manufacturers and other business interests worked hard on their end, Kallet traversed Washington, trying to drum up support for a version of the bill that more accurately reflected his organization's goals. This proved to be quite a challenge. Although several members of Congress sympathized with Kallet and with what he and other consumer activists had tried to accomplish, few wanted to throw their weight behind the measure.[123]

Consequently, S 2000, which was introduced in early 1934 as a replacement for S 1944, provided less stringent advertising regulation than its predecessor had. The first revision changed the criteria for false and misleading advertising. Contrary to S 1944, S 2000 left no room for consumers' input in determining whether an advertisement should be deemed false because of ambiguity or inference. The revised bill demanded that "substantial medical opinion or demonstrable scientific fact" be consulted before an ad could be said to meet the preceding criteria. The new measure also contained a proposal to establish health and food advisory committees to aid the Department of Agriculture in determining any complaint's merits. Advertisers who might have worried that these committees would be staffed by Schlink and his supporters found comfort in the explicit assurance that the government-appointed posts would have several business-friendly individuals on board. Also stipulated in the revised draft was the promise that no publisher, advertising agency, or broadcaster should be adjudged guilty of disseminating false or misleading advertisements. Another clear improvement from advertisers' perspective was S 2000's intent to give substantially less power to the secretary of agriculture. Although S 1944 had demanded formula disclosure on all proprietary drugs and a provision that allowed factory inspection by the secretary of agriculture, both stipulations were absent from S 2000.[124] Large segments of the advertising community expressed relief regarding the developments. "It looked pretty bad three months ago," reflected a *Printers' Ink* writer, "when the then Tugwell Bill, being an Administration measure, seemed slated for inevitable enactment. But the moderates got in their work and now we have the Copeland Bill [S 2000]."[125]

CR and other consumer advocates, of course, were unimpressed with the Copeland bill.[126] "The bill is bad," reflected Kallet, "largely because the politicians and the courts in which hand the protection of consumers would remain are willing servants of the business interests and have little genuine interest in the public welfare."[127] Neither did the changes please Tugwell, who argued that S 2000 severely weakened the original bill's intent.[128] He reached his breaking point when the president intervened and sided with Copeland when he wanted to change a provision in the original bill that Tugwell wanted to keep intact. "Senator Copeland, after our conversation the other day," observed the assistant secretary of agriculture in a letter to Roosevelt, "apparently thought he had a mandate from you to kill every provision of the F & D [Food and Drug] bill which would be of any use. He has virtually allowed the people who have been making the personal attacks on me all summer to rewrite it to suit themselves; in fact they wrote the language now incorporated in it. In view of everything, I am going to be compelled to announce my own withdrawal and to explain how Senator Copeland has handed our measure over to our opponents who would have been regulated under it."[129]

In early 1934 the Emergency Conference of Consumer Organizations, with its impressive roster of intellectual leaders, demanded that Copeland's law be scrapped in favor of a bill that provided more adequate consumer protection. "The twice revised bill shows that Dr. Copeland has taken excellent advantage of the opportunity thus afforded him to emasculate the original bill," protested the group.[130] The best solution would be to remove Copeland from any responsibilities with the food and drug legislation. Also helping to drum up liberal support for a new bill was the People's Lobby, a radical group that fought for public enlightenment and in the public's interest, led by lobbyist Benjamin Marsh.[131]

To many members of the advertising community the Tugwell bill expressed the Roosevelt administration's hostility toward advertising and business.[132] Although the president quite clearly favored some form of advertising regulation, he was by no means against advertising per se. Roosevelt was less in favor of strict advertising regulations than some of his critics gave him credit for, and this became increasingly evident when he not only failed to endorse S 1944 but also nixed some of its less stringent versions as well.[133] Needless to say, members of the advertising community were quite pleased with these developments. They were not particularly upset that Tugwell, whom they clearly did not like, appeared to be on the outs with Roosevelt.[134] "The President is a master of politics, and he understands quite well the advantages of dropping an unpopular member of the official family after he has demonstrated that he is not in good standing with the public," *Advertising Age*'s editors observed, speculating that the confrontation meant weaker presidential support for Tugwell's ideas.[135]

Another round of minor changes resulted in yet another bill, and S 2800, which replaced S 2000, was even more to the advertising community's liking. The new bill offered no provisions for mandatory grading of goods—a clear victory for major food manufacturers. "The Copeland bill as it now stands," commented a writer for *Printers' Ink*, "is so vastly superior to the original Tugwell measure—a glaring monstrosity in the way of legislation, if there ever was one—that most advertisers will probably accept it with little further argument."[136] Not surprisingly, the changes failed to impress the proprietary industry, who through the Joint Committee for Sound and Democratic Consumer Legislation decried the bill as a bureaucratic piece of legislation that did not reflect the American people's will.[137]

The first half of 1934 saw several new measures to replace the Copeland bill. The Black bill (HR 6376) proposed to amend the Food and Drugs Act of 1906 in a manner that drug interests generally approved of, whereas the main goal behind another bill introduced by Sirovich (HR 7426) was to fight the grading provisions outlined in the Copeland bill. Yet another contender was the McCarran-Jenckes bill (S 2858), a measure written with food manufacturers' interests in mind.[138] Broadcasters, although offering reserved approval for S 2000, had objected to its definition of repetitious dissemination of false advertising by means of radio broadcasting as a "public nuisance." Because the Federal Radio Commission was mandated to deny licensing renewals to any station that constituted a public nuisance, broadcasters feared that a station associated with commercial messages of the same category could unjustifiably be refused a broadcasting renewal. Broadcasters preferred the Black bill because it sanctioned the FTC's established practice in regard to radio advertising.[139] When the Senate Commerce Committee convened for a hearing on S 2800 in February 1934, it became evident that other constituencies opposed the bill as well. Major women's groups, such as the American Home Economics Association, for example, protested S 2800's removal of a provision in the Tugwell bill for government food grading. Although S 2800 was a major victory for food manufacturers, who had fought the CAB's grading proposal and resisted its inclusion in S 1944, they still preferred the McCarran-Jenckes bill and battled against S 2800's passage.[140]

Declaring S 2800 "worthless," CR offered a new set of objections.[141] Consumers, maintained Kallet, who had emerged as the organization's spokesperson on the matter, have the right to demand a certain degree of protection from a food, drug, and cosmetic bill, but S 2800, which allowed industry profits to take precedence over consumers' safety, did not even come close to providing this protection.[142] "I do not believe that Congress can or will fully protect and serve the public in this or any other bill," James Rorty asserted. "Why? The reason, in my belief, is that adequate legislation cannot be passed in the face of the tremendous opposition of the food, drug, cosmetics, advertising and publishing interests."[143] Kallet agreed and was particularly upset that S 2800 served purely as a retroactive measure against false and misleading advertising. It contained no measure to prevent such advertising from appearing in the first place. Frustration with the legislative developments prompted CR to introduce its own legislation, the radical Boland bill (HR 8316). To prevent false and misleading advertising from reaching the public, the bill required that advertisers register their products and claims with a Board of Labeling, Packaging, and Advertising Control.[144] Unfortunately for CR, the bill did not receive much support among lawmakers.

Support for S 2800 could be found among major advertising organizations and in some media circles. The AAAA, for example, viewed the measure as "going a long way in protecting the honest advertiser" but also suggested a few changes, including lenient treatment of advertising puffery that would offer "much needed relief" for the industry.[145] The AFA reluctantly concurred. "Those provisions which deal with advertising are far from perfect," its board acknowledged, "but it appears they will work out in a reasonably satisfactory manner since it must be assumed that the law enforcement agencies will be intelligent and just."[146] The Association for National Advertisers offered no endorsement. The National Editorial Association approved of the bill, whereas the National Publishers' Association stayed noncommittal.[147]

A hearing before the Senate Commerce Committee on S 2800 was held in late February and early March 1934. Unfortunately for consumer groups, however, Hubert D. Stephens, a staunchly pro-industry Mississippi Democrat who for some time had been working to dismember the Copeland bill, chaired the hearing. Dominating the three-day session were long testimonies from large food and drug companies. Consumer groups were not given the same opportunity. On the second day Alice Edwards from the American Home Economics Association estimated that during nine hours of testimony, only twenty-five to thirty-five minutes had been devoted to the consumer's point of view. Kallet's request to testify on behalf of CR, for example, was ignored by Stephens. Tired of such treatment, Kallet took the drastic step of telegraphing Roosevelt about the senator's conduct. "Representatives of consumers for whose protection a food and drug bill has been drawn," he reported, "are being refused a fair hearing by the Senate Committee now holding hearings on the bill. Will you not use your influence to see that the obvious procommercial bias of the committee does not permit these hearings to end and a bill to go through without consumers being given full opportunity to state their criticisms."[148]

When finally given a say at the hearing, Kallet was questioned at length about CR: how it was financed, the size of its staff, and how its directors and officers were chosen. He was asked to file for the record a complete list of CR's organizers, officers, and past and present directors.[149] Kallet began his statement by reading the telegram he had sent to Roosevelt. Stephens, however, ruled that this constituted an unfair attack on the committee members and refused to accept it into the record. Kallet, he demanded, should confine his comments to S 2800. Arguing that consumers had a right to know, Kallet began his prepared statement by criticizing the manner in which the bill was being handled and went so far as to compare manufacturers to gangsters. This, quite obviously, did not sit well with Stephens, who exploded into a rage, refused to accept the statement, and threatened to cut Kallet off.[150] The same restrictions were not placed on CR's critics, however. When one attacked Kallet's comments as "destructive," Stephens not only appeared to agree but also allowed the remarks to be included in the record. Unlike Kallet's diatribe, he maintained, these comments were acceptable because they criticized an organization as a whole. For the portion of his statement that was allowed on the record, Kallet pointed to CR's concerns in connection with certain advertising practices, including some for products that Copeland had helped promote.[151]

Copeland himself, interestingly enough, did not appear particularly troubled by the many personal attacks on him. At some level it seemed as if he had never considered problematic his dual roles as promoter of products with questionable claims and senator in charge of a law that aimed to outlaw such practices. "Personally," he noted after the S 2800 hearing, "I am more concerned over the public health than with anything else in the world. A lifetime of activity in this field has demonstrated to me that nothing within the purvue [sic] of a legislator is more important to Americans than protection against doubtful claims and actual fraud in the sale of products that may serve to undermine health."[152] Although acknowledging that some interests might oppose parts of the bill or the measure in its entirety, a confident Copeland reported that S 2800 was out of committee in early March 1934. "Of course," the senator remarked sternly, "there are those who continue in bitter opposition to the bill. But, in my opinion, they are largely those who would be in opposition to any attempt whatever at regulation. We cannot hope to please them, and of course, have no desire to please them."[153]

CR leaders were frustrated, to put it mildly. The organization blamed the commercial mass media for not providing the public with fair coverage of the issues. "The economic welfare of the newspapers," one member argued, "is too dependent upon those very interests to which an investigation would be particularly offensive."[154] Nor did CR let Washington, D.C., off the hook. In spring 1934, as its criticism of the NRA and the CAB was escalating, CR concluded that the government's support for a food and drug law that would offer consumers the fullest amount of protection possible was not particularly solid.[155] "Consumers," claimed a frustrated Schlink, "did not get going in time to save the Copeland bill because Assistant Secretary Tugwell spent the first months of his activities out of touch with consumers and in touch with patent medicine, food and cosmetic manufacturers, directly against our counsel that at the very best consumers would need a long time to get into action on a subject on which manufacturers, better staffed and equipped and with media and publicity and propaganda at their disposal, were fully prepared to go into action very quickly and very powerfully."[156] CR even went so far as to suggest that Tugwell's later and very public opposition to S 2800 was a well-orchestrated stunt to mislead the public about the administration's stance concerning corporate power and manipulation. "In an obvious effort to throw the critics off the track," claimed CR representatives, "Professor Tugwell publicly protested to the White House against the measure which Professor Cavers had drafted under his direction. Verily, it required a brain trust to think that one up."[157] The truth, according to the organization, was that unlike consumer groups, who had very little influence over what was going on in Washington, D.C., industry representatives had been granted long and secret conferences with Copeland, with officials in the FDA, and with the president.[158]

The original Tugwell bill, according to Kallet, had become "a delightful puppet show with the quack medicine men and their colleagues manipulating the strings which move the pliant and gesturing little figures of Roosevelt, Tugwell, Chief Campbell of the Food and Drug Administration, and some hundreds of Senators and Congressmen."[159] Within less than a year, the bill to amend the 1906 food and drug legislation had lost almost every provision to which the medicine, food, and cosmetic industries had objected. These included food grading, voluntary factory inspections, medicine ingredient labels, false-advertising definitions, and prohibitions against medicine advertisements for diseases for which self-medication might be dangerous.[160] Unfortunately for those who wanted to see the bill pass, the president decided that other issues were more important. When a busy Congress adjourned in June 1934, S 2800 had won only tentative consideration on the Senate floor, and the House committee had been unable to give it any attention whatsoever.[161]

Conclusion

The fight over the Tugwell bill and its many permutations forced the advertising industry into a more direct confrontation with the consumer movement's, and particularly CR's, demands. The need to protect consumers from false and misleading advertising along with the need to provide legal guidelines for grading and labeling of food and cosmetics had been on CR's agenda for several years. By 1933 the organization's demands were articulated through the Tugwell bill. The advertising community was obviously none too pleased. The various legislative measures to prohibit advertisements that cloaked their claims in ambiguity and led consumers to false inferences fell uncomfortably close to the industry's practice of playing on consumers' emotions. Advertisers did all they could to crush the bill. Gradually, the spirit of consumer protection embedded in the Tugwell bill was chipped away by the advertising industry and its allies, who lobbied hard and heavy to have their demands incorporated into new versions of the bill. The responsibility for this development rested not with advertisers alone, however. Much to CR's disappointment, members of Roosevelt's administration, including the president himself, did not fight the consumers' fight. In a manner that fully reflected their weak support of the CAB, administrators did very little to stop business from dominating the legislative process.

By 1935 the basic outline of a law to amend the Food and Drugs Act of 1906 had emerged. Yet it would require three more years of wrangling and fine-tuning on Capitol Hill before the Wheeler-Lea Amendment was passed into law in 1938. In those intervening years the advertising industry began to develop a far more sophisticated notion of the importance of public relations to its political success.

4

A Consumer Movement Divided:
The Birth of Consumers Union
of the United States Inc.

By the mid-1930s even the most optimistic consumer activist had come to realize that consumer protection in the form of strict federal regulation was not forthcoming. Given that its key objectives had served as a model for the original Tugwell bill, Consumers' Research Inc. (CR) was greatly disappointed by the battle's outcome. As if the legislative limbo was not enough, summer 1935 brought yet another challenge to the budding consumer movement. A labor strike caused CR to split into two distinct fractions, each fighting for consumers' loyalty. Those who remained at CR became increasingly insistent on viewing consumers as a distinct group that shared few interests with U.S. manufacturers and almost none with organized labor. More than ever CR focused its efforts on securing consumers' right to cost-effective products of high quality and gradually removed itself from direct involvement with the advertising regulatory struggle in Washington, D.C.[1] Consumers Union Inc. (CU), the new consumer group born from the strike, took the opposite approach. Much to CR's dismay, CU sought to link consumer issues with broader social concerns and showed a strong desire to cooperate with labor interests.

The mid-1930s also brought yet another perspective on the best way to educate consumers. The split in the consumer movement suggested a less-than-unified approach to this issue, and business quickly recognized this as an opportunity. The result was a large campaign to create an explicitly pro-business consumer movement designed to educate U.S. consumers on the benefits of free enterprise, including advertising's value. In the second half of the decade, three major approaches to consumer education, each opposing the ideology of the others, emerged.

The CR Strike

From its modest beginning in the late 1920s CR grew steadily. By 1935 the organization boasted fifty-five thousand members and had made a social and economic impact that belied its numbers. Although established to run a testing service and publish newsletters, CR regularly responded to individual requests for help and information. By 1933 the pressures on the relatively new organization were such that Frederick J. Schlink moved CR from New York City to much larger facilities in a vacant piano factory near Washington, New Jersey, some one hundred miles away. Many workers, upset over having to pay for their own move, decided to quit, whereas others, considering themselves fortunate to have work at all during the Depression, hung on. Unfortunately for Schlink, the locale change did not stop the flow of public requests. Before long the journey to CR's New Jersey headquarters had turned into a pilgrimage for people interested in consumer issues.[2]

Schlink's strategy for handling the many demands and pressures was to run an unusually tight ship. A lot of responsibility rested on his shoulders, and he often found himself in situations in which swift and far-reaching decisions about the group's future, goals, and potential allies needed to be made. One approach for maintaining the fullest possible control involved constantly altering CR's corporate composition. Early on he had dropped Stuart Chase because the author did not spend enough time on consumer issues, and he frequently fired members appointed to the advisory committee, called the Council of Advisors, if he did not like their advice. By 1933 the board had been reduced to only five members.[3] The board was further altered in fall 1934 when longtime member Arthur Kallet was removed while he was away on a lecture tour and replaced by M. C. Phillips, the author of *Skin Deep,* who had married Schlink in 1932.[4]

Not everyone supported Schlink's leadership methods. Many board members resigned after run-ins with the brash CR head, who showed an intense determination to build a consumer movement strictly according to his own precepts.[5] Although some found Schlink's philosophy off-putting, others were fascinated by his drive and convictions. Belonging to the latter group was J. B. Matthews, a colorful character who upon being appointed to CR's board in 1933 would emerge as one of Schlink's strongest supporters. After a stint as a missionary in Java, Matthews had returned to New York and had undergone a series of transformations. He first embraced pacifism but later turned his attention to the labor movement. Upon exploring both Communism and Socialism, he found great fulfillment in working for CR. A brilliant speaker, Matthews managed to attract a contingent of liberal lawyers, including Milton Handler, who assisted CR during the Tugwell bill drafting.[6]

The constant liquidation of individuals who failed to meet Schlink's standards extended to the organization's staff, and this created a great deal of insecurity and instability. Concerns and complaints, however, did not receive much sympathy from Schlink, who believed that any person found worthy to work for CR should appreciate the honor and not ask for much in return.[7] Workers, unsurprisingly, failed to share this view. Many did not find their rural surroundings and the around-the-clock company of their co-workers entirely satisfying, so they quit. For others, resignations were motivated by Schlink's insensitivity to their financial needs. As late as 1935 CR workers were paid an average weekly wage of only $13.13, but Schlink, who earned several times this amount, did not understand their demands for higher pay. He argued that if CR workers followed his advice, they would buy more wisely and have no need for a larger paycheck.[8] Schlink also insisted on hiring part-time and temporary workers, placing all new employees on a six-month probation period, and enforcing strict rules for those hired permanently. Schlink had a habit of playing people against each other, a tactic that kept workers constantly on edge. The presence of Phillips, working as the organization's office manager, did not exactly calm matters either.[9] The inevitable result of these practices was high turnover. By fall 1933 CR had lost close to 30 percent of its staff.[10] Of the forty employees who came to New Jersey with Schlink in May 1933, only six (exclusively executives and board members) remained in early fall 1935. Over this two-year period at least sixty staff members had come and gone.[11]

Other official attitudes at CR that stemmed from the political upheaval across the country stifled workers. Since the Russian Revolution in 1917, Communism had gained steady support in the United States, yet the Communist Party engaged in only limited outreach to attract new members. With a few exceptions the Communist International and its many national sections had proceeded upon the theory that workers alone would furnish the armies of revolution. By the mid-1930s, however, the party had begun to actively solicit members, and this approach was not always welcome. Many Americans watched what they viewed as "the first large scale attempt to involve the middle-class in the revolutionary movement" with fear.[12] In summer and fall 1935, when a nationwide series of seemingly spontaneous strikes broke out in response to high meat prices, Schlink and his allies in CR began to suspect that Communists had targeted U.S. consumer organizations, with their many middle-class members, as perfect recruiting spots.[13]

Thus, when rumors of labor unrest at CR began to percolate in summer 1935, Matthews's response was quick and defensive. Viewing the accusations as an unjustified attack on a successful organization, Matthews brushed them off as unsubstantiated. He insisted that the workers were well treated and that they had a "bona fide" labor union to take care of their interests.[14] "There is now a union among the employees at CR," he wrote in July 1935, "and I can assure you that it is recognized by the Board of Directors as a perfectly legitimate employee activity."[15] Because CR did not actually have a union at this time, its employees surely interpreted his words as encouraging. That summer they forged ahead with their organizing plans. In late August they informed CR officials that the American Federation of Labor (AFL) had recognized their efforts toward forming a union. Considering Schlink's need to control the organization, workers might have anticipated a lukewarm response, but few could have predicted the extremely hostile reaction that Schlink, Matthews, and Phillips displayed toward the new chapter of the AFL's Technical, Editorial, and Office Assistants' Union.

Immediately after presenting the contract for AFL charter number 20055 to the CR board, sparks began to fly. Within a few hours CR fired the three employees who had led the unionization effort. When pressed by union representatives, Schlink claimed that the three men, all still in their probation period, were fired for different reasons. John Kilpatrick was let go because of work incompetence, and CR simply no longer required the services of Donald Rogers and John Heasty, the union's president. Later, in an obvious attempt at bolstering their argument, Schlink and Matthews also claimed that finances and overstaffing had played a part in the firing decisions.[16]

The union's request for a meeting with CR's board of directors to discuss the employees' cases and to negotiate a settlement was futile. When Walter Trumbull, an AFL organizer who had been working with the CR union, contacted CR's lawyer Oscar S. Cox about meeting with CR's board of directors, Schlink, Matthews, and Phillips flew into a rage. A board meeting was called, and the three agreed that whoever in the employees' union had gone to Trumbull and gotten him to request the meeting was guilty of blackmail and would be fired.[17] They determined that Dewey H. Palmer, the only other board member at the meeting, was the guilty party. By sharing information about the employees' union with liberal individuals in the trade press who were in a strategic position to publish information that could harm CR, Palmer had shown the kind of disloyalty that justified his removal from the board. Adding to their conviction was Palmer's staunch defense of the union and his refusal to turn his back on the workers' demands.[18] Schlink, Matthews, and Phillips were similarly angry with Kallet, who had come out in full support of the workers. The board majority of three accused him of having shown great disloyalty to CR by discussing the union with outsiders without the board's approval. They decided that Kallet, who already had been demoted from his board position, should now be removed from CR's roster entirely.[19]

The staff was outraged. Sixty of the sixty-eight employees rushed to sign a petition asking for Palmer's reinstatement.[20] The following day Schlink called a staff meeting at which Matthews made a passionate plea for support. Unfortunately for the board, however, a secret ballot revealed that less than one-quarter of CR's forty-five workers agreed with its handling of the matter. Instead of discrediting the union and scaring workers away from its activities, the board's actions had the opposite effect. Workers flocked to the union in protest and threatened to go on strike unless CR's leadership met their demands.[21]

Although acknowledging the union's existence, CR leaders refused to negotiate. Matthews was particularly aggressive in his attacks. He accused the union's leaders not only of employing gangster and racketeering strategies to attract members but also of forcing CR workers to accept its agenda. Union leaders demanded that Matthews and his fellow CR officials withdraw or at least substantiate their charges. If this was not done immediately, Local 20055 intended to enlist the aid of liberal labor leaders as well as the editors of the *Nation* and the *New Republic* in an effort to expose the accusations' bogus nature. The union's strategy, at least at this early point, was to place most of the blame on Matthews, who was considered unfit to be a CR board member. That Matthews, who earlier in his career had gone on record in favor of militant labor organizations, would help initiate and support a fierce attack against an organization of his employees' choosing was nothing short of bewildering to labor activists. "You have accused of racketeering a Union among whose entire membership there is not one person who receives or asks for a penny of recompense for Union work, and whose policies have been so approved by the entire staff of Consumers' Research that in a secret ballot three-fourths voted in support of the Union," scolded the union delegation.[22]

On September 5, with no solution in sight, forty-one of CR's union employees went on strike. Citing the culmination of labor difficulties over the past three years and an increasingly dictatorial leadership as their most important grievances, the strikers called for the reinstatement of Heasty, Rogers, and Kilpatrick and asked for a signed agreement to protect CR workers against firings on whim, for personal dislike, because of minor differences in opinion, and for no reason at all. The union demanded a retraction of Matthews's racketeering charges; the removal from the board of Matthews and Phillips, "who have shown themselves interested only in personal aggrandizement"; and the reestablishment of a representative board of directors with the real interests of impoverished "consumer-workers" at heart. The union also insisted that Palmer be reinstated as a board member. If CR would give in to the first three demands immediately, the union promised to end picketing and send its members back to work.[23] Other issues to be ironed out were the strikers' request for a thirty-five-hour work week, a guaranteed minimum salary of fifteen dollars a week, and a one-dollar increase every six months until a weekly salary of twenty-five dollars had been reached. The union also insisted that all strikers be paid in full for the time they had been on strike and that their employer put an end to the yellow-dog contract that prevented CR employees from joining other political organizations.[24]

CR showed no intention of giving in to these demands, and the strike, which at times turned violent, continued for weeks. CR wielded all the tools used traditionally by employers to harm and discredit strikers. "There are large groups in this country," stressed a writer for *Consumers' Research Bulletin*, "who will swallow hook, bait and sinker any lie or atrocity which it perpetrates, on the ground that 'workers can do no wrong.' Any and all measures of protection which CR takes against lies or atrocities are, according to the Union, just so many manifestations of the usual 'capitalist tactic.' If CR refuses to be intimidated by vicious assaults upon its officers and loyal employees, it's just a 'capitalist tactic.' In short, if CR opens its mouth to offer any account whatever of the Union's behavior (even from the Union's own documentary record), it's just a 'capitalist tactic.'"[25] Striking workers, according to CR accounts, had gone so far as to throw rocks at CR leaders and workers who crossed picket lines and had attacked the homes of three nonunion employees. In one case, claimed the organization, stones had been slung through a front window and barely missed the crib where a three-week-old baby lay sleeping.[26]

Union leaders admitted that some minor, and regrettable, cases of violence had occurred, but they were quick to point out that a great deal of the overall injuries had been committed at the hands of hired CR constables. "Newspapers, in order to make a good story," stressed strike leader Susan Jenkins, "will seize upon anything of this nature and play it up to the

Overturned car during the 1935 Consumers' Research strike. Reprinted with permission from the Consumers' Research Collection, Special Collections and University Archives, Rutgers University Libraries.

point where it becomes fantastic. . . . The CR Board has pirculated [*sic*] and released accusations of violence against the Union where none existed, in an attempt to turn public sympathy against the strike. Actually, the violence has been predominantly on the other side, largely concealed under the forms of legality."[27]

Although strikers were upset by Matthews's accusations that union members had beaten children and were planning to bomb the CR plant, they were perhaps equally disturbed by his sudden and intense contempt for unions.[28] "When you consider that J. B. Matthews before the strike had applied for and secured the endorsement of local organized labor in his campaign as Democratic candidate for State Assembly," mused Jenkins to a supporter, "you will realize that the sentiment of local labor unions against him was very strong, since they felt, rightly, that he had betrayed them."[29] Kallet concurred. "The most astonishing thing about this strike," he reflected, "is that the people who are outdoing the coal and steel barons in their attempts to break the strike are men who once professed their friendship for labor and their devotion to social and economic reform. Their actions constitute one of the most complete betrayals in the history of American liberalism."[30]

The strikers received strong support from many CR subscribers, who expressed dismay and bewilderment over the situation. "It is indeed surprising," one CR supporter admonished Schlink, "that you, who have so long upbraided even the most progressive persons in the Home Economics and Consumer education movement for their failure to take a forthright stand in favor of the consumer and of labor, should now use the methods of big business in attempting to solve your own labor difficulties. This casts serious doubts on your sincerity in all the causes you have so ardently advocated. I am confident that the entire consumer defense movement will experience the same doubts."[31] Such letters pleased the striking workers no end. Part of their strategy was to enlist the help of subscribers in an effort to pressure CR into accepting the union's demands. After all, claimed Kallet, because subscribers financially supported the organization, they should also be exercising final authority over its activities.[32]

In response CR's management only intensified its attack on the strikers, who were running out of money for food, fuel, and shelter and were in dire need of general operating funds.[33] Specifically designed to exhaust the union's resources was a plan to obtain injunctions against strikers who picketed the CR plant. For a union with absolutely no funds, the prospect of being dragged through a long and possibly expensive litigation was anything but enticing.[34]

Much of CR's adverse reaction to the union had been fueled by the suspicion that it served as a smoke screen for the Communist Party and that the real motive behind the strike was to secure the organization for the party. In mid-October, and with public sympathy for the striking workers mounting, Matthews testified in a sworn affidavit that he held information that would prove such an infiltration plan. Matthews told of attending a secret meeting in New York during summer 1935 with Susan Jenkins, Kallet, and other people he considered to be Communist sympathizers. Matthews recalled that at Jenkins's request every person had declared confidence in the Communist Party and sympathy with its broad purposes. He also remembered that Kallet admitted to having attended frequent meetings with Communist Party leaders and expressed his belief in the possibility of organizing consumers for effective social action. According to Matthews's recollection, Palmer, who had also been present at the meeting, had agreed with Kallet and made it clear that CR should be placed under the leadership of the Communist Party. Palmer, according to Matthews, was particularly worried about the obstacle that CR's plan to initiate the Consumers' Party could come to represent.

Kallet, who according to Matthews's affidavit had acted with Palmer's full support, used the meeting to launch a bitter attack upon Schlink, whom he

Striking workers at Consumers' Research, 1935. Reprinted with permission from the Consumers' Research Collection, Special Collections and University Archives, Rutgers University Libraries.

accused not only of being an elitist snob with few sympathies for the working class but also of being viciously antilabor. "The farther we got into the discussion," reminisced Matthews, "the more apparent it became that the group had been called together at the instance of Susan Jenkins and Arthur Kallet, with the definite purpose of making plans for the capture of Consumers' Research and the bringing of all of its work and projects as closely as possible under the control of the Communist Party."[35] The difficulty of substantiating these claims did not hinder Matthews. Because of its subversive nature, he explained, the group did not document its activities. People at the meeting were forewarned that if all members of the group did not observe absolute secrecy, it would become necessary for the other members to deny that a meeting had been held. The offending member would therefore be placed in the position of "concocting a fabulous fiction."[36]

Although it had received more than 150 offers of arbitration by mid-October, CR management did not acknowledge any of them. The union, however, had eagerly sought such means of negotiation and had not turned down a single proposal. Given CR's low level of trust and confidence in the government, it should come as no surprise that the organization even turned down the Department of Labor's offer to arbitrate.[37] The conflict came to a head in late November when the newly created National Labor Relations Board charged CR with unfair labor practices. Based on the available evidence, the trial examiner found CR guilty of intentionally trying to discredit the union and of attempting to prevent its employees' self-organization. Denying the result of the seven-day trial, CR moved to have the National Labor Relations Board dismissed from negotiations on the grounds that sections of the National Labor Relations Act were unconstitutional and that the board was without jurisdiction over CR's activities because they did not constitute interstate commerce.[38]

Schlink's Response

The advertising industry's first response to the CR strike, observed the liberal trade journal *Tide,* was "a deep, hearty laugh. It was too perfect." That Schlink, whom many perceived as the "champion of the under-dog, champion of the misguided consumer, avowed radical, labor sympathizer, anticapitalist" who "shouted, thundered against advertising as an anti-social force," would suddenly attack labor unions and turn into a red-baiter was big news.[39] Although business and advertisers took great delight in CR's predicament, they were not alone in being somewhat confused as well. To the general public Schlink's reaction came as a surprise.[40]

What appears to have been a sudden shift in Schlink's attitude toward labor has been the subject of vigorous scholarly debate. Some claim that Schlink never experienced a transformation. "Observers," according to the historian Lawrence B. Glickman, "mistook CR's belligerence for political militance, its condemnation of advertising for economic radicalism, and its call for a consumers' movement for unequivocal support of the Popular Front." CR's leaders, he argues, "were not guilty of false advertising; they never claimed to hold the political and economic beliefs that both the Left and Right assigned them."[41] They simply wanted consumers to protect themselves from getting exploited but did not see this function as part of a larger revolutionary movement.

The public confusion was understandable, however. First of all, as would become crystalline as CR's labor problems escalated, the organization's leadership did not adhere to a uniform political view. As long as product testing dominated the organization's efforts and its political activities were pegged to this function, differing political opinions among the leaders rarely made it to the forefront. This seemingly united effort to challenge corporate interests and demand their regulation was read as a radical effort to challenge the status quo by the general public, when it was instead merely the by-product of CR's testing practices.

Adding to the mistaken apprehension of the situation was the sense of a drastically changed Schlink. Although it is possible that Schlink never intended his CR work as a radical statement, the public might have assumed that his political views, expressed through support for Norman Thomas, the Socialist candidate in the 1928 presidential election, and a speaking engagement before the League of Industrial Democracy, played a key role in his consumer activism.[42]

Also confusing was Schlink's newfound hostility toward labor. Although never a strong defender of workers' rights, Schlink, at least during CR's early years, held an open, even accommodating, attitude toward organized labor. In the early 1930s he was all in favor of developing a separate bulletin that occasionally would "specialize not on the quality of the product, but *on the quality of the human relations and the social policies of the various concerns reported on.*"[43] At this point his reservations were not based on disregard for labor issues but motivated by a concern that such activities might be beyond the organization's expertise and detract from its desire to detail technical aspects of product testing.[44] Monitoring labor conditions, he told fellow board member Bradford Young, was a strictly humanitarian consumer activity, nearly religious in its function, "and our function is technological and economic, and only indirectly religious in quality."[45] Referring to previous attempts by the National Consumers' League (NCL), Schlink also worried that mixing labor policies with quality issues might backfire and hurt, rather than help, workers. For example, unfavorable comments about products produced at a plant with good labor policies might jeopardize the relationship between manufacturers and those organizations trying to improve industry labor conditions.[46] By 1934, however, CR gave up on establishing a collaborative system with other groups on this issue and started referring concerned individuals to the National Foundation of Religion and Labor, an organization led by Bradford Young that had taken an interest in the matter.[47]

Schlink's experiences with the National Recovery Administration (NRA) may have contributed to what would eventually escalate into his complete contempt for organized labor. The NRA's failure to recognize consumers' needs coupled with the frustrated effort to create a Department of the Consumer not only spurred Schlink's resentment toward the Roosevelt administration but also intensified his contempt for business and created an enemy out of labor. Indeed, insofar as Schlink regarded labor as the consumer movement's natural ally, its lack of support enraged him far more than business's predictable antagonism did.

It did not take long, then, before Schlink wanted just as little to do with labor as he did with business. Witnessing the NRA's actions in spring and summer 1933 contributed to his distrust. "Frankly," he huffed in a letter to Mark Starr, the educational director for the International Ladies Garment Workers' Union, "if the labor movement took over society tomorrow, we think that the consumer on the whole (that is, the average citizen) would probably be just as badly off under such a regime as he now is under capitalism."[48]

"As a matter of fact," he stated in February 1935, "we have in our files material indicating that labor is antagonistic to the consumer in some instances and, on account of its developing trend to make friends in high places and enemies only among those who can't fight back, more likely to think class conflict is with the consumer than with its traditional enemy, the boss."[49]

With Schlink at its helm, CR was also disappointed over what it perceived as labor's disinterest in consumer issues. Early on the organization had attempted to reach out to labor by offering group subscriptions at a reduced rate. Of the several thousand groups contacted, only three responded positively. By late 1934 only one group, the Postal Clerks' Union in Brooklyn, New York, with its 150 members, was still subscribing. Although they remained interested in attracting labor groups, CR leaders concluded that concentrating too much on this effort would waste time and energy.[50] "On the whole," reflected Phillips, "conservative labor groups are antagonistic to the consumer approach because they allege that to teach a man to spend his money wisely is to make him satisfied with his present wages so that he will not strive for higher wages in general. The radical labor groups see the consumer approach as completely bourgeois and, therefore, unimportant."[51] Really, Phillips asserted, what served a person as a worker (in terms of efficiency and labor-cutting devices) did not always serve a person as a consumer. Although making biscuits from a Bisquick mix might be a good labor-saving tactic for you as a cook, this worker-friendly strategy could hurt you as a consumer because Bisquick was not recommended by *Consumers' Research Bulletin*.[52] Such examples, she affirmed, demonstrated very clearly that "the workers' interest is not identical with the consumers' interest."[53]

Schlink and Phillips were not the only CR leaders to undergo a change in attitude toward labor. Even more striking was the shift by Matthews. As late as 1935 Matthews, who was considered one of CR's most radical leaders, wrote *Partners in Plunder: The Cost of Business Dictatorship* with Ruth Shallcross.[54]

Equating the conflict between business and the salaried "consumer-workers" with a "clash of classes," the two authors warned that business interests, whom they described as an "out-and-out fascist regime," were tightening their grip on social life and politics with the government's support. "The present Administration at Washington, like its predecessors," claimed the authors, "is completely under the control of, and in another sense effectively a partner of, those who work for profits (not wages and salaries) against the interests of consumer-workers."[55] Considering consumption-related concerns paramount to the struggling classes, Matthews and Shallcross promoted CR's work as an important tool in winning the fight. If anything, the book, which denounced the AFL as reactionary, was more left leaning than large segments of the labor movement. Few could have anticipated that within a few months of the book's publication Matthews would join Schlink and Phillips as an extremely staunch management defender.

"Strikes when other people have them," reported a writer for the liberal trade journal *Tide,* "are simply the natural process by which labor tries to get its say-so in the economic setup—hence [Matthews's] current iron resistance, his willingness to face a strike when any advertiser could have told him that to do so is to irreparably injure not only himself but the whole of his last seven years of work" was baffling.[56] The writer predicted two end-of-strike scenarios. The most drastic outcome could be CR's complete destruction. If the organization did survive, however, its failure to garner support from the many middle- and upper-middle-class subscribers who backed labor might spell its doom.[57] At the time, few predicted that instead a new viable consumer organization would emerge from the strike.

Consumers Union of the United States Inc.

CR's hostile attitude and blanket refusal to negotiate with the union left the striking workers with few choices. They decided to break all ties with CR and start their own consumer organization. The new group, they promised, would not fall into CR's trap of neglecting the worker's place in the "so-called consumer oriented society."[58] Naming itself Consumers Union of the United States Inc. (CU), the group appointed Kallet its leader. Joining him were Palmer, Colston E. Warne, and a large group of former CR employees and board members.

Although its initial hope of attracting almost all of CR's members was not realized, CU managed to sign up several thousand subscribers in a relatively short time. The new organization also sought funds from liberal foundations such as the Twentieth Century Fund, the Elmhirst Fund, and the Christian Social Justice Fund. Within a couple of months of its founding CU also enjoyed the endorsement and contributions of many influential individuals.[59] True to its promise of a more worker-friendly environment and having learned a hard lesson from CR, CU passed a bylaw stipulating clear procedures for the election of directors and also for their eventual removal. In contrast to CR, which had operated with a quorum of two (which, in theory, meant that the husband-and-wife team of Schlink and Phillips could make all decisions), CU set the quorum at seven board members. At first everybody, regardless of position, made ten dollars per week. Minimum pay was later raised to fifteen dollars per week, and although people's wages began to diverge, the staff was unionized; it had a contract and was represented on the board of directors.[60]

In May 1936 CU published the first issue of what would become a monthly newsletter called *Consumers Union Reports* (*CUR*).[61] Much like the bulletins put out by CR, *CUR* placed commodities into categories such as "Best Buy," "Acceptable," and "Non-Acceptable." Unlike CR, however, which had only toyed with creating a link between consumption and production of consumer commodities by providing information about manufacturing conditions, CU carried the idea into practice. The first issue of *CUR* featured an article called "Consumers' Goods Makers Unfair to Labor," which included a list of manufacturers facing union complaints.[62] CU, in other words, viewed itself as more than just a rating service for commodities. In addition to its technical aspects, CU also tried to bridge a desire to help consumers maintain a decent living with a broader political, and definitely prolabor, agenda. Although research and testing on consumer goods helped consumers buy their food, clothing, and other products more efficiently, the new consumer organization did not feel it had done its job if consumers had merely saved a few pennies, or even a few dollars, by buying one brand over another. "Decent living standards for ultimate consumers will never be maintained simply by reports on the quality and the price of products," CU concluded. "By reporting on the labor conditions under which consumer goods are produced; by letting consumers know what products are manufactured under good labor conditions so that when possible they can favor them in making their purchases; by letting them know what products are produced under unfair conditions so that consumers can avoid such products; Consumers Union hopes to add what pressure it can to the fight for higher wages and for the unionization and the collective bargaining which are labor's bulwark against declining standards of living."[63]

Despite more than a little confusion about the differences between CR and CU and some criticism about CU's prolabor attitude, the new consumer organization experienced tremendous growth. Between May and October 1936, for example, its membership increased from thirty-five hundred to fifteen thousand, with members in every state and in some foreign countries as well.[64] Many wrote CU to express their support and their preference for *CUR* over *Consumers' Research Bulletin.*[65] Upset over CU's success, and even considering suing the organization for name and concept infringement, CR nevertheless continued its familiar pattern of testing products and publishing the results.[66] CR's leaders, however, never passed up an opportunity to publicly criticize CU or its board members whom they accused of having a "Communist bias."[67] The organization's testing practices became favorite targets for scorn. "In some cases," Schlink argued, "their findings are more like a grotesque imitation of technical reports than anything to be taken seriously."[68]

CR's accusations were not unfounded. Due to its limited budget, CU was confined to testing items such as soap, suntan lotion, pencils, and tissue paper: objects that were inexpensive to obtain and that could be tested through everyday use by staff or in experiments conducted in its tiny laboratory. Unfortunately for the new organization, however, even its own technicians complained about the unscientific testing methods, and in 1939 a frustrated Dewey H. Palmer left his position as technical supervisor. Protesting the subordination of testing processes to political advocacy work, Professor Charles Marlies left CU's board of directors at the same time.[69]

The business community was quick to catch on to CU's limitations. It had considered CR a nuisance and its attacks on advertising a threat, and it liked CU even less. Some expressed grave doubts about CU's competency to test products and dispense advice; some accused CU of being a racket, shaking down legitimate businesses for bribes and hush money.[70] Doing their best to keep readers' attention on the pending legislation of food, drug, and cosmetics regulation, many *CUR* writers illustrated problems that CU hoped a new law would solve. In the July 1936 issue of the magazine the organization unleashed a particularly strong diatribe against *Good Housekeeping*'s testing facility, the Good Housekeeping Institute. Declaring the institute to be "one of the greatest frauds now being perpetrated on American consumers," *CUR* set out to demonstrate that many products advertised in *Good Housekeeping*, including Fleischmann's Yeast and Grayban hair coloring, made false or misleading claims. Products such as Saraka (a laxative) and Lysol (advertised as a safe and effective germicide and contraceptive), for example, could actually pose a danger to consumers' health.[71] The owners of *Good Housekeeping*, the Hearst Corporation, did not appreciate this attack and accused Consumers Union of "prolonging the Depression by destroying confidence in the institution of advertising."[72] It did not take long before other media interests, concerned about their advertisers, joined the chorus.

It had been clear to CU from the very beginning that its survival as an organization depended upon its ability to attract members. Advertising for membership presented itself as an immediate solution, and CU initially had no problems getting newspapers and (liberal) magazines to accept its ads for new subscribers. By early 1937, however, major newspapers including the *New York Times* were beginning to reject CU's advertising. Claiming that it had received complaints about CU's testing practices, the *New York Times* refused to accept more ads until the organization's credibility could be assured, and its editors suggested that CU agree to a blanket investigation by the National Better Business Bureau (NBBB).[73] From CU's perspective, this was exceptionally problematic. The NBBB, with its close ties to major business interests, was far from neutral. Its board of directors consisted of powerful individuals from the advertising and magazine industries, including *Good Housekeeping*'s business manager. Not only did CU leaders think they could predict the outcome of such an investigation but they also worried about having their files and methods investigated by the same people who stood to gain by having their operations muzzled. Predicting the NBBB's report to be "a foregone conclusion," Kallet eyed no other solution than to refuse the investigation and withdraw CU's advertising from the *New York Times*.[74] This, however, was not enough to ease the situation. By June 1937 other newspapers and national magazines had started to reject CU's ads. Although CR had faced advertising boycotts early in its history, the group did not come to CU's rescue. To the contrary, those at CR, which by now had few problems placing its ads, seemed to take a certain delight in the situation, doing everything in their power to ridicule and discredit their former colleagues.[75]

In response CU began to map strategies to best meet the attacks. Suggestions included enlisting sympathetic columnists to write on the issue, convincing members of Congress to make speeches, and picketing. CU's legal advisor, Abraham J. Isserman, seriously questioned the legality of mass media's blanket refusal of CU's ads and intended to check with the Federal Trade Commission to see if the practice was banned.[76] Considering CU's critical view of advertising, some business leaders exulted in preventing the organization from using this form of marketing for itself. For an organization determined to bring the "low-down" on nationally advertised goods and services, remarked one observer, it seemed rather hypocritical for it to spend large portions of its income on advertising. Moreover, maintained the vice president of *Printers' Ink,* referring to some *CUR* stories he found inaccurate, "I should think you folks would be wise and to lean over backwards in trying to maintain the same standards of ethics and real truthfulness that many of the leaders in advertising have so long and diligently striven for, with some degree, though admittedly not complete, success."[77]

By 1939, and with Kallet assuming greater responsibility for CU's testing operations, the organization confronted industry opposition by establishing a chemical, electrical, bacteriological, and textile-testing lab.[78] It also announced its intention to put on a proconsumer exhibit during the 1939 New York World's Fair. The fair was a collaboration between business and government intended to help New York City recover from the Depression. Promising to help "Building the World of Tomorrow," the fair promoted a vision of an American future in which large corporations would create prosperity for all. Recognizing the importance of consumption in this process, a specially created Production and Distribution Zone at the fair included a Consumers Building. Many consumer-movement leaders were invited to serve on the Advisory Committee on Consumer Interests and help plan the event.[79] "This affair," stressed CU president Colston E. Warne, "might give us the opportunity to insert a critical note toward the usual advertising ballyhoo that constitutes the center of the arena of a twentieth century world's fair."[80]

The prospect of CU's presence at the fair distressed many advertising interests, however. A nightmare scenario in which CU started attacking the other exhibitors in public had them petrified. The fair's organizers willingly admitted that they were "up against advertising pressure which could not be very well resisted" to ban CU's presence. So the executive committee in charge of planning demanded that all participating groups refrain from passing judgment on the other exhibitors and let "each organization state its viewpoint concerning the consumer in a manner which it deemed fit."[81] Thus, the organizers made it very clear that to participate, CU needed to omit anything "destructive" from its exhibits. Considering the opposition to their participation, CU leaders fretted that after committing ten thousand dollars of the group's scarce resources to secure a role in the venture, commercial interests might invent some "obnoxious" reason they should not be allowed to exhibit.[82] These concerns were not unfounded. In October 1938, only months before the fair's opening, the Advisory Committee on Consumer

Interests was informed that its chair had been replaced by the president of the Associated Grocery Manufacturers, who was not particularly sympathetic to a critical agenda. Many consumer leaders quit in protest.[83]

In the end, CU was left with the only noncommercial consumer exhibit at the fair. The organization's display helped dramatize fraud in the marketplace and offered tips on how consumers could best protect themselves.[84] Although it provided a significant forum for exhibits extolling the virtues of business and advertising, including one called "Advertising's Influence on American Life and Business" sponsored by the McFadden Publishing Group, the fair was not an economic success. To recoup losses the fair was reconvened in 1940, this time without CU's contribution. The "World of Fashion" had replaced the consumer organization's exhibit.[85]

Despite this snub, CU still maintained its impressive number of members. In only its first year and with the first annual membership meeting only a couple of weeks away, CU counted more than thirty-five thousand subscribers in April 1937 and planned an eventful convention with one thousand members in attendance.[86] The summer brought more encouraging news. By June the membership numbers had climbed to forty thousand, and by December the total had reached fifty thousand. This meant that the organization needed only another ten thousand subscribers to match CR in size.[87] Building coalitions between CU and working-class consumers turned out to be more difficult than the new organization had anticipated, however. Unlike regular annual memberships, which were sold at three dollars, CU offered memberships at a reduced price to low-income individuals and people qualifying for membership through a larger group. This proved to be a huge disappointment for CU, as neither low-income individuals nor unions flocked to join.[88]

In addition to its technical work, during this period CU lobbied to pass the still-pending food and drug legislation, sent requested speakers to various community meetings, and created educational material for classroom use.[89] The organization also played an instrumental role in organizing the Consumers' National Council, a coordinating agency for more than forty organizations that concerned themselves with consumer issues. The group counted the American Association of University Women, the American Home Economics Association, and the NCL among its members. CR, on the other hand, refused to participate in the Consumers' National Council.[90]

Perhaps as a way of reasserting itself into the consumer movement limelight, CR decided to publish a monthly magazine called *Consumers' Digest*. Bearing a striking resemblance to the layout in *Reader's Digest*, the magazine, published initially in January 1937, consisted mainly of reprints from *Consumers' Research Bulletin*. Unlike the latter, which rated products and found some better than others, however, *Consumers' Digest* named only those products that it recommended. In addition to providing an ideological platform for CR's antilabor and anti-Communist agenda, the new journal helped keep Schlink's demand for a Department of the Consumer in the public eye.[91] Schlink also unveiled a revised view of advertising. "With advertising *per se* we have no quarrel," stated Schlink. "*No one can reasonably deny that under the stimulus of advertising there has been an increase in the consumption of many meritorious products and an improvement in the standard of living of those who have used them.* Our criticism of advertising practices is directed toward its obvious, and often flagrant, failure to safeguard the consumer's interest in matter of quality, need for the product, its suitability for his uses, and freedom from needless hazards of harm."[92] *Printers' Ink,* which less than three years earlier had bemoaned CR's views on advertising, was now almost jubilant.[93] Although the journal still covered "the usual malarkey about advertising, arsenic and saving your anti-freeze in a bottle for next winter," reflected a journalist from the trade press, "Mr. Schlink is no longer on the side of the angels. It means he is a lone wolf; no leader but a sniper in an isolated bush."[94]

Advertising as a Public Relations Tool for Business

The splitting of CR into two consumer organizations not only created animosity in the consumer movement's ranks but also enabled new participants to enter the arena with greater ease. By the mid-1930s business and advertising interests, who for a long time had resorted to false attacks to defend against the consumer movement's demands, were starting to reevaluate their strategies. Exactly how to align consumer education with corporate needs was the key problem, and to meet this challenge industry looked to the rapidly growing field of public relations.

To understand the context facing the advertising industry we need to appreciate the broader developments in business's use of PR during this time. The change was characterized by a gradual shift away from the heavy-handed use of propaganda toward campaigns with more educational emphases. Instead of merely bragging about benign and useful functions, business increased its use of advertising to explain its views and perspectives to the public. This strategy departed from the "institutional advertising" that had been around since the turn of the century and had become increasingly popular in the 1920s. Unlike institutional advertising, which aimed at reassuring consumers of a firm's sound and friendly nature without actually promoting specific products, "public relations advertising" had a much broader scope. It attempted to sell a certain set of social principles and educate the American people to business's helpful and important role in society.[95]

Many business leaders began to acknowledge that selling business itself and its contributions to the entire economic system was just as important as selling its products. They also realized that to be effective, such PR, instead of serving as palliatives for corporations who neglected their corporate health, needed to follow a strategy and be consistent.[96] To yield a successful result, PR had to be established as a "fundamental system of business hygiene" and not just dispensed in individual doses as damage control.[97] Although industry might have learned to create favorable opinions of its products, it had been largely unsuccessful in creating goodwill for the business behind the products, and this is where strategically designed advertising could do a world of good.[98] A defensive stance, counterattacks, and blatant propaganda designed to discredit the New Deal and the consumer movement were no longer considered the best strategies for winning consumers. "The sooner we stop thinking of public relations as a job of mass hypnotism which will make the public think the way we want it to think," stressed the advertising executive Edgar Kobak, "the better for all of us."[99]

The National Association of Manufacturers (NAM) emerged as a trendsetter in this respect. Beginning in 1933 and under the leadership of its president, Robert Lund, the association undertook a massive effort to improve the public's perception of U.S. manufacturers. Working under the assumption that most of the public's misgivings against business were based on misunderstandings, the NAM designed a PR campaign that allowed industry to "tell its story" by educating the American people about industry and the benefits it bestowed upon society.[100] Many of the individual advertising campaigns that resulted concentrated not so much on the merits of individual products, services, and companies as on the contribution of these companies to the general betterment of the United States. Campaigns by the NAM, AT&T, and the U.S. Chamber of Commerce aimed to familiarize consumers with the role of big business in society and asked them to associate industry with "the American Way." The Lord and Thomas advertising agency prepared a series of full-page NAM advertisements that explained the organization's view on political and social issues of the day. The association's take on "Machines and Employment," "Taxation," the "American Standard of Living," and "America's Tomorrow" were made available to members for publication at their own expense.[101]

In 1936 General Motors designed the traveling exhibit Parade in Progress and took it on a twenty-thousand-mile trip across the country. Tying the exhibit together was *Previews of Science,* a film show depicting the glorious future of a society based on free-enterprise principles. Other large companies such as Du Pont, General Electric, Westinghouse, Goodyear, and AT&T also designed individual PR strategies.[102]

Before long, almost all businesses engaged in some form of PR activity, and most national advertisers established emergency budgets in case PR advertising should became necessary. Manufacturers also relied on a variety of PR methods designed to take advantage of free publicity. A growing need to "interpret" various aspects of business to the public prompted many advertising agencies to create PR departments to provide clients with more "rounded" services. One such service was to show clients how tax-deductible institutional copy could be used more effectively.[103]

The business community's faith in advertising's ability to help educate the public was both flattering and reassuring to those who had worked hard for advertising's acceptance. The use of advertising to improve the public's faith in business, therefore, suggested that advertising, despite the withering attack it was taking from the consumer movement, had not lost its esteem in business circles.[104] "More definitely now than ever before, advertising is industry's voice," concluded a writer in *Printers' Ink.* "Advertising confronts an opportunity to correct befogged and biased opinion. That which the press agents have done, surreptitiously and often not particularly well, for a handful of clients, advertising can do for all business."[105] The advertising executive Bruce Barton concurred. "We have a story to tell," he declared enthusiastically. "We have great benefits to confer upon the people if they will give us the opportunity; but we must persuade them that we are more reliable than the politicians; that we will work for them more cheaply and with more satisfaction. This story should be told, with all the imagination and art of which modern advertising is capable. It should be told just as continuously as the people are told that Ivory Soap floats or that children cry for Castoria."[106] Business, according to the American Association of Advertising Agencies (AAAA), needed to use advertising as "a mouthpiece and interpreter" for industry leaders.[107] Acting in full agreement with these goals, the Advertising Federation of America (AFA) and the Association of National Advertisers stressed the urgent need to "sell" the public on an industry interpretation of business and called for a broad campaign to this effect.[108] "We have an obligation to tell it, to explain and interpret what industry has done for the well being of the people of America," gushed AFA president Chester H. Lang, "so that they may judge for themselves whether they shall believe in us or not—whether they shall continue to believe in the American system. If we give them the 'facts,'" he concluded, "I have no misgivings concerning their verdict."[109] Advertising, according to *Printers' Ink,* could serve as a "most potent force" in building better PR for U.S. business.[110]

Not all industry observers were convinced that an extensive use of advertising was the best way to go, however. Because part of the public viewed advertising as just another trick to "outsmart the buyer" or "[pull] the wool over consumers' eyes," some speculated that it might not be the best PR vehicle. Advertising's reputation for treating consumers as "high-grade morons" was also problematic.[111] Reports that part of the public was growing suspicious of PR and regarded it as purely "the attempt to give oneself a good reputation, whether one deserved [it] or not" added to the business worries.[112]

Advertising's New PR in the Late 1930s

The consumer movement may have been severely tested, but its many demands, including advertising's federal regulation, still had strong support. Astute PR strategies were needed to counteract consumers' might. The advertising industry slowly began to accept that to attack the consumer movement as it became larger and more muscular could be read as an indirect attack on the very consumers who supported this movement. For business leaders and advertisers to attack, rather than respond to, organized consumer demands might suggest an unwillingness to serve the public.[113]

Although it had helped businesses build better relations with the public, advertising had been less successful in doing so for itself. Part of the problem, of course, stemmed from the danger in explaining advertising's true economic role to the public. It was not just tricky to admit that its main functions were to deemphasize price and product comparisons and build brand loyalties; the strategy could play directly into the consumer movement's hands as well. Instead of emphasizing this function, the industry elected to stress advertising's role in bringing modernity, a variety of conveniences, and a higher standard of living to the masses. Before long, advertising trade organizations poured their combined efforts into fixing advertising's credibility problem. Influenced by these new PR strategies, the advertising community no longer viewed self-regulation as the only way to improve public perceptions. Instead of focusing on the eradication of fraudulent and misleading advertisements, advertising took a cue from the NAM's efforts and shifted to a strategy whereby educating the public about the benign and useful functions of advertising took center stage. "The first step in the direction of improved public relations for advertising, of course, is the establishment of effective measures for control within the industry of objectionable advertising," reflected *Advertising Age*'s editors. "The next is presenting on a [broad] scale, a statement of policy which will impress the public with the fact that advertising, in its proper function, is essentially mutual in character, serving the seller best only when it also renders a valid service to the buyer. These two objectives seem to us to be not only desirable, but well within the limits of practicable achievement."[114]

In 1934, and as a reaction to the consumer movement's growing popularity, speakers at the AFA's annual convention had called for organized outreach to schools, clubs, associations, and consumer organizations. Members were encouraged to use speakers, radio, newspapers, and other media to educate Americans about the social and business benefits of advertising as well as advertising's "indispensable character." Also recommended was the formation of a PR group to "aid in the dissemination of the facts and right understanding in regard to the utility and operation of advertising."[115] Such measures, experts argued, were necessary to shield the industry "against decay from within and unfair attacks from without."[116] Part of advertising's problem, its defenders claimed, was that consumers judged it on face value and lacked a clear understanding of its larger function. "Were it possible through some magic to eliminate all questionable copy, there still would remain criticism because there is so little understanding of Advertising," concluded one industry spokesman.[117] Advertising, claimed industry leaders, served valuable social and economic functions. Informing large numbers of people about products' availability led to mass demand, mass production, and cheaper and more easily available goods; it also introduced consumers to new products that helped improve the quality of their lives and their health.[118]

One of the advertising industry's biggest PR nightmares, at least in the mid-1930s, was its inability—or perhaps its unwillingness—to address the heavy use of emotional appeals in ads. On this important point the consumer movement and the advertising community did not see eye to eye. The industry's inability to explain the necessity of emotional appeals and limited factual information in advertisements contradicted its strategy of explaining itself to the public and ran counter to the rapidly growing realization that, to be successful, PR had to deal more directly with consumers' concerns.[119] Because parity advertising played such a major part in business marketing strategies, the advertising community exhibited an extremely defensive attitude when criticized on this point. Instead of admitting that parity advertising was the direct result of product competition's nature in an oligopolistic economy, industry defenders argued that the emotional appeals associated with parity advertising had come about due to some inherent characteristic in the American consumer. "Illusions," stated AAAA president John Benson, "are what men live by and if advertising by illusion can create a desire for better things, thereby creating more jobs and a sounder economic structure, it is doing America a real service."[120] Others, such as Malcolm P. McNair, the director of research at the Harvard Graduate School of Business Administration, indirectly attributed America's superiority as a consumer society to ads' emotional appeals. Advertising in the United States constituted a much greater social force than it did in Europe, he argued, not because the volume differed but because the appeals did. Although frequently flamboyant, pseudoscientific, and even misleading, American toothpaste advertising, for example, could be credited with some great indirect results. After all, he asked, did not Americans have the best teeth of people living in any civilized nation?[121]

The benefits, according to advertising community representatives, did not stop there. The use of emotional appeals was a great example of "a completely democratic institution," according to the advertising-executive-turned-professor James W. Young. "It holds an election in which you and I vote every day as we pass our money across the counter for advertised products."[122] The advantages went far beyond these principles, Young argued. Emotional advertising inspired people's hopes and dreams and improved their everyday existence. "So in a jar of face cream," the professor rhapsodized, "the advertiser may pack a dream of youth more priceless to some than the rarest unguents of the Orient. Or in a carton of breakfast food he may enclose an ambition to be another Babe Ruth, more satisfying to your boy than all its calories."[123] The consumer movement's demand for detailed product information completely missed the most important point, claimed *Advertising Age*. Advertising was not intended as a catalog or description of a product's qualities and characteristics, nor was product information its primary function. "Persuasion, which is mainly an appeal to the emotions rather than to reason, is the primary purpose of advertising," maintained the trade journal's editors.[124] "Advertising is a symbol of economic freedom," offered a writer in *Banking*. "[It] is the promoter of free enterprise, the voice of free competition and the symbol of free choice. It is as democratic, as flexible, as vulnerable, and as permanent as the American system."[125]

To get people to appreciate advertising and value its function, the advertising industry invested in an entire promotional program. In addition to employing speakers' bureaus and motion pictures, it used its considerable influence over radio broadcasting to see that the programming had a pro-advertising sentiment.[126] For example, in June 1936, on the twenty-fifth anniversary of the truth-in-advertising movement, NBC broadcast a program on advertising's greatness and benevolence. The AFA urged NBC to go a step further in promoting the event. "You have a number of very fine preachers on the air on that day and if you could give us their names, we could send them material regarding the program for that day so that in their programs they could include a message regarding 'Truth in Advertising.' Some of them may want to make their sermons or talks in tune with the subject and others may want to mention the subject as a part of their talk," urged the federation's leaders. Although the result is not exactly clear, evidence suggests that NBC accepted the idea.[127]

Without actually changing its ways, the advertising industry wanted to convey the impression that it was listening to the public's concerns and working to meet its demands. Exactly how to accomplish this task was the big, but not impossible, challenge. The discontent that the consumer movement had fueled could be turned to the advertising industry's advantage. Because the movement's quest for change had been largely unsuccessful, a frustrated public might be interested in leveraging a deal with advertisers. "Lectures and radio talks have not done enough to stem the tide," observed a *Business Week* writer, "and now advertisers are discussing more effective measures. For a long time there has been talk that the industry itself might furnish consumers with some reliable buying service, modeled after that of the more radical consumer organization."[128]

Although the consumer movement had no doubt fueled consumer discontent, the editor of *Printers' Ink* argued, its quest for change had been largely unsuccessful, and advertisers stood a good chance of winning the battle.[129] "The women are consumers; and the depression made them conscious of their rights and powers as such," concurred another trade magazine. "The moment that happened, the consumer movement became important to you [advertisers]. Fortunately for the trade, the women are hard to convince. Neither Mr. Schlink nor Mr. Kallet nor Mr. Warbasse [a leader of the cooperative movement] can deliver their vote, and they are ready now, as they ever were, to cooperate with any businessman who will talk turkey."[130]

Thus, in addition to PR advertising, lectures, and radio broadcasts, the advertising industry began actively undermining consumer organizations by creating industry front groups that claimed to serve consumers but had building up business as their ulterior motive. Similar to the larger PR effort to sell the public on business's role and value, the new advertising approach was intended to be a long-term effort to replace people's reliance on the consumer movement and make them look to the advertising industry for answers. "The 'right-wingers' in advertising circles," concluded *Advertising and Selling*, "aren't looking at the problem as a one-shot, one-time affair . . . they are building programs for the long pull."[131]

Conclusion

By the mid- to late 1930s the consumer movement had split into two distinct camps. Although CU, which was the more activist oriented, refused to consider consumer issues in isolation and insisted on a link to organized labor, CR increased its determination to elevate consumers' rights as a worthy cause unrelated to business and labor. The advertising industry, which had emerged as a third group claiming to represent the consumers' interests, insisted on linking consumer education with a business agenda. The advertising industry's initial attempts at preventing the consumer movement's impact had failed, as had its attempts at "explaining" advertising to the public. Its sovereignty among politicians could not be equaled in the court of public opinion. The industry's next PR strategy, which focused on replacing people's confidence in the consumer movement with faith in the advertising industry's ability to provide the same information, would prove far more effective. "It is a familiar pattern," reflected *CUR*'s editor, that "no one fights reform so bitterly as the one who stands most in need of it."[132]

5

Defining the Consumer Agenda:
The Business Community
Joins the Fray

The very nature of advertising in an economy dominated by oligopolistic markets suggests that advertising would find itself in a perpetual PR war to establish its legitimacy and undermine its foes. Indeed, by 1939 the industry's various trade organizations had established permanent PR programs and had propelled these activities to the pinnacle of their missions.[1] Advertisers argued, in effect, that not only did they know more about consumers' needs and wants than did consumer groups but they also knew more than consumers themselves. Contrary to the consumer movement's call for product facts and information, the industry maintained that the average consumer was incapable of understanding technical terms. It accused consumer groups of providing unreliable and inconsistent data and stressed that advertising, because it talked a language people could understand, was better suited for educating consumers.[2]

From 1935 to 1938 advertising established a sophisticated probusiness alternative consumer movement to undermine and discredit the claims of autonomous consumer groups. Through public conferences, radio programs, and publications, advertisers aggressively propagated the notion that advertising was synonymous with freedom and democracy and was a "natural" U.S. institution. The immediate goal behind these PR activities was to render the pending food and drug legislation as ineffective on regulating advertising and business as possible. Their long-term goal was to marginalize, even nullify, the consumer movement and minimize the possibility of future threats to advertising's modus operandi.

The Rise of Commercially Backed Consumer Groups

Although survey research into consumers' wants and needs had served as a valuable marketing tool since before World War I, not until the late 1920s and early 1930s did it develop into a strategy to secure business dominance. Instead of functioning as a two-way method for interpreting the public's view of business and vice versa, consumer behavior began to be studied by such groups as the Psychological Corporation, which was led by the Yale-trained psychologist Henry Link, as a means of manipulating it. Enlisting the help of undergraduate and graduate students across the country to conduct surveys, the Psychological Corporation issued the quarterly *Psychological Sales Barometer* that monitored consumers' attitudes, brand preferences, and ability to recall advertising slogans. What Link and other pollsters hailed as "the *Vox Populi,* speaking wisdom through 'chi-squares,'"[3] others, such as Robert S. Lynd, criticized as an example of "democracy working in reverse."[4] The one-way flow of communication and business's ability to set the parameters for legitimate debate did not empower the public to form opinions. On the contrary, it served primarily as a tool to justify a business-dominated agenda.[5] The National Industrial Information Committee, a public information agency formed by the National Association of Manufacturers (NAM), stressed the importance of "keeping a finger on the pulse of public opinion" by using the mass media and other means of communication to correct "misconceptions" about business that surveys revealed.[6] This strategy of producing self-serving data, which later would help set the parameters for future discussions, was heavily used in advertising's dealings with the public. Beyond the creation of self-serving polls, business elaborated on a series of established PR strategies. The use of industry front groups—or third-party groups—the proven technique of divide and conquer, and the application of money and media access to overwhelm the consumer movement were all part of the industry's arsenal.

One of the first attempts at creating an industry front group based on the consumer movement's strategies was set in motion by the Collier Publishing Company. In 1937 the publisher, which operated as a separate division in the Crowell-Collier Publishing Company, established its Consumer Division, a politically conservative bureau led by the editor of the *Women's Home Companion,* Anna Steese Richardson. Prior to leading the Consumer Division, Richardson had directed the company's Good Citizenship Bureau and had, in this capacity, spent months touring the country speaking to various women's groups. Her plea to American clubwomen was for a better understanding of advertising. Better food on the table, healthier skin, and improved oral health were not due to the work of home economics teachers, doctors, or dentists, she argued, but rather to the influence of educational advertisements that suggested more nutritious food combinations and taught people how to clean their skin and teeth.[7] According to Richardson, the slow business recovery in the United States resulted from the uncritical acceptance of Consumers' Research Inc.'s (CR's) work and its supporters. "These groups, with a complete lack of knowledge of the facts of advertising and big business, have sought to rob the American woman of her faith in advertising and her confidence in business," she contended. "Until she gets back that faith through an unbiased study of the facts, and the application of her own common sense to the situation, we cannot hope for prosperity."[8] The consumer movement's success in poisoning the minds of the clubwomen of the United States loomed so large, complained Richardson, that whenever she addressed the League of Women Voters, the American Home Economics Association, or the American Association of University Women, she felt as if she was beating her "bare hands against [the] stone wall of prejudice."[9] Although the millions of women exposed to CR's propaganda believed the information to be well intended, its actual purpose, according to Richardson, was to increase sales of consumer advocacy books like *100,000,000 Guinea Pigs* and make CR's organizers rich.[10]

According to critics, however, the ultimate objective behind Collier's Consumer Division was to "'channel consumer thought' in such a manner as to make it harmless to big business and national advertisers."[11] As the Consumer Division's director, Richardson conducted an exhaustive survey of consumer activities and used the findings to launch a detailed program to counter supposedly left-leaning consumer groups and ally leading advertisers with the more "constructive side of the consumer movement."[12] The result of the study was published in a 1937 pamphlet entitled *Advertising and the Consumer Movement,* which characterized CR, Consumers Union of the United States Inc. (CU), Cooperative Distributors, and the Inter-Mountain Consumers' Service as "Professional Consumer Groups" with axes to grind against advertising. The pamphlet warned that these groups' influence was rapidly spreading and that "destructive and misleading propaganda against branded goods [had] encouraged unscrupulous manufacturers and merchants to foist unbranded products of inferior quality on the consumer public," causing "millions of young people [to be] taught to distrust American business methods." Collier proudly announced that its Consumer Division would back its "obligations to its reading public and to the honest manufacturers who stand behind its advertising pages." The publisher promised to "act as a clearing house through which American business [could] tell a clear story of what it [was] doing to provide even better products and services to its consumers."[13] Its advertising director, J. A. Welch, insisted that the Consumer Division would serve a helpful function by offsetting some of the consumer movement's "subversive propaganda."[14]

The publisher's strategy was fortified by a budget ranging somewhere between sixty thousand and one hundred thousand dollars. The division supplied consumer groups with study material and provided discussion leaders with information on topics including foods, textiles, labeling, and business costs.[15] Richardson called on business to "combat the dissemination of misinformation through consumer groups" and stressed that the latter not only hurt advertisers' immediate sales efforts but also had another and possibly more threatening effect.[16] As she put it: "The women who are being fed this type of stuff [consumer information from groups like CU] are voters. As constituents, they command the ear of congressmen and state legislators. Led by propagandists, they telephone, write, telegraph and petition their representatives. You can thank them for many of the measures which harass and handicap business men, for the steady growth of sentiment toward cooperatives and government control of business."[17]

Although stating that her organization had no quarrel with "the legitimate consumer movement," Richardson acknowledged that it set out to attack the "small groups of aggressive, self-appointed leaders of the consumer movement—because under the guise of protecting the consumer they are apparently lining their own pockets or advancing their own political interests." In 1939 the Consumer Division designed an extensive ad campaign to educate the public on advertising. Not limiting the effort to its own publications, which included the *Women's Home Companion, American Magazine, Collier's, National Weekly,* and *Country Home Magazine,* the publisher offered the extensive program to other publications at cost. Much to its delight, more than six thousand daily and weekly newspapers eventually accepted the offer.[18] "Month after month," explained the publisher, the ads featuring "interviews between typical consumers and famous business leaders have brought home to the public a clearer concept of advertising . . . its influence on prices, its essential honesty, its social benefits."[19]

For example, "What has advertising ever done for me?" was the rhetorical question posed to J. A. Zehntbauer, president of Jantzen Knitting Mills, by Mrs. Howard George from Newberg, Oregon, in the September 1939 issue of the *Women's Home Companion.* In this advertisement the eager bathing suit manufacturer elaborated on the direct relationship between swimwear advertising and the immense popularity of "the country's newest and biggest outdoor sport"—swimming. "Gradually," Zehntbauer lectured, "advertising made people realize it was proper to dress sensibly for swimming. And it wasn't long before America had a fine new source of pleasure and health." He added, "Yes, Mrs. George, advertising can be an enormous social benefit. It is constantly working, directly and indirectly, for greater happiness, greater freedom, better living for all. Fact is, you'd have a hard time finding a single person in this country whom advertising hasn't helped in some very substantial way."[20]

Collier's consumer activities were not limited to educational material along traditional lines. In 1937 it promised one hundred dollars for the advertising play that best presented an "adequate and convincing exposition of advertising as an economic and social force" to consumer groups.[21] Richardson's persistent lobbying to get NBC to broadcast the winning play, entitled *Meet the Consumer,* paid off. Margaret Cuthbert, NBC's director of women's activities, strongly recommended the play and offered to have her employer pay the actors. She also encouraged the radio network to cooperate with other Crowell ventures.[22]

Richardson never let pass a chance to attack the consumer movement, which invariably she characterized as a group of self-appointed protectors and professional agitators. Claiming to represent the interest of average consumers, she castigated CR and CU not only for being out of touch with consumers' interests but also for being "pseudo-educational groups." Manufacturers, she argued, were more in tune with consumers' needs, plus their elaborate product testing ensured quality. "The finest investigations made in America today are not made by so-called protectors of consumers but by the manufacturers who know that unless they keep up the standards of their products, they cannot meet competition nor hold the trade of Mrs. America."[23] Why, she asked, would consumers trust "men who have never made up a payroll or lain awake nights wondering how they could keep their factories or stores going"?[24] This approach was so effective that a writer for *CUR* concluded, "The Crowell family of magazines is the fountain-head of one of the best-organized, most active anti-consumer machine-gun nests that the advertising interests have yet set up."[25]

By championing themselves and manufacturers as consumer experts, these industry fronts hoped to steer the public away from independent assessments. Right-wing consumer groups intended to flex their financial muscles and capitalize on their easy access to mass media to win consumers' loyalties. These groups wanted to overwhelm and discredit the original consumer groups and mold consumer behavior into actions consistent with, and financially beneficial to, business interests. Industry observers recognized that this transformation would not be easy. Aggressive sales techniques had to be traded for more sophisticated tactics. "Advertising is not awake to its possibilities in consumer education," declared one advertising spokesman, "to not one of the hundreds of possibilities that are inherent in such education."[26] It would not be long, however, before a large segment of the advertising industry realized that rather than fighting the consumer movement, it should instead beat it at its own game.

The mid- to late 1930s witnessed a rapid increase of commercially backed consumer groups motivated to set the agenda for consumer issues. By 1937 *Public Opinion Quarterly* was warning its readers about the ideological differences behind the many similar-sounding groups even though all claimed to serve in the consumer's best interest.[27] The Consumer's Advertising Council, which was founded by the American Association of Advertising Agencies (AAAA) in 1938 to "stem the tide of misunderstanding" about advertising that it accused the consumer movement of causing, is one prominent example. Much like the Consumer Division just discussed, the Consumer's Advertising Council focused on the critical perspective on advertising that many women's club members seemed to have adopted. "How far their ideas reach down among the masses who read and buy from advertising, we don't know [but] we would like to find out," commented AAAA president John Benson. "There is grave danger in it. These leaders among women are influential in their own communities; what they think and say is important; in a local sense they make opinion." Benson was determined to turn the consumer movement's momentum against itself. "Many of the [club] women are intelligent and fair minded; anxious merely to get their money's worth. Naturally they are interested in advertising as a guide to value. Many have been misled about it. They want to know the truth. They want to think well of advertising. It is up to us to give them facts, both benefits and abuses, and a clearer understanding of its true function. The menace thus becomes an opportunity, which it would be folly indeed for us to miss."[28] Heavily funded by advertising, publishing, and business interests, the Consumer's Advertising Council was entrusted to supply data about advertising and advertised products to consumer organizations and to help create a favorable opinion about advertising, all while keeping anti-advertising sentiments at bay.[29]

Soon large retailers, who wanted consumers to trust them, their testing institutes, and their advertising over the consumer movement's advice, developed an interest in consumer education. Although dismayed over the many radical proposals set forth by consumer activists, they eyed exploiting the movement's energy and ambition. As retailers soon discovered, properly channeled consumer discontent actually could be used to further their own agenda.[30] R. H. Macy and Co. emerged as an expert at this strategy. The venerable department store chain offered monthly "consumer clinics" to familiarize clubwomen with Macy's merchandise-testing procedures.[31] Macy's flagship store in New York City, according to *Sales Management* magazine, had also "found many a way to turn the sour grapes of the consumer movement into jam for its bread." Its *Consumer Quiz Club,* a fifteen-minute, five-days-a-week broadcast, attracted hordes of women eager to be questioned on their knowledge of what and how to buy and have that knowledge augmented by that of experts (Macy's experts, naturally).[32] Retail interests even went so far as to thank the consumer movement for providing them with one of the greatest sales opportunities ever offered and urged all retailers to capitalize on its popularity.[33]

Just as ominous as Macy's self-serving pitch to middle-class customers was the Advisory Committee on Ultimate Consumer Goods, sponsored by the American Standards Association and the Consumer-Retailer Dry Goods Association. This special project, suggested by Harold Brightman of L. Bamberger in Newark, New Jersey, emerged when two business-backed consumer groups combined to further the goals of retail interests.

Another group reflecting retailers' concerns was the Consumers Foundation, supported by the Institute of Distribution and the *National Consumer News,* a monthly magazine edited by Crump Smith. The *National Consumer News,* transformed into the house organ for the foundation, vigorously solicited advertising and set its goal at one million paid subscriptions. In contrast to *CUR* and *Consumers' Research Bulletin,* which accepted no advertising whatsoever, Smith's *National Consumer News* accepted ads at the rate of $540 a page.[34] With a pressrun of seventy-five thousand for the first forty-four-page issue, Smith was well on his way toward establishing what he described as "The Golden Cord—Between Business and the New Consumer Consciousness."[35] Although acknowledging Smith's right to publish whatever he wanted, CU members were upset that his magazine operated under the guise of helping consumers. In fact, contended the consumer organization, the magazine's real purpose appeared to be the promotion of an alternative, and voluntary, labeling system to replace the grade-labeling proposal in the pending food and drug bill. It did not escape CU's attention that the first issue of the *National Consumer News* devoted its entire center spread to a full-color advertisement for Del Monte's proposal for new "informative" labeling and that one article entitled "Informative Labels Are Adopted—Del Monte, Libby Aid Buyer" paraphrased the same Del Monte ad, a Del Monte publicity statement on the merits of "informative" and "descriptive" labeling, and Libby's plan for achieving this particular industry goal.[36]

Unlike CU, CR was surprisingly undisturbed by Smith's magazine. "We subscribe to *National Consumer News,* ourselves," wrote M. C. Phillips to a CR member in Arizona. "We think that on the whole their sheet is fairly innocuous, but not especially useful to consumers. There are rumors in advertising magazines and trade journals that they are subsidized by the chain stores. However, we believe from what little we have seen of their stuff that it is not bad as far as it goes."[37] A couple of years later Smith began to offer a confidential publication called *Consumer Movement Trends.* For an annual membership fee of one hundred dollars—here targeted at a business readership—Smith promised to supply a weekly news bulletin reporting on developments within the consumer movement, a monthly inquiry on the headline consumer question of the month (interpreted in terms of business needs), and a quarterly summary of business-consumer relations. For those willing to pay an additional fee, *Consumer Movement Trends* offered surveys about the consumer movement's activities and gave counsel on specific problems involving consumer relations.[38]

The list goes on. The National Consumer-Retailer Council was founded in 1937 and promoted itself as a nonprofit forum for national consumer organization representatives and retailing interests to "discuss their common problems." The council not only stressed its dedication to consumer education but also its willingness to cooperate with large women's organizations such as the American Association of University Women, the American Home Economics Association, the national board of the Young Women's Christian Association, and the National Council of Jewish Women. Many of the largest retail stores in the United States supported the council, which received its funding from membership dues and subscriptions, retail stores and associations, consumer organizations, foundations, advertisers, manufacturers, and individuals. For retailers, the council promised to provide "a practical and fundamental long range public relations program in the public interest," whereas consumers were promised the opportunity to "enlist the support of business men in achieving many of the practical steps involved in raising the levels of living of the American people." Despite its proclaimed willingness to cooperate with (select) consumer groups, the council's high priority on developing advertising as a more effective buying and selling tool and its dedication to the "maintenance of the American system of business enterprise" suggest that the parameters for legitimate discussion had been drawn by retail interests a priori. The consumer presence was largely cosmetic: a token to legitimize the council for mainstream consumers. Judging from the National Consumer-Retailer Council's setup and goals, its most important function was to provide retailers with tips for their marketing strategies.[39] The "'most constructive and significant developments' of the consumer movement during the last two years," concluded the council's leaders in 1939, "have been the willingness of several of the great national women's organizations to cooperate with business through the agency of the National Consumer[-]Retailer Council and recognition by many business organizations that 'sensible efforts on the part of consumer groups to improve business practices, including advertising, can no longer be construed as attempts to destroy business.'" The National Consumer-Retailer Council also kept a close eye on the consumer movement's growing popularity.[40] In response to these actions by business interests, Robert S. Lynd warned that these were mere attempts at "channel[ing] consumer thought" to make it harmless for big business and national advertisers.[41]

Ironically, the commercially backed consumer movement did not shy away from appropriating ideas and strategies from Professor Lynd's participant-observer methods. One industry representative, Mabel Crews Ringwald, suggested that advertising interests should use Lynd's scholarship as a blueprint for a scientific analysis of the consumer and "the movement devoted to her interests." She recommended that advertisers employ women as "confidential public relations officers." To do "what no man could possibly do in the way of customer research," Ringwald proposed scientific participant-observer studies of various women's clubs to chart their concerns about advertising and consumer issues.[42] It would be beneficial, claimed Ringwald, "to mix with other women of all social levels as a sister-under-the-skin, to sit in at their social, cultural and uplift gatherings, to chart their chatter about what they buy, where and why, to watch them when exposed to advertising, printed, spoken and displayed, and most of all in the retail store where frankness flourishes and consumer preferences crystallize."[43]

The job of developing good working relations with women's clubs frequently fell on the advertising community's female members.[44] In 1937 women's advertising clubs in Buffalo, Chicago, Cleveland, Detroit, Lansing, Milwaukee, St. Louis, and Toledo designed a five-point program to foster improved consumer understanding of advertising and sound advertising practices and legislation. The plan included a central speakers' bureau that provided women's clubs with lecturers to explain advertising from an industry perspective. Distribution of written material covering the industry's view on advertising was part of the program, which also called on each advertising club to adopt a consumer relations strategy designed to "restore public confidence in advertising."[45]

By the late 1930s major department stores, the National Better Business Bureau (NBBB), and several retailers had started providing consumers with buying guides that at least one industry representative deemed more helpful and sincere than those issued by the government.[46] "We as manufacturers know more about the consumer than these spokesmen do, or than the consumer himself does, as the result of our many transactions with him," argued one advertising executive. Because consumer organizations provided unreliable and inconsistent information, business had an obligation to mount a counteroffensive through its own consumer groups.[47] Many manufacturers viewed retailers' efforts with great interest and unusual seriousness. "It is even possible that some advertising agencies will eventually discover that the consumer movement is important to somebody besides a few 'lady agitators' and 'crackpot' editors of advertising papers," mused C. B. Larrabee in *Printers' Ink.* "The possibilities for the development of such a movement are tremendous. And whether the manufacturer and his advertising agent like it or not they will have to give it some attention."[48]

The Committee on Consumer Relations in Advertising, a group begun by the AAAA and sponsored to the tune of one million dollars by its members, answered the call. The committee engaged in fact-finding and research on the economics of advertising and consumption and viewed its most important objective as that of working with consumer groups to shape public opinion toward advertising. Among other programs, the effort included a study to determine what factors were involved in teachers' decisions to accept or reject educational material prepared by business firms.[49]

Not to be outdone, the NAM and the AAAA proposed a joint project to gain confidence, loyalty, and support from clubwomen in such prominent groups as the General Federation of Women's Clubs, the National Council of Women, and the League of Women Voters. The *Women's Home Companion* and the *New York Herald Tribune* were also key in spreading the word about the organizations' activities.[50] The problem, however, according to Lammont Du Pont, the president of Du Pont de Nemours and Company and an active member of the NAM, was that the industry's message did not reach the entire population. "The weakness of all these programs," he observed, "lies in the fact that the particular class of people who need the educating most are the ones who are not at all likely to see or read the material which is put out. The lower stratum of society does not read that kind of thing in newspaper[s] or periodicals. . . . It seems to me that about the only way to write the class of thing[s] I have in mind is through humorous articles tuned down to their level."[51]

The American Family Robinson, a popular radio program that used its characters to deliver the NAM's anti–New Deal messages, fit the bill. Each story line in the soap opera, which by 1936 was broadcast twice a week on 225 radio stations, reflected a conservative view on key issues. The "avowed purpose" of *The American Family Robinson,* according to the NAM, was to present "the fundamental principle that freedom of speech and of the press, freedom of religion and freedom of enterprise are inseparable and must continue to be if the system of democratic government under which this country has flourished is to be preserved."[52]

Business-Consumer Conferences

Much of the tension between consumer groups and business played out at a series of conferences in the late 1930s. In 1937 Stephens College in Missouri accepted a generous offer from the Alfred P. Sloan Foundation to establish an Institute for Consumer Education. In addition to planning college courses, textbooks, pamphlets, radio programs, motion pictures, and magazine articles,[53] the institute was to organize conferences that would bring business, education, government, and consumer representatives together for discussions.[54] The institute also developed a library, established a consumer-oriented curriculum, published a monthly newsletter, distributed booklets, conducted research related to teaching consumer education, and arranged for the Annual National Conference on Consumer Education.[55]

Prior to the establishment of the Institute for Consumer Education, only a few largely unsuccessful attempts had been made to consolidate the consumer movement into a unified front. A conference to secure popular support for governmental consumer agencies had started in 1933 but quickly petered out. Yet another effort had been made in 1936 when several consumer-minded groups in New York City formed the Consumers' National Federation. Although it managed to hold several conferences and secure a couple of interviews with Franklin D. Roosevelt, its impact and visibility were questionable. Thus, the Institute for Consumer Education represented a fresh attempt at unifying the consumer movement's many factions and also provided room for business-backed groups to present their solutions to consumer-related problems.[56]

The institute's first conference in spring 1939 attracted more than five hundred leaders from business, educational organizations, the consumer movement—including CU—and government agencies for a discussion of what would be the "Next Step in Consumer Education." People from thirty-one states descended on Missouri, where CU president Colston E. Warne and three staff members had also found their way. Talks and discussions, not surprisingly, revealed a deep rift between business and consumer advocates on approaches to consumer education. Much to the advertising industry's dismay, the executive director of the institute, Harold S. Sloan, sided with the consumer movement's demands. He supported restriction, even elimination, of advertising testimonials and advocated limiting advertising copy to strictly factual statements. This did not sit well with advertising interests. John Benson defended the industry's practices, arguing that emotional appeals provided a much-needed psychological uplift to consumers, who were too shallow or too stupid to understand facts.[57]

Benson's arrogant (and now familiar) argument could not conceal a lingering consumer dissatisfaction with advertising, however. A 1939 survey, sponsored by Pet Milk, found, for example, that 81 percent of the respondents believed that advertisements led people to buy things they either could not use or did not need. It also concluded that 56 percent of the respondents favored grade labeling, that 59 percent wished for stricter laws to govern advertising, and that nearly half (45 percent) of the respondents desired a Department of the Consumer. Advertisers, when asked for their opinion of the consumer movement's growth, mentioned "general discontent with social and economic conditions," a "critical attitude towards business," "consumer co-ops and their anti-advertising propaganda," and "growth in number of educational courses in schools and colleges" as the most important reasons for the movement's strength.[58]

Advertisers upset with the institute's attitude and its unwillingness to take a more pro-advertising stand went directly to Alfred P. Sloan and insisted that his foundation withdraw its support. Unfortunately for commercial interests, however, Sloan had assured his brother Harold that he would not allow outsiders' opinions to interfere with the institute's operation. Thus, the Institute for Consumer Education survived its first round of attacks.[59]

The animosity between business and the consumer movement was far from resolved when the Institute for Consumer Education concluded its second conference the following year. The avowed purpose of this meeting was to bring about cooperative understanding between producers and advertisers, on the one hand, and the many divergent groups making up the consumer movement, on the other hand.[60] One major obstacle to improved relations and closer cooperation between the factions, noted *Advertising Age,* was the general level of mistrust. Educators and consumers maintained that the advertising community held a hostile and largely condescending attitude toward the consumer movement and accused it of evading consumers' demands. Conversely, the advertising community regarded educators and consumer representatives as impractical demagogues who were largely unaware of business's problems. Indeed, as the conference revealed, many industry representatives confessed to being so frightened of the consumer movement that they were afraid to speak honestly.[61]

As on most other issues Frederick J. Schlink diverged from CU's opinions, and after examining the list of attendees he declined his invitation to attend the conference. "Frankly," stated the president of CR, "I don't think anything significant for consumers can come from a meeting of 'big names,' particularly second- or third-string government employees, and Communists and left wing sympathizers—when the people concerned are not directly and actually interested in consumers for the consumers' sake, but are in many cases devoted to using consumers as a take-off for some other end."[62] The only way to reach common ground, according to Schlink, was through a straightforward dialogue between producers and consumers. Marxist theoreticians needed to be left out. "There is, in my mind, much more to be gained by discussing specific criticisms which refrigerator manufacturers, say, have of the tests made by Consumers' Research," he contended, "than by listening to an economist like Colston Warne deliver a sermon on this week's Communist Party line interpreting the common objectives of consumer and labor."[63]

C. B. Larrabee of *Printers' Ink,* who had been among the first to encourage business recognition of the consumer movement, came away from the conference slightly more encouraged than many of his colleagues. He observed:

> If there was an outstanding important lesson to be learned by business from the conference it was that by and large the educators are not Reds, nor even Pinks. They are, rather, a group of pretty intelligent, pretty fair-minded, pretty wholesomely skeptical people who are at bottom honestly interested in making the world a better place for themselves and their pupils to live in. No one can object to that. And it forms a pretty good foundation on which business can build a mutuality of understanding—once business can convince the educators that it, too, is just as interested in a better world. . . . But up to the present moment too many business men seem to be bound to go about the convincing in the hard way.[64]

As another insider observed, "the day of the consumer who, it might be mentioned again, is also the customer, is here. It is well to plan future activities with that thought in mind."[65] But Larrabee, obviously not entirely satisfied with the conference's outcome, took advantage of a 1940 meeting about the consumer movement held at the Chemists Club in New York City to ridicule CR and James Rorty and complain that the public so critical of business seemed to accept the competency of CR and CU without question.[66]

NBC's conference representative, W. G. Preston, warned business against belittling, attacking, and talking down to the consumer movement. "Although the demagogues were not too convincing," he cautioned, "it is obvious that they are going to control the movement unless business, and the advertising world in particular, does a more intelligent job of public relations not only directly with the consumer but more particularly with the vertical pressure groups. It is obvious that the consumer movement has realized that its best approach for dissemination of information is through so-called 'education.'"[67] Women's organizations were a preferred forum for this purpose, and Preston was impressed with their willingness to cooperate with broadcasters. He was, however, disturbed that broadcasters were having "their hands full apologizing for, and defending to the consumer movement, the unfortunate choices of representatives which the various business trade associations send to these meetings."[68]

Following the Institute for Consumer Education's example, the NBBB organized the Business-Consumer Relations Conference on Advertising and Selling Practices in 1939 to create "mutual understanding" among business, education, consumers, government, and educational institutions. Stressing the interdependence of these groups and how unfair, dishonest, or unequal dealings on the part of anyone could upset the balance of society, the NBBB invited representatives from major advertising groups, women's organizations, colleges and universities, and trade organizations. CU and CR were conspicuously absent.[69] Realizing this obvious exclusion, some women's organizations expressed severe doubts about the organizers' intentions. "My first reaction was to refuse," noted one invited guest, "however [I] decided it was better to be on the inside than on the outside in such meetings. You might possibly have some influence in shaping policies if you were on the inside; you would probably have none if you were on the outside."[70] Alice Edwards, the former executive secretary of the Home Economics Association, was of a similar opinion.[71] "When the National Association of Better Business Bureau wrote asking that I be a member of their Advisory Council of Business-Consumer Relations Conference, I consented because I thought that such a connection would give me an opportunity to become better acquainted with their organization," explained Margaret G. Reid, a consumption economics professor from Iowa State College, in a letter to CU. But "when the tentative program was sent, I made comments which were none too favorable. The vague topics which had been listed were very unenlightening and the speakers seemed likely to be neither inspiring nor informed. I feel that the meeting will be far from satisfactory if consumer organizations are not present. I see no reason why members of Consumers Union should not be there."[72]

Despite the lackluster topics, conference attendees hotly debated the extent to which government should be involved in consumer education.[73] "I think the point to hammer away at," noted Donald E. Montgomery from the Consumer's Division of the Agricultural Adjustment Administration, "is that both business and consumers shall speak for themselves, that neither shall pretend it is speaking for the other and that on this basis they stand ready to argue, bargain and negotiate any issues that are of interest to both. If we can get that idea across clearly we rule out the business groups who think they are the guardians of the consumer interest."[74] A second meeting with similar objectives and with participants from the same groups took place the following year.[75]

The Advertising Federation of America (AFA) welcomed the effort as a constructive and unbiased attempt at making advertising serve as an informative consumer guide.[76] Whereas the same organization only a few years earlier had exhibited a rather defensive and uncooperative attitude toward the consumer movement, it now reached out and even encouraged cooperation with the more mainstream consumer groups.[77] By 1940 the AFA had initiated a full-fledged program for "better consumer education." "Propaganda and lack of knowledge are a bad combination," warned an AFA leader. "They threaten the status of advertising as a useful tool of business. Articles, speeches, teaching material, and best-seller books persuade the public to beware of advertised goods. Advertising itself is described as an economic waste, an unwholesome influence, and a burden upon society. Some Government officials and legislators are already swung over to the enemies of advertising."[78]

Fighting destructive propaganda was only a part of the battle. "Building a sound understanding" of advertising among the public was the long-term, and more important, goal. Radio, newspapers, and periodicals played a vital role in the AFA's educational program, which was designed to convince the public of advertised products' reliability and advertising's sound economic and social functions. A fifteen-part series called *Short Talks on Advertising* was broadcast over 278 radio stations. At the same time, the AFA placed syndicated articles in more than two thousand newspapers and periodicals. Other efforts included a speakers' bureau as well as numerous discussion groups and consumer-advertising forums. "The AFA," boasted a group leader, "has the facilities and the channels for safeguarding the force that makes business."[79]

Attacks on the "So-Called Consumer Movement"

The AFA realized that its goal of selling advertising as an economic and social service could not be accomplished unless it met the consumer movement at least halfway. "Judged from speeches-in-public and talk-in-private, advertising leaders are in almost 100% agreement that the discontent of organized consumer groups is the No. 1 marketing problem of the day," concluded a *Business Week* writer in 1939 after the AFA issued a resolution to cooperate with mainstream consumer groups.[80] This move was prompted by rumors that the consumer movement's radical elements were getting a stranglehold on the critical segment of middle-class women and their organizations. Addressing the Advertising Club of Boston, AFA president Allen Rose warned fellow advertisers against "destructive elements" of "a new social order" and their attempts at gaining control over the "true consumer movement."[81]

Probably as a means of delegitimizing consumer groups with contrasting political agendas, the advertising industry during this period increasingly began referring to adversarial consumer groups as part of the "so-called consumer movement."[82] Industry representatives, however, fully realized that in order to possibly diffuse the most radical consumer critique of advertising, it was important to form good relationships with the mainstream segments of the consumer movement. At another convention, this one in 1940, the AAAA held a town hall meeting with representatives from groups as diverse as CU and Crowell-Collier Publishing Company. Government representatives were also present at the meeting, which an *Advertising Age* writer described as "one of the most comprehensive, intelligently presented and thought provoking episodes in the drama of the consumer movement to date."[83] The consumer movement was also high on the agenda when the Association of National Advertisers held its annual convention in late 1939. Similarly, the Advertising Research Foundation, a venture jointly sponsored by the association and the AAAA, concluded that the consumer movement was far from fizzling and that its impact among educators was especially pronounced.[84]

Despite the many conferences and pledges to hear consumers' demands, the advertising industry's strategies for handling the consumer movement were far from cooperative. Because it intended to co-opt the movement, advertising tried to push consumer groups toward conflicting goals and thereby foil them all. The AFA worked only with what it considered the business-friendly, or "legitimate," segment of the consumer movement. Soon its leaders agreed that the *consumer movement* had outlived itself as a term and that the *consumer-advertiser movement* or the *consumer education movement* more accurately described contemporary consumer education.[85] The undefined nature of what constituted the consumer movement justified this approach. "The 'consumer movement' still needs quotation marks," concluded the editors of *Advertising Age,* "because it has not yet reached a phase in its development where the words mean exactly or nearly the same thing to all segments of any particular group."[86] In the same vein, a writer for *Broadcasting* warned that the "the so-called consumer movement" deserved close watching.[87] An editor of *Advertising Age* used the same term and charged members of the "so-called consumer movement" joining government elements that considered business's profit motive antisocial.[88] In this manner the industry subtly expressed its disdain for "radical" consumers.

This approach ignored the admonitions of John M. Cassels, the director of the Institute for Consumer Education. Much like the institute's executive director, Harold P. Sloan, Cassels sympathized with the consumer movement and had used the 1939 NBBB conference as an opportunity to criticize business's dealings with consumer advocates. Cassels objected to the heavy-handed attempts by business to crush the consumer movement by referring to all involved as "reds" and "communists," and he was equally distressed by business's concerted attempts to control or subvert the movement. "In some cases consumer organizations have been deliberately set up and financed by business groups to promote their own particular interests," cautioned Cassels. "In other cases pressure or persuasion has been exerted on the leaders of organizations already in existence. Very commonly booklets, films and other types of business materials prepared by business concerns for use in the education of consumers are definitely colored by considerations relating to their own interests as sellers. It is this kind of activity by particular groups, which, more than anything else stands in the way of the establishment of right relations between business and consumer education."[89] Indeed, some consumer advocates warned business against wasting its money on creating pseudoadvocacy groups to attack consumer organizations, suggesting that it might only deepen consumers' antagonism.[90]

Meanwhile, support for the Institute for Consumer Education's annual conferences was picking up steam. The 1941 conference, entitled "Consumer Education for Life Problems," was attended by even a larger number of people than had shown up the previous year.[91] The significant volume of

CU material and heavy promotion of the group's activities at the event disturbed both advertising interests and CR. The institute, according to a CR report, provided a melting pot in which "transmission-belt" organizations for the Communist Party could dump their ideologies, literature, and agendas and appear "perfectly acceptable" to unsuspecting women's organizations. "The entire conference," the CR writer contended, "was a one-sided picture of what is *not* being done for consumers, an evil which can apparently be speedily cured by a federal Consumer Department in Washington."[92] The Sloan Foundation and Stephens College administrators were beginning to share these critical sentiments. Much like CR, the institute's leaders expressed unhappiness with CU's practice of conducting its own off-campus luncheons during conferences, which allegedly divided the audience and undermined attempts to foster general consumer agreement. Advertising interests were also unimpressed with Cassels's conciliatory attitude toward the consumer movement and his willingness to let CU and other radical consumer advocates dominate the conferences. Perhaps as a result of this discord, the institute's third consumer conference in 1941 turned out to be its last.[93]

Taking another tack, the Advertising Research Foundation commissioned a survey that suggested that failure to blunt the consumer movement's impact might reduce the effectiveness of all advertising and "deal a serious blow" to those advertisers most frequently attacked. It also found that a majority of the public favored grade labeling, were ignorant about the ratio between advertising expenditures and a product's price, believed that advertising led people to buy things they did not want or need, and favored stricter advertising regulation. Much like the Pet Milk survey conducted the previous year, the poll disclosed that almost half of the respondents desired a Department of the Consumer. "The advertiser who views this whole movement lightly is unwittingly looking straight into the mouth of a loaded cannon," warned the polling expert George Gallup. The survey maker counseled advertisers to adhere to some of the consumer movement's demands. Suggested Gallup:

> I may be mistaken, but perhaps the time has come, because of this widespread discussion of advertising, when it will prove effective, in a dollar and cents way, to give the public more facts about products in advertising. It is just possible that with the ingenuity we have in this profession we can give people the facts they seem to want and still make advertising inviting and otherwise palatable. Likewise it is just possible that a little more money spent on product research could make some products, especially those now under fire by the leaders of the consumer movements, not such conspicuous targets. In short, I believe there

is not necessarily any great basic conflict between advertisers and consumers. As a matter of fact, I think it is possible for us all to lie in the same bed.

Gallup concluded that the consumer movement had the strongest impact on people in high-income brackets, those with "higher intelligence," urban dwellers, and young people. He predicted that the movement would "continue to grow and to flourish" and that educators would play a large part in that process.[94]

The Battle for Schools, Colleges, and Universities

The case for the institution of advertising became prominent in U.S. schools in the late 1930s. On the one hand, and most significant, firms aggressively distributed educational material touting their products in schools. This made advertising and commercialism appear as "natural" instructions to students. On the other hand, the advertising industry promoted pro-advertising material for classroom use as well. Ever since Horace Mann had initiated nonsectarian schools in the early nineteenth century, groups with widely different agendas had fought to control what schools should be required and allowed to teach. By the 1920s advertisers and commercial interests had entered the fray.[95] In their first study of Middletown in the mid-1920s Robert S. Lynd and Helen Merrell Lynd had detected an increasing tendency toward a commercial agenda in school curricula that showed no indication of easing with time.[96] Not only were schools being targeted by advertisers but few efforts were made to equip children with necessary skills for a consumer society. And even when teachers did try to educate them, the subtle and not-so-subtle pressure of commercial forces worked against their efforts. Recognizing the problem early on, CR set out to combat advertising's influences on children. To help students see through the hype and the added costs associated with brand names, the consumer organization encouraged teachers to assign laboratory projects focused on commercial products. This would help students discover that brand-name vanishing creams, which could run as high as four dollars a pound, could be produced in the lab for only six cents a pound and that a less expensive shaving cream might give exactly the same comfort as a popular and heavily advertised brand that was priced much higher. When comparing the price and quality of nationally advertised brands, students would discover that these commodities did not differ substantially in terms of uniqueness, quality, or utility from their less-well-known but far cheaper competitors.[97] "May I suggest," responded Dewey H. Palmer to a request for help from the Department of Public Instruction in Harrisburg, Pennsylvania, in 1932, "that your classes could carry on very interesting experiments by making a first-hand stud[y] of advertising and selling methods. Give various groups of students the problem of determining the amount of scientific information they can get about a product sold in the average grocery-store or drug store. Have the students study the labels and advertising claims of these products, and if time permits, in a few cases make simple tests that will reveal the useful properties of such materials and the price-cost relationship of the ingredients."[98] The proposition was met with a favorable response.[99]

Just as problematic, argued Proctor W. Maynard, an economics teacher, was that high school textbooks were written from the producer's point of view and were not intended to make students wiser consumers. If all economics teachers in the United States were willing to undertake a concerted effort to educate students about their role and rights as consumers, the country would be able to "lift itself by its own bootstraps."[100] Advertisers and manufacturers, needless to say, did not share this view. Even before World War I advertisers had warned that encouraging customers not to buy brand names might lead to factory closings and worker layoffs. If anything, this attitude was expressed even more firmly in the 1930s.[101]

To make it possible for teachers to discuss consumption problems by looking at the relative value of goods (and certain services) as determined by unbiased and scientific data, CR offered schools a chance to sign its confidential agreement and pay one dollar for a limited amount of CR material specifically selected for students. For the fall semester 1932, CR made four handbooks available for classroom use.[102] By January 1933 some five hundred students from sixteen colleges and universities and two preparatory schools had taken advantage of the offer.[103]

Before long the nation's schools, colleges, and universities became a critical battleground in the fight over advertising's role in U.S. life. Advertisers recognized that these institutions held unsurpassed opportunities to influence young minds. That millions of students would mature into consumers, community leaders, and voters did not pass unnoticed. The advertising industry's own statistics seemed to indicate that "anti-advertising propaganda" in the form of "doctrines" from CR was already being taught at major universities. This represented a serious challenge to the industry. "It seems to me," observed one ad executive in reply to reputed anti-advertising attitudes at the University of Wisconsin, "that when some of the professors refer to the criticisms of F. J. Schlink and Stuart Chase they are only trying to help their students get wisdom. But the trouble is a little wisdom is a dangerous thing . . . in a university classroom as well as in a business office."[104]

The advertising industry took a great interest in the issue and was outraged to find that what it termed anti-advertising propaganda was being taught in public schools and at many colleges and universities. "Anti-advertising propaganda, once started, has a way of spreading with startling rapidity," worried one advertising association's leadership, "especially since the professional propagandists have directed their attacks upon colleges, scientists and in general people who are members of organizations interested in social, political and economic problems."[105] Others argued that educators were intrinsically more likely than other citizens to read anti-advertising propaganda in the form of consumer books, to be influenced by such material, and to take its claims at face value.[106] "How University scholars feel about business is important to business men," confirmed John Benson. "For centuries clear thinking was kept alive by the schools. To be useful to the world, consumer education must not be conducted in a classroom filled with bias or resentment."[107]

The industry trade press reported that popular economics textbooks presented a disturbing picture for advertisers and that many students were becoming increasingly skeptical of advertising. "Inflammables in the lower deck cargo are burning," warned NBBB officials dramatically. "Is it the best defense of advertising to pass it off with charges that the fire was started by fanatics; or should some effort be made to find out what makes the fire burn? Is it safe to assume that it will burn itself out; or should the pumps be started?" The NBBB's answer was to call for increased efforts to limit the consumer movement's influence in schools.[108] Professors on the whole were considered negative or at best critical toward the workings of advertising and business. A 1938 *Printers' Ink* survey concluded that although most economics professors held unflattering views of advertising their opinions were not of the Communist variety. Still, the advertising industry's deeply held suspicions about educators were not assuaged.[109]

The industry was offended when a University of Chicago faculty member argued that advertisers were willing to improve themselves only to the extent of avoiding public criticism and government control.[110] *Advertising Age*'s editors reasoned that it would be absurd for the advertising community to resent "intelligent and constructive" criticism, but that many academics exceeded justified boundaries by attacking advertising as an economic function.[111] "The challenges of the academic critics of advertising must not go unanswered," proclaimed G. D. Crain, publisher of *Advertising Age*. "All persons interested in advertising should learn what is being taught in the schools in their communities and should work with the teachers and correct impressions that are responsible for sweeping condemnations."[112] The trade journal followed up with a series of articles designed to measure anti-advertisement sentiments and classroom treatment of advertising on several major university campuses.[113] Business schools in general, and the Harvard School of Business Administration in particular, provided a welcome exception to naysayers, for they treated advertising in an exceptionally complimentary manner. Neil H. Borden, a professor of advertising at Harvard, stressed, for example, that he favored advertising criticism only to the extent that it did not challenge the very economic structure from which advertising drew its legitimacy.[114]

To counteract antibusiness sentiments in schools and universities, the advertising industry launched programs to even the score and possibly tip the balance in its favor. "Progressive advertisers have an unusual opportunity to take advantage of a school situation which makes it mandatory in many instances to depend upon good supplementary material for daily discussion," suggested a writer for *Advertising and Selling,* pointing out that many schools, due to financial cuts, had limited funds for up-to-date textbooks. This enabled major manufacturers such as Heinz, General Foods, Hershey, American Can, and Calvert to provide classrooms with commercially sponsored material that would subtly aim at making advertising appear useful and productive. For example, General Motors published a set of four inspirational books for use in science classes, among them *Transportation Progress* and *Chemistry and Wheels.* "This kind of circulation builds up an acceptance among all ages and both sexes for all pupils [taking] general science," an advertising expert insisted.[115] "With a few changes in context and presentation these might be listed as textbooks."[116] The purpose of such classroom materials, of course, was transparent: to encourage student identification of the manufacturers' products and services. Advertisers wanted to do more than influence these future consumers' buying habits; they wanted to make students dependent on, and grow trusting of, advertising as consumer education. A related goal was to establish a generally positive view of business and advertising in students' minds. Unfortunately for advertisers, however, many school systems had rules banning the dissemination of advertising material in classrooms. Advertisers determined to get their material adopted eagerly surveyed teachers' criteria for use of commercially sponsored teaching aids and kept product plugs to a minimum.[117]

These industry booklets for students included a multitude on makeup, hair care, shaving, and clothes. *The Romance of Copper, The Romance of Modern Decoration,* and *The Romance of Rubber* were typical of these attempts at replacing traditional textbooks with commercially sponsored material.[118]

This booklet for classroom use was developed by Canco. From *Grade Teacher*, February 1939, p. 43.

The possibilities were not lost on advertisers. At the beginning of the 1933–34 school year the twenty-three million children supervised by about seven hundred thousand teachers presented a vast specialized market. Advertisers eager to reach this group were advised to tailor their educational aids to meet teachers' criteria, consult state syllabi, send questionnaires to educators, and personally call on school superintendents and principals to gauge their interest in buying "enrichment material." Many manufacturers placed ads in teachers' journals to get their products into the educational arena and make some money to boot. E. W. Clapp of Southern Pacific received about five thousand inquiries for maps, selling at twenty-five cents each, after placing one ad in a school publication. Similarly, the Spool Cotton Company received more than fifteen thousand coupons from teachers requesting one million "Spool pets"; the ad cost less then one thousand dollars but brought in five thousand dollars in stamps, coins, and bills for the animals with wooden spool bodies and cardboard faces and tails.[119] Typically, the money came from school funds for miscellaneous purchases, from teachers' own pockets, and from schoolchildren and their families.

Although many advertisers successfully sold their teaching aides, others, possibly in an effort to cast a wider net, elected to provide free material. More than two hundred thousand adults and nine million children, for example, requested the Lifebuoy Wash-Up Chart and a complimentary School Size Lifebuoy bar of soap for the company's wash-up campaign. After taking a chart home and keeping track of daily washing habits, students were awarded stars for perfect records and given a chance to appear on the classroom honor roll. "As each chart covers a period of four weeks, each record makes four round trips between school and home—coming to the parents' attention each time," noted the pleased soap manufacturer. An advertisement by Lambert Pharmaceuticals drew seventy-six thousand requests for more than two million outline drawings of children gargling with Listerine. After coloring the drawings in school, students were encouraged to bring their artwork home "so that the parents may see them." One teacher recounted building an entire exhibit around commercially sponsored material. Cards, bottles, and samples explained how products, ranging from Waterman fountain pens to Hershey chocolates, were made. Charts sponsored by Kellogg, the United Fruit Company, the Wheatena Company, and the Wilson Company told the stories of breakfast cereal, bananas, wheat, and meats. *Jack's Trip around the World* and *The Hidden Parasol* from the Colgate-Palmolive-Peet Company described imaginary journeys to countries where soap ingredients were produced, and *The Tale of the Brownie* by the Simplex Shoe Company emphasized the value of sensible and comfortable shoes for children.[120] By 1937 food manufacturers alone spent an estimated several hundred million dollars each year on educational material.[121] The advertising industry zeroed in on teachers of home economics—the very heart and soul of consumerism.

Until the 1920s nearly all home economists worked as teachers, but following World War I many were recruited by business. As home economists were put in charge of manufacturers' test kitchens, conducted product promotion, and provided outreach or consultation for commodities firms, their educational focus shifted. In 1924 the American Home Economics Association created its own Economics of Business division. "Home economists envisioned an ideal consumer society in which producers manufactured high-quality goods for healthful ways of living and consumers made systematic purchasing choices based on careful considerations of budget and long-term benefits," notes the historian Carolyn M. Goldstein. As interpreters or diplomats in the marketplace, home economists, nearly all of them women, worried about

FREE

Chart for
your
Classroom

The Story of Corn and Corn Flakes

Courtesy of the KELLOGG COMPANY Battle Creek, Michigan.
The world's largest manufacturer of ready-to-eat cereals.

HERE'S *The Story of Corn* in picture form. With easy-to-read explanatory notes. Indians are shown planting, cultivating and husking corn by primitive methods. Other illustrations show various stages in making Kellogg's Corn Flakes.

Kellogg's Corn Flakes are fine for children. Energy-giving— and easy to digest. Crisp and delicious for breakfast, lunch and the after-school snack.

The Story of Corn makes an interesting exhibit for your classroom. When ordering, mention the number you wish for your pupils.

Material for classroom use developed by Kellogg. Printed by permission from Kellogg.

some companies' manipulative selling methods but were assured that their dual role of enlightening business to the needs of consumers and informing consumers about valuable products would eventually pay off for the public.[122] Industry-supported teaching material, then, was not only seen as a help to financially strapped schools but also cast as a useful tool for building relationships between manufacturers and students, who, after all, were tomorrow's consumers.[123]

Left-leaning consumer advocates viewed the issue differently. Indeed, most distrusted the practice and claimed that manufacturers were actually bribing home economics teachers into accepting commercially backed material. Reporting from the American Home Economics Association's national convention in 1934, CR's Dewey Palmer decried the heavy promotion of trademarks and the "oh-so-benevolent corporation that gives [home economics teachers] free dinners at the Waldorf!"[124] Although deeply concerned about the relentless targeting of home economics teachers, CR was also bothered by teachers' seemingly unconcerned attitude about passing commercial information on to students. "I have met a large number of the leaders of the [home economics] profession," said Schlink, "and found, with a few honorable exceptions among them, a singular lack of interest in the social significance of their work."[125]

In the hope of establishing a generally positive view of business and advertising in students' minds, advertisers began channeling their educational material through legitimate-sounding "consumer" organizations they established. For example, the sole purpose behind one advertising outfit calling itself the Home Makers' Educational Service was to supply educators with free charts, pamphlets, and product samples.[126] As early as 1930 the people in charge of the service bragged about having more than fourteen thousand home economics teachers on its list who could reach more than two million students.[127] The *Home-Makers Bulletin,* the organization's newsletter, offered suggestions for how teachers could incorporate product samples into their lessons, make frequent references to the sponsor's brand names, and quiz students on their knowledge of the manufacturer's products. An essay instructing students about the tradition of taking afternoon tea, for example, was sponsored by India Tea and provided frequent references to the brand. Similarly, the Resinol Chemical Company, maker of soap and skin ointment, offered a lesson in skin care and quizzed students on "why Resinol Soap and Ointment [are] so desirable."[128]

Some teachers were impressed: "Hires Root Beer Extract was stressed [in *Home-Makers Bulletin*] as a wholesome beverage," wrote one satisfied home economics teacher. "The girls were deeply interested and more Root Beer is made in the homes than ever before due to the samples and discussions in the Home Economics classes. . . . After the sample is used they buy from the stores regularly."[129] The advantage with the Home Makers' Educational Service, boasted its proprietor, Gerald B. Wadsworth, is that "when a Home Economics teacher has proven the merits of a product by actual demonstration, she does not merely ask for it—she *demands* it, as do [anywhere] from 25 to 500 of her pupils, according to the size of her class."[130]

During 1936 the National Canners Association responded to more than one hundred thousand requests from educators. Estimating that each teacher's class had forty students, the association boasted that its campaign had reached about four million students that year. Manufacturers, needless to say, were eager to see the immediate impact of their marketing efforts on sales and soon developed research methods to investigate.[131] In 1935 Sunkist's food bulletins, charts, and textbooks on the orange industry were sent to millions of schoolchildren upon their teachers' requests. The citrus producer also prepared two "educational" motion pictures, *Golden Orange* and *The Secret of Citrus.* The former, specifically produced for young students, depicted California orange production and the health benefits of eating citrus fruits and was shown to an audience of more than two million, whereas *The Secret of Citrus* was viewed by women's groups as well as more than one million students in home economics classes.[132]

The intense effort to blanket U.S. schools with business-backed material concerned some educators. "Booklets which are provided by commercial firms for use in the classroom also contain unsubstantiated, false, and misleading material," warned one, pointing to a study in which 75 percent of the three hundred surveyed booklets had been found to contain questionable statements. Thirty-seven percent of the material had false statements, 43 percent made unsubstantiated claims, and more than half of the booklets included misleading statements.[133] Upon learning about the *Home-Makers Bulletin* from CR, Marion F. Breck, the Delaware state supervisor of home economics, surveyed home economics teachers and found that those teachers ranked highest for excellence in the state used this service more critically than other teachers did.[134] The highest-rated teachers, according to his survey, seldom read the *Home-Makers Bulletin* and rarely used its lessons. They were also less likely than other teachers to hand out advertising folders and comment on product samples. Whereas highly ranked teachers were somewhat lukewarm in their endorsements of the service, members of the lower-rated group of teachers relied on the service, claiming that it was beneficial, that students liked the recipes, and that students valued the additional information.[135]

Teachers often felt pressured by students, parents, and community members to include hands-on projects. Because little or no money was available for such tasks, teachers were forced to rely on advertisers' material.[136] "Every parent knows the abuses of the child's confidence in this way, and I am constantly hearing about new aspects of it which I would not have thought of," complained Schlink in 1938, telling of teachers who were intimidated into not providing their students with information about consumer issues.[137]

Also problematic for consumer advocates were the flourishing business-backed "institutes" and "foundations." With lofty-sounding boards of directors and names like the American Economic Foundation, the Edison Electric Institute, the Audible Arts, and the Cleanliness Institute, these PR councils implied "white-tiled laboratories" and dedicated scientists "giving their all for humanity," whereas in reality they represented only the interests of those funding them.[138] Many groups targeted the Parent-Teacher Association for commercial plugs. "It is easy to see how the educational system of the country is helpless when the Edison Electric Institute, the school equipment manufacturers, or anyone else with an axe to grind is more or less automatically selected as the preferred agency to address bodies of teachers," Schlink observed.[139]

Advertisers observed that if school texts and school activities could sell products, they could also be used to sell the institution of advertising—a situation characterized as having "almost unlimited opportunities" for advertisers. "The alert advertiser can furnish material that will make possible many worth-while school activities," promised an industry analyst, "and at the same time promote the sale of his products through the teacher, child and parent."[140]

Advertising Age's student essay competition, inaugurated in 1936, was also part of the industry's strategy "to encourage sane thinking about advertising."[141] High school students had "How Advertising Helps the Consumer" as a topic, and college students were asked their opinions on advertising's economic value.[142] The successful advertising ploy attracted some thirteen hundred entries from forty-two states, and several teachers made the essay part of their required curriculum.[143] The contest became an annual tradition, although in 1939 the topic morphed into "How Advertising Benefits the Consumer." The trade journal claimed that this change was better suited to meet challenges from the consumer movement, whose impact seemed to be spreading widely and vigorously.[144] Pall Mall Cigarettes designed its own contest for college students, offering cash prizes for the best Pall Mall advertisements.[145]

Yet another effort involved distribution of a dictation exercise book in five thousand schools and colleges where stenography was taught. The book, to be used by an estimated six million students, included one exercise promoting the industry's position on advertising's economic and social functions.[146] *Criticism, Suggestions, and Advice,* a publication for "teachers and students" put out by the Curtis Publishing Company, encouraged student activity based on *Saturday Evening Post* ads. One article, on "gaze motion in advertising," invited students to closely study a series of ads. "How many of the attractive persons on page 5 are looking at the General Tire? What relation has the gaze motion in the Metropolitan Life advertisement to the rest of the advertisement on page 7? And, how long can you study the gaze motion in the Log Cabin Syrup advertisement and still keep your balance?" the author asked.[147] In addition, high school and college students were promised prizes for their various observations about different ads and for their efforts at "Complet[ing] the Ad-writer's Job."[148]

The advertising community took advantage of radio's immense popularity as well. Du Pont's *Cavalcade of America* was first broadcast on CBS from 1935 to 1939 but was moved to NBC's Blue and Red Networks for the 1940 fall season. The half-hour show offered tales of famous Americans who, according to Du Pont, had made great contributions to the nation's development. By emphasizing entrepreneurial and business success stories, the program aimed at elevating corporate America's role and function in history.[149] The series featured programs such as *The Seeing Eye,* about an organization that trained guide dogs for the blind, and *The Willingness to Share,* which showcased the patriotism and generosity of Du Pont's contribution to military munitions for the coming war.[150] To be fair, *Cavalcade of America* differed from other commercially sponsored programs in that its scripts were intelligent and well crafted and its commercial plug was extremely subdued. Prominent writers such as Marquis James, Carl Sandburg, Robert Sherwood, Douglas Southall Freeman, Alexander Woollcott, Marc Connelly, William Saroyan, and Maxwell Anderson all contributed scripts.[151] Well-known liberal intellectuals such as James Rowland Angell, Walter Lippmann, and Frank Monaghan willingly touted the series on behalf of Du Pont, pointing to the importance of giving young people the "birthright" of learning about "the line of great men who performed great deeds. . . . No nation can live and remain a nation if the people in it cease to remember and no longer respect their own history," the narration intoned. Du Pont declared that "the aim of *Cavalcade* [was] not to reconstruct the minute details of historical archeology, but to recapture and reproduce the significant patterns of those lives which have built the America in which we glory."[152]

It should come as no surprise that Du Pont viewed the chemical industry as having played an especially important role in shaping the United States. One program, for example, touted Fabrikoid, a new plastic fabric coating. In addition to promoting its many applications and great social benefits, it also made sure to mention how production of Fabrikoid had greatly boosted the local economy and benefited the people of Newburgh, New York. "And so it can be seen that the *Du Pont Company*'s work in developing coated fabrics benefits not only the millions who use these products but a great many other people who help to make them," concluded the commercial announcement for this particular *Cavalcade of America* program. "This story of two-way service gives added meaning to the Du Pont pledge—'Better Things for Better Living . . . Through Chemistry.'"[153]

Since the program's first airing in 1935, Du Pont had promoted the series to educators. Some history teachers made the series required listening for their students; others assigned composition work based on the broadcasts. Even science teachers recommended the "stories of chemistry," which were part of each program, as an adjunct to classroom work.[154] The program responded to the call by *Advertising Age* to sell Americans on business through dramatic human-interest stories not only by entertaining its audience but also by reaching out to future consumers.[155]

The CBS version of the series resulted in a dozen permanent recordings that were distributed at cost to schools, colleges, and the interested public through the Association of School Film Libraries, an educational organization subsidized by the Carnegie Institution. The Milton Bradley Company, publishers of school textbooks, compiled sixteen scripts from the program and published them in book form as *Cavalcade of America*. Approximately ten thousand copies were sold at two dollars each. A second book containing twenty scripts was published in 1938. Identically priced, it sold only three thousand copies.[156] In light of these declining sales, Du Pont's move of the series from CBS to NBC suggested a renewed effort to reach the educational market. For example, fifty thousand promotional pamphlets aimed at educators were mailed out shortly before the show's NBC premiere in October 1940.[157] Two new textbooks based on *Cavalcade of America* scripts were published the same year. In Texas the powerful state board of education purchased forty thousand copies of the first book for use throughout the school system.[158] "I think it [*Cavalcade of America*] is doing a great deal of good, generally, for the American tradition and particularly for the Dupont Company as an American institution," observed Dixon Ryan Fox, a *Cavalcade of America* consultant and president of New York's Union College, in a letter to Roy S. Durstine at the Batten, Barton, Durstine, and Osborn advertising agency. Thanks to *Cavalcade of America*'s ability to improve relations with the public, undergraduates who only a few years earlier had seen the Du Pont name as a sinister symbol of warmongering had changed their opinion of the company. Pointing to Union College's proud tradition as an engineering and chemistry college, the educator suggested the possibility of creating a Du Pont Professor of Chemistry.[159]

Those critical of schools' increasing commercialization did not let advertisers' attempts at consumer indoctrination pass unnoticed. Robert S. Lynd and Helen Merrell Lynd had warned against these trends as early as the mid-1920s, when the practices had barely begun. By the 1930s the Lynds were joined by others who perceived the same societal dangers.[160] Some detractors worried that advertising saturation in schools prevented students from getting even the most elementary consumer education. Others argued that the public school system had never raised for discussion the question of whether it should provide a forum for business to sell its products and ideas. "Business pressure groups have increasingly come to treat public education as an extension of their long-established private system of consumer education," reflected CU's president, Colston E. Warne. "Samples of [advertisers'] merchandise are to be given to the children through cooperating teachers. Charts and pamphlets tell the child why he should use Coty's perfumes, Talon zippers, Ivory soap, Pet Milk, Crisco, or Jell-O and Kellogg's cornflakes. Teachers are cordially invited to join the staff of this major department of American consumer education and to share in spreading the knowledge of our fairyland of nylon and cellophane."[161] But seeing thirty-seven million elementary and high school students with an estimated annual buying power of one hundred dollars each deafened advertisers to any criticisms of their methods. They wanted to cultivate and maintain this valuable audience.[162]

Conclusion

Although it is obviously impossible to measure the direct impact of advertising's many PR efforts, it is safe, nevertheless, to conclude that by the late 1930s large segments of the consuming public had been exposed to manufacturers' spin on consumer issues. Corporate PR, however, was not the only challenge facing the consumer movement. The split of CR combined with Schlink's refusal to cooperate or make compromises challenged the ideologically diverse consumer movement. The second stage in the battle over advertising regulation, or what would eventually materialize as the 1938 Wheeler-Lea Amendment, proved to be an easy battle for the advertising industry to win.

6

Legislative Closure:
The Wheeler-Lea Amendment

If popular antagonism to advertising in the second half of the 1930s seemingly grew, and certainly did not diminish, the status of legislation for federal advertising regulation did not reflect this sentiment. The advertising industry had largely eliminated the threat of advertising's aggressive regulation by 1935, and the consumer movement effectively had been removed as a viable lobbying force on Capitol Hill. By the latter part of 1935 it had become increasingly obvious that business interests dominated the debate. The consumer movement was fragmented and less able to present a united front. Its most radical wing believed that subsequent versions of the Tugwell bill offered too little consumer protection, whereas mainstream consumer advocates more willingly submitted to compromises. Partly because of these conflicting approaches, consumer advocates were squeezed out of the picture, and consumer protection ceased to be the debate's central issue.

Nevertheless, the advertising industry was eager to get the matter of permanent legislation resolved and out of the public eye. Industry and government officials, on the other hand, still argued about how the ultimate law to regulate advertising should be framed. Between 1935 and 1938 these issues were hammered out, and eventually a compromise was reached that met the strictures of the advertising industry. The struggle was long and convoluted, however, and at the outset no one could have predicted the exact outcome.

Copeland and S 5

During 1935 a new—and, for advertising interests, an increasingly lenient—version of the original Tugwell bill was prepared. A relieved Association of

National Advertisers noted that in S 5, almost all major objections to S 1944 had been resolved. The definition of false advertising in this latest Copeland bill had been greatly simplified and made easier on advertisers, compulsory government grading and voluntary factory inspections at manufacturers' expense had been dropped, and the secretary of agriculture, who had been given huge discretionary powers under the Tugwell bill, had been replaced with advisory committees on which advertisers had a say. S 5 also spared manufacturers from disclosing formulas and recipes. Much to media owners' relief, the Copeland bill stated quite clearly that blame for false advertising rested with advertisers alone.[1] Members of the advertising community expressed even greater satisfaction with S 5 than its predecessors, and many were eager to have it enacted in the hope of warding off stronger regulations.[2]

Food and drug manufacturers, however, were largely opposed to the measure. They proposed that S 5 be rewritten to incorporate elements of the new McCarran bill (S 580), a measure giving advertisers more leverage in their product claims. Around the same time yet another advertiser-friendly measure referred to as the Mead bill (HR 3972) entered the legislative hopper. It proposed a minor revision of the Federal Food and Drugs Act of 1906 and gave the Federal Trade Commission (FTC) regulatory power.

These legislative variations divided the advertising community into two major camps. The majority group desired S 5 or a new law combining S 5 and S 580, whereas the Association of National Advertisers and the Proprietary Association, to the extent that they wanted regulation at all, urged Congress to pass the Mead bill in its purest form. Not overly enthusiastic about any of the proposed legislation, *Printers' Ink* suggested another possibility: a bill built on a combination of S 5, the Mead bill, and S 580, which would make "an almost perfect foods, drugs and cosmetics law."[3]

This desire to push competing agendas caused concern among manufacturers, advertisers, and other business leaders. "This is no time for one association to put forward one bill and another association to put forward another bill while the Department of Agriculture puts forward a third bill and various obliging Congressmen and Senators put forth other bills," warned *Printers' Ink*. "If consumer education is needed, let us make it a united effort rather than a renewal of the spectacle of five or six different groups intermittently firing shotguns none too carefully aimed and which, through a perhaps too studied carelessness, come perilously close to plugging holes in the hides of all, sinners and saints alike."[4]

The advertising industry had also started to realize that endless debate over revisions and highly publicized hearings did not exactly constitute the best form of public relations. "Just between us," stated the Advertising Fed-

eration of America's (AFA's) Edgar Kobak in a letter to the NBC lobbyist
Frank Russell, "the quicker we get a bill, the quicker the agitation against bad
advertising will subside. Every time there is a hearing it makes swell publicity
for men like [Arthur] Kallet."[5] Industry leaders were eager to get the matter
of permanent regulation out of the public eye.

Another reason for advertisers' increasingly conciliatory attitude toward any
legislation was Secretary of Agriculture Henry A. Wallace's promise that these
new measures would provide ample room for advertising self-regulation. This
was the industry's preferred means of handling false and misleading advertising, and most of its members approved of the proposal to install an advisory
committee to the Department of Agriculture. The proposed committee would
help set false and misleading copy practices with the help of media owners who
accepted food, drug, and cosmetics advertising.[6] Drug manufacturers were
still not impressed. S 5, argued a proprietary representative, "is a 'monstrous
piece of bad draftsmanship—arbitrary, tyrannical, vague, uncertain.' . . . [It]
reflects the belief that the American character is bankrupt."[7]

Royal S. Copeland continued to lobby for passage of S 5, however. During
the debate he went so far as to bring to the Senate floor an exhibit showing the
dangers associated with unregulated drug advertising: the so-called chamber
of horrors exhibit that had been shown at the 1933 Chicago World's Fair and
to various women's clubs across the country to elicit support for the Tugwell
bill a year or so earlier. Amid bottles and packages of food and drugs that he
claimed to be fraudulent, dangerous, or both, Copeland solicited votes for a
measure that he promised would give "a degree of safety to women, babies,
and children" against crooked advertisers and manufacturers of adulterated foods.[8] Unfortunately for Copeland, this dramatic dog-and-pony show
prompted Joshua W. Bailey of North Carolina and Joel Bennett "Champ"
Clark of Missouri, two Democrats with strong ties to drug industries, to force
through several amendments that, according to most consumer advocates,
gave consumers even less protection, although Charles Wesley Dunn, the
author of the McCarran bill and a drug industry proponent, claimed the
opposite.[9] One amendment curbed the Department of Agriculture's power
to make mass seizures of misbranded goods and modified S 5's definition
of adulterated foods to better suit food and drug manufacturers. The new
definition of false advertising was now so broad that it would be virtually
impossible to prosecute any advertiser for dissemination of false or misleading ads. For example, the new bill stipulated that a drug's therapeutic
representation was false only if in every particular it was not sustained by
demonstrable scientific facts or substantial medical opinion.

An upset Copeland retaliated by accusing Bailey of being beholden to the patent-medicine lobby.[10] Given his own questionable endorsement of Fleischmann's Yeast, this was not one of Copeland's smartest moves. "Even the Senator from New York," noted a vengeful Bailey, "has spoken not unfavorably of some of these [medicinal] articles over the radio."[11] Realizing that S 5 would encounter severe resistance, Copeland, in a last-ditch effort to gain time to rustle up more support for the measure, requested that it not be put up for a vote during its scheduled time in spring 1935.[12] Realizing that in its present wording his bill would have a limited chance of being passed by the Senate, Copeland agreed to a rewritten version that incorporated some amendments proposed by Bailey and Clark. Pleased with the changes, the editor of *Printers' Ink* promoted the measure in glowing terms, describing it as a "highly satisfactory and valuable piece of lawmaking—almost statesmanlike in certain respects." Copeland did not agree. Much like his harshest consumer-advocate critics, the senator maintained that the new version of S 5 had been so diluted that he wanted no more to do with it.[13]

By now, however, most media and advertising groups, with the exception of the AFA, which had a heavy proportion of drug manufacturers, supported the bill.[14] The major stumbling block for advertisers was one of the few carryovers from the original Tugwell bill (S 1944): the stipulation that entrusted the Department of Agriculture with the power to simultaneously confiscate products in multiple states regardless of whether misleading ads appeared in all locations. This, according to Lee Bristol of Bristol-Myers, constituted government censorship of private business and ought to be removed from S 5.[15] The Proprietary Association agreed, arguing that the clause delegated too much power to the Department of Agriculture by giving it broad and arbitrary powers to seize products. False advertising, asserted the drug manufacturers, should be dealt with as misbranding and be halted by injunctive proceedings overseen by the FTC and not, as proposed in the newest Copeland bill, become the basis for criminal procedure against advertisers.[16] Speaking on behalf of the drug-manufacturing industry, Bristol also expressed concerns about the bill's proposed advisory health and food committees. His fear was that these committees, designed to help the government identify false or misleading advertisements, would be staffed by physicians opposed to self-medication.[17] Drug manufacturers, in other words, feared that physicians would be overzealous in adjudicating. Copeland fought long and hard to keep the seizure provision in the bill, seeking the support of major women's groups in the process. Copeland had from the beginning enjoyed considerable support from these organizations, but their endorsement was

far from automatic. Many let it be known that S 5's failure to secure mandatory product grading and labeling was greatly disappointing.[18]

Consumer advocates were also concerned that the numerous rewritings
and amendments had resulted in proposed legislation that was a far cry from
the original Tugwell bill introduced two years earlier. As consumer protection ceased to be the central issue, the principal consumer groups were given
only a limited role in the ensuing congressional deliberations, and they were
almost entirely dissatisfied with the outcome. At the Senate hearing on the
bill in early 1935 Kallet, who had wanted Consumers' Research Inc. (CR) to
send out letters to all its subscribers informing them how best to affect the
legislative process but was vetoed, stressed the impossibility of designing a
bill protecting manufacturers and consumers simultaneously. "As the bill is
drawn," he predicted, "it will protect the industries, and judging from the
testimony that has been presented and the reports in the trade press, and what
precedes these hearings, apparently the great emphasis has been on how to
protect the industry."[19] As had been the case during the hearing on S 2800 a
year earlier, Kallet's questions about Copeland's commercial endorsements
were brushed aside as an "indulge[nce] in personality" by Clark, who presided over the hearing.[20]

Clark's behavior so provoked Frederick J. Schlink that he contacted Franklin D. Roosevelt, alerting him to the hearing's lopsided nature. Although business lobbies were given ample time to present their case, consumer interests
were once again pushed to the side. The "belief is becoming current in many
quarters that your administration is moving rapidly toward a policy of suppression of evidence and opinion when dealing with matters that vitally affect
the health[,] purchasing power and even lives of unorganized millions of
consumers," Schlink contended. He argued that "the dictatorial suppression
of the rights of the weaker parties to be heard on matters of legislation" was
"a dangerous encroachment upon Democratic institutions." He pointed to
the large following of demagogues such as Senator Huey Long and Father
Charles Coughlin and argued that it reflected the common citizen's "growing distrust of his ability to register his protest through regular channels of
political expression."[21] The hearing so outraged the executive secretary of
the People's Lobby, B. C. March, that he declared his intent to join Long in
starting an investigation into what profiteering interests kept the Democratic
Party from protecting consumers.[22]

Roosevelt refused to get involved. He determined that the issue was "wholly
a matter for the Senate" and recommended that Schlink's telegram be sent
to Clark.[23] The New Republic howled: "What became of that part of the

New Deal program which was to confer new benefits on the consumer and give him added protection against the unscrupulous forces in business?"[24] Effective consumer protection under the Copeland bill was becoming less probable by the day. At the House hearing in July and August 1935 CR cited "pressure from precisely the gentlemen who are guilty of all the other adulterations and misbrandings" as the main force behind the bill's wording and claimed that anyone making a comparison between the original Tugwell bill and S 5 could see that this "adulterated and misbranded" bill no longer offered consumers protection.[25]

At the same time that S 5 was sent to the House Committee on Interstate and Foreign Commerce for new hearings and a gamut of amendments and revisions, Senator David I. Walsh of Massachusetts introduced a bill with a twist on the issue. More than an amended Food and Drugs Act, the Walsh bill (S 2909) placed regulatory power over advertising with the FTC rather than the Food and Drug Administration (FDA). It expanded the FTC's jurisdiction to crack down on misleading advertising not just when it affected business competition but when such practices hurt consumers as well. A companion bill (HR 8744) was introduced simultaneously in the House by Richard B. Russell Jr. of Georgia.[26]

Working behind the scenes, the still-hopeful CR tried diligently to secure a public, as opposed to an executive, hearing on S 5. Wise from previous experiences, the consumer organization feared that a closed hearing would provide yet another opportunity to silence and marginalize those objecting to the current legislative trajectory. CR leaders reasoned that if the hearing was made public, concessions to industry demands could at least be subjected to scrutiny. "We are all pretty well persuaded by now that our only possible importance in this situation is the educational one of showing what happens and how it happens in a pseudo-democracy," reflected a somewhat discouraged Schlink in one of his last civil exchanges with Kallet, "because quite obviously to the extent that our influence is feared the tactic used would be that which has already been mentioned several times—to keep us out of the situation so far as feasible, so as to avoid our focusing any publicity light on the pseudo qualities of the democracy."[27]

Drug and food manufacturers' fingerprints were all over the amended S 5 that came before the House. Although CR was given the public hearing it so desired, business was still afforded preferential treatment. True to his established pattern, Virgil Chapman, the committee's chair, was both aggrieved and offended when Kallet questioned the motives of many members of Congress who appeared before the committee on behalf of various business interests.

Manufacturers and other business executives were given far more time than consumer advocates, but Chapman claimed that Kallet had exceeded his allotted time and forbade him from completing his testimony.[28]

The final version of S 5 was able to garner more support than S 1944 and S 2800 before it. Although the American Medical Association and CR wanted the bill made more stringent, most women's groups, media owners, and advertising organizations wanted the bill passed. Drug manufacturers expressed reluctance.[29] The editor of *Printers' Ink,* now speaking for the moderate majority, urged unity and stressed the importance of having any bill passed. Although he did not consider S 5 perfect, the editor spoke for a large segment of the advertising community when he stressed the necessity of getting a federal law on the books. The advertising industry had good reason to take this stance: The delay in passing a federal law had led several state governments to begin proposing independent statutes. Conflicting state laws could cause serious trouble for interstate commerce. The advertising community looked on this prospect with anxiety. Some blamed drug manufacturers' categorical opposition to any form of regulation for this unfortunate development. "It is perfectly obvious that some of these gentlemen [drug manufacturers] do not want any new law at all," wrote the exasperated editor of *Printers' Ink.* "If Moses himself could descend from Mount Sinai with a perfect measure it would be no more satisfactory to them than was the fantastic Tugwell bill (S 1944)."[30] Consumer advocates were much less enthusiastic about S 5. "If the Copeland bill, bearing the name of a senator who has been a paid employee of patent medicine advertisers," were to pass, warned Kallet, "those officials and consumers who favor the bill because they consider it better than the present law, are in for their share of astonishment."[31]

S 5 supporters' fears that the bill would have problems passing the House were not unfounded. This, of course, was not because they expected consumer advocates to influence the outcome but rather because they suspected that the overworked legislative body would give the bill low priority. They also knew for a certainty that the House was highly suspicious of anything emanating from the Department of Agriculture, especially a bill associated even remotely with Rexford G. Tugwell.[32]

The FDA versus the FTC

In 1935 legislation hit a snag over whether the FDA or the FTC should direct advertising regulation. Further complicating the issue was the competitive history of these two government bodies. Judge Ewin L. Davis, the FTC's head, claimed that his commission should be given jurisdiction over false and misleading advertising. This agreement, he argued, extended naturally from the FTC's legal jurisdiction. Davis proposed that S 5 abandon all references to advertising regulation and that such regulation be left to the FTC in an amended version of the Federal Trade Commission Act of 1914.

FTC supporters viewed S 5 as an attempt by the FDA to usurp the commission's power by taking administrative control over food, drug, and cosmetics advertising. The general advertising community, with the exception of the Institute of Medicine Manufacturers, the National Association of Retail Druggists, and possibly one or two other organizations, in contrast, wanted the regulatory power to rest with the FDA. In their view advertising regulation was a more logical extension of the FDA's jurisdiction to control food and drug labels than of the FTC's control of unfair business practices.[33] The FTC's quest for power was a concern not only for Tugwell but also for Roosevelt, who regarded Davis's maneuvering as undesirable as well as inappropriate. The judge had first shared his ambitions for the FTC during the Senate hearing on S 2800 in March 1934, and this, according to Tugwell, was contrary to instructions that forbade one governmental agency from appearing before Congress to actively oppose a measure advocated by another department.[34]

Drug manufacturers constituted a small but powerful group who persistently advanced the FTC's cause. One reason was their fear that the FDA, which in their view boasted vigorous reformers with a clear antibusiness bias, would hobble their industry.[36] They worried that the FDA, which could impose criminal sanctions and act quickly and decisively, would prove all too effective in dealing with false and misleading advertising. The FTC's sluggish bureaucracy, combined with its rather unimpressive sanctioning record and limited authority to dole out punishments, spurred drug manufacturers' enthusiasm for the commission as a new controlling agency. Their preference also stemmed from the greater difficulty they had encountered in attempting to manipulate cabinet departments like the FDA, which was part of the Department of Agriculture, than independent agencies like the FTC.[37] Drug interests were comfortable with the FTC, which was not in a position to penalize offenders and could only, through its cease and desist orders, tell advertisers to "sin no more." They had no desire to be regulated under a potentially more hostile body like the FDA. This was not enough to satisfy consumer advocates. As Tugwell himself noted, "adequate consumer protection demands a criminal law like the Food and Drugs Act under a unified administrative control."[38]

In constructing their lobbying strategies drug manufacturers capitalized on the knowledge that many members of Congress harbored an intense dislike for the FDA and calculated that the FTC could count more friends and influence among legislators.[39] "The big thing that was wrong with the Copeland Bill from the very beginning was that, through it, the officers and employees of the Department of Agriculture set themselves up to tell the whole advertising world what it could and could not do," maintained a writer for *Printers' Ink*. "Theoretically, at least, the tail should never wag the dog; but this is exactly what was attempted."[40] "I understand," acknowledged Bailey, who had emerged as a strong supporter of U.S. drug industries, "the Department of Agriculture was created for the purpose of fostering agriculture in the United States and not for the purpose of governing advertising in the United States."[41] FDA officials, however, asserted that the FTC would prove quite ineffective in a regulatory capacity because it lacked the necessary testing facilities to properly identify false and misleading advertising. "I do not approve the proposal that provisions against false advertising be enforced by the cease and desist order procedure of the Federal Trade Commission. This procedure is time-consuming," complained Tugwell in a letter to Bailey. "It carries no penalty and has no deterrent effect on the evader and chiseler."[42]

Viewed through consumers' eyes, the new version of S 5 was abysmal. Consumer protection had plainly ceased to be a central issue, and the debate had shifted to wrangling over the advertising community's interests. Still, consumer advocates were not willing to back out. In the following months Copeland tried to come up with a food, drug, and cosmetics bill that would please as many of the competing parties as possible and still stand a chance of being enacted. Copeland realized, however, that any proposed measure would face a tough fight on governmental oversight of advertising.

The senator's solution was to introduce a new version of S 5 as an amendment to, rather than an amended version of, the Food and Drugs Act of 1906. Copeland hoped that this strategy would prevent the FTC from usurping authoritative power because the 1906 law firmly established that the FDA was in charge. The new proposal gave the FDA control over advertising of items it already regulated under the Food and Drugs Act. In presenting the measure to Congress as an amendment, Copeland hoped that the existing powers of the FDA would be undeniable. This approach would not appear to be a request for the wholesale grant of power that a new bill might suggest; it would discourage tinkering; it would, according to Copeland and his supporters, demonstrate more convincingly why and how through thirty years of routine operation the FDA had become specially equipped to regulate advertising in the food and drug fields.

The new version gave consumer advocates a spark of hope. The amended S 5 authorized the FDA to seek, and any U.S. district court to grant, injunctions against the dissemination of false or misleading advertising of any food, drug, or cosmetic. Whereas earlier versions of the bill had prohibited the courts from seeking injunctions until an advertiser had committed multiple violations, the rewritten S 5 envisioned this option to enable the FDA to stop false advertising more swiftly and, in theory, reduce the need for civil suits. The bill proposed that criminal provisions should be applied only in cases in which injunctions were openly violated; it rejected a provision that would have made misleading advertising a criminal offense.[43] Much to the dismay of John Benson, the president of the American Association of Advertising Agencies (AAAA), this was proposed as law even in those cases in which advertisements did not affect public health.[44] Although trusting the FDA with authoritative power over false and misleading advertising, Copeland's new bill specifically refrained from disturbing the existing authority of the FTC to move against advertisers for unfair competition.[45] The Chapman bill (HR 300), a measure quite similar to the old S 5 but with stiffer penalties for ads that involved "danger to health or gross deception," was introduced around the same time.[46]

Most supporters of the old S 5 came out more or less in favor of the new S 5. Some women's organizations objected, however, to the new version's omission of mandatory grade labeling and therefore favored the Chapman bill and its efforts to make mandatory labeling into law.[47] The same groups also complained that the new Copeland bill limited the FDA to single seizures of misbranded goods and replaced actual penalties for false advertising with mere injunctions. They also did not like the bill's proposal to exempt manufacturers from false advertising charges if a scientific expert confirmed their claims.

Unfortunately for those holding out for his support, Roosevelt did not endorse S 5 in its new version because he did not view the bill as an improvement over the 1906 measure it was trying to amend. In some respects, according to the president, the changes actually weakened the existing law. Many politicians who wanted the bill to pass were upset with the president and what they termed "militant" women's groups.[48] "The crusading clique in the Department of Agriculture—comprising part of the personnel of the Food and Drug Administration—probably wishes now that it had not been quite so energetic in enlisting feminine resistance to the Copeland bill," crowed

Printer's Ink. Eager to place blame, the journal's editor accused women's groups and their lobbying strategies of alienating S 5 supporters. A real possibility now was that legislators might retaliate by favoring the FTC over the FDA.[49]

One thing was certain: The FTC and its supporters were not ready to retreat. In no sense was the FTC willing to relinquish the extended power S 5 had augured. In late 1936 its leaders officially recommended to Congress that the existing FTC law be amended to give the agency broader powers to protect the consuming public and address unfair competition.[50] "There is more than interdepartmental jealousy involved in F.T.C. lobbying against the Food and Drug Administration," claimed Jay Franklin of the *Washington Star*. "Its personnel is mainly of . . . politicians who have found it a mighty snug harbor in the stormy weather of post-panic politics. It carries weight on Capitol Hill if not at the other end of Pennsylvania Avenue." To support his allegations, and to add more fuel to the fire set by the FTC's enemies, Franklin pointed to several other new bills designed to expand the commission's power.[51] Even advertisers were split on whether the FDA or the FTC should serve as advertising's regulatory body.

Passage of the Wheeler-Lea Amendment

By 1937 consumer protection—the original focus and intent of the bill—was all but absent from the legislative discussions. The Washington, D.C., correspondent for *Printers' Ink* blamed consumers' "self-appointed evangelists" for singling the revised S 5 out for attack just because it represented "a reasonable and fairly practicable compromise under which enforcement agencies and affected industries may find it possible to function with a decent regard for the public interest." This insider argued that consumer advocates failed to represent the public's view on advertising regulation and accused them of using consumer protection as a smokescreen for (unspecified) selfish interests.[52]

In early March 1937 the Senate Commerce Committee decided to report out of committee a slightly amended S 5, which passed the Senate by a unanimous vote. The new amendment, introduced by Idaho's William E. Borah, concerned a much-debated section of the bill on multiple product seizures. The provision further diminished the FDA's power by prohibiting it from seizing falsely advertised goods in locations where such advertising had not occurred. Seizures, stated the newly amended S 5, needed to be restricted to areas where the alleged violation had taken place.[53]

In the House the bill faced competition from the Chapman bill and also from the Coffee bill (HR 5286). Unlike the Copeland bill, which had evolved into a measure with very little preventive effect, the Coffee bill sought strict labeling regulations and prevention of false and misleading advertising to make the law's enforcement easier. Drafted with Consumers Union of the United States Inc.'s (CU's) encouragement by Will Maslow, a lawyer experienced in food and drug regulation, the bill called for licensing manufacturers, registering proprietary products, labeling informatively, and preventing false and misleading advertising. Unimpressed, *Printers' Ink* characterized this latest legal variation as "malicious," "childish," and one that would "consume expensive Congressional time."[54] CU, however, voiced its objection to all the other pending bills and demanded a congressional investigation of "the lobby which has operated against the passage of effective food, drug, and cosmetic legislation."[55]

The House rejected all the measures, including the amended S 5, in favor of the Lea bill (HR 3143), which was an amended version of the Trade Commission Act of 1914. The Lea bill proposed to give the FTC control over all advertising in all media but delegated enforcement of technical phases such as labeling and testing to the FDA. Introduced by California's Clarence F. Lea, the bill defined an advertisement as false if it misrepresented the character, quality, or therapeutic effect of an advertised commodity. The proposed law distinguished between ads that were false in a material respect and those that were injurious to consumers' health. It authorized cease and desist orders to prevent dissemination of the former and allowed the FTC to seek injunctions against the latter. In other words, the law was less concerned about advertisements that hurt consumers' pocketbooks than those that endangered consumers' health.[56]

In an expansion of the commission's duty to monitor fair business practices, the Lea bill gave the FTC power over all "unlawful and . . . unfair trade practice" in commerce and the right to exercise that power for consumers' protection.[57] The bill further proposed that the FTC judge advertisements not only in terms of the representations they "made or suggested" but also on their failure to reveal important facts. Unlike S 1944, which burdened advertisers with the difficult task of proving their ads' truthfulness, the Lea bill placed this responsibility with the FTC. Under the Lea measure publishers, radio broadcasters, and advertising agencies could not be held accountable for false advertising unless they refused to reveal the advertiser's identity. Although the bill proposed fines for the dissemination of false advertising, it did not propose prison terms for such offenses.[58]

Major advertisers expressed concerns about authorizing the FTC to obtain injunctions against any person, partnership, or corporation engaging in, or about to engage in, publication of misleading advertisements. They also objected to a provision that made failure to reveal important facts about an advertised product an offense. Many industry leaders correctly discerned that the FTC's means for dealing with false and misleading advertising practices would fail to restore consumers' confidence. The commission's power to issue cease and desist orders did not differ much from the advertising industry's own (and largely ineffective) efforts to address questionable advertising practices, which had led Congress to undertake this regulatory legislation in the first place.

The Lea bill entrusted the FTC with more power than had ever been bestowed on any regulatory organization, federal or otherwise. It gave the commission authority not only to move against an advertiser as the result of copy already in print or on the air but also to interfere if it suspected that advertisements about to be issued were likely to induce use of injurious products.[59] The FTC was on a quest. The Lea bill expanded its power, and the recent passage of the O'Mahoney bill (S 10) to establish a federal licensing system for corporations engaging in interstate commerce and the Tydings bill (S 100) to amend the Federal Trade Commission Act were all part of the FTC's strategy to wrest power from other government bureaus, commissions, and agencies.[60] The Lea bill proposed to let the FTC police false and misleading advertising and left the FDA in charge of false and misleading branding and labels. All regulatory power over advertising, in other words, was given to the FTC, whereas the FDA was left with no more power than it already held under the Food and Drugs Act of 1906. Many critics, including Charles Wesley Dunn, the attorney who had aided the food and drug industries in the legislative battle and had helped draft the McCarran-Jenckes bill, argued that the new legislation was a poorly camouflaged attempt at replacing the FDA with the FTC.[61]

The 1914 law had forced the FTC to endure time-consuming and frequently ineffective procedures to prove and punish unfair business practices. The Lea bill promised to change this. Supporters of the proposed law maintained that it would provide swifter and more effective action against false advertising that would result in increased consumer protection.[62] House members were split in their opinions. Many were concerned about increasing the FTC's investigative powers. They fretted that the bill would provide the FTC with carte blanche "to go on fishing expeditions into private files" and business matters on its own initiative. In the end, they feared, the FTC might come to hold unrestricted power over business.[63] Consumer advocates voiced their own set of concerns. They believed the FTC members were too sympathetic toward patent-medicine makers and were particularly suspicious of the eager endorsements bestowed on this government body by conservative drug interests, who had been among the first to insist that unless a law to regulate advertising could be avoided, such regulatory powers should reside in the FTC.[64]

Ewin Davis of the FTC soon proved himself a master at defending his bureaucratic turf; his efforts were instrumental in saving regulation of food, drug, and cosmetics advertising for the FTC. He received strong support from drug makers, who had organized forces at an early stage to bring pressure on Congress. Their heavy patronage of small local newspapers gave them leverage to induce editorial support for themselves and unfavorable publicity for the FDA. Drug interests also maintained a powerful Washington, D.C., lobby and attempted to sway the votes of members of Congress already susceptible to their advances.

Much of the animosity toward the Lea bill in the House had disappeared when the measure came up for a vote in June 1937. The brief debate ended after Samuel D. McReynolds of Texas asked for loyalty from his fellow representatives: "Now members of the House, what are you going to do about it? Are you going to . . . leave it with the Federal Trade Commission with such men as Judge Davis and other men from this House on that Commission?" His speech was greeted with applause. The subsequent vote pleased McReynolds: 190 members of the House voted in favor, with only 70 opposed.[65] The bill went to the House Committee on Interstate and Foreign Commerce around the same time that the Wheeler bill (S 1077) was reported on favorably by the Senate Commerce Committee. Theoretically, at least, S 1077 was intended as a companion bill to Lea's legislation.[66]

S 1077 passed the Senate in summer 1937 and was sent to the House Interstate and Foreign Commerce Committee. The Wheeler bill differed from the Lea bill in that it did not grant the FTC authority over advertising of foods, drugs, and cosmetics and provided stricter penalties for violating advertisers. Lea, who also chaired the House Interstate and Foreign Commerce Committee, feared that Burton Wheeler's measure would face a stiff contest in the House. His offensive strategy was to strike out the complete text of the Wheeler bill except for the title, substitute the text with that of the Lea bill, report the new legislation out of committee again as S 1077, and rename it the Wheeler-Lea bill. The measure's text on food, drug, and cosmetics advertising was lifted from the food and drug provision in S 5 but gave jurisdiction over such advertising to the FTC rather than the FDA.[67] Lea's parliamentary move was designed to avoid having the bill come before the Senate again. Moreover, when the Wheeler-Lea bill went to conference, it was sent to the Senate Committee on Interstate Commerce, which was chaired by Wheeler, rather than to the Senate Committee on Commerce, chaired by Copeland.[68] The Wheeler-Lea bill passed the House on a standing vote, 107 to 10, in January 1938. It was written into law in March after the Senate voted in its favor.[69] The first action against an advertiser under the new law was launched in September of the same year.[70]

Although it entrusted regulatory powers over advertising to the FTC, the Wheeler-Lea Amendment merely outlined the parameters of the commission's jurisdiction and had not solved the need for a revised Food and Drugs Act. A modified version of S 5 proved to be a solution to that problem. Written into law in June 1938, the measure amended the 1906 act but did not regulate advertising of food, drugs, and cosmetics.[71] The amended act required stricter labels from food, drugs, and cosmetics. Manufacturers had to disclose the distributor's name. Drug makers were required to list the active ingredients of their products, and all foods made of two or more ingredients had to reveal their common names on their labels. Industry lawyers, who so ably had influenced the course of the five-year legislative battle, were largely pleased. Considering some of the alternative measures that might have been passed, they were happy to have a law that did not seriously interfere with the marketing of most goods and that helped honest manufacturers by hindering quack nostrums from entering the market.[72]

ADVERTISING REGULATION UNDER THE WHEELER-LEA AMENDMENT

The Wheeler-Lea Amendment's purpose was to strengthen and supplement the Federal Trade Commission Act of 1914. The amendment principally extended the FTC's jurisdiction to protect consumers as well as competitors against injuries resulting from deceptive acts and practices in interstate (but not in local) commerce.[73] The new provisions were directed against two broad categories of business practices. One was the use of unfair methods of competition and unfair or deceptive acts or practices in commerce. The other was the use of false or misleading advertising of foods, drugs, and cosmetics.[74] As such, the amended law opened up a whole new arena for FTC activity and gave it an opportunity to regain the power and respect that had been whittled away during its attempts to regulate competition.[75] The FTC was no longer limited to issuing cease and desist orders; now, in certain situations, it could impose substantial penalties. The commission had also gained the long-desired right to intervene in cases in which consumers' interests were at stake.

Consumer advocates, however, were not enthusiastic about the benefits conferred by the new law. Some argued that the measure's inability to impose more severe penalties prevented it from protecting the public against false and misleading advertising. They claimed that the law was "without teeth" and that merely issuing cease and desist orders would prove "absolutely ineffective" in preventing false and misleading advertising from appearing in the first place.[76] A 1940 survey conducted by the advertising industry did indeed reveal consumer dissatisfaction. Of the five thousand people interviewed, 59 percent were in favor of additional advertising regulations.[77]

Neither did the new advertising regulatory law impress Copeland. Instead of providing the public with increased protection against false and misleading advertising practices, he contended, the Wheeler-Lea Amendment actually made such protection less likely. Indeed, after all the turmoil, the legislation had made "no substantial advance in the authority to deal with false advertising over what has been contained in the FTC act for more than 20 years."[78] Wheeler, in contrast, argued that Copeland's interpretation of the law was based on a misunderstanding. In terms of consumer protection, Wheeler maintained, the new law represented a huge improvement. Previously the FTC could regulate unfair advertising practice only on behalf of business, but it now could issue cease and desist orders on behalf of the consuming public even if no person had already been harmed or injured by the advertised products.[79] Undeniably, however, the Wheeler-Lea Amendment put the burden of proving the false or misleading nature of an advertisement on the government instead of forcing advertisers to censor their ads' claims. This was a powerful legal distinction that advertising reformers understood would go a long way toward undermining the possibility of rigorous federal advertising regulation.[80]

The passage of the new amendment and, to a lesser extent, the new Food, Drugs, and Cosmetics Act, presented the advertising industry with a new set of legal restrictions. These were, however, much milder than the industry had first feared, and the law hardly affected the large majority of advertisers.[81] Even the editor of *Printers' Ink,* who had long and consistently opposed the FTC's role as advertising administrator, had to admit that business could live with the law because there was "nothing particularly vicious" about it. These sentiments were shared by advertising-executive-turned-politician Bruce Barton.[82] Charles Wesley Dunn agreed too, although he expressed fear that the Wheeler-Lea Amendment gave the FTC too much power to attack fundamental trade practices. This, in his opinion, permitted the commission to become an arbiter of business conduct. He readily admitted, however, that the new amendment was quite acceptable to food, drug, and cosmetics manufacturers. Celebrating the new law as a "marvelous piece of legislation" that was likely to increase advertising's power was John Benson.[83] The advertising community apparently realized that in comparison to some of the more stringent regulation proposals that had circulated, the Wheeler-Lea Amendment allowed it to breathe a deep sigh of relief.

Unimpressed with the new law, CU complained that its complicated and drawn-out legal procedures further prevented consumers' protection in the marketplace. Upon discovering a case of misleading advertising, the FTC would issue a notice for a hearing to the advertiser and give the advertiser at least thirty days to prepare for it. After the hearing the commission members would spend several months, even years, deliberating the merits of issuing a cease and desist order. If, upon weighing the evidence, the members decided to issue an order, the advertiser was given a two-month grace period to decide whether to follow the order or to appeal the decision to the U.S. Circuit Court of Appeals. If an appeal was denied, the advertiser would have another month's grace period in which to deliberate the merits of appealing the case to the U.S. Supreme Court. If denied an appeal by the Supreme Court, yet another thirty days would have to elapse before the order went into effect. In the meantime the advertiser might continue to expose consumers to false advertising claims, and cause some to waste their money and risk their health.[84] Advertisers who continued their false or misleading advertisements after one court had handed down a cease and desist order faced a five-thousand-dollar fine and six months' imprisonment for the first offense. For a second offense, the penalties were doubled.[85] "The only new feature of the Wheeler[-]Lea Bill, as far as protection of the consumer is concerned," admitted a J. Walter Thompson advertising executive, "is that the Commission through the Trial Examiner's office now is empowered to undertake prosecution of persons or corporations for violation of the law without the necessity of establishing an actual or potential injury to a competitor."[86]

Despite its byzantine procedures, the law was not entirely toothless. One of the first persons to test its applicability was M. C. Phillips. Less than two months after the passage of the Wheeler-Lea Amendment, Phillips contacted the FTC about an advertisement for Pond's Cold Cream, which she charged claimed falsely to nourish the skin. The test of the FTC's willingness to act on complaints from individual consumers, an action that CR strongly recommended, was crowned with success. Upon reviewing the case, the FTC issued a cease and desist order against the manufacturer. The commission also asked the manufacturers of eighteen other cosmetics products who were making unsubstantiated claims about their products' ability to prevent baldness or remove freckles to halt their ads.[87] Also receiving a cease and desist order was Standard Brands. In fall 1938 the FTC decided that advertisements for the company's Fleischmann's Yeast, the very product that Copeland had promoted on the radio, made crude and misleading claims. Agreeing with the consumer advocates who had argued this for years, the FTC did not believe the product's claim of being a cure-all for vitamin deficiencies, digestive problems, pimples, tooth malformation, and everything in between.[88]

Although the FTC managed to crack down on the advertising practices of some big national advertisers, the mass media, with their close financial ties to these manufacturers, did not publicize the cease and desist orders. Because of this, the lengthy appeals procedure might be well underway before the public ever learned, for example, that the FTC had found several advertising claims by Listerine antiseptic to be unsubstantiated or that it had ordered a stop to Helena Rubenstein's claims that its Eye Lash Grower Cream would cause the lashes to grow and that one of its face powders would prevent skin blemishes.[89]

The immediate and somewhat ironic result of the law on advertising copy was a tendency to glamorize products and employ indirect assertion. Because it was relatively easy to check the truthfulness of verbal claims, advertisements relied more heavily on illustrations to get around the law. Although most advertising agencies were instructed to design copy that complied with the law, they still used techniques to sidestep product claims that the amended version of the Federal Trade Commission Act had rendered illegal. "It was obvious," the historian Otis Pease argues, "that a pictorial illustration could frequently pass muster where a verbal presentation would not, that a promise of reward as a result of purchasing the product could often be enhanced by being left unspecified and thereby innocent of legal transgression."[90] This sneaky behavior revealed the shortcomings of the new law as well as its general failure to encourage advertisers to provide consumers with more factual information.

CU, which had emerged as the law's most vocal opponent, cited four distinct problems with the Wheeler-Lea Amendment. The FTC lacked sufficient funds to effectively enforce the law, and its drawn-out legislative process followed by only mild penalties for violating advertisers was equally problematic. Also concerning CU was the FTC itself. The consumer organization considered the commission prejudiced in favor of business and thus not the best defender of consumers' interests. The fourth major concern was the Wheeler-Lea Amendment's failure to require advertisers to provide more facts and information about their products. The latter, of course, had fueled the legislative battle when the original Tugwell bill was drafted in 1933.[91]

Not surprisingly, the resolution of these same issues satisfied advertising interests. In March 1939 John Benson not only praised the law as "a very fortunate thing for advertising" but also claimed that it served a great public benefit. The AAAA president pointed to "dozens and dozens" of cases in which exaggerated assertions and exclamatory boasting had been replaced with straightforward, matter-of-fact assertions.[92]

In reality the new law represented little hardship for the vast majority of advertisers. During the first two years of the law's existence the FTC investigated some eight hundred new cases. Combined with those pending before the amendment went into effect and a few that were reopened, the commission investigated a total of 1,137 cases between March 1938 and May 1940. In all, these resulted in a total of seventeen injunctions and a single criminal prosecution that involved an abortifacient believed to seriously endanger users' lives; the latter resulted in a guilty plea and a one-thousand-dollar fine.[93] Not surprisingly, this outcome encouraged *Advertising and Selling* to assure wary advertisers that the FTC did not believe in advertising's severe regulation. Although the commission demanded that truth should be the basis of advertising, it also allowed a reasonable amount of commercial hyperbole. Moreover, concluded a writer for the trade journal, the advertising community should be grateful that it was the FTC rather than the FDA that had finally won the right to regulate advertising: "During the first year following passage of the Wheeler-Lea amendment it [the FTC] referred only three cases to the Department of Justice for prosecution. Contrast this with six criminal, and 245 civil cases referred by the Food and Drug Administration during the first year of the new Food and Drug Act."[94]

Nevertheless, the advertising industry knew it could never take the FTC's lax regulation for granted. This gave it incentive to constantly lobby the White House, the FTC, and Congress to ensure that the FTC never got too carried away with regulating advertising in the public interest. In this sense, the Wheeler-Lea Amendment gave rise to the advertising industry's need for a permanent and prominent lobbying presence in Washington, D.C., just as commercial broadcasters, securities traders, and other regulated industries had. Not only did the industry consider advertising regulation a threat but it also realized that regulation was favored by a substantial segment of the public. Manufacturers and their advertising agencies understood that it would be politically impossible to eliminate advertising regulation in the climate of the 1930s and that future battles would be fought largely at the FTC and in the courts, not on the floor of Congress or in the White House. In 1942, just four years after passage of the Wheeler-Lea Amendment, the U.S. Supreme Court for the first time considered the argument that federal advertising regulation should be deemed unconstitutional on the ground that the First Amendment protected commercial speech. The Court ruled 9–0 in *Valentine v. Chrestensen* that advertising was not protected speech and that regulation was therefore constitutional.[95]

Conclusion

In spite of demands from consumer groups, New Dealers, and government regulatory agencies, advertisers survived the five-year legislative battle over advertising regulation with surprising ease. Although both the Tugwell bill and the Wheeler-Lea Amendment claimed to protect consumers against false and misleading advertising, the two measures were drastically different. The former was drafted with consumer protection in mind; the latter reflected the advertising community's successful five-year effort to render such protection painless for business interests. The original intent of the Tugwell bill was to revise the Food and Drugs Act of 1906 and increase protection for consumers; this goal was largely acknowledged in the early discussions surrounding the measure. By 1936, however, the debate had shifted and business considerations had taken control. In contrast to the Tugwell bill, which had attempted to regulate not only false advertising but also advertising that created a misleading impression, the Wheeler-Lea Amendment protected consumers only from explicitly fraudulent advertising claims. The passage of the new law effectively subdued public discussions concerning the extent to which advertisements had an obligation to inform and educate consumers. The final version left an enormous gray area in which advertisers could practice misleading advertising even as they obeyed the letter of the law.

Similarly, the amendment to the FTC act provided rather weak consumer protection, but the consumer movement did not fight against this measure once it was written into law. The five-year struggle had made it clear that those fighting the institution of advertising were sure to lose. Yet the advertising industry was in no mood to rest on its laurels. To the contrary, following passage of the Wheeler-Lea Amendment the industry was more concerned than ever that unless it became even more vigilant in protecting and promoting advertising's public image, a measure far worse than the Wheeler-Lea Amendment might be passed into law.

Legislative threats were far from the advertising industry's only challenge, however. Part of the industry's strategy after the passage of the new law included a careful cultivation of public opinion. The many PR programs that had emerged in the early 1930s now formed the basis for a more permanent strategy intended to prevent future attacks. Before the bombing of Pearl Harbor on December 7, 1941, when advertising interests began to make the case that criticism against advertising as an economic system was unpatriotic, the crusade against advertising's foes had resulted in a new series of accusations against the left-leaning wing of the U.S. consumer movement and had created some very curious bedfellows.

7

Red-Baiting the
Consumer Movement

Although advertising's federal regulation was essentially established in 1938, in subsequent years the advertising industry redoubled its public relations efforts to improve consumers' perceptions. By the late 1930s business groups and trade organizations had established permanent PR programs, and several pegged them as requiring high priority. Many efforts to create coalitions with mainstream consumer groups had been fairly successful, although considerable debate on the best strategy still erupted.[1] Whereas politically moderate business groups stressed increased cooperation, conservative peers adopted a more militant approach. They accused segments of the consumer movement of being part of a Communist plot designed to destroy capitalism and the American way. Increasingly, through public conferences, radio programs, and publications, conservative business interests, led by groups such as the National Association of Manufacturers (NAM) and the Advertising Federation of America (AFA), aggressively propagated the notion that advertising and capitalism were synonymous with freedom and democracy and were "natural" American institutions. No longer satisfied with merely supplying advertising-supported teaching material, these groups sought to have a greater say over the public school curriculum. They continued to offer teaching materials to promote advertising's role in a free society but also systematically scrutinized teachers and textbooks for sentiments incongruent with a conservative interpretation of the American system.

The strategy to secure the teaching of a probusiness agenda to the nation's youth was part of a larger attempt to rid the country of Communist influences. In 1939 the Dies Committee—forerunner of the House Un-American

Activities Committee—targeted the consumer movement for investigation. Helping behind the scenes was a delighted Frederick J. Schlink, who thought nothing of building alliances with some of his former adversaries in the business community. Humiliated by the 1935 strike and its aftermath, Schlink and his Consumers' Research Inc. (CR) colleagues finally spied a chance to publicly embarrass Consumers Union of the United States Inc. (CU). The radical implications of the consumer movement's attack on advertising were revealed when CU was among the first victims of the committee's investigations in 1939. Despite the accusations, however, much of the advertising community no longer considered the consumer movement a threat. Consequently, the right-wing attempt to drag left-leaning consumer advocates through the mud as well as its plot to control the classroom were ineffective.

The Dies Committee

The mid- to late 1930s was not an easy period for CR. The 1935 strike had severely tarnished its image in many supporters' eyes, and, even more humiliating, the organization witnessed CU's growth and success. Within a few years, CU had surpassed CR in size and possibly also in public influence. By 1939, when CR counted sixty thousand members, CU had managed to attract seventy-five thousand people to its prolabor consumer cause.[2] As leaders of CR, J. B. Matthews, M. C. Phillips, and Schlink were not merely upset. They were ready to take drastic measures to discredit CU and its organizers. Their methods included repeatedly ridiculing CU's testing practices and constantly documenting its alleged Communist sympathies.

In a climate of Communist fears and obsessions with "subversive activities," CR was far from the only organization interested in slinging mud. The conservative U.S. Chamber of Commerce, for example, championed attempts to hunt down and vilify "Reds." Even before CR's strike the Chamber of Commerce had issued a special report entitled "Combating Subversive Activities in the United States." A year later the business organization demanded that Congress enact laws to criminalize advocating the violent overthrow of the government and insisted that all writings promoting such teachings be banned from the U.S. postal system. Aliens promoting said actions should be deported and denied the right to become U.S. citizens, and people who tried to promote insubordination or disaffection in the U.S. armed forces should be punished. The Chamber of Commerce resolution also called for a special agency in the Department of Justice to investigate these matters. The Chamber of Commerce distributed booklets such as *The American Economic*

System Compared with Collectivism and Dictatorship and *Combating Subversive Activities in the United States* to groups and individuals upon request and issued a mimeographed bulletin called *Safeguards against Subversive Activities* to keep its members up-to-date on subversive activities around the world and legislative measures to help stop their proliferation.[3] Although it defined both Communist and Fascist activities as subversive, it was quite obvious that the Chamber of Commerce was far more worried about the former. Whereas the August 1936 issue of *Safeguards against Subversive Activities* included a lengthy summary of world Communist activity during the first six months of 1936, the Chamber of Commerce, with many U.S. industrialists as members, had few qualms about holding its ninth general meeting in Berlin in summer 1937.[4] "The Hitler dictatorship in Germany," concluded the Chamber of Commerce leadership, "is of a totally different character [than Communism in Russia]. It justifies itself to Germany and to Europe as a bulward [*sic*] against bolshevism."[5]

After several years of discussion in 1938 the House of Representatives finally created a committee to investigate alleged unpatriotic propaganda and appointed Martin Dies, a Democrat from Texas, as its chair. Critics argued that it functioned as a sounding board for every antilabor zealot in the country and that its primary purpose was to destroy organized labor, defame the New Deal, and harass left-wing and liberal organizations until they folded. Some protested that the committee itself employed Fascist techniques by "stampeding the people by shouting 'Communist.'" One critic characterized Dies as the "hatchet-man of 'the native American fascist,'" maintaining that his occasional swipes at Fascism were merely camouflage designed to obscure the committee's Fascist nature.[6] Dies and his supporters on and off the committee were self-righteous and energetic, and they used their considerable power to "cleanse" political organizations and labor unions of Communists and fellow travelers.[7]

Joining Dies in investigating "the extent, character, and objects of un-American propaganda activities in the United States" and "the diffusion within the United States of subversive and un-American propaganda" were Arthur D. Healy of Massachusetts, John Dempsey from New Mexico, Alabama's Joe Starnes, Harold G. Mosier of Ohio, Noah M. Mason of Illinois, and New Jersey's J. Parnell Thomas.[8] During fall 1938 the committee conducted hearings in Washington, D.C., New York City, and on the West Coast. Although Fascist groups, even by conservatives' own estimates, enjoyed large memberships, the Dies Committee focused primarily on Communist sympathizers.[9] At first the committee spent most of its time on causes of forced union membership. These investigations failed to attract much attention, and many, including Dies himself, doubted that the committee would survive another session of Congress. At this point Matthews, who by now had made a complete turn to the political Right, arrived in Washington, D.C. Still hurting from the CR strike, Matthews was quick to realize the Dies Committee's potential not only for cracking down on labor unions and exposing subversive Communist activities but also for getting back at old enemies in the consumer movement.[10] Dies was so impressed with Matthews's drive, knowledge, and intensity that he hired him as his research director. Under Matthews's hand the committee quickly commanded the attention of several influential, and very conservative, business leaders, most of whom were affiliated with the NAM, the Chamber of Commerce, or both.[11] In spite of having left CR for work in Washington, D.C., Matthews stayed in close contact with his former colleges and wasted no time in turning Schlink's crusade into the Dies Committee's mission. Much like his former boss, Matthews claimed that Communists had infiltrated large segments of the U.S. consumer movement and that CU housed the most subversive elements. In fact, hardly an aspect of CU's conduct escaped CR's criticism.

In the early days of CR, Schlink explained in a lengthy letter to Dies, liberal individuals had been helpful to the organization. And whereas some wanted nothing in return, others had expected to control CR's ideology as it grew in size and popularity. Conflicts soon arose between the people who supported Schlink's vision of CR as a scientific agency devoted to truth and those who desired to drag politics into the picture. CU, he argued, was not formed to serve consumers but to promote Communism and act as a front group. Thus, product testing, the heart and soul of CR's activities, was not a high priority for CU, which used its shoddy testing services only as bait to attract members to its left-wing causes. CU's insistence on boycotting products from countries such as Germany and Japan, for example, should not be seen as a fight against Fascism but, rather, as an expression of radicalism.[12] He also warned that CU worked with Communist leaders to indoctrinate young children and unsuspecting schoolteachers with subversive, radical ideas.[13]

Even CU's application for membership on the Advisory Committee on Ultimate Consumer Goods for the American Standards Association was interpreted as suspect; it was an attempt to infiltrate a "non-radical, non-liberal, non-political, quasi-public agency" for subversive purposes. Because the advisory committee functioned as a clearinghouse for information on industry technical standards, Schlink explained, CU might use its membership as an excuse to obtain information that could help the militant labor movement organize strikes and, more generally, paralyze U.S. industry.[14]

Although he clearly targeted CU as the ringleader, Schlink also claimed that other consumer organizations, including the Consumers' National Federation, the League of Women Shoppers, and the Milk Consumers Protective League, were serving as Communist fronts. "I realize that the consumer movement may look unimportant to the Dies committee as compared with Communist activity in the Army, Navy and State department, and other vital branches of the government," Schlink acknowledged to Dies Committee member J. Parnell Thomas. He begged the committee members not to be fooled by the Communist Party's strategy to lure the middle classes through front organizations.[15] Although the Dies Committee might have driven the Communist Party underground, it had not ended its activities. Instead of operating in the open, it was now hiding in pseudoconsumer organizations.[16]

Schlink also fired against the consumer councils of the Agricultural Adjustment Administration, the City-Wide Tenants Council, the [National] Consumers' League, the Progressive Women's Councils, the People's League for Abundance, and the Federation of Architects, Engineers, Chemists, and Technicians. Also suspicious, he claimed, were the activities of the Institute for Propaganda Analysis, a group formed in 1937 to examine propaganda.[17] Schlink accused it of being far more concerned with subversive activities of the Fascist variety than with Communist-inspired behavior.[18] The institute, he claimed, deliberately made left-wing propaganda look "weak, poor, poorly financed, socially unimportant," and incapable of having a subversive effect while at the same time painting right-wing and centrist propaganda as "scheming, heinous, diabolical," and "dangerously subversive to American ways of thought."[19]

CR's campaign to smear CU was not without challenges. In spite of CR's attempts to distance itself from CU, many consumers were confused about their differences. Needless to say, this did not sit well with CR and Schlink.[20] Nothing, stated the organization's leaders, could be more deceitful than fostering the illusion that all agencies critical of advertising were agents of Moscow.[21] CR's leaders argued in a parody that evoked CU's mission statement:

> If [we] were really trying to overthrow the American political and economic system, we wouldn't be content with trying to help people get the best products for their money. We would play up the products which are poor and of poor value and are thus *not recommended*. We would discuss the labor conditions under which products were made—not evaluating working conditions in fact, but basing our approval or disapproval on whether or not a particular factory had a contract with the C.I.O. We would urge consumer boycotts of manufacturers and even small shopkeepers on the slightest provocation to help the leftists' cause in Timbuktu, Xanadu, or Patagonia.[22]

Unlike Communist-friendly consumer groups, CR claimed to fight all forms of totalitarian influences and support private enterprise against the "State-dominated system of industry and trade."[23]

With help and support from Matthews, it was just a matter of time before Dies and the other committee members agreed that certain aspects of the consumer movement were un-American and up to no good. Thus, in early November 1939 at the annual convention of the Associated Grocery Association, Dies announced his intention to give the consumer movement, or at least the part accused of harboring Communist tendencies, a closer look. He also filed a request for a one-hundred-thousand-dollar grant to carry on the committee's work for another year after its mandate expired in early January 1940. Advertisers were not sure what to think. Considering some of the other issues that Dies could have singled out, the consumer movement seemed quite insignificant. When Dies investigated the consumer movement, warned a writer for *Business Week,* he should keep in mind that business's interests in consumer groups had expanded far beyond discrediting the radical ones. "Business is now interested in converting consumer energy to its own uses—in establishing common aims and objectives, and in refining those business practices which have caused customer dissatisfaction in the past." Many, in fact, were beginning to suspect that Matthews was using his position as prize investigator with the Dies Committee purely to settle an old score with Arthur Kallet.[24]

Not all business interests, however, were on speaking terms with the consumer movement. Some, including the NAM and the Hearst Corporation, rushed to support the Dies Committee. In the past CR had rebuked the Hearst publication *Good Housekeeping* for its advertising practices. In *Skin Deep* M. C. Phillips had attacked the magazine's practice of accepting advertising for false, misleading, and even dangerous cosmetics. Now, in its eagerness to get back at CU through the Dies Committee, CR displayed an uncharacteristically short institutional memory.

The Matthews Report

In August 1939 the Federal Trade Commission (FTC) lodged a complaint against *Good Housekeeping*'s publisher, accusing it of deceiving and misleading readers by issuing guarantees and seals of approval to advertisers who spouted grossly exaggerated or false claims. Taking its newly acquired mandate seriously, the FTC had spent the months since the passage of the Wheeler-Lea Amendment investigating fraudulent advertising. Through this process the commission had determined that many ads carried by Hearst's *Good Housekeeping* (including those for Lambert's Listerine) contained false claims, and it issued cease and desist orders against the manufacturers. Just as detrimental to the publication's reputation was the FTC's ruling that *Good Housekeeping* had provided several falsely advertised products (including Fleischmann's Yeast and Welch's Grape Juice) with its seal of approval. And much to the magazine's dismay and embarrassment, the FTC estimated that about 80 of its regular and prominent national advertisers were guilty of false or misleading advertising practices.[25] So outraged was Richard E. Berlin, executive vice president at Hearst magazines, that he eventually sent telegrams to three thousand advertisers and publishers in which he claimed that the FTC's charges were the result of a Communist plot. "Certain subversive elements, pretending to serve the consuming public but actually motivated by Communistic theories," stated the telegram, "have persistently been attacking the institution of advertising and Good Housekeeping [*sic*] in particular as a leading medium in the advertising field. . . . We believe that the underlying motive of these attacks on advertising is to destroy the freedom of the American press by first destroying its principal source of revenues—advertising. We believe this subversive movement must now be publicly exposed."[26]

Joining forces with Berlin was a group of influential business leaders with their own reasons for diminishing the consumer movement's power. Leading the crusade on behalf of the NAM was its former president, Robert Lund, now the head of Lambert Pharmaceuticals, and George E. Sokolsky, a columnist and radio announcer whose loyalties lay with the far right. A former radical, Sokolsky had, according to the liberal advertising journal *Tide,* "tasted the cup which advertising thinks its critics want, and could testify he found it bitter."[27] Sokolsky was a lucid writer whose credits included working for *Liberty* magazine and the NAM's campaign for the American way. In the latter capacity Sokolsky had written numerous columns, conducted many interviews, and helped produce the dozens of radio broadcasts that the NAM had aired to defend free enterprise. From his vantage point, Sokolsky viewed the consumer movement as a Communist plot intent on destroying capitalism.[28] For his work for the NAM Sokolsky earned a tidy sum. He also collected sizable honoraria as a writer, lecturer, and publicity agent for Republic Steel and as a speechwriter for Earnest Weir, a conservative steel magnate who backed the NAM's ideological work.[29]

In November 1939 Lund, Matthews, and Berlin were joined by a small group including Schlink and Henry P. Bristol, an official of the Bristol-Myers drug company, for a private dinner party at Sokolsky's home. George Gallup, the vice president of the Young and Rubicam advertising agency, and Paul S. Willis, the president of the Associated Grocery Manufacturers of America, were also on the short guest list. At this meeting, according to persistent rumors, Matthews read his official statement of how he intended to utilize his position within the Dies Committee to disclose Communist infiltration in "so-called consumer organizations and groups," a choice of terms that strongly resembled the language used by business interests to destroy the same groups. In response some of the powerful businessmen present vowed to withhold advertising from publications that refused to give Matthews's investigation their fullest possible attention.[30]

On December 3 Matthews submitted a report to Dies, who acted as a one-man subcommittee at a hearing at which only he and Matthews were present. The peculiar circumstances, however, did not prevent Dies and Matthews from announcing that the report had been placed in the records of the full committee.[31] The report's purpose, according to Matthews, was to name organizations in which Communists played a major role. He claimed to have unveiled a Communist strategy of taking advantage of consumers' dissatisfaction in the marketplace and using this discontent to build a revolutionary, Moscow-directed movement. "Communists," argued Matthews, "understand that advertising performs an indispensible [sic] function in the mass production economy and that advertising as an economic process, wholly apart from questions which have to do with good or bad advertising copy, is as essential a part of the distributive mechanism as are railroads and retail outlets. Therefore, communists believe that to sabotage and destroy advertising, and through its destruction to undermine and help destroy the capitalist system of free enterprise, is a revolutionary tactic worthy of a great deal of attention."[32] The Dies Committee, he promised, now held enough evidence to demonstrate that most popular attacks upon advertising were the direct result of Communist propaganda from consumer organizations. "The technique of revolution requires the Party to work in every way possible to discredit—rather than repair where weaknesses exist—the economic structure of free enterprise in the United States," warned Matthews.[33]

Among the groups specifically accused of serving as Communist fronts was the League of Women Shoppers, an organization that employed Susan Jenkins, one of the leaders behind the 1935 strike at CR,[34] and the Committee for Boycott against Japanese Aggression along with its leader, Ben Gold. The Labor Research Association, the Transport Workers Union, the American League for Peace and Democracy, and the American Youth Congress, including their organizers, as well as Joseph P. Lash, the executive secretary of the

American Student Union, and Kathleen McInerny, the former leader of the League of Women Shoppers, were similarly accused. Other groups, such as Against the High Cost of Living, the Milk Consumers Protective Committee, the Consumer-Farmer Milk Cooperative, the New York Consumers Council, the Consumers' National Federation, and the *Consumers' Guide* published by the Department of Agriculture were painted as "transition belts" used by the Communist Party to spread propaganda. The weightiest charges in Matthews's report, however, were leveled at CU and Kallet. Matthews claimed that Kallet, through numerous writings, comments, and associations, had demonstrated a true commitment to Communist ideals. Matthews also maintained that federal officials had cooperated with Communists and that federal funds had been used for subversive purposes. He accused Donald E. Montgomery, head of the Agricultural Adjustment Administration's Consumers' Division, of leading a Communist-inspired crusade against advertising. Montgomery's affiliation with the Consumers' National Federation was taken as "proof" that the "attack" on *Good Housekeeping* was part of an extended Communist consumer plot to eliminate advertising.[35] CR—where Matthews's wife was still employed—and his former boss, Schlink, were spared from the brunt of the general accusations.

At the same time that he denied all charges, Kallet also found the situation somewhat ironic. The allegations by this former CR colleague were the same ones trade organizations had been hurling at them both only few years earlier. Then their defense had been united. A distraught Kallet took issue with Matthews's report: "I want to state emphatically that neither Consumers Union, as an organization, nor myself as an individual, nor to the best of my knowledge anyone else connected with Consumers Union, has ever had any connection with the Communist party or is even aware of any such broad destructive movement as Mr. Matthews seems to find in operation." In particular Kallet questioned why the Dies Committee considered CU's work so "subversive" in nature. "We cannot believe," he fumed, "that making comparative tests of consumer goods and reporting the test findings, which is the work we do, is in any way subversive or destructive."[35]

Others singled out reacted similarly. Susan Jenkins, for example, denied having organized the League of Women Shoppers. Neither did she appreciate that Matthews had promoted her to the sole leader of the CR strike. Much like Kallet, Jenkins denied any connection with the Communist Party. "I am not and have not been a communist or a fellow-traveler," she insisted.[36] The Consumers National Federation also refuted the charges. "The Consumers' National Federation is not a Communist organization nor a 'transition belt,' nor do its policies in any way reflect Communist nor any other political control," claimed Chair Helen Hall and Vice Chair Robert S. Lynd on behalf of the group. "It is not un-American to be poor nor to serve the poor."[37] Donald E. Montgomery was equally upset, terming the Communist allegations "preposterous canard[s]."[38]

CU's legal counsel, as well as others targeted by the report, scrutinized the document with an eye toward possible action. Demanding a congressional investigation into Matthews's unethical behavior to see if he should be severed from the federal payroll was considered. Whereas CU leaders claimed not to be surprised to see the NAM and proprietary drug manufacturers' fingerprints on the Dies report, they did confess to being disappointed that Schlink, a pioneer of consumer testing, should have involved himself in the undertaking. Not only had Matthews succeeded in maneuvering Schlink into an antilabor stand four years earlier, observed a *Consumer's Union Reports* (*CUR*) writer, but "it now seems that Mr. Schlink has been led into an anticonsumer stand as well."[39]

Fearful of how the report would play out in the advertising-supported mass media, which still did not accept CU's advertisements, the concerned consumer group reached out to its members for support. "You *must* tell your friends the real meaning of the Matthews attack," urged CU's leadership. "You *must* do your best to help CU grow by bringing in new members. It is too bad that CU cannot do its work, and CU members cannot get the fruits of it, in peace. But Mr. Matthews and his like would have it otherwise; and the challenge must be met."[40]

Much to CU's satisfaction, however, its fear of massive media support for the Dies report was severely alarmist. The general consensus among newspapers and the business press was that the accusations were way out of proportion to the evidence.[41] The main exceptions were Hearst's newspapers, which did their best to fuel the committee's activities.[42] According to *Advertising and Selling,* the report and its author lacked credibility. The trade journal claimed that Matthews's efforts at labeling the entire consumer movement as Communistic were unfair and generally unsupported. Questioning Matthews's political background, the editors expressed concern with persistent rumors that manufacturers and the ultraconservative Sokolsky had been allowed to edit the report before it was made public and that Schlink had been involved in the chicanery.[43]

Even *Printers' Ink,* a publication that had been very critical toward the consumer movement in the past, recommended that advertisers take the report with a grain of salt, especially in light of Matthews's background. "The fact that Mr. Matthews has attempted to show the communistic bias of a number of consumer organizations does not mean that the whole consumer movement and all the individuals in it are tarred with a red brush," warned one of its writers.[44] *Advertising Age*'s editors concurred: "We believe it would be a mistake of policy for the advertising field to assume that the movement as a whole can be dismissed as of communistic origin. Its development has been over too large an area and has embraced too many organizations of unquestioned standing to make this a satisfactory solution of the problem." Although "radical elements" might use criticism of advertising as a wedge to attack business as a whole, its editors stressed that the safest and surest method of supporting the economic, political, and social institutions of the United States was the use of legitimate channels by democratic means.[45] Others questioned the committee's motives as well. "What is Communistic about wanting to make your purchase as economic as possible?" asked one critic. "In the past, that desire was always considered admirable. Has it suddenly become subversive?"[46] Mainstream women's groups were particularly angered by the smear campaign. "Congressman Dies may not realize it yet, but he has just made the greatest mistake of his entire un-American activities career," remarked two *St. Louis Star-Times* writers. "He has ignored the oldest adage of smart politicians, lawyers, newspaper editors and others who have to get along with folks—namely, never to assail a woman."[47] Although the same report only a year or so earlier may have been hailed in the business community, it now fell flat. Matthews, one observer concluded, had "blunted his weapon by a premature release and ambiguity of statement."[48]

This, of course, was far from the reaction that Matthews had hoped for. Not only did the attempt to impugn CU and Kallet backfire but also the well-calculated plot to elevate CR above the controversy seemed to unravel. Not coincidentally, the Matthews report had not accused CR of Communist activities, but far from all detected this omission. CR officials despaired that many casual observers failed to realize the difference between CR and the groups that the Dies Committee now portrayed as Communist-inspired. But by the late 1930s, more than four years after the bifurcating strike, CR held high hopes that the public would be able to differentiate it from CU. Unfortunately for Schlink and his supporters, the public remained ignorant about the differences between CU and CR and their history. Not all, for example, had kept up with Matthews's political turnaround, and many still associated him with his radical opinions and writings, including *Partners in Plunder,* which he had published only a few years earlier. Neither had it been very long since Schlink himself had promoted ideas that were seen as left of center. In other words, that CR and its officials had moved to the right on the political spectrum might have been difficult for many citizens to fathom. Unfortunately for CR, much of its strategy was predicated on the public's knowledge about its political orientation.

In the first months after the publication of the Matthews report, CR's leaders saw it necessary to launch a campaign to clear up confusion about the differences between itself—a "genuine" consumer organization—and "pseudo" consumer groups.[49] A tendency among the mass media to ignore this distinction and lump CR with the groups it so loathed infuriated the organization's leadership.[50] "At the present moment," complained Schlink, "the writing of articles and speeches on consumer questions seems to be going through a phase when this confusion is being encouraged."[51] Although some commentators tried to foster the idea that all consumer groups were agents of Moscow, others (including certain business journals) seemed to embrace the illusion that no groups were so inclined. Refusing to acknowledge that charges against the consumer movement's left wing had failed to stick, Schlink chastised the press for its failure to support his plan. He accused advertising trade journals of not daring to publicly identify Communist-directed consumer organizations out of fear that advertising might take yet another hit from the public as a result. Just as problematic from Schlink's perspective was the tendency to lump all consumer groups (including CR) together as Communist-inspired.[52] Unlike CU and the other pseudoconsumer groups mentioned in the Dies report, Schlink explained, CR did not try to mow down U.S. industry but worked within the system to improve it.[53] Although many, including groups and individuals in the advertising community, urged for a stop to the Dies investigations, Schlink argued to the contrary. He strongly urged the committee to intensify its probe and purge the consumer movement of Communists.[54]

One of CU's first reactions to the Matthews report was an intense undertaking to identify the report's rationale and expose those responsible for it. In spring 1940, some four months after the report had been made public, the consumer organization presented the results of its investigation. According to its report, conclusive evidence of collusion existed "between at least one member of the Special Committee's staff (which was made up of one man; namely J. B. Matthews) and interests known to be hostile to and even competitive with many of the consumer groups and individuals cited in the Report."[55] CU had been suspicious of Matthews's involvement with the Dies Committee from the very start. In 1938 it had presented the Dies Committee with evidence of perjury by Matthews in his testimony before that very committee.[56]

Although Matthews might have been correct in his claim that some people connected with the consumer movement were fellow travelers, he provided little hard evidence to support the characterization. He was also largely unsuccessful in proving his broader accusation that the consumer movement was largely inspired by Communist ideology and that this had influenced the federal case against *Good Housekeeping*. "What began as a statement that the consumer movement was a front for Communists," observes the advertising historian Otis Pease, "ended with a well-hedged insinuation that the federal case against *Good Housekeeping* was being conducted by subversives."[57]

Another peculiarity of Matthews's report was the highly irregular circumstances of its release. After Matthews had submitted the report solely to Dies, it took five days before the report was made available to the press on December 8. Although all members of the full Dies Committee were in Washington, D.C., they were not informed about the report's existence until they read about it in the press. Three committee members were so infuriated that they refused to sign the report and successfully fought a battle against making it part of the official record.[58] "In short," argues Pease, "one is compelled to infer that the report was intended largely to satisfy purposes of publicity which required that it appear to have received official endorsement when it had not and when to have received such endorsement would have fatally exposed it to the scrutiny of an official hearing."[59]

CU's investigation also produced strong evidence that Richard E. Berlin had been using the report to retaliate against the FTC's treatment of *Good Housekeeping*. CU concluded that Berlin's fingerprints were all over the document. When comparing mimeographed versions of the report that Berlin had sent to advertisers, manufacturers, and the trade press, CU workers discovered that these contained the same typing, spacing, and printing irregularities found in the official report given by Matthews to the committee. Moreover, the two reports were also printed with the same color ink on the same type of paper. A document expert hired by CU concluded that the two reports in all likelihood had been printed in the Hearst Magazine offices. Moreover, Berlin's report was not only stapled to and included with the rest of the report but also released to the public one day before the Matthews report was released from the Dies Committee's office and two days before it appeared in any newspaper.[60]

As he defended the Dies Committee's work of exposing Communist, Nazi, and Fascist activities in the United States, committee member Jerry Voorhis stressed that such investigations should have been conducted during full and open hearings and launched on the basis of compelling evidence. Refusing to have any association with such underhanded tactics, the congressman suspected that the entire report was purely and simply Matthews's opinion. Voorhis described Matthews as a man "who in spite of his past connections with a [consumer] organization other than those attacked in the report sits as sole investigator, judge and juror on the whole consumers [sic] protective and cooperative movement in America. If anything is un-democratic in the world certainly this procedure is."[61] He added, "I believe the committee is put in a very difficult position by releasing a report which attempts to brand as Communist intrigue, protests against high milk prices, the teaching of young women to be wise buyers, or the efforts of consumers to secure the honesty in advertising which every reputable merchant and business man in America desires as much as the consumers do."[62]

Thus, the potentially sensational report on Communist subversion of the consumer movement did not prove as effective as Dies and Matthews had hoped. Most members of the advertising community were not willing to support the Dies Committee's extreme rhetoric and shoddy methodology. "Nowhere in this country as far as I have been able to discover, is there any significant support for the scrapping of capitalism," reflected the well-known journalist Stanley High. "To argue that the desire to change is a sign of communistic or un-American activities will neither frighten nor fool anyone. The American public is too well versed in the facts of recent history to be side tracked by a label. Moreover, the surest way to destroy the still-prevailing belief in the capitalistic system would be for capitalists to give the impression that to advocate change is unpatriotic and to effect change is impossible." In his opinion, the practice of labeling the consumer movement as Communistic could easily backfire and hurt business.[63]

Similarly, Paul S. Willis, the president of the Associated Grocery Manufacturers of America and a guest at the by-now-infamous Sokolsky dinner, contended that although some Communists or fellow travelers had indeed infiltrated the consumer movement and although some consumer organizations could be characterized as Communistic, the overwhelming majority of housewives and clubwomen involved with the consumer movement were "the finest type of Americans—patriotic, civic-minded and sincere." And it was with this group, he added, that business wanted to cooperate.[64]

This sentiment, however, was not shared by the most right-wing factions of U.S. business. Conservative business organizations such as the National Association of Manufacturers (NAM) and the Advertising Federation of America (AFA) were not as willing to make peace with the consumer movement's left wing because they did not view their prolabor sympathies as simply prob-

An artistic parody on the hunt for Communists in the consumer movement. *New York Mirror,* December 12, 1939.

lematic; for the AFA in particular, the persistent criticism of advertising as an institution was simply unacceptable.[65] Because the left-leaning critique of advertising was seen as a direct attack on free enterprise, conservative business groups were not willing to give up the fight. On the contrary, they actively promoted freedom and democracy as synonymous with free enterprise and the NAM's definition of the American way into the early 1940s. During the last few years before the United States became officially involved in World War II, the campaigns on behalf of business would reach large segments of the U.S. population and would mark a major attempt to challenge the consumer movement's influence.

The Conservative Crusade to Rid Schools of Reds

Even though Matthews's campaign against CU had overshot its target, powerful forces opposed to the consumer movement remained. By 1937 *Your Money's Worth* had sold an estimated one hundred thousand copies, and two hundred fifty thousand individuals and institutions had bought *100,000,000 Guinea Pigs*, which by spring 1936 had gone through nineteen printings. Other consumer books such as *Skin Deep* (1934), *American Chamber of Horrors* (1936), *40,000,000 Guinea Pig Children* (1937), *Eat, Drink, and Be Wary* (1936), and *Guinea Pigs No More* (1936) also found a ready audience.[66] A 1937 study concluded that the average library carried several copies of each book and that an interest in consumer titles was on the rise.[67] This trend was confirmed by the publisher of *100,000,000 Guinea Pigs*, who reported that an imposing portion of the quarter-million books had gone to public libraries, where it was among the most frequently requested titles. The public library in Southbridge, Massachusetts, for example, kept a two-year patron waiting list, which made *100,000,000 Guinea Pigs* the library's most requested book to date.[68] The movement was reaching all social strata, including schools and colleges, where the middle-class consumers of tomorrow were being educated.[69] In fall 1939 a study of five thousand citizens, including a high percentage of teachers, revealed much to the industry's horror that 83 percent of the educators had read *100,000,000 Guinea Pigs* and similar books. More than half the teachers admitted to changing their buying habits as a result of this literature. Teachers also confessed to being eager readers of consumer reports and bulletins, and they considered that information unbiased. The poll concluded that the consumer movement had its strongest followers among teachers and consumers in the upper-income brackets.[70] And teachers did not keep their consumer information to themselves. Another study, this one conducted by the AFA's Advertising Research Foundation in fall 1939, concluded that three thousand teachers were employed full-time to teach consumer subjects in U.S. schools.[71]

In spite of advertisers' intense efforts to reach students in schools, many business interests still worried that not enough was being done to counteract the consumer movement's influence on the educational arena.[72] "The business of the nation," warned Anna Steese Richardson, the director of Crowell Publishing's Consumer Division, "is faced with a serious menace from a mass of thoroughly unreliable and misleading information being disseminated by school teachers to pupils in high schools and colleges." Judging from her many trips around the country and a new study suggesting that students had been so affected by so-called antibusiness propaganda that they held advertising and U.S. business in low regard, Richardson was convinced that action had to be taken.[73]

The response of advertisers was part of the broader campaign to push pro-capitalist material in schools. The NAM had kept an eye on the educational arena for some time. In an effort to boost its PR, the group had established an elaborate program for sending speakers to civic and educational groups, including teachers' associations. The goal, according to the NAM, was to reach the "so-called 'opinion molding' audiences where the factual story of industry . . . viewpoint[s] and philosophy [were] least understood."[74] As part of this effort, the organization offered four films and a nine-volume series of booklets entitled *You and Industry* designed for the educational market.[75]

In 1938 it formed the Committee on Educational Cooperation (CEC) to foster understanding and appreciation of free enterprise among future generations. Much to the business organization's delight, Dean William F. Russell of Columbia University's Teachers College, an institution responsible for training more than 50 percent of all educators in public school supervisory positions throughout the country, responded favorably. During its first year the CEC started a cooperative effort with Teachers College to produce conferences to correct "fallacious thinking about private enterprise" among educators.[76] Before long the CEC had launched an aggressive campaign to organize local conferences to promote its program in elementary schools and institutions of higher learning.[77] "Personally," remarked Lammont Du Pont, the CEC's chair, "I am highly enthusiastic about the possibility of extending this process (under the MOBILIZATION FOR UNDERSTANDING PRIVATE ENTERPRISE) to include hundreds of similar conferences between educators and industrialists all over the country."[78]

In addition to indoctrinating educators, the NAM encouraged business executives to get personally involved in the crusade. By visiting schools and giving talks that demonstrated to students and teachers that the industrialist was "a human being with problems" but was "sincerely interested in finding out about the work the students are doing and the problems which they encounter," these business leaders would provide "good public relations, and an opportunity to learn first hand what students are being taught and what they are not being taught."[79] Concerned that U.S. schoolchildren might be losing track of the American way, the CEC stressed the need to revitalize the teaching of "the history of government, and political, economic and religious philosophy" in the nation's schools. "We modern Americans," urged CEC leaders, "have grown lazy, complacent and smug in our enjoyment of our heritage of freedom. If we want to pass that heritage down to our children, it is high time that we arouse ourselves from lethargy, acquire a thorough understanding of the concepts that underlie our American system, and proceed to inculcate that philosophy in the hearts and minds of the oncoming generation."[80]

Schoolchildren, concurred Alfred T. Falk, the director of the AFA's Bureau of Research and Education, were discouraged from recognizing America's glorious history and the Founding Fathers' good intentions. They were told that the U.S. system was unsatisfactory because it benefited only the ruling class and that change, especially through government and social organizations, was necessary.[81] To reclaim education for business interests, the CEC proposed that every educational institution, from elementary schools on up, adopt a curriculum called "The Roots of Liberty." In addition to providing age-appropriate courses in the mechanics of government, this curriculum would "delve deep into the historical and spiritual foundations of the American system of government, free enterprise and religious liberty, and thus revive that sense of patriotic pride in [the nation's] institutions which characterized the early decades of [the] country's history."[82] The only way to fight the propaganda of collectivism, claimed the NAM, was through education. Although educators should not ignore the shortcomings of free enterprise, they should also be obligated to teach their students about the system's strengths and advantages and demonstrate that its advantages outweighed its shortcomings. Academic freedom, the NAM concluded, ended "where academic license begins to undermine the vital concept of representative democracy—with its inseparable concomitants—free enterprise and civil, especially religious, liberty."[83] In fact, this principle was so important that it needed to be applied with equal pertinence to teachers' words in the classroom and to the textbooks being used.[84]

These efforts went far further than what business had attempted in the past, and many educators hotly objected to such an obvious ploy. Leaders of the National Education Association of the United States, for example, contended that efforts to dictate what teachers could and could not say interfered with the basic principles of academic freedom. "The cause of academic freedom, like the cause of free speech in general, is the cause of effective democracy," insisted the organization's leaders. "Both freedoms exist to promote the rule of intelligence in our democratic affairs."[85] To instill them with intellectual integrity, students needed to be exposed to a wide range of opinion on any given issue.

Not so, argued the CEC. The teacher was a hired person, employed by the public through a school or community board of supervisors. Thus, asserted Lammont Du Pont, "the public has a perfect right to deny academic freedom to its teachers, and cannot be held in violation of the Constitutional provision regarding free speech."[86] Teachers, he continued, should be told that criticism of certain principles and policies was forbidden and that selection of all classroom material should be left to the school governing body.[87] "When parents send their children to school, they have a right to expect unbiased education and truthful teaching. It is the responsibility of school authorities to see that they get it," concurred Alfred T. Falk. Because schools were the property of the people, he reasoned, the democratic principle of academic freedom did not confer upon individual educators the personal privilege of using the schoolroom for propagating their pet prejudices or social theories.[88]

The Chamber of Commerce and the Bankers Association were early supporters of the CEC, as was the Federation of Sales Executives, which took a strong interest in educating schoolchildren about free enterprise.[89] By 1940 the federation had begun distributing a weekly newsletter called *Young America* to students in grades six through nine. With a circulation of three hundred thousand, the publication was read by an estimated one million people, including teachers and parents. According to the publisher, the newsletter was designed to carry industry's message into the classroom and help teachers facilitate a discussion about U.S. business and its contribution to social life. Each week featured an article on particular aspects of "the American way of life and free enterprise." The basic policy of *Young America,* maintained the federation, was to teach "*Americanism.*"[90]

During 1940 alone, the NAM had distributed at least 175,000 posters, 15,000 copies of nontheatrical films, and 3.5 million booklets.[91] The NAM estimated that its study material was reaching between two-thirds and three-quarters of all U.S. high school students and somewhere between one-third and one-half of all children enrolled in junior high school.[92] The association was particularly happy to discover that the material appealed to parents and teachers alike. "Anyone visiting the high schools and junior high schools of America today will find N.A.M. posters particularly evident," concluded the group's leaders. "They are to be seen on class bulletin boards, in school corridors, in school shops and elsewhere."[93] The director of social studies of the Gary, Indiana, school system had one of the American Way series posters on the wall next to his desk, and in another high school, this one in Parkersburg,

West Virginia, the most central bulletin board of the corridor prominently displayed the NAM's "I'm Glad I'm an American" poster.[94] As 1940 came to a close, the NAM declared its school service program a huge success.

Much like the NAM, the AFA considered educational programs vital. Because "today's young people will be tomorrow's business leaders," concluded the AFA's leaders, "it is essential that they be well grounded in the problems of industry and in the basic philosophy of the private enterprise system."[95] To expose students to "the constructive side of the story," AFA leaders urged local advertising clubs to make sure that school libraries were supplied with materials that put the industrial system of the United States in a positive light and provided students with a business perspective on advertising's role and function. The federation encouraged direct contact between students and industry representatives and promoted the use of films and slide shows along with debates and essay contests to help keep an educational focus on these issues.[96]

It did not take long for these efforts to snowball. Textbooks had long been of keen interest to the NAM, but in 1940 the CEC decided to make them into a specific focus for investigation. The effort received backing from business-oriented groups on the Right, including the AFA and the New York State Economic Council, as well as conservative educators. Schlink, too, viewed this as yet another chance to get back at his numerous enemies in the consumer movement.

Harold Rugg and *An Introduction to Problems of American Culture*

Although many educators at Teachers College accommodated the CEC, some influential and quite radical educators did not share its vision. The rumor in business circles, or at least among NAM members, was that educators such as John Dewey, George S. Counts, and William Heard Kilpatrick were subversive elements under Moscow's control. "A trustee of a prominent university," complained a NAM member in a report on Teachers College, "was told by the heads of the Russian Government that they considered Columbia University and Teachers College their main stronghold in the United States."[97] Although this member estimated that only 40, or slightly more than 10 percent, of the 350 faculty members at Teachers College belonged to the radical fraction, NAM leaders were worried.[98] One educator in particular had them very concerned; it did not take long before Harold Rugg was singled out for a series of aggressive attacks.

In the early 1930s, after teaching a set of experimental classes at Columbia

University's Lincoln School, Rugg had become convinced that high school students could obtain a better grasp of history, civics, geography, and economics if the subjects were integrated and taught as social science. Rugg wrote several textbooks, including a series called *An Introduction to Problems of American Culture,* specifically for this purpose. Although the books explored a wide variety of issues, their discussion of advertising caught conservative business interests' attention. The latter were aghast to discover that Rugg encouraged students to question advertising's role in society and that he accused advertising of creating demands for unnecessary products and playing upon consumers' fears and vanities.[99] This did not sit well with the NAM. Rugg's textbooks, argued critics, were nothing short of propaganda for "a new social order." The material was presented in a way that directed students' thinking and controlled their conclusions. "If parents still have faith in private enterprise and other fundamental principles underlying our Republic; and, if they still believe our schools should be training centers in factual knowledge and sound Americanism rather than hotbeds of propaganda for educator-reformers, then in my opinion, the Rugg system, lock, stock and barrel, should be barred from every publicly supported school in the United States," affirmed one detractor.[100]

Combining forces in 1939, the NAM and the AFA launched a large campaign to rid schools of Communist-infiltrated school texts and, in particular, to purge schools of Rugg's work.[101] The attack began in reaction to *An Introduction to Problems of American Culture* but quickly ballooned to a condemnation of all his textbooks. Estimating that Rugg's texts were used in four thousand two hundred schools and read by three million high school students across the country, Alfred T. Falk expressed great concern about the author's ability to indoctrinate students with propaganda against advertising.[102] Supporting the fight against "subversive" textbooks, Norman S. Rose, the president of the AFA and the advertising manager at the *Christian Science Monitor,* used a 1940 speech given at the New York World Fair's Goodrich Arena to announce that "textbooks used by thousands of American school children attacked American business, American advertising, [and] time-tried and time-honored American ways of living and prospering."[103] The public schools, stressed another critic, needed to rid itself of "all those who use the classroom for their own political purposes."[104] Still others accused Rugg of being "the Fifth Columnist in America" and suspected him of being "financed by the Russian government." Even people who had not read the books made passionate pleas against them. Campaigns against the professor's work resulted in incidents of hysteria, even book burnings. The vice president of the school board in Bradner, Ohio, for example, publicly burned Rugg's books, and two school board members in Binghamton, New York, advocated torching their district's set.[105]

The conservative New York State Economic Council joined the AFA's textbook crusade and created the American Parents Committee on Education to deal with the issue. Members included prominent industry leaders such as Lammont Du Pont; A. W. Erickson, the board chair of the New York–based advertising agency McCann Erickson Inc.; and Alfred P. Sloan, president of General Motors. For a small fee, this committee distributed information about the Rugg series and other "subversive" textbooks to any interested party. It also offered help and support to groups and individuals in their quest to remove Communist-inspired material from their local public schools.[106] New York State Economic Council president Mervin K. Hart, in fact, went so far as to accuse Rugg's books of being one of the most effective Communist front efforts in the United States.[107] Echoing these sentiments, the ultraconservative American Legion published a pamphlet entitled *Treason in the Textbooks*. A cartoon on the front cover pictured Rugg as a slant-eyed devil putting eyeglasses (with pink lenses, naturally) on schoolchildren. Somewhat clumsily the caption warned: "The 'Frontier Thinkers' are trying to sell our youth the idea that the American way of life has failed."[108] Around this same time Schlink eyed yet another chance to get back at former allies and joined in the feeding frenzy. At a November 1940 conference of twelve hundred Catholic educators he delivered an address on the "Infiltration of Communism in Education."[109]

In late 1940, as part of its plan to garner "Understanding of Private Enterprise," the NAM established a program to help manufacturers and private citizens learn about the textbooks used in their local schools. Fearing a public backlash if the enterprise could be traced back directly to it, the NAM enlisted the help of Ralph W. Roby, a professor of economics at Columbia University and the business editor of *Newsweek* magazine. Although the NAM paid Roby to conduct a survey of public school textbooks, its leaders insisted that they did not influence Roby's evaluations. Assessments were entirely his own and not a business-orchestrated effort to "whitewash private enterprise." Aided by his staff, Roby claimed to review all books based on their merits, evaluating each book's general thesis, educational standards, and research quality. Under no circumstances, assured the NAM, would Roby classify books as simply "good" or "bad."[110] Still, and this is the point at which the investigation got a bit sticky, Roby was encouraged by the NAM to use quotes from the various books to illustrate their attitudes toward the "American form of government" and "the private enterprise system."[111] But, as Lammont Du Pont warned in anticipation of public criticism, a quotation taken out of context could be used to illustrate almost any point. To assure the integrity of the project, and hopefully deflect criticism, the NAM stressed that Roby understood each book and did not misunderstand its thesis.[112] NAM president H. W. Prentis Jr. rushed to provide reassurance. Nothing was biased about the investigation. "Either you must *want* to present a biased picture, or you must be so uninformed that you do not realize you are misrepresenting the situation," he argued. "Neither of these factors is present in our textbook project."[113]

Nevertheless, the NAM maintained, certain questions needed to guide the investigation. How, for example, did each school district determine which textbooks to use? Was this choice left to individual teachers, the school's entire faculty, the principal, or the school system as a whole? To what extent were appropriate laypeople consulted? Also important, according to the same set of standards, was if the textbooks provided an unbiased presentation of a particular subject or, when no unbiased books were available, if teachers sought supplementary material (provided by business) to secure a more balanced picture. Yardsticks for analyzing the authoritativeness and lack of bias in textbooks should include the author's credentials and political bent as well as his or her ability to be objective. If dealing with a controversial issue, a school's evaluation of a particular book should include an assessment of its age appropriateness.[114] "I recognize that what we are doing is fraught with danger," noted one NAM executive, "but these are dangerous times and the stake is Democracy itself."[115]

Although manufacturers continued their mission they were not as successful in influencing public opinion as they had hoped. In fact, the initial campaign to investigate six hundred textbooks received a lukewarm industry response and largely backfired with the public. Many groups, including teachers' and publishers' organizations, reacted negatively to the campaign. Educators and consumer leaders viewed the enterprise as an infringement upon "the right of teachers to teach the truth as they see it" and helped expose it for what it was, "namely . . . an effort to convert the schools into alleyways for the propaganda of business."[116] Several influential educators supported this view and rejected business's interference with school curricula, censorship of teaching freedom, and attempts to label noncompliant teachers as Reds or subversive. Advertising journals such as *Advertising and Selling,* and even the more conservative *Printers' Ink,* advised business to keep its hands off textbooks.[117] Although in his survey Roby criticized a majority of books for being antibusiness and thus un-American in tone, he reluctantly admitted to locating only a few traces of Communist Party doctrines in the books.

Conclusion

In spite of their many efforts, the NAM, the AFA, and other conservative business interests did not garner much support for their attacks on the consumer movement. By the end of the 1930s the general public, and even many advertising interests, refused to acknowledge the U.S. consumer movement as a Communist-infiltrated operation. Thus, the many attempts to unveil a Communist conspiracy, ranging from the abuse of the Dies Committee's congressional privileges to the investigations of educators and school material, largely failed. To some extent this was due to the temper of the times; although the United States was hardly a bastion of left-wing politics on the eve of World War II, it was more progressive than it had been for at least a generation. When the Red-hunting campaigns returned in the late 1940s and early 1950s, the nation's mood had changed and the campaigns were able to reshape business and consumer groups.

But when those Red Scare campaigns returned, the consumer movement was no longer a target comparable to organized labor; indeed, it was not even a target at all. By 1940, clearly, the massive amount of outreach and cooperation between the business community and the consumer movement had led Americans to recognize and be more accepting of consumer activism in their daily activities. Thus, viewing the consumer movement as Communist or subversive was not congruent with their own experiences. One writer for *Printers' Ink* put it well in late 1940: "Today there are many indications that consumers and business have a better and more sympathetic understanding of each other's problems. Even Consumers Union, which has been most vociferous in its strictures on business, has calmed down considerably. Wider experience has shown consumer advocates that there are no such things as pure blacks or whites, particularly in such a complicated field as the relations between consumers and business."[118]

This social acceptance, however, came at a price. Although mainstreaming protected consumer advocates from attack, it also downplayed, even marginalized, some of the movement's original demands and concerns. Whereas in the early 1930s advocates were dedicated to reforming advertising radically so that commercial information would serve the public more than it did business, by the end of the decade they had come to accept that advertising, for better or for worse, was entrenched in the political economy. After the passage of the Wheeler-Lea Amendment in 1938 the parameters for advertising's legitimate discussion appeared to have been established anew, and in this sphere the radical critique that had first inspired the consumer movement did not fit. Although under this arrangement the consumer movement was protected against right-wing accusations of Communist infiltration, it also had little impact on the status quo. On a certain level, most consumer advocates seemed resigned to their position and considered a token presence better than none at all.

Epilogue

Although the advertising industry's strategy to control its practices was crowned with success, its PR program was far from foolproof. The start of World War II in early fall 1939 further complicated its plans for garnering public support. Even before the United States became actively involved in the war a large portion of all raw materials were tagged for war-related products and equipment, which left the consumer market with fewer products. The gradual shift from a consumer economy to a defense economy posed new questions about advertising's role and function. Manufacturers, fearing that promoting consumer products when raw materials were scarce might lead to black markets or even inflation, worried that advertising during such circumstances might be considered unpatriotic and reflect poorly on the industry.

It did not take long, however, before advertisers arrived at an almost perfect PR plan for the war. Organizing its forces under what would be known as the Advertising Council—or the War Advertising Council between 1943 and 1945—the advertising industry pooled its resources to aid the government's home-front program. In exchange for tax benefits, advertisers used their campaigns to encourage citizens to join the armed forces, seek work in war production industries, ration, and plant victory gardens. Although manufacturers for the consumer market had less to sell, they could justify their product advertising on the ground that it served a patriotic function. That continuous advertising allowed them to keep their brands before the public for the war's duration and provided a great tax shelter further enhanced its attractiveness. Moreover, and just as important, the practice earned the industry a reputation of "helping America win the war," and its collaborative experience with the Office of War Information facilitated close relationships between the advertising industry and key figures in Washington, D.C.

To avoid watching its PR gains from the 1930s dwindle, the advertising industry sharpened its techniques and waited to wield them in new arenas. The Advertising Council initially worked to secure advertisers' right to practice throughout the war despite major shortages and the logical assumption that consumer-product advertising would therefore stimulate demand, spur inflation, and prove counterproductive to the war effort. The council defended advertising's privileged wartime position, arguing that it was performing an indispensable patriotic duty. Its unstated but overarching goal was to have the U.S. public internalize a view of advertising as a democratic institution instrumental to the defeat of the Axis powers. By the war's end the Advertising Council asked how an institution that had contributed close to one billion dollars to the war effort, cooperated with the government against enemies of the United States, and promoted world peace to boot could ever be viewed in an unfavorable light. The Advertising Council's purpose, as Frank W. Fox argues, was to promote "the ad behind the ad," that is, to use advertising to sell not only products but also the institutions and ideology behind them.[1]

The few objections to this collaboration between government and business came mainly from Consumers Union of the United States Inc. (CU). Speaking on behalf of the consumer organization, President Colston E. Warne offered no objection to government advertising but showed resentment toward a system in which advertisers were given tax breaks for what amounted to goodwill advertising.[2] This criticism fell on deaf ears, however, and throughout the war CU vowed to help consumers during a time of price controls, rationing, and material shortages.[3] With a less receptive audience for its criticism of advertising and little prospect of instituting tangible changes, advertising reform quickly faded in prominence at CU. It had already all but vanished at Consumers' Research Inc. (CR).

By the end of the war in 1945 the advertising industry found itself in a quite favorable position and faced the postwar era with renewed enthusiasm. Due in part to the Advertising Council's work, the advertising industry enjoyed improved relations with the public and, as the sociologist C. Wright Mills pointed out, the intimate working relationship between business, industry, and government leaders had become more congenial.[4] Recognizing the Advertising Council's PR value, the advertising industry decided to make it a permanent fixture of the postwar era. No longer affiliated with the government, the postwar Advertising Council was free to chart its own course. Whereas the council's wartime campaigns had asked people to plant vegetables and buy War Bonds to express their patriotism, its postwar campaigns commercialized this noble sentiment. Patriotism was now tied to the unconditional acceptance of free enterprise, which some now termed "People's Capitalism."[5] The Advertising Council's new intent, observes the historian Robert Griffith, was to "promote an image of advertising as a responsible and civic-spirited industry, of the U.S. economy as a uniquely productive system of free enterprise, and of America as a dynamic, classless, and benignly consensual society."[6] The Advertising Council's postwar campaigns, including its unabashed flag-waving and unconditional declaration of "true Americanism," helped to stifle and mute advertising criticism. On the heels of a world war, many hesitated to attack an institution claiming to epitomize Americanism, and when dissident opinion became intolerable in the late 1940s and early 1950s, even fewer voices spoke out.[7] If in the 1930s advertising had been a controversial, even scorned, undertaking in the minds of many Americans, twenty years later it was firmly entrenched in democracy, a fixture of "the good life" and "the American dream."

Over time advertising's legitimacy in locating itself in the firmament of U.S. society would increase. In 1942, for example, when First Amendment protection for commercial speech was brought before the U.S. Supreme Court, the justices ruled unanimously against advertisers.[8] Gradually, however, as many social institutions became increasingly beholden to advertisers, commercial speech won a series of important judicial victories. As shopping malls replaced Main Street as the central site for commerce and congregation, mall owners fought several successful legal battles to prevent political opinions and politically controversial ideas from entering the new public spheres. Such ideas, it was believed, might interfere with the mall visitors' shopping experience and ability to express their freedom (of choice) as consumers.[9] Although advertising today still does not enjoy the same First Amendment protection that political speech does, the day when this will happen might not be far away.[10] As its practices become cemented in law it will be officially labeled off-limits to political scrutiny and debate.

And just when legal protection for commercial speech was expanding, the laws that regulate advertising and protect consumers against false and misleading promotional information were stagnating. Today, as in 1938, the Wheeler-Lea Amendment to the Federal Trade Commission Act controls advertising regulation. Even when the law was written it was criticized for providing weak consumer protection. When one considers the massive increase in advertising and commercialization since then, the law looks even less well equipped to protect consumers today.[11] Regardless of the letter of the law, however, with advertising regulation the key factor is how aggressively the government wishes to pursue the matter. In a political environment in which business interests are dominant and consumer interests are dormant, one should expect relatively lax regulation. And that is exactly what has happened.

This point is never far from my narrative. Consumer activism is the straw the stirs the drink of public activism around advertising regulation. When advertising and corporations fostered a supportive environment for their ideas, consumer activism, which in the 1930s had served as a counterforce to these influences, declined. A scarcity of consumer products during the war had forced CU to put product testing on the back burner and to prioritize consumer guidance. As the war ended, pent-up consumer demand combined with the availability of new products revitalized the need for commodity testing. Wartime savings had also enabled many Americans to participate in the postwar consumer boom and increase their standard of living. Between 1946 and 1950, for example, Americans purchased 21.4 million automobiles, more than 20 million refrigerators, 5.5 million electric stoves, and 11.6 million television sets.[12]

The sudden popularity of television put people in even closer proximity to advertising, and, as Lawrence R. Samuel and other scholars argue, the seamless merging of entertainment and commercial values in this new medium helped fan the flames of consumerism and spending in postwar America.[13] In sharp contrast to the discourse surrounding the introduction of radio a couple of decades earlier, television faced no serious challenges to its purely commercial nature.[14] To some extent the decline and eventual muzzling of commercial broadcasting's opponents from the 1930s through the 1940s paralleled the transformation of the consumer movement over the same decades. Both movements sought federal legislation to alter the course of major industries in the 1930s—and both lost. Those who wished to be considered legitimate advocates for reform thereafter had to accept commercial broadcasting and advertising as necessary institutions. The federal government, convinced that increased levels of advertising would boost consumption, combat economic sluggishness, and raise the standard of living, supported television's commercialization.[15]

The general absence of public objection to this new commercial medium did not necessarily mean that such sentiments did not exist or that everyone welcomed the more commercialized culture.[16] Today an increasing number of scholars contend that most histories of postwar America fail to account for the psychological complexity of those years, including the vitality and variety of subordinate cultures that flourished. "If consensus did indeed characterize America's national culture in the 1950s," Robert Griffith remarked, "it was perhaps to a degree we have not fully appreciated, a consensus manufactured by America's corporate leaders, packaged by the advertising industry, and merchandized through the channels of mass communication."[17]

Advertising was arguably seen as less problematic in the postwar era than it had been previously, and it is quite possible that the postwar economic prosperity helped shield the industry from a new wave of consumer attacks. Although specific advertisements were lampooned for being loud, annoying, or obnoxious, few critics questioned advertising as an institution—and no one called for the kind of draconian regulation of advertising that was propounded by many in the 1930s. That the country did not experience another economic depression after World War II does not fully explain the general shift in advertising criticism, however. If an economic upturn indicates consumer contentment with advertising, how can we account for the radical critique of advertising that emerged in the late 1920s at the height of another economic boom? One difference is that in contrast to the 1920s, the postwar era was marked by the advertising industry's intensive PR strategies, which had managed to channel advertising into unthreatening forms that did not belie the industry's claims of being a democratic and necessary U.S. institution.

Decreased consumer militancy coupled with new consumption patterns also affected CU. Many consumers became interested in learning as much as possible about products before they purchased them, and the circulation of *Consumer Reports* skyrocketed. In March 1944 the magazine had a circulation of only fifty-five thousand, but by June 1949 the number had increased to two hundred seventy-five thousand. Despite the fivefold increase in circulation, the magazine's leaders were frustrated in their efforts to reach a socioeconomic cross section of U.S. consumers and continued to appeal primarily to professional middle- and upper-middle-income individuals.[18]

Between 1944 and 1949 *Consumer Reports* emerged as a unique U.S. institution and also as the only ongoing success of the 1930s consumer movement. That this huge demand for product testing developed in a more conservative political climate, however, forced a major transition for CU. Excited over this renewed interest and weary from the organization's experiences with the Dies Committee and subsequent allegations of un-American activities that lasted into the 1950s, Arthur Kallet led a fight to intensify CU's testing component but left the task of organizing consumers to others. In the late 1930s CU had established a permanent presence in Washington, D.C., to help the organization stay informed about the latest capital news and also keep the consumer's point of view before lawmakers. But Kallet was no longer comfortable with CU's role in legislative battles and turned his back on anything that could be interpreted as political. He was so committed to this agenda, in fact, that he objected to CU's rating of the labor conditions under which featured products were made and developed a rather hostile attitude toward unions even though these issues had been of utmost importance to him when CU was formed some twenty years earlier. Kallet also worried that maintaining CU as a membership-based organization might leave it open to further right-wing accusations of harboring Communist sympathizers. The organization would be much better served, he argued, if *Consumer Reports* could be converted into a subscription- and newsstand-based publication.

In 1954, after thirteen years as a target of Red-baiting, CU was finally cleared of Communist charges, but the experience had taken its toll. As time went on it became increasingly obvious that Kallet's vision of CU diverged wildly from the other officers' views, and in 1957, amid massive turmoil, Kallet was removed from his post as director. Although the organization's transformation into a pure product-testing agency was prevented, CU did not embrace activism as it had done in the past. Throughout the late 1950s and into the 1960s, the group expanded its increasingly successful testing operation and *Consumer Reports.* All was not lost from a consumer activism perspective, however. By the late 1990s, the organization again let its presence be known on Capitol Hill as it lobbied for laws to protect consumers of prescription drugs and telecommunication services.[19]

CR had a much less satisfying postwar experience. Represented by Frederick J. Schlink, M. C. Phillips, and J. B. Matthews, CR continued its attacks on CU throughout the 1950s. The organization's membership leveled off at around one hundred thousand (with an occasional push to more than one hundred fifty thousand) until April 1980, when M. Stanton Evans took over the daily operations. Schlink, by then in his late eighties, continued to head CR's testing facilities until Evans closed them down. By the late 1990s CR's monthly newsletter, reaching only 15,000 members, no longer focused on commodity testing but instead addressed policy issues affecting consumers.[20]

During this bleak period a few consumer victories were won, however. A Consumers' Bill of Rights and a presidential advisor for consumer affairs were instituted in 1964. And in 1967 the Consumer Federation of America was established to cooperate with a wide range of consumer-interest groups and to represent consumer interests and demands before Congress and federal regulatory agencies.[21] Obviously, compared with the 1930s the postwar era was by no means a hotbed of consumer activism. Not until the 1960s did the United States experience yet another intense wave of politically organized consumers. Throughout the 1960s and early 1970s consumer organizations witnessed steady support for their demands, and during the 1970s a variety of national consumer groups, each with specialized interests and a few with charismatic leaders, emerged.

The most influential person in the 1960s and 1970s consumer movement was without doubt Ralph Nader. In 1963 the young lawyer published *Unsafe at Any Speed,* a highly acclaimed and widely discussed exposé of the auto industry and its utter disregard for consumer safety.[22] The book indicted unsafe automobile designs and targeted General Motors' Corvair as a particularly glaring example. When it became publicly known that General Motors had hired private detectives to dig up information that might discredit Nader, a Senate subcommittee was set up to investigate. The outcome was a personal apology from the president of General Motors and a handsome financial settlement that Nader used to start the Center for the Study of Responsive Law.[23]

Nader transformed the interest in consumer issues into a movement that could effectively counter the power held by business in the marketplace. During the latter part of the 1960s he helped uncover abuses committed by U.S. businesses and the government against individual consumers, and in 1968 he recruited a task force of students to investigate the Federal Trade Commission (FTC). Business interests, he found, were manipulating the agency to the extent that it failed to fulfill its mandate. Hoping to invigorate the citizenry to fight corporate power and make businesses accountable to the people, Nader experimented with new strategies of citizen action. His efforts had a strong impact, and in the period between 1967 and 1973 Congress enacted more than twenty-five laws to regulate corporate conduct in consumer and environmental fields.[24]

The difference between CU and the new wave of consumer activism led by Nader was quite obvious. By the 1970s CU virtually shunned activism and focused primarily on consumer-product testing. By 1971 the circulation of *Consumer Reports* had reached two million copies, and its rating service was so influential that it could make or break a product. The makers of Maytag washing machines and Volkswagen cars, for example, attributed their ability to penetrate hitherto oligopolistic markets to the publication's favorable ratings.[25] Nader, who in the late 1960s had been elected to CU's board of directors, grew increasingly impatient with the organization's nonactivist bent. "There is a division of philosophy on the Board as to how much energy and resources are to be directed toward changing major consumer injustices through consumer action instead of just informing some consumers about some of them," he observed in his 1975 resignation letter. "Neither the majority of the Board, nor most of the upper management nor the employees' union leadership wants to urge or see the fundamental changes needed to make a truly Consumers Union of power, presence and priority."[26] The lack of commitment to activism and outreach, responded Colston E. Warne for CU, was due to the unprofitable nature of these enterprises. "The drop in renewals and new orders plus the comments we received from members indicate quite clearly that *Consumer Reports* should revert to the time-honored manner of reporting on testing and general consumer information rather than using the funds they provide for an advocacy role."[27] This difference in outlook illustrated quite clearly how far CU had fallen from the glory days of the 1930s, when it evinced a militancy that Nader wished to resurrect. "I can better use the 10 days a year, which would be spent on CU matters, in other pursuits within the consumer movement—more broadly defined," Nader concluded.[28]

A watershed in the third era of consumer activity was the 1978 defeat of legislation to create a consumer-advocacy agency. The idea of a Department of the Consumer to parallel the Departments of Commerce and Labor had first been introduced back in the early 1930s. In the 1970s and under the leadership of Nader, however, attention shifted from the creation of an agency without regulatory powers to one entrusted with monitoring the activities of other government agencies and, if necessary, the authority to intervene in their regulatory decision making on consumers' behalf. Nader pushed for this particular structure because he believed that regulatory responsibility was incompatible with advocacy activity. The Consumer Federation of America and many of its member organizations, CU, the Nader network, and about one hundred trade groups worked diligently to get the advocacy organization established. Much to their dismay, however, the plan soon faced opposition from a broad coalition of business interests. Opponents in the business community envisioned an agency with extensive powers and the ability to intervene in all aspects of government. They claimed that the proposed agency would create a new bureaucracy, increase the complexity of regulatory hearings, and force the disclosure of trade secrets. In the end, they managed to defeat the plan.[29]

From the late 1960s to the mid-1970s consumer activists were successful in Congress, but during the Jimmy Carter administration they started to lose momentum. Some scholars offer public disenchantment with government as a possible explanation whereas others point to a rejuvenated Republican Party as the reason. The (re)discovery of intense political lobbying and extensive PR by the business community point toward other reasons for consumer activism's decline.[30]

Faced with a largely sympathetic political environment since the late 1940s, the business community had fallen into complacency, so when public criticism of its conduct emerged in the 1960s, corporate America initially failed to appreciate its significance. After all, business was still providing the public with what it most wanted: a steady increase in real living standards. Even in the 1960s political activity on business's behalf was not considered necessary, so lobbying efforts, by contemporary standards, were limited. Well-funded trade organizations to defend business's interests were not a high priority. By the mid-1970s, however, business woke up to regulation's restraints, costs, burdens, and bureaucracies. This creeping government encroachment upon its autonomy had to be resisted by direct political action.[31] This brings us to the final piece of this book's puzzle: corporate public relations. Many techniques that the advertising industry, along with broadcasting and telecommunications, had helped develop became widely adopted across the corporate sector. Managing public thought became mandatory corporate policy.

The U.S. Chamber of Commerce, which by the 1960s was frequently dismissed as a feeble and out-of-date organ, met the challenge. Between 1974 and 1980 the business organization doubled its membership to one hundred sixty thousand and tripled its annual budget to sixty-eight million dollars. Through aggressive new leadership the Chamber of Commerce pioneered for business the seeding of political action committees (PACs), direct mail, and technologically sophisticated grassroots-organizing techniques, many of them shamelessly copied from public-interest groups.[32] Organized labor, the inventor of PACs, soon found its efforts overshadowed by business might. Whereas 201 prolabor PACs hit Washington, D.C., in 1974 compared with 89 corporate sponsored PACs, by 1978 the 784 corporate PACs and another 500 or so PACs associated with trade associations or other businesses vastly outweighed the 217 sponsored by labor.[33]

Business interests also increased their influence in Washington, D.C. Between 1968 and 1978 the number of corporations with public affairs offices there skyrocketed from one hundred to more than five hundred, and many groups grew substantially in size. Trade organizations also increased their Washington, D.C., presence. In 1977 an average of one association a week relocated its main office to the nation's capital, bringing the total number of trade associations headquartered there to two thousand. And in 1973 the National Association of Manufacturers (NAM) moved its headquarters to Washington, D.C., as part of an effort to upgrade its lobbying activities.[34] Between 1970 and 1986 business representatives were three times more likely to testify at House and Senate hearings than were major consumer organizations. The presence of business PACs and lobbying groups intensified during the 1980s. In addition to lobbying, corporations realized that they could use PAC money to support business-friendly candidates to defeat politicians that did not favor unrestricted business power, and shareholders and employees were encouraged to raise funds for PACs. Neither did other grassroots strategies such as Nader's strength in dealing with the press pass unnoticed. By the mid-1970s an increasing number of CEOs were receiving formal training in handling the public and the mass media.[35]

Another dimension of the corporate response to the gains made by left-wing, liberal forces during the 1960s and 1970s took place on an ideological level. In addition to increased lobbying and press manipulation, business also engaged in an organized attempt to influence intellectual and public opinion. This surge in advocacy advertising, geared toward the mass media, universities, and institutions both public and private, worked to counter the anticorporate attitude that business claimed to have detected in the mass media. By the end of the 1970s, according to the political scientist David Vogel, major corporate advertisers were spending about one-third of all their advertising dollars on selling consumers the business system, industry, and political ideology behind their commodities.[36] In a manner that echoed their plotting in the 1930s, corporations concerned about unfriendly teachers increased their endeavors to influence university education and research. Far from giving unrestricted grants to schools and universities on the basis of their academic reputation, corporations cooperated only with schools, departments, institutions, and faculty that appeared likely to support and promote corporate objectives and values.

Finally, to counteract the funding that public interest and left-leaning organizations had traditionally received from liberal interest groups, business established its own foundations to promote its conservative ideology. Grants from these institutions helped established conservative associations and fostered new ones. These business-backed foundations also produced an impressive array of newsletters, reports, magazines, books, and pamphlets and made sure they were both visible and available to scholars and journalists interested in public-policy issues affecting business. By the end of the 1970s, argues Vogel, this ideological onslaught by business interests had helped pave the way for the neoliberal belief that regulation by markets was inevitably superior to regulation by government in the public interest. Neoliberalism, then, made the consumer movement anathema or at the very least irrelevant.[37]

The business-sponsored drive toward neoliberalism reached center stage with the election of Ronald Reagan in 1980, and by that time the third wave of consumer activism was rapidly retreating. Not only did Reagan make a series of deregulatory decisions that adversely affected consumers but he also cut funding to consumer-protection agencies and eliminated most grants and contracts to consumer groups. CU, the Consumer Federation of America, and Public Citizen, the Nader flagship organization, suffered financially. Neither was most of the 1990s a good period for consumer activists. Although some people in the movement hailed Bill Clinton for his success in regulating telemarketing, he was also instrumental in passing legislation, including the 1996 Telecommunications Act, that was detrimental to consumers. From a consumer's point of view, some critics argue, Clinton's record was not very impressive.[38]

As the United States entered the 1980s, business was grabbing increased recognition for its claim that commercial speech deserved the same First Amendment protection that political opinions enjoyed.[39] Unlike the second wave of consumer activism, which specifically targeted advertising, the third wave focused primarily on corporate reform and ignored advertising's encroachments on free speech's territory. The advertising critique that emerged in the 1960s rarely, if ever, questioned advertising's economic function but concentrated instead on its symbolic nature: how certain advertising images helped shape people's views of themselves, others, and society in general. One of the first people to contemplate advertising's adverse influences on the individual was Vance Packard. Much like consumer advocates of the 1930s, Packard was concerned about the advertising industry's penchant for probing consumers' fears and pandering to their (unconscious) longings. In contrast to consumer advocates, however, Packard did not urge for legislation or regulation to prohibit this practice but merely alerted consumers about its pitfalls in his 1958 book *The Hidden Persuaders*.[40] A sign of the advertising industry's ideological dominance in the postwar era was that in his book—probably the most widely read and discussed attack on the industry prior to the 1970s—Packard did not even posit the notion that an outraged public has the right to demand institutional change.

Advertising's role in manipulating women was also a central theme in Betty Friedan's groundbreaking book *The Feminine Mystique,* which signaled the beginning of a feminist critique of advertising that pushed women into domesticity and consumption.[41] In numerous books and articles published in the late 1960s and later, writers argued that advertising's power to define female beauty had a devastating impact on women's self-esteem and that it also affected children adversely. Advertising's damaging effect on women remains central to contemporary feminist scholarship.[42] In contrast to consumer advocates of the 1930s, who believed that people had a right to make demands on advertising, even some of the most radical feminists wanted merely to see the images of women altered so that they would be less stereotypical and therefore less harmful. Ad content otherwise was not considered within the realm of what could be changed. And the less optimistic feminist critics simply hoped to equip consumers with enough knowledge and self-esteem to resist the advertised messages. This, however, did not mean that consumers' battle against advertising had been lost.

Indeed, judging from the history of consumer activism, its prominence is periodic, taking shape every thirty years or so. Looking back, we can see how consumer activism in the Progressive Era was followed by the 1930s consumer movement and then by yet another movement some thirty years later. Not surprisingly, many consumer activists looked to the late 1990s with renewed hope for change. And a new consumer movement did manifest itself by the end of the decade. This militant movement rose up in response to the futility of the inside-the-Beltway consumer activism drowned by the tidal wave of business lobbying power and politicians awash in campaign contributions. These new consumer activists are more than willing to demonstrate as well as agitate for legislation.

This fourth wave of consumer activism addresses all the issues that concerned previous consumer movements. Sweatshop conditions, child labor, environmental regulation, food safety (genetically engineered foods), corporate power (the World Trade Organization, the International Monetary Fund, the World Bank), and overcommercialization are among its major focuses. Its heterogeneity hearkens back to the first wave of consumer activists in the Progressive Era and their emphasis on labor conditions and public health across all classes. One main difference between the recent wave of consumer activism and those of the past is its global focus. Whereas past generations of consumer activists concentrated their efforts on national problems, the new wave of activism tends to look at consumer issues from a global perspective and is frequently referred to as the antiglobalization movement. Despite this characterization, its proponents are not necessarily xenophobic or nationalistic; they simply oppose globalization that serves investors and corporate interests, not globalization per se.

Much like those in the 1930s consumer movement, contemporary consumer activists are increasingly concerned with the direct and indirect effects of commercialism. They worry about its influence on cultural and social institutions such as the mass media and the educational system.[43] Ironically enough, given that we live in the so-called information age, corporate conduct, including its commercial strategies, is more difficult to monitor than ever. Because commercial values have become entrenched in our everyday life and commercial speech is gaining increased First Amendment protection, consumer advocates and citizens face a greater challenge in gaining a critical perspective on commercialism. In many respects corporate branding behaves like an aggressive virus: It outpaces its critics and is financially well equipped to fend off any activist remedy.[44]

Whereas past consumer movements were mostly able to keep a fairly narrow focus, the latest wave of consumer activism fights commercialism on so many fronts that it often must spread itself thin. The extent to which it will be able to sustain itself depends to a large degree on its ability to build coalitions with other groups. As we saw in the 1930s, however, this strategy is not without risk because it can provide business with a chance to interject its own brand of consumer activism and effectively alter the contest. Given the escalating public concerns over advertising and commercialization, however, this might be a risk worth taking.

Key Players

Advertising Council. Known as the War Advertising Council between 1943 and 1945, this group began as an attempt by the advertising industry to pool its resources to aid the government's home-front program. Advertisers launched campaigns to encourage armed forces enrollment, war production industries work, rationing, and victory gardens and received tax benefits in exchange. Flushed with its success and positive public sentiment, the council in its postwar campaigns tied patriotism to unbridled free enterprise and helped stifle advertising criticism.

Advertising Federation of America (AFA). Established in 1929 after the demise of the Associated Advertising Clubs of the World, this group's primary objective was to formulate general business policies for national advertising associations and major advertising clubs. The AFA also worked to standardize advertising rates and contracting practices, invested in research, and effected change in state advertising bills. In 1934 it led the charge for industry self-regulation and backed plans by other business organizations to keep control of advertising. It organized outreach to schools, clubs, associations, and consumer organizations to combat the growing number of consumer advocates and eventually cooperated only with what it considered the legitimate segments of the consumer movement. In 1968 the AFA changed its name to the American Advertising Federation.

American Association of Advertising Agencies (AAAA). This organization was founded in 1917 to protect the interests of the large advertising agencies most closely connected with national advertising. Its Consumer's Advertising Council and its Committee on Consumer Relations in Advertising were designed as PR attempts to stop criticism of advertising.

Association of National Advertisers. In 1915 this group splintered from the Associated Advertising Clubs of the World and eventually rose to prominence as the official voice for national advertising interests.

John Benson. He served as president of the American Association of Advertising Agencies during the tumultuous 1930s and emerged as a vocal defender of the advertising industry.

Stuart Chase. A writer critical of business and advertising, he teamed with Frederick J. Schlink in 1927 for the exposé *Your Money's Worth: A Study in the Waste of the Consumer's Dollars.* With Schlink he founded Consumers' Research (CR) in 1929. Chase resigned as president of the national group in 1932 to concentrate on his writing.

Committee on Educational Cooperation (CEC). Formed by the NAM in 1938, the organization was designed to expound the benefits of free enterprise. Its aggressive program garnered favor with Columbia University's Teachers College, which trained many public school educators, as well as other leaders in elementary and higher education. Its newsletters, posters, and films reached more than half of all high school students and at least one-third of all junior high school students.

Committee on Public Information (CPI). Also known as the Creel Commission after its leader, George Creel, this organization was established by Woodrow Wilson in 1917 to mount an extensive propaganda campaign to mobilize U.S. support for World War I.

Consumer Division of Crowell Publishing. Helmed by the editor of the *Women's Home Companion,* Anna Steese Richardson, this conservative bureau was established in 1937 to serve as an industry front group. Through a series of programs and outreach efforts it tried to prove to the public that manufacturers, not the government or consumer groups, should provide information about products.

Consumers' Advisory Board (CAB). An advisory body to the National Recovery Administration, the CAB was charged with protecting consumers' interests. Constantly criticized by Frederick J. Schlink for being out of touch, the group had a limited budget and diffuse support, so it could serve only as an ineffectual voice for consumers.

Consumers' Research Inc. (CR). Formed by Stuart Chase and Frederick J. Schlink in 1929, this consumer advocacy group focused on product testing and educating consumers. Until a strike fractured its membership in 1935, it reigned as the champion of consumers. After the group's testing facilities were closed down in the early 1980s, its monthly newsletter focused on policy issues affecting consumers. In addition to a confidential list of product ratings, CR published *Consumers' Research General Bulletin* (renamed *Consumers' Research Bulletin* in 1935) and, beginning in 1937, *Consumers' Digest.*

Consumers Union of the United States Inc. (CU). Born from a 1935 strike at CR and incorporated in 1936, this group was founded by Arthur Kallet, Colston E. Warne, and other Consumers' Research members. Committed to product testing and consumer protection, it published *Consumers Union Reports.* Unlike CR, CU was strongly committed to linking its activities with larger political struggles. In 1942, *Consumers Union Reports* was renamed *Consumer Reports.* This publication is still the most popular consumer magazine in the United States and the only ongoing success of the 1930s consumer movement.

Royal S. Copeland. A Democratic senator from New York, Copeland spent ten years practicing medicine in Michigan. When he chaired an allegedly impartial hearing on amendments to the Federal Food and Drugs Act of 1906, his conservatism and his commercial endorsements of products with dubious health claims made him the perfect target for Arthur Kallet and others at Consumers' Research. Although he championed his own legislation, he later withdrew his support when the bill was watered down by business interests.

Martin Dies. As chair of the Dies Committee, the forerunner of the House Un-American Activities Committee, this Democrat from Texas worked to discredit organized labor, dismantle the New Deal, and disband liberal and leftist organizations. Steered initially by J. B. Matthews, Dies presented unconvincing evidence to reveal and remove Communism from the consumer movement.

Food and Drug Administration (FDA). Entrusted with regulating advertising through the Federal Food and Drugs Act of 1906, this body was one candidate for controlling false and misleading advertising. Concerned about its power, however, business leaders worked diligently to make sure the FDA did not control advertising.

Federal Food and Drugs Act of 1906. This law established the FDA's jurisdiction over labeling and branding, but not advertising, of food and drugs.

Federal Trade Commission (FTC). Under the Federal Trade Commission Act of 1914, this body was given the power to investigate business misconduct. Its power to regulate advertising was initially limited to cases in which the promotional strategies of one business hurt that of a competitor. The Wheeler-Lea Amendment extended its regulatory power. The FTC could now impose substantial penalties and intervene when consumers' interests were at stake, albeit after a lengthy and laborious investigation and appeals process.

Institute for Consumer Education. In 1937, Missouri's Stephens College capitalized on an offer from the Alfred P. Sloan Foundation to found this institution to publish and distribute consumer-oriented materials, conduct research, and serve as a unified front for the consumer movement. Dropped after 1941, its Annual National Conference on Consumer Education brought business, education, government, and consumer representatives together for discussions.

Arthur Kallet. An engineer from the American Standards Association, he joined Consumers' Research (CR) as its secretary. With Frederick J. Schlink he wrote *100,000,000 Guinea Pigs,* an indictment of business that became a best seller, and penned his own advocacy book, *Counterfeit,* in 1935. During the legislative hearings to amend the Federal Food and Drugs Act of 1906, he represented CR and fought bitterly against business's attempts at undermining consumer protection in the new law. He was castigated by Frederick J. Schlink, J. B. Matthews, and M. C. Phillips during the CR strike for siding with the workers and was ousted from the organization. With Colston E. Warne, Dewey H. Palmer, and other CR members, he founded CU, where he served as the organization's first director. By the mid-1950s and scarred by persistent right-wing attacks, Kallet tried to turn CU into a testing outfit only. His views were not endorsed by the organization, and he was removed as director in 1957.

C. B. Larrabee. Although he served as the editor of the conservative trade journal *Printers' Ink,* he nevertheless was among the first in the industry to urge business to take the consumer movement seriously.

Robert S. Lynd. With Helen Merrell Lynd he coauthored *Middletown* and *Middletown in Transition,* sociological studies of a homogeneous town that demonstrated the advance of commercialism on American society. He was later selected as a member of the CAB and formed the Consumers' National Council to act as a national coordinator and clearinghouse for consumer information.

J. B. Matthews. With Ruth Shallcross he wrote *Partners in Plunder: The Cost of Business Dictatorship,* an all-out condemnation of business interests, and he also worked to draft advertising regulations. As a brilliant speaker, he brought verve to CR, of which he was made vice president in 1933, but his aggression in handling the 1935 strike fractured the troubled organization. Because he had previously championed workers and was viewed as one of the group's most radical leaders, his about-face and industry-derived scare tactics were shocking. After he left CR, he worked in Washington, D.C., with Martin Dies to try to bring down CU and other consumer groups by charging them with harboring Communists.

National Association of Manufacturers (NAM). Established in 1895 to protect business interests, this group initiated a huge PR program in 1933 under the leadership of its president, Robert Lund. Attributing the industry's bad image to public misunderstanding, the NAM designed radio, advertising, and PR campaigns to showcase the benefits business had bestowed upon society and to rail against the New Deal. Its program to survey public school textbooks, led by Ralph W. Roby, was perhaps its most concerted academic effort to appear to be unbiased while attempting to sway public opinion. In 1938 it formed the Committee on Educational Cooperation to promote appreciation of free enterprise in schools.

National Better Business Bureau (NBBB). Formed from local advertising clubs across the country in 1925, this group handled consumer complaints, investigated questionable advertising practices, and enforced national advertising standards. It was part of the advertising industry's public relations efforts to get the public to accept this business practice, but its inability to impose sanctions severely limited its effectiveness.

National Consumers' League (NCL). This organization, founded in 1899, emphasized the link between production and consumption and drew middle-class women into what had previously been a working-class struggle. Members labored relentlessly to improve working conditions in factories by passing legislation and granting approval of a white label to those garments produced in factories that refused to employ children, paid its workers fair wages, and treated workers well.

National Recovery Administration (NRA). Established in 1933 in the Franklin Delano Roosevelt administration, this body, headed by Gen. Hugh S. Johnson, was mandated to reorganize and rehabilitate industry by banning unfair competitive practices, creating rules for fair practices, controlling unemployment, ameliorating labor standards, raising or maintaining wages, and standardizing working hours. The NRA also arbitrated codes on minimum prices, competitive practices, maximum work hours, minimum wages, and output levels. Its Blue Eagle advertising program offered a trademark to businesses affiliated with organizations that had signed code agreements with the NRA.

Dewey H. Palmer. As a board member and technical supervisor for CR he faced the ire of Frederick J. Schlink, J. B. Matthews, and M. C. Phillips when he dared to defend the workers during the 1935 strike. Accused of harboring Communist sympathies, he was booted from the group. With Arthur Kallet, Colston E. Warne, and other CR members he helped found CU but left the organization in 1939.

M. C. Phillips. A CR associate and board member, Phillips published *Skin Deep,* her critique of the cosmetics industry, in 1934. Promoted to a board member when her husband, Frederick J. Schlink, held the reins, she bolstered her husband's iron control and played a key role in the 1935 strike. She also served the organization in several editorial capacities and was one of the first to test the mettle of the FTC's new powers under the 1938 Wheeler-Lea Amendment and successfully halted deceptive ads after charging that Pond's Cold Cream employed false advertising.

James Rorty. In *Our Master's Voice: Advertising,* his scathing 1934 critique, Rorty portrayed the industry as an antidemocratic institution that allowed corporations to control the economy and the voting public. He later aligned himself with Cooperative Distributors, a short-lived consumer advocacy group that tested products, published a bulletin with results, and sold the approved products wholesale and by mail order to the public.

Frederick J. Schlink. When he was working as an engineer for the American Engineering Standards Committee (later renamed the American Standards Association), Schlink met Stuart Chase and decided to collaborate on the scathing book *Your*

Money's Worth: A Study in the Waste of the Consumer's Dollars. The success of this partnership led them to form CR, with Schlink as technical director and leader of the organization. His tyrannical rule, buttressed by M. C. Phillips, his wife, fractured the organization and contributed to a strike in 1935. His anger toward the workers, his allegations of Communism, and his newfound contempt for organized labor matched his slide toward the political right. After the strike he joined with J. B. Matthews to smear members of CU and other consumer groups as Communists. He remained CR's leader until 1980 and then headed its testing facilities for a few years until they were closed down by his successor.

Rexford G. Tugwell. As the assistant secretary of agriculture in 1933, Tugwell spearheaded the movement to revise the Federal Food and Drugs Act of 1906. Through his scholarly work Tugwell had already established himself as a champion of consumer rights and as a foe of corporate greed. Despite his concerted efforts to reform advertising, which resulted in numerous bills attached to his name, his frustration over the process caused him to withdraw from the fray.

Tugwell bill (S 1944). Introduced in 1933 to protect the public against false and misleading advertising of foods, drugs, and cosmetics, the bill signaled the beginning of a five-year struggle over federal legislation of advertising that culminated in the 1938 Wheeler-Lea Amendment.

U.S. Chamber of Commerce. Attacks led by this conservative probusiness group preceded the Communist "witch hunt" headed by Martin Dies. Even before 1935 it demanded laws to criminalize advocating the violent overthrow of the government, wanted such writings banned from the U.S. postal system, suggested that aliens promoting said actions should be deported, and urged punishment for those who tried to promote insubordination or disaffection in the U.S. armed forces. Not surprisingly, it supported the Committee on Educational Cooperation and other efforts to promote business.

Colston E. Warne. First an economics professor, he served as a member of CR's advisory board (1929–35), sided with striking workers, and left the organization to form CU in 1936. Warne served CU as its president and on the board of directors from 1936 to 1980.

Legislative Developments, 1933–38

1933

S 1592—CAPPER BILL

Prepared by advertising and publishing interests to prevent the stringent censorship of advertising expressed in S 1944. Introduced in the Senate by Arthur Capper (R-Kans.).

S 1944—TUGWELL BILL

Prevented misbranding and false advertising of food, drugs, and cosmetics. Prepared by the Department of Agriculture. Introduced in the Senate by Royal S. Copeland (D-N.Y.). Introduced in the House by William I. Sirovich (D-N.Y.). Senate hearing held in December 1933.

1934

HR 6376—BLACK BILL

Prepared by proprietary industries as an alternative to S 1944. Introduced in the House by Loring M. Black (D-N.Y.). Introduced in the Senate by Hubert D. Stephens (D-Miss.).

S 2858—MCCARRAN-JENCKES BILL

Reflected the interests of food and pharmaceutical industries. Introduced in the Senate by Patrick A. McCarran (D-Nev.). Introduced in the House by Virginia Ellis Jenckes (D-Ind.).

S 2000—TUGWELL BILL/COPELAND BILL

Revised version of S 1944 that required stricter criteria for false advertising.

HR 7426—SIROVICH BILL

Proposed a relaxation of S 2000's grading requirements. Introduced in the House by William I. Sirovich.

HR 8316—BOLAND BILL

Proposed more regulation of industry than envisioned in S 1944. Prepared for Consumers' Research Inc. Introduced in the House by Patrick J. Boland (D-Mass.).

S 2800—COPELAND BILL

Revised version of S 2000 that removed mandatory grading. Senate hearing held in February and March 1934. Won only tentative support in the Senate and no attention from the House.

1935

S 5—COPELAND BILL

Revised version of S 2800 that simplified the definition of false advertising, dropped compulsory government grading, and struck a provision for voluntary factory inspections at manufacturers' expense. Senate hearing held in March 1935. House hearing held in August 1935. Passed Senate in June 1936.

S 580—MCCARRAN BILL

Reflected the interests of the food and pharmaceutical industries. Introduced in the Senate by Patrick A. McCarran.

HR 3972—MEAD BILL

Reflected the interests of the proprietary industry. Introduced in the Senate by James Michael Mead (D-N.Y.).

HR 8941

A version of HR 3972 introduced in the House by Virginia Ellis Jenckes. House hearing held in August 1935.

S 2909—WALSH BILL

Gave the Federal Trade Commission (FTC) the power to regulate advertising. Introduced in the Senate by David I. Walsh (D-Mass.).

HR 8744

S 2909's companion bill. Introduced in the House by Richard Russell Jr. (D-Ga.).

1937–38

S 5—REVISED VERSION

Did not regulate advertising of food, drugs, and cosmetics. Resubmitted to the Senate as an amendment to the Federal Food and Drugs Act of 1906 by Royal S. Copeland in January 1937. Passed the Senate in March 1937. Passed the House in June 1938 to become law.

HR 300—CHAPMAN BILL

Nearly identical to the version of S 5 passed by the Senate in June 1936. Introduced in the House by Virgil M. Chapman (D-Ky.).

HR 5286—COFFEE BILL

Reflected the concerns and demands of Consumers Union of the United States Inc. Introduced in the House by John M. Coffee (D-Wash.).

HR 3143—LEA BILL

Gave the FTC control over advertising of food, drugs, and cosmetics but gave the Food and Drug Administration (FDA) control over labeling and testing. Introduced in the House by Clarence F. Lea (D-Ga.). Passed the House in June 1937.

S 1077—WHEELER BILL

Theoretically a companion bill to HR 3143 but gave the FDA, not the FTC, power over advertising of food, drugs, and cosmetics. Introduced in the Senate by Burton Wheeler (D-Mont.). Passed the Senate in June 1937.

S 1077—WHEELER-LEA BILL

Contained the exact text of the Lea bill but regulated advertising of food, drugs, and cosmetics by amending the 1914 Federal Trade Commission Act. Introduced in the House by Burton Wheeler. Passed the House in January 1938. Passed the Senate in March 1938 to become law.

Notes

Preface

1. The total advertising expenditures on all media in 2003, according to *Advertising Age,* was $245.48 billion; see Advertising Age, *Fact Pack 2005 Edition: A Supplement to Advertising Age 3rd Annual Guide to Advertising & Marketing* (New York: Advertising Age, 2005), 14 (www.adage.com/images/random/FactPack2005.pdf; accessed July 21, 2005). Although they do not agree about the effects, scholars from all political camps concur that people are exposed to a massive amount of advertising messages on a daily basis; see, for example, Matthew P. McAllister, *The Commercialization of American Culture: New Advertising Control and Democratic Media* (Thousand Oaks, Calif.: Sage Publications, 1996), 38; Michael Dawson, *The Consumer Trap: Big Business Marketing in American Life* (Urbana: University of Illinois Press, 2003), chap. 6; and James B. Twitchell, *Adcult U.S.A.: The Triumph of Advertising in American Culture* (New York: Columbia University Press, 1996), 2. For a discussion of the tension between advertising and democratic principles, see Robert W. McChesney, *Rich Media, Poor Democracy: Communication Politics in Dubious Times* (Urbana: University of Illinois Press, 1999); Robert W. McChesney, *Corporate Media and the Threat to Democracy* (New York: Seven Stories Press, 1997); and Robert W. McChesney, *The Problem of the Media: U.S. Communication Politics in the Twenty-First Century* (New York: Monthly Review Press, 2004). For a general discussion of advertising influences in the lives of young children and teenagers, see Susan Linn, *Consuming Kids: The Hostile Takeover of Childhood* (New York: New Press, 2004); and Alissa Quart, *Branded: The Buying and Selling of Teenagers* (New York: Perseus, 2003).

2. Stuart Elliot, "A Survey of Consumer Attitudes Reveals the Depth of the Challenge that the Agencies Face," *New York Times,* sec. C, April 14, 2004, 8.

3. Twitchell, *Adcult U.S.A.,* 1.

4. Robert W. McChesney, *Telecommunication, Mass Media, and Democracy: The Battle for Control of U.S. Broadcasting, 1928–1935* (New York: Oxford University Press, 1993). For an account of the revived movement to challenge corporate media domination, see McChesney, *The Problem of the Media,* chap. 7.

5. For a discussion of Edward L. Bernays's PR strategies and philosophies, see Edward L. Bernays, *Crystallizing Public Opinion* (1923; repr., New York: Liveright, 1961); Edward L. Bernays, *Propaganda* (New York: Liveright, 1928); Stuart Ewen, *PR! The Social History of Spin* (New York: Basic Books, 1996), 163–73; and Alan R. Raucher, *Public Relations and Business, 1900–1929* (Baltimore: Johns Hopkins University Press, 1968), 126–31.

6. John Stauber and Sheldon Rampton, *Trust Us, We're Experts: How Industry Manipulates Science and Gambles with Your Future* (New York: Tarcher/Putnam, 2001), 17–22; Fraser P. Seitel, *The Practice of Public Relations* (Upper Saddle River, N.J.: Pearson Prentice Hall, 2004), 330.

7. For an excellent discussion of women's contributions to the 1930s consumer movement, see Lizabeth Cohen, *A Consumers' Republic: The Politics of Mass Consumption in Postwar America* (New York: Alfred A. Knopf, 2003).

8. Thorstein Veblen, *The Engineer and the Price System* (1921; repr., New York: Viking Press, 1938); Thorstein Veblen, *Absentee Ownership and Business Enterprise in Recent Times: The Case of America* (1923; repr., New York: Viking Press, 1954); Paul A. Baran and Paul M. Sweezy, *Monopoly Capital* (New York: Monthly Review Press, 1966), 115–31.

Chapter 1: The Rise of a Corporate Culture

1. Richard Hofstadter, *The Age of Reform: From Bryan to F.D.R.* (1955; repr., New York: Vintage Books, 1960), 174.

2. For a discussion of advertising's role in creating national markets, see Susan Strasser, *Satisfaction Guaranteed: The Making of the American Mass Market* (New York: Pantheon Books, 1989); Richard S. Tedlow, *New and Improved: The Story of Mass Marketing in America* (New York: Basic Books, 1990); and Daniel Pope, *The Making of Modern Advertising* (New York: Basic Books, 1983), chap. 2.

3. For a discussion of the rise of corporations in America, see William G. Roy, *Socializing Capital: The Rise of the Large Industrial Corporation in America* (Princeton, N.J.: Princeton University Press, 1997).

4. Naomi Lamoreaux, *The Great Merger Movement in American Business, 1885–1904* (Cambridge: Cambridge University Press, 1985), 1.

5. Ibid., 108; Richard L. McCormick, "The Discovery that Business Corrupts Politics: A Reappraisal of the Origins of Progressivism," *American Historical Review* 86, no. 2 (April 1981): 247–74.

6. Lamoreaux, *Great Merger Movement,* 3.

7. The classic statements remain Thorstein Veblen, *The Engineers and the Price*

System (1921; repr., New York: Viking Press, 1938); and Thorstein Veblen, *Absentee Ownership and Business Enterprise in Recent Times: The Case of America* (1923; repr., New York: Viking Press, 1954). See also Baran and Sweezy, *Monopoly Capital;* and Merle Curti, "The Changing Concept of Human Nature in the Literature of American Advertising," *Business History Review* 41, no. 4 (Winter 1967): 346.

8. Stephen Fox, *The Mirror Makers: A History of American Advertising and Its Creators* (1984; repr., Urbana: University of Illinois Press, 1997), 39.

9. Juliann Sivulka, *Soap, Sex, and Cigarettes: A Cultural History of American Advertising* (Belmont, Calif.: Wadsworth, 1998), 47; Fox, *Mirror Makers,* 38–39.

10. Pope, *Making of Modern Advertising,* 23. For a discussion of business expenditures on advertising between 1880 and 1942, see Martha L. Olney, *Buy Now, Pay Later: Advertising, Credit, and Consumer Durables in the 1920s* (Chapel Hill: University of North Carolina Press, 1991), chap. 5.

11. Gerald J. Baldasty, *The Commercialization of News in the Nineteenth Century* (Madison: University of Wisconsin Press, 1992), 59–60. See also McChesney, *Corporate Media,* 9–17.

12. Pope, *Making of Modern Advertising,* 30; Baldasty, *Commercialization of News,* 59.

13. For a discussion of the rise of a national magazine industry, see Louis Filler, *The Muckrakers* (1968; repr., Stanford, Calif.: Stanford University Press, 1993); Matthew Schneirov, *The Dream of a New Social Order: Popular Magazines in America, 1893–1914* (New York: Columbia University Press, 1994); and Richard Ohman, *Selling Culture: Magazines, Markets, and Class at the Turn of the Twentieth Century* (London: Verso, 1998), chap. 2.

14. Ohmann, *Selling Culture,* 83–85; Pope, *Making of Modern Advertising,* 43–45; Sivulka, *Soap, Sex, and Cigarettes,* 82–83; Strasser, *Satisfaction Guaranteed,* 91.

15. Strasser, *Satisfaction Guaranteed,* 83–88.

16. Juliann Sivulka, *Stronger than Dirt: A Cultural History of Advertising Personal Hygiene in America, 1875 to 1940* (New York: Humanity Books, 2001), 121–22.

17. Strasser, *Satisfaction Guaranteed,* 30–31.

18. Melvin Anshen, "The Rediscovery of the Consumer," *Journal of Marketing* (January 1941): 248–53, clipping in box 22, folder 13, Consumers' Research Papers, Special Collections and University Archives, Rutgers University, New Brunswick, N.J.

19. Strasser, *Satisfaction Guaranteed,* 255.

20. Ibid. See also Stuart Ewen, *Captains of Consciousness: Advertising and the Social Roots of Consumer Culture* (New York: McGraw-Hill, 1976), 115; and Stuart Ewen and Elizabeth Ewen, *Channels of Desire: Mass Images and the Shaping of American Consciousness* (New York: McGraw-Hill, 1982), 57–63.

21. Kathy Peiss, *Cheap Amusements: Working Women and Leisure in Turn-of-the-Century New York* (Philadelphia: Temple University Press, 1986); Andrew R. Heinze, *Adapting to Abundance: Jewish Immigrants, Mass Consumption, and the Search for*

American Identity (New York: Columbia University Press, 1990). Contemporary scholars, most notably Simon N. Patten, also celebrated commercialization as a liberating social force; see, for example, Simon N. Patten, *The New Basis of Civilization,* ed. Daniel M. Fox (Cambridge, Mass.: Belknap Press of Harvard University Press, 1968).

22. Roland Marchand, *Advertising the American Dream: Making Way for Modernity, 1920–1940* (Berkeley: University of California Press, 1985), 217–22.

23. Charles McGovern, "Consumption and Citizenship in the United States, 1900–1940," in *Getting and Spending: European and American Consumer Societies in the Twentieth Century,* ed. Susan Strasser, Charles McGovern, and Matthias Judt (Cambridge: Cambridge University Press, 1998), 50.

24. Stuart Ewen, *PR! The Social History of Spin* (New York: Basic Books, 1996), 42–43. For a general discussion of middle-class tensions in reaction to modernism, see T. J. Jackson Lears, *No Place of Grace: Antimodernism and the Transformation of American Culture, 1880–1920* (1983; repr., Chicago: University of Chicago Press, 1994).

25. For an excellent discussion of the Progressive movement see Michael McGerr, *A Fierce Discontent: The Rise and Fall of the Progressive Movement in America, 1870–1920* (New York: Free Press, 2003); Hofstadter, *Age of Reform,* chap. 6.

26. James Harvey Young, *The Medical Messiahs: A Social History of Health Quackery in Twentieth-Century America* (1967; repr., Princeton, N.J.: Princeton University Press, 1992), 32–35.

27. Filler, *Muckrakers,* 148–49.

28. T. J. Jackson Lears, *Fables of Abundance: A Cultural History of Advertising in America* (New York: Basic Books, 1994), 156–57.

29. Filler, *Muckrakers,* 147–48. For a quick summary of the events leading up to the passage of the Federal Food and Drugs Act of 1906, see Robert O. Herrmann and Robert N. Mayer, "U.S. Consumer Movement: History and Dynamics," in *Encyclopedia of the Consumer Movement,* ed. Stephen Brobeck (Santa Barbara, Calif.: ABC-CLIO, 1997), 585–87.

30. Upton Sinclair, *The Jungle* (1906; repr., Urbana: University of Illinois Press, 1988).

31. Filler, *Muckrakers,* 167; Herrmann and Mayer, "U.S. Consumer Movement," 584.

32. Louis Filler, *Crusaders for American Liberalism* (1939; repr., Yellow Springs, Ohio: Antioch Press, 1950), 148, 151; Young, *Medical Messiahs,* 29–30.

33. Baldasty, *Commercialization of News,* 60, 75–80.

34. See Upton Sinclair, *The Brass Check* (1919; repr., Urbana: University of Illinois Press, 2002).

35. Filler, *Muckrakers,* 341.

36. Although Louis Filler claims that heavy pressure from advertisers led to the muckraking tradition's demise, other scholars argue that this is a simplistic view of

the matter. Matthew Schneirov, for example, contends that other factors, not least a public fatigue with muckraking exposés, led to their demise; see Filler, *Crusaders*, 359; Schneirov, *Dream of a New Social Order*, 252–55.

37. Young, *Medical Messiahs*, 35.

38. Ralph M. Gaedeke, "The Muckraking Era," in *Consumerism: Viewpoints from Business, Government, and the Public Interest*, ed. Ralph M. Gaedeke and Warren W. Etcheson (San Francisco: Canfield Press, 1972), 58.

39. Kathryn Kish Sklar, "The Consumers' White Label Campaign and the National Consumers' League, 1898–1918," in *Getting and Spending*, 25. See also Alice Rosenberg Wolfe, "Women, Consumerism, and the National Consumers' League in the Progressive Era, 1900–1923," *Labor History* 16, no. 5 (Summer 1975): 378–92; and Kathryn Kish Sklar, *Florence Kelly and the Nation's Work: The Rise of Women's Political Culture, 1830–1900* (New Haven, Conn.: Yale University Press, 1995), 309–11.

40. C. B. Larrabee, "That Cooperative Gap," *Printers' Ink*, September 20, 1934, 9. For a more in-depth treatment of consumer cooperatives, see Helen Sorenson, *The Consumer Movement: What It Is and What It Means* (New York: Harper and Brothers, 1941); and Steven Leikin, "The Citizen Producer: The Rise and Fall of Working-Class Cooperatives in the United States," in *Consumers against Capitalism? Consumer Cooperation in Europe, North America, and Japan, 1840–1990*, ed. Ellen Furlough and Carl Strikwerda (Lanham, Md.: Rowman and Littlefield, 1999), 93–113.

41. Alex Carey, *Taking the Risk Out of Democracy: Corporate Propaganda versus Freedom and Liberty* (Urbana: University of Illinois Press, 1997), chaps. 1–2.

42. Richard S. Tedlow, *Keeping the Corporate Image: Public Relations and Business, 1900–1950* (Greenwich, Conn.: JAI Press, 1979), 15–16.

43. Ewen, *PR!* chap. 3.

44. Roland Marchand, *Creating the Corporate Soul: The Rise of Public Relations and Corporate Imagery in American Big Business* (Berkeley: University of California Press, 1998), 42–43. For an excellent account of Ivy Lee's career, see Alan R. Raucher, *Public Relations and Business, 1900–1929* (Baltimore: Johns Hopkins University Press, 1968), chap. 2.

45. Marchand, *Creating the Corporate Soul*, 43–44.

46. Edward L. Bernays, *Crystallizing Public Opinion* (1923; repr., New York: Liveright, 1961), chap. 3. See also Edward L. Bernays, *Propaganda* (New York: Liveright, 1928).

47. Ewen, *PR!* 80 (emphasis in the original).

48. Stephen L. Vaughn, *Holding Fast the Inner Lanes: Democracy, Nationalism, and the Committee on Public Information* (Chapel Hill: University of North Carolina Press, 1980), 192.

49. Creel quoted in Ewen, *PR!* 112–13. See also Robert Jackall and Janice M. Hirota, *Advertising, Public Relations, and the Ethos of Advocacy* (Chicago: University of Chicago Press, 2000), chap. 1; and Vaughn, *Holding Fast*, chap. 8.

50. Jackall and Hirota, *Advertising,* 23.

51. Vaughn, *Holding Fast,* 191.

52. Raymond Rubicam, "Advertising in the Last War—And This," *Broadcasting,* June 9, 1941, 12.

53. Although men dominated the field of advertising, women were attracted to the profession as well. Advertising provided them with career opportunities that they could not easily obtain elsewhere. Their status and salaries tended to be far below those of their male colleagues, however; see Marchand, *Advertising the American Dream,* 33–35.

54. *New Republic* quoted in Lynda Maddox and Eric J. Zanot, "The Image of the Advertising Practitioner as Presented in the Mass Media, 1900–1972," *American Journalism* 2, no. 2 (1985): 118.

55. Marchand, *Advertising the American Dream,* 6.

56. Frank W. Fox, *Madison Avenue Goes to War* (Provo, Utah: Brigham Young University Press, 1975), 11–12; "Ad Field Pledges Aid in Emergency," *New York Times,* May 29, 1941, 33; "Advertisers Face Price Cost Hazard," *New York Times,* October 27, 1940, 7; "Advertising: Federation Maps Code by Recovery Act," *News-Week,* July 15, 1933, 25. Accusations of tax evasion during World War I had been poorly received by certain members of the advertising community. Industry defenders argued that advertising expenditures actually dropped during the first year the excess-profits tax was in effect and that the advertising spurt that occurred between November 1918 and July 1920 tapered off a year and a half before the excess-profits tax was repealed. This view attributes the wartime advertising eruption to a variety of factors. One explanation is that the government's use of advertising to promote the sale of government war bonds inspired manufacturers who previously did not use advertising to do so. Manufacturers' need to recapture goodwill, their desire to introduce new products to take advantage of production facilities that had expanded during the war, and their extended use of advertising in response to the Department of Labor's call for more advertising to keep business going and prevent unemployment are also suggested as alternative reasons for the surge. For a discussion of these issues, see L. D. H. Weld, "Excess Profits Tax Had Little Influence on Advertising during First World War," *Printers' Ink,* February 14, 1941, 13–14.

57. Otis Pease argues that until at least the 1930s, national advertising executives were less concerned with their public popularity than with their professional standing with business clients; see *The Responsibilities of American Advertising: Private Control and Public Influence, 1920–1940* (New Haven, Conn.: Yale University Press, 1958), 8.

58. Ibid.; "The AFA Is Looking Up," *Advertising Age,* July 23, 1945, 12; Louise MacLeod to H. H. Haupt, April 11, 1945, box 1, AFA 1942–55 folder, Bruce Barton Papers, Wisconsin Center for Historical Research, State Historical Society of Wisconsin, Madison. By 1937 the AFA had approximately ten thousand members and counted organizations such as the Newspaper Advertising Executive Association, the National Newspaper Promotion Association, the American Association of Adver-

tising Agencies, the Public Utilities Advertising Association, the Premium Advertising Association of America, the Outdoor Advertising Association of America, the National Association of Broadcasters, and the Associated Business Papers Inc., as well as several advertising clubs and women's advertising clubs from major cities, among its members. Frank Gale to Stephen Early, memo, May 3, 1937, box 602, Advertising Federation of America folder, President's Personal Files, Franklin D. Roosevelt Library, Hyde Park, N.Y. In 1968, after merging with the Associated Advertising Clubs of the World, the AFA changed its name to the American Advertising Federation.

59. Pease, *Responsibilities of American Advertising,* 8–9. For the history of the Association of National Advertisers, see Phil Thompson, "Phil Thompson Remembers," *Advertising and Selling,* October 1944, 48; and Phil Thompson, "Phil Thompson Remembers," *Advertising and Selling,* November 1944, 56.

60. Ewen, *Captains of Consciousness,* 73–76. Sociologist Michael Schudson uses *capitalist realism* as a term for advertising; see *Advertising: The Uneasy Persuasion; Its Dubious Impact on American Society* (New York: Basic Books, 1984), 5–6, chap. 9.

61. Ewen, *PR!* 127.

62. Curti, "Changing Concept of Human Nature," 334–57; James Rorty, "Call for Mr. Throttlebottom!" *Nation,* January 10, 1934, 37–39.

63. J. Michael Sproule, "Propaganda Studies in American Social Science: The Rise and Fall of the Critical Paradigm," *Quarterly Journal of Speech* 73, no. 1 (February 1987): 60–78. Freud, however, was not happy with the advertising industry's appropriation of his work. He complained that commercial interests, including the public relations practitioner Edward L. Bernays, who was his nephew, failed to recognize that the behavior of organized groups differed from that of crowds; see Raucher, *Public Relations and Business,* 133–34.

64. Michael McMahon, "An American Courtship: Psychologists and Advertising Theory in the Progressive Era," *American Studies* 13, no. 2 (Fall 1972): 5–18; Lears, *Fables of Abundance,* 208.

65. This view of consumers, although increasingly dominant among advertising practitioners between 1910 and 1930, was not uniformly accepted, however; see Curti, "Changing Concept of Human Nature," 345–53.

66. *Printers' Ink* quoted in Lears, *Fables of Abundance,* 209.

67. Roland Marchand argues, however, that industry trade publications frequently warned advertising practitioners against setting the consumer audience's "mental age" too low; see Marchand, *Advertising the American Dream,* 67.

68. Ibid., 50.

69. Ibid., 336.

70. Ibid., 69–72.

71. Lears, *Fables of Abundance,* 209.

72. Pope, *Making of Modern Advertising,* 247–50; Curti, "Changing Concept of Human Nature," 344.

73. Marchand, *Advertising the American Dream,* 66–67.

74. Lears, *Fables of Abundance,* 196–98.

75. Wallace Boren, "Bad Taste in Advertising," 9, J. Walter Thompson Forum, January 21, 1936, J. Walter Thompson Company Staff Meeting Minutes, box 7, folder 1, J. Walter Thompson Company Archives, Hartman Center for Sales, Advertising, and Marketing History in the Rare Book, Manuscript, and Special Collections Library, Duke University, Durham, N.C.

76. Boren, "Bad Taste," 6; Lears, *Fables of Abundance,* 197. Marchand elaborates on this point in *Advertising the American Dream,* chaps. 1–3.

77. Boren, "Bad Taste," 6.

78. "Resolved by the A.F.A.," *Printers' Ink,* July 1, 1937, 68.

79. Charles Margee Adams, "Who Bred These Utopias?" *North American Review,* no. 240 (June 1935): 14.

80. Peggy J. Kreshel argues that efforts to inject "science" into advertising practices in the 1910s and 1920s were undertaken not just to improve advertising as a marketing tool. "Scientific research" also served as an important public relations tool for elevating advertising from a trade to a profession; see "The 'Culture' of J. Walter Thompson, 1915–1925," *Public Relations Review* 16, no. 8 (Fall 1990): 80–98. Alan Raucher also supports this view; see *Public Relations and Business,* 116.

81. "Truth in Advertising," *Printers' Ink,* January 16, 1936, 37.

82. Robert S. Lynd and Helen Merrell Lynd, *Middletown* (1929; repr., New York: Harcourt, Brace, and World, 1967); Robert S. Lynd and Helen Merrell Lynd, *Middletown in Transition* (1937; repr., New York: Harcourt, Brace, Jovanovich, 1965). See also Robert S. Lynd with the assistance of Alice C. Hanson, "The People as Consumers," in *Recent Social Trends in the United States,* ed. Research Committee on Social Trends (New York: Whittlesey House, 1934), 857–911.

Chapter 2: Advertising Challenged

1. Landon R. Y. Storrs, *Civilizing Capitalism: The National Consumers' League, Women's Activism, and Labor Standards in the New Deal Era* (Chapel Hill: The University of North Carolina Press, 2000); Kathryn Kish Sklar, "The Consumers' White Label Campaign and the National Consumers' League, 1898–1918," in *Getting and Spending: European and American Consumer Societies in the Twentieth Century,* ed. Susan Strasser, Charles McGovern, and Matthias Judt (Cambridge: Cambridge University Press, 1998), 17–35.

2. Arthur S. Link, "What Happened to the Progressive Movement in the 1920s?" *American Historical Review* 64, no. 4 (July 1959): 833–51; Allen F. Davis, "Welfare and World War I," *American Quarterly* 19, no. 3 (Autumn 1967): 516–33.

3. Robert S. Lynd with the assistance of Alice C. Hanson, "The People as Consumers," in *Recent Social Trends in the United States,* ed. Research Committee on Social Trends (New York: Whittlesey House, 1934), 876.

4. Hayagreeva Roa, "Caveat Emptor: The Construction of Nonprofit Consumer

Watchdog Organizations," *American Journal of Sociology* 103, no. 4 (January 1998): 926.

5. Edward Podolsky, "The Gospel of the Advertiser," *Commonweal*, April 5, 1935, 641.

6. Roland Marchand, *Advertising the American Dream: Making Way for Modernity, 1920–1940* (Berkeley: University of California Press, 1985), 336.

7. "About People," n.d., 5, 2, box 17, Some Things We Have Learned 1946–51 folder, Company Publications, Correspondence 1937–76, J. Walter Thompson Company Archives, Hartman Center for Sales, Advertising, and Marketing History in the Rare Book, Manuscript, and Special Collections Library, Duke University, Durham, N.C.

8. Roa, "Caveat Emptor," 927.

9. "Discuss Wants of Consumers at N.Y. Hearing," *Advertising Age*, March 11, 1933, 2. Alice I. Edwards, executive secretary of the American Home Economics Association, argued that advertising tended to stress insignificant features that frequently proved to be of no value to consumers; see "Four A's Ponder Public Attitude on Advertising," *Sales Management*, June 1, 1934, 518–19.

10. See, for example, Ruth DeForest Lamb, *American Chamber of Horrors* (New York: Farrar and Rinehart, 1936).

11. Robert S. Lynd, "The Consumer Becomes a 'Problem,'" *Annals of the American Academy of Political and Social Science* 173 (May 1934): 4.

12. Richard L. D. Morse, ed., *The Consumer Movement: Lectures by Colston E. Warne* (Manhattan, Kans.: Family Economics Trust Press, 1983), 17–21; "A Consumer—From Amateur to Professional: A Consumer Becomes Consumer Conscious," n.d., folder 92, box 22, Consumers' Research Papers, Special Collections and University Archives, Rutgers University, New Brunswick, N.J. (hereafter referred to as CR Papers). See also Roa, "Caveat Emptor."

13. Morse, *Consumer Movement*, 19.

14. Ibid., 21.

15. "A Consumer—From Amateur to Professional."

16. Robert N. Mayer, *The Consumer Movement* (Boston: Twayne, 1989), 21; Norman Isaac Silber, *Test and Protest: The Influence of Consumers Union* (New York: Holmes and Meier, 1983), 18. See also Edith Ayres, "Private Organizations Working for the Consumer," *Annals of the American Academy of Political and Social Science* 173 (May 1934): 158–65.

17. Morse, *Consumer Movement*, 25; "Consumer v. Producer: A Libel Suit against the Authors of *Your Money's Worth*," *Consumers' Research General Bulletin*, October 1934, 9–12; "Ethics of Advertising Agencies," *Consumers' Research General Bulletin*, May 1932, 2; M. C. Phillips to Daisy A. Davis, March 1, 1934, box 16, folder 8, CR Papers.

18. Otis Pease, *The Responsibilities of American Advertising: Private Control and Public Influence, 1920–1940* (New Haven, Conn.: Yale University Press, 1958), 98–99.

19. Morse, *Consumer Movement,* 27.

20. J. P. Cunningham, "How to Conserve Working Capital of Advertising," *Printers' Ink,* November 14, 1935, 69.

21. "'Guinea Pigs' Called Danger to Advertising," *Advertising Age,* March 11, 1933, 15.

22. Arthur Kallet and Frederick J. Schlink, *100,000,000 Guinea Pigs* (New York: Vanguard Press, 1933), 15.

23. "Skin Deep," *Tide,* December 1934, 10–11.

24. Edward L. Bernays, "Evaluation of the Consumer Movement," n.d., box 76, folder 11, National Broadcasting Company Papers, Wisconsin Center for Historical Research, State Historical Society of Wisconsin, Madison; C. B. Larrabee, "Guinea Pig Books," *Printers' Ink,* April 16, 1936, 71–73; James Henle, "Who Hurts Advertising?" *Printers' Ink,* October 22, 1936, 33.

25. "Four A's Ponder Public Attitude on Advertising," 518–19.

26. Colston E. Warne, "Present Day Advertising—The Consumer's Viewpoint," *Annals of the American Academy of Political and Social Science* 173 (May 1934): 71.

27. Stephen Fox, *The Mirror Makers: A History of American Advertising and Its Creators* (1984; repr., Urbana: University of Illinois Press, 1997), 88–90.

28. Public resentment toward "bad taste" in advertising picked up momentum in the mid-1920s; see Pease, *Responsibilities of American Advertising,* chap. 3; and Marchand, *Advertising the American Dream,* chap. 4.

29. Charles Margee Adams, "Who Bred These Utopias?" *North American Review,* no. 240 (June 1935): 14.

30. Marchand, *Advertising the American Dream,* 314. For an excellent discussion of consumer activists' views on commercial radio see Kathy M. Newman, *Radio Active: Advertising and Consumer Activism, 1935–1947* (Berkeley and Los Angeles: University of California Press, 2004), chap. 2.

31. Frederick J. Schlink to Daisy Davis, March 9, 1934, box 16, folder 8, CR Papers; M. C. Phillips to Daisy A. Davis, March 1, 1943, box 16, folder 8, CR Papers. For another script by Dorothy Tolbert, see "Wise and Otherwise," n.d., box 247, folder 14, CR Papers.

32. For a treatment of early radio serial listeners and their sponsor loyalty, see Marilyn Lavin, "Creating Consumers in the 1930s: Irna Phillips and the Radio Soap Opera," *Journal of Consumer Research* 22, no. 1 (June 1995): 75–89.

33. "Radio Cracks Down," *Printers' Ink,* March 21, 1935, 114.

34. Warne, "Present Day Advertising," 72.

35. A. H. Brandow to the Federal Radio Commission, March 18, 1934; Emma J. Wollaston to the Federal Radio Commission, April 7, 1934; Harold Cooke to the Federal Radio Commission, February 27, 1934; and I. S. Mullen to Eugene Sykes, May 3, 1934, all in box 271, Office of the Executive Director, General Correspondence, 63–2, Federal Communications Commission Papers, Record Group 173, National Archives II, College Park, Md.

36. For a discussion of these points, see Robert W. McChesney, *Telecommunications, Mass Media, and Democracy: The Battle for the Control of U.S. Broadcasting, 1928–1935* (New York: Oxford University Press, 1993), particularly chaps. 5–9.

37. Roy S. Durstine, "A Challenge to All Snipers," *Printers' Ink,* May 9, 1935, 76, 80–81.

38. John Benson, "The True Function of Advertising," *Advertising and Selling,* July 4, 1935, 20.

39. Ibid., 36.

40. "Public Sentiment Now Favorable to Advertising," *Advertising Age,* August 13, 1932, 6; "Readers Want Advertising," *Advertising Age,* February 11, 1933, 4; "Consumers Have Faith in Advertising," *Advertising Age,* January 20, 1934, 4. Industry leaders admitted that some manufacturers engaged in questionable advertising practices. They maintained, however, that only between 5 and 10 percent of all advertisers were responsible for giving the entire industry a bad reputation; see, for example, Cunningham, "How to Conserve Working Capital," 69.

41. "Readers Want Advertising."

42. Charles Coolidge Parlin, "Advertising and Its Critics," address delivered at the Conference on Distribution, Boston, September 20, 1937, box 122, folder 22, CR Papers.

43. "Advertised Brands as a Protection to the Consumer," *Advertising Age,* August 6, 1932, 4.

44. "Consumers Have Faith in Advertising."

45. T. J. Jackson Lears, *Fables of Abundance: A Cultural History of Advertising in America* (New York: Basic Books, 1994), 198.

46. Gilbert Hodges, "Advertising Must Fight as Well as Clean Up," *Printers' Ink,* April 19, 1934, 33. See also "Advertising—Brief Survey and Current Status," *Index* 19, no. 1 (March 1939): 15–21.

47. James Rorty, "Advertising and the Depression," *Nation,* December 20, 1933, 703.

48. Lears, *Fables of Abundance,* 233.

49. Rorty, "Advertising and the Depression," 703.

50. "Can We Help Advertising's Unemployed?" *Advertising Age,* December 17, 1932, 4.

51. Robert R. Troxell to Frederick J. Schlink, July 2, 1935, box 21, folder 15, CR Papers.

52. "Let's Face the Music," *Printers' Ink,* March 8, 1934, 104.

53. C. B. Larrabee, "This Consumer Revolt and How to Meet It," *Printers' Ink,* April 19, 1934, 10. See also G. A. Nichols, "Agency Men Invite, and Get Cracks on Chin," *Printers' Ink,* May 31, 1934, 25–26; M. C. Phillips to J. B. Matthews, April 24, 1934, box 414, folder 3, CR Papers.

54. C. B. Larrabee, "Mr. Schlink," *Printers' Ink,* February 1, 1934, 37.

55. "Those Guinea Pig Engineers," *Printers' Ink,* February 1, 1934, 37.

56. Larrabee, "This Consumer Revolt"; Cunningham, "How to Conserve Working Capital," 69–71; Robert Tinsman, "The Renewal of Faith in Advertising," *Advertising and Selling,* January 19, 1933, 21; "Durstine Challenges Consumer Research at Washington Meeting," *Advertising Age,* May 6, 1935, 1–2.

57. Earnest Elmo Calkins, "What Kind of Regulation Does Advertising Need?" *Advertising and Selling,* December 7, 1933, 15–16.

58. "Those Guinea Pig Engineers," 37.

59. Raymond Pearl, "A Biologist Dissects 100,000,000 Guinea Pigs," *Printers' Ink,* May 25, 1933, 33.

60. James Rorty, *Our Master's Voice: Advertising* (1934; repr., New York: Arno Press, 1976).

61. "Comrade Rorty Lifts the Lid," *Printers' Ink,* May 10, 1934, 92. For a treatment of Rorty's life and career, see Daniel Pope, "His Master's Voice: James Rorty and the Critique of Advertising," *Maryland Historian* 19, no. 1 (Spring-Summer 1988): 5–15.

62. Frederick J. Schlink to Roy Dickinson, May 9, 1934, box 22, folder 6, CR Papers; Roy Dickinson to Frederick J. Schlink, May 2, 1934, box 22, folder 6, CR Papers. See also Frederick J. Schlink to Malcolm Cowley, May 1934, box 22, folder 3, CR Papers.

63. Roy Dickinson to Frederick J. Schlink, February 19, 1934, box 22, folder 7, CR Papers; internal handwritten memo to "$," January or February 1934, box 22, folder 7, CR Papers. The review of Arthur Kallet's 1935 book *Counterfeit* in *Printers' Ink* reflected the terse relationship between CR and the trade publication; see Arthur Kallet, *Counterfeit: Not Your Money but What It Buys* (New York: Vanguard Press, 1935); "Bigger and Better Consumers," *Printers' Ink,* February 22, 1934, 99–100; C. B. Larrabee, "Counterfeit," *Printers' Ink,* June 6, 1935, 29.

64. James Rorty to Frank L. Palmer, May 3, 1934, box 22, folder 3, CR Papers.

65. Dewey H. Palmer to James H. Rorty, June 14, 1934, box 22, folder 6, CR papers; Frederick J. Schlink to Malcolm Cowley, May 7, 1934, box 22, folder 7, CR Papers.

66. Morse, *Consumer Movement,* 42–43. For information on the 1930s cooperative movement, including the advertising industry's reactions, see, for example, Lizabeth Cohen, *A Consumers' Republic: The Politics of Mass Consumption in Postwar America* (New York: Alfred A. Knopf, 2003), 49–53; Helen Sorenson, *The Consumer Movement: What It Is and What It Means* (New York: Harper and Brothers, 1941), chap. 6; Richard Giles, "What Is Co-operative," *Printers' Ink,* October 15, 1936, 6–8; Charles F. Phillips, "The Co-operative Scare," *Printers' Ink,* March 18, 1937, 61; C. B. Larrabee, "Watch the Co-ops!" *Printers' Ink,* December 26, 1935, 21; Gordon Cook, "To Halt Consumer Co-ops," *Printers' Ink,* August 19, 1937, 58; "Warbasse Tells Steady Rise of Consumer Co-ops," *Advertising Age,* September 30, 1935, 1; "Advertisers Ponder New Deal Trend toward Co-ops," *Advertising Age,* July 20, 1936, 1; "Co-ops March On," *Printers' Ink,* October 20, 1938, 30; Kenneth Hinshaw, "That Co-op Bogey," *Printers' Ink,* August 6, 1936, 7; Richard Giles, "Co-ops and Politics," *Printers' Ink,* August 13,

1936, 15–17; C. B. Larrabee, "That Co-operative Gap," *Printers' Ink,* September 20, 1934, 7; H. Erbes Jr., "How a Co-op Co-ops," *Printers' Ink,* November 10, 1938, 13–16; and "Co-op Catalog Shows How Movement Is Progressing," *Advertising Age,* September 9, 1940, 16.

67. The Good Housekeeping Institute was perhaps the largest and best known among the so-called consumer institutes connected with women's magazines. Others included the Delineator Institute, operated by *Delineator* magazine, and similar services were provided by the *Ladies' Home Journal* and the *Women's Home Companion.* Most were known and used only by the readers of a particular magazine, although manufacturers who earned the Good Housekeeping Star, the symbol of *Good Housekeeping*'s approval, liked to display this on their products and in their ads. The various institutes tended to rely on their own laboratories for product testing. Test procedures, however, were rarely made public, and this made it difficult for readers to determine precisely what tests had been completed. Focusing on the positive attributes of their advertised products, institutes failed to issue warnings about poorly made merchandise and rarely pointed to the price-quality ratio of a product. For a discussion of these issues, see Edith Ayres, "Private Organizations Working for the Consumer," 159–60.

68. "Skin Deep," 10–11. For more information on this issue, see various correspondence in box 3, folder 3, Arthur Kallet Papers, Consumers Union Archives, Yonkers, N.Y.

69. "*Harper's* and *Time* Refuse CR's Advertising," *Consumers' Research General Bulletin,* May 1932, 6; "*Time* and *News-Week* Can't Afford to Print CR's Advertising," *Consumers' Research Bulletin,* January 1935, 19–20.

70. Lizabeth Cohen, "The New Deal State and the Making of Citizen Consumers," in *Getting and Spending,* 111–25.

71. Sorenson, *Consumer Movement,* 14.

72. Cohen, "New Deal State"; Cohen, *Consumers' Republic,* 54–56; Alan Brinkley, *The End of Reform: New Deal Liberalism in Recession and War* (New York: Vintage Books, 1996), 72–77; Meg Jacobs, "Pocketbook Politics: Democracy and the Market in Twentieth-Century America," in *The Democratic Experience,* ed. Meg Jacobs, William J. Novak, and Julian E. Zelizer (Princeton, N.J.: Princeton University Press, 2003), 258–59.

73. "The Consumers' Place in the Organization of the New Deal," n.d., 11, box 11, CAB General Files, Correspondence (General A) folder, General Files of the Consumers' Advisory Board 1934–35—Correspondence A-B, Records of the Consumers' Division, Records of the National Recovery Administration, Record Group 9, National Archives, Washington, D.C. (hereafter referred to as Consumers' Division Records).

74. Meg Jacobs, "'Democracy's Third Estate': New Deal Politics and the Construction of a 'Consuming Public,'" *International Labor and Working Class History* 55 (Spring 1999): 35–36.

75. "Gov't and Business," *Tide*, June 1935, 15.

76. Sorenson, *Consumer Movement*, 17–18.

77. William E. Leuchtenburg, *Franklin D. Roosevelt and the New Deal* (New York: Harper and Row, 1963), 64–69; Wilson Compton, "The Test of Industrial Organization and NRA: An Address Delivered before the Meeting of the American Trade Association Executives," May 1, 1934, box 11, CAB General Files, Correspondence (General A) folder, General Files of the Consumers' Advisory Board 1934–35—Correspondence A-B, Consumers' Division Records.

78. Cohen, "New Deal State," 118.

79. Persia Campbell, *Consumer Representation and the New Deal* (New York: S. King, 1940), chap. 1; Alan Brinkley, *The End of Reform*, 71.

80. Robert S. Lynd quoted in Margaret Winfield Stewart, "The Consumer and the N.R.A.," *Social Forces* 12, no. 4 (May 1934): 586 (emphasis in the original).

81. Frederick J. Schlink to W. A. Ross, December 22, 1933, box 183, folder 14, CR Papers.

82. See, for example, A. B. Walton to Robert J. Bulkley, February 14, 1934, box 11, CAB General Files, Correspondence (General A) folder, General Files of the Consumers' Advisory Board 1934–35—Correspondence A-B, Consumers' Division Records; "The Little Fellow," *Tide*, February 1934, 8–9.

83. Campbell, *Consumer Representation*, 56.

84. "Definition at Last," *Printers' Ink*, May 24, 1934, 100. See also Pease, *Responsibilities of American Advertising*, 120.

85. The CAB (1933–35) included the following members: Mary Rumsey (first chairwoman), William F. Ogden (executive director), Emily Newell Blair (second chairwoman), Frank Graham, Belle Sherwin (president of the National League of Women Voters), William Thorp, Louis Bean, Dexter M. Keezer, Corwin Edwards, and Thomas C. Blaisdell. Among the consulting members were Frederick C. Howe, Gardiner C. Means, Robert S. Lynd, George Stocking, Walton Hamilton, Paul H. Douglas, Huston Thompson, and Stacy May; see Pease, *Responsibilities of American Advertising*, 120n10.

86. Campbell, *Consumer Representation*, 44.

87. Ibid., 11; Robert S. Lynd to Frederick J. Schlink, October 6, 1934, box 92, folder 27, CR Papers; Robert S. Lynd to Frederick J. Schlink, n.d., box 368, folder 18, CR Papers.

88. Campbell, *Consumer Representation*, 44.

89. Jacobs, "'Democracy's Third Estate,'" 41. See also Persia Campbell, *The Consumer Interest: A Study in Consumer Economics* (New York: Harper and Brothers, 1949), 623–33; "Prices and Profits," *Tide*, December 1933, 48; "Consumer Groups," *Tide*, February 1934, 10–11.

90. "Consumer Councils," *Printers' Ink*, January 25, 1934, 98.

91. "Consumer Groups," 11.

92. "Government Grades versus Advertised Brands," *Advertising Age,* February 3, 1934, 4.

93. Quoted in "Lasker Visions U.S. Rule of Advertising Fatal," *Advertising Age,* September 29, 1934, 23.

94. Campbell, *Consumer Interest,* 61.

95. Louis F. Cahn, "NRA Can Help Individuals Only as It Helps Nation," *Printers' Ink,* September 7, 1933, 71–72.

96. See "Advertising under the Industrial Recovery Bill," *Advertising Age,* June 10, 1933, 4; C. B. Larrabee, "Industrial Recovery Bill a Boon to Honest Advertising," *Printers' Ink,* June 22, 1933, 3; Chester M. Wright, "NRA Codes Won't Harm the Decent Advertiser," *Printers' Ink,* May 24, 1934, 21; and "Study Effects of Industry Bill on Advertising Field," *Advertising Age,* June 10, 1933, 1.

97. H. J. Kenner, *The Fight for Truth in Advertising* (New York: Round Table Press, 1936).

98. "Advertising Is Called an Aid to Government," *Advertising Age,* June 23, 1933, 20; "Roosevelt Asks Advertisers' Aid," *New York Times,* June 27, 1933, 3. For a copy of the president's statement, see Stephen Early to Edgar Kobak, June 15, 1934, box 602, Advertising Federation of America folder, FDR Personal Files (hereafter referred to as FDR Personal Files). It turned out, however, that the president's message was prepared by the AFA. See Daniel C. Roper to Stephen Early, June 13, 1934, box 602, Advertising Federation of America folder, FDR Personal Files.

99. Larrabee, "Industrial Recovery Bill a Boon."

100. William H. Rankin, "A New Deal for Advertising," *Printers' Ink,* July 6, 1933, 82.

101. "Advertising Is Asked to Aid in Recovery Effort," *Advertising Age,* July 29, 1933, 1.

102. "Rush Formation of Advertising Group for NRA," *Advertising Age,* September 2, 1933, 1.

103. "Buy Now Because—," *Business Week,* October 14, 1933, 5; Julian Chase, "Advertising Today Is a Patriotic Duty," *Automotive Industries,* July 15, 1933, 63; "'Buy Now' Campaign Spurs Advertising," *New York Times,* October 7, 1933, 21; "New NRA Advertising Drive," *Printers' Ink,* October 5, 1933, 6; Earnest Elmo Calkins, "Courageous Selling and What It Can Mean to Recovery," *Advertising and Selling,* February 1, 1934, 16–17.

104. Hugh S. Johnson, "Praise from the General," *Printers' Ink,* July 19, 1934, 63; Roy Dickinson, "Advertising Methods to Be Used to Speed Recovery," *Printers' Ink,* July 27, 1933, 29–31; "Advertisers NRA Report to President Roosevelt," *Printers' Ink,* October 19, 1933, 58. For a discussion of Johnson's role in the code-building process, see Leuchtenburg, *Franklin D. Roosevelt,* 64–68.

105. "Advertising Displaces Ballyhoo in NRA Program," *Printers' Ink,* October 12, 1933, 3; "Buy Now Because—."

106. "Advertising Displaces Ballyhoo," 5 (emphasis in the original).

107. Ibid., 3.

108. Frederick J. Schlink, "What the Government Does and Might Do for the Consumer," *Annals of the American Academy of Political and Social Science* 173 (May 1934): 125–43.

109. For more on the Fascism comparison, see Frederick J. Schlink, "The New Deal and the Consumer," July 12, 1934, box 27, folder 9, CR Papers; Frederick J. Schlink to Henry Ellenbogen, April 17, 1934, box 367, folder 9, CR Papers; and Frederick J. Schlink to Alfred M. Bingham, August 7, 1934, box 328, folder 9, CR Papers.

110. Frederick J. Schlink, "How the Consumer Was Betrayed: The Acid Test of the New Deal Liberals," September 1934, 4, box 328, folder 15, CR Papers; "Notes on NIRA—For Consumers," *Consumers' Research General Bulletin,* October 1933, 1–5; Frederick J. Schlink to Robert S. Lynd, April 19, 1934, box 368, folder 9, CR Papers.

111. "That Great NRA Illusion: The Consumers' Advisory Board," *Consumers' Research General Bulletin,* October 1934, 6.

112. Schlink, "How the Consumer Was Betrayed," 4; see also "Excerpts from Subscriber's Letter," April 25, 1934, box 368, folder 18, CR Papers; Frederick J. Schlink to Robert S. Lynd, April 19, 1934, box 368, folder 18, CR Papers. "Excerpts from Subscriber's Letter" provides a somewhat detailed account of Schlink's criticism of Ramsey and his attempts to get her removed from the CAB.

113. Frank L. Palmer to Frederick J. Schlink, July 21, 1933, box 367, folder 29, CR Papers.

114. Ibid.; Frederick J. Schlink to Frank L. Palmer, July 25, 1933, box 367, folder 29, CR Papers. See also Frederick Press, "Consumers Finally Represented on Consumers' Board," *Federal Press Eastern Weekly Newsletter,* July 20, 1933, box 367, folder 29, CR Papers.

115. Schlink to Palmer, July 25, 1933, box 367, folder 29, CR papers. See also Frederick J. Schlink to Mrs. John (Genevieve Forbes) Herrick, December 20, 1933, box 369, folder 23, CR Papers.

116. "Minutes of the Special Meeting of the Board of Directors of Consumers' Research Inc.," October 18, 1933, box 3, folder 2, Kallet Papers. Johnson did not offer Schlink the appointment. For more on this incident, see miscellaneous correspondence in box 369, folder 24, CR Papers. See also Frederick J. Schlink to Robert S. Lynd, January 8, 1934, box 368, folder 18, CR Papers; Theodore Kain to Hugh S. Johnson, February 24, 1934, box 369, folder 24, CR Papers; and M. C. Phillips to Melville J. Herskevits, February 6, 1934, box 369, folder 24, CR Papers.

117. Schlink, "New Deal and the Consumer," 2.

118. Frederick J. Schlink to Henry Ellenbogen, April 17, 1934, box 367, folder 29, CR Papers.

119. Malcolm Ross to Josephine F. Eddy, July 19, 1934, box 10, CAB General Files, Correspondence (General A) folder, General Files of the Consumers' Advisory Board 1934–35, Cooperatives—Correspondence A, Consumers' Division Records.

120. "That Great NRA Illusion," 5.

121. "F. J. Schlink vs Howard Y. Williams," script of radio interview on station WEVD, August 23, 1933, box 367, folder 29, CR Papers.

122. Campbell, *Consumer Representation,* 60–61, 68–69; "Incredible Relentless," *Tide,* January 1934, 22–23. For an organizational chart of the proposed Department of the Consumer, see "Suggested Plan for the Department of the Consumer," *Consumers' Research General Bulletin,* July 1934, 23. Although Howe, Lynd, and Tugwell occupied high positions in the Roosevelt administration, Rorty, Kallet, and Schlink had few institutional loyalties and less to lose from rigorous attacks on the NRA's consumer policy.

123. J. Charles Laue to Franklin D. Roosevelt, December 11, 1933, box 183, folder 11, CR Papers. See also Consumers' Research Inc., "A Proposed Act to Establish a Federal Department of the Consumer," March 1935, box 183, folder 12, CR Papers.

124. Frederick J. Schlink, "An Open Letter to President Roosevelt," November 20, 1933, box 3, folder 6, Kallet Papers, copy in box 183, folder 13, CR Papers.

125. "Needed: A Department of the Consumer," *Consumers' Research General Bulletin,* January 1934, 2.

126. M. C. Phillips to James W. Matthews, May 29, 1935, box 328, folder 9, CR Papers.

127. Robert S. Lynd, "New Deal Consumer: A Study at Close Range," *Printers' Ink,* March 22, 1934, 41–42; "CAB Grading Program," *Printers' Ink,* September 20, 1934, 88; "Keep Up Fight on Grading," *Printers' Ink,* March 14, 1935, 100–102. See also Lynd, "The Consumer Becomes a 'Problem.'"

128. Lynd, "New Deal Consumer," 42.

129. "CAB Grading Program," 88.

130. Bernhard Lichtenberg, "Some Advertising Facts for Government Skeptics," *Printers' Ink,* February 22, 1934, 84. See also "Government Grades versus Advertised Brands."

131. "Consumer Groups," 10–11.

132. Lears, *Fables of Abundance,* 224–31.

133. Lynd, "New Deal Consumer," 42.

134. Frederick J. Schlink, "Safeguarding the Consumer's Interest—An Essential Element in National Recovery," *Annals of the American Academy of Political and Social Science* 172 (March 1934): 117.

135. Pease, *Responsibilities of American Advertising,* 121; "NRA Hits A-B-C Labels," *Printers' Ink,* January 24, 1935, 73; Paul S. Willis, "Why Food Industry Fights A-B-C Labeling," *Printers' Ink,* January 31, 1935, 69–70; "CAB Grading Program," 86; "Keep Up Fight on Grading," 100; "U.S. Grading Expands," *Printers' Ink,* August 23, 1934, 20; Lynd, "New Deal Consumer."

136. "CAB Grading Program," 86.

137. Alfred T. Falk quoted in "Consumers' Doom," *Printers' Ink,* March 1, 1934, 86.

138. Lichtenberg, "Some Advertising Facts," 84.

139. "What the Consumer Thinks of Advertising—A Lowdown," *Sales Management,* April 10, 1934, 322–25. For the advertising industry's reaction to this survey, see "What Advertising Men Think of Consumers," *Sales Management,* May 1, 1934, 442.

140. Pease, *Responsibilities of American Advertising,* 120. The CAB's fight to win government acceptance for consumer cooperatives also was met with defeat; see, for example, Meyer Parodneck, "Co-op Movement Has Rapid Growth in Europe," *Printers' Ink,* March 28, 1935, 86; "Canonizing the Co-ops," *Printers' Ink,* July 25, 1935, 94; "Warbasse Tells Steady Rise"; Larrabee, "Watch the Co-ops"; and Larrabee, "That Co-operative Gap." For in-depth treatments of these issues, see, for example, Sorenson, *Consumer Movement,* chap. 8; Suzanne Rebecca White, "Chemistry and Controversy: Regulating the Use of Chemicals in Foods, 1883–1959" (Ph.D. diss., Emory University, 1994), chap. 6; Peter Barton Hutt and Peter Barton Hutt II, "A History of Government Regulation of Adulteration and Misbranding of Food," *Food, Drug and Cosmetic Law Journal* 39, no. 1 (January 1984): 2–73; "A.N.A. on Labeling," *Business Week,* December 13, 1941, 66–67; "Checkup on A-B-C," *Business Week,* May 17, 1941, 62–64; and "Chains Use Grades," *Business Week,* November 30, 1940, 27–28.

Chapter 3: The Drive for Federal Advertising Regulation, 1933–35

1. Robert S. Lynd, "The Consumer Becomes a 'Problem,'" *Annals of the American Academy of Political and Social Science* 173 (May 1934): 1–6.

2. "Outstanding Advantage to Consumers of Senate Bill 2800 over Present Food and Drug Act," 1934, box 25, Food and Drug Legislation folder, Royal S. Copeland Papers, Bentley Historical Library, University of Michigan, Ann Arbor (hereafter referred to as Copeland Papers).

3. "The Consumer's Weak Position in the Law," *Consumers' Research General Bulletin,* September 1931, 3; "W. G. Campbell Stresses Need for Stronger Pure Food Legislation," U.S. Department of Agriculture Office of Information press release, September 4, 1931, box 3, folder 1, Arthur Kallet Papers, Consumers Union Archives, Yonkers, N.Y. (hereafter referred to as Kallet Papers).

4. Editorial, *Nation,* December 27, 1933, 719.

5. Association of University Women, "Scientific Consumer Purchasing: A Study Outline Covering Some Recent Developments in Production and Distribution Which Affects the Consumer," n.d., box 10, CAB General Files, Correspondence (General A) folder, General Files of the Consumers' Advisory Board, 1934–35, Cooperatives—Correspondence A, Records of the Consumers' Division, Records of the National Recovery Administration, Record Group 9, Washington, D.C.; Richard S. Tedlow, "From Competitor to Consumer: The Changing Focus of Federal Regulation of Advertising, 1914–1938," *Business History Review* 55, no. 1 (Spring 1981): 35–58. See also memo marked "Confidential," J. Walter Thompson Forum, October 25, 1938, J. Walter Thompson Company Staff Meeting Minutes, box 7, folder 4, J. Walter Thompson

Papers, Special Collections Library, Duke University, Durham, N.C.; "False Advertising and the Federal Trade Commission," undated and unsigned memo, box 25, Food and Drug Legislation folder, Copeland Papers; and James Harvey Young, *The Medical Messiahs: A Social History of Health Quackery in Twentieth-Century America* (1967; repr., Princeton, N.J.: Princeton University Press, 1992), 124–27.

6. "The Case for the Tugwell Bill," *Advertising and Selling,* October 26, 1933, 13–14.

7. Consumers' Research, "Draft of Resolution for Consideration by Clubs, Societies, and Other Groups Interested in Reform of State and National Food and Drug Laws," late 1932 or early 1933, box 356, folder 10, Consumers' Research Papers, Special Collections and University Archives, Rutgers University, New Brunswick, N.J. (hereafter referred to as CR Papers).

8. Frederick J. Schlink to Milton Handler, March 13, 1933, box 356, folder 11, CR Papers; [Frederick J. Schlink?] to David F. Cavers, May 10, 1933, box 356, folder 11, CR Papers.

9. Milton Handler to Frederick J. Schlink, March 9, 1933, box 356, folder 11, CR Papers.

10. Frederick J. Schlink to Rexford G. Tugwell, March 7, 1933, box 6, Consumers' Research folder, Rexford G. Tugwell Papers, Franklin D. Roosevelt Library, Hyde Park, N.Y. (hereafter referred to as Tugwell Papers; emphasis in the original).

11. Ibid.

12. "Sidelights on the Food and Drugs Act," *Consumers' Research General Bulletin,* October 1933, 10; Consumers' Research, "Draft of Resolution."

13. David F. Carver to Frederick J. Schlink, March 8, 1933, box 356, folder 11, CR Papers.

14. Bernhard Sternsher, *Rexford Tugwell and the New Deal* (New Brunswick, N.J.: Rutgers University Press, 1964), 24, 228–29; William S. Groom, "Tugwell's Mischievous Ideas about Advertising," *Printers' Ink,* March 1, 1934, 32–34.

15. Rexford G. Tugwell, "A New Ideal for the Consumer," address delivered at the Columbia Alumni Luncheon, Columbia University, New York City, February 12, 1934, box 56, A New Deal for the Consumer folder, Tugwell Papers.

16. Handler to Schlink, March 9, 1933.

17. "Foods, Drugs, Teeth," *Business Week,* May 24, 1933, 12; "Administration Bill Penalizes 'Ambiguity' and 'Inference' in Ads," *Printers' Ink,* June 8, 1933, 11–12; "Cosmetics Are Written into Food, Drug Act," *Advertising Age,* May 20, 1933, 9; Allen Heald, "What Kind of Regulation Would the Tugwell Bill Provide?" *Advertising and Selling,* December 21, 1933, 14.

18. Representatives for the advertising industry argued that the grading provision would severely hurt advertising. If passed into law, such a provision would deflate the value of brands and trademarks and render consumers dependent on government standards and qualifications; see, for example, "Tugwell Bill Would End Value of Brands and Trade Marks," *Printers' Ink,* December 14, 1933, 6; Roy Dickinson,

"At the Tugwell Hearings," *Printers' Ink,* December 14, 1934, 85; and Earnest Elmo Calkins, "Another Look at the Pure Food Bill," *Good Housekeeping,* December 1933, 90. S 1944 also proposed changes in food labeling. It required that all product ingredients be disclosed on a product's label. Most women's organizations endorsed this stipulation whereas manufacturers claimed that such formula revelations would hurt the value of private brands; see Catherine Hackett, "The New Deal and Advertising—Two Points of View: A Housewife Praises," *Forum,* February 1934, 98–101; and John G. Sterling, "The New Deal and Advertising—Two Points of View: A Business Man Condemns," *Forum,* February 1934, 102–4.

19. Heald, "What Kind of Regulation."

20. "Nine Objections to the Tugwell Bill—With Their Answers," *Advertising and Selling,* November 23, 1933, 13–15.

21. "New Bill Worries Advertising Trade," *New York Times,* April 9, 1933, 15.

22. "Food and Drugs," *Tide,* May 1933, 8–9.

23. "Federal Regulation of Advertising," *Advertising Age,* April 29, 1933, 4.

24. "Enemies of the Consumer," *Consumers' Research General Bulletin,* October 1933, 22.

25. Ibid.

26. "Fine the Dishonest Advertiser or Lock Him Up," *Printers' Ink,* June 22, 1933, 60.

27. "Defense of 'Opinion,' 'Ambiguity' in Advertising Law," *Printers' Ink,* August 24, 1933, 43; "Administration Bill Penalizes"; Heald, "What Kind of Regulation."

28. In spite of the increasing use of emotional appeals in advertising copy, it would be inaccurate to assume that all advertisers used this strategy. In 1929, for example, *Tide* and the *Ladies' Home Journal* surveyed one hundred full-page advertisements. They concluded that more than half (56 percent) did not rely on emotional appeals; see Otis Pease, *The Responsibilities of American Advertising: Private Control and Public Influence, 1920–1940* (New Haven, Conn.: Yale University Press, 1958), 35n39.

29. Lee H. Bristol, "Capper Bill Insures against Rule by Bureaucrats," *Printers' Ink,* May 25, 1933, 41.

30. Ibid.

31. "More Better Business Bureaus Back P. I. Statute," *Printers' Ink,* June 8, 1933, 32–33; "Capper Bill Seen as Powerful Aid to Honest Advertising," *Printers' Ink,* August 17, 1933, 89; "Capper Advertising Bill Draws Strong Support," *Printers' Ink,* August 17, 1933, 58; "Strong Support for P. I. Statute," *Printers' Ink,* June 1, 1933, 78–79.

32. "Thumbscrews," *Tide,* June 1935, 18; Pease, *Responsibilities of American Advertising,* 119.

33. "Advertising or Tugwell," *Business Week,* October 28, 1933, 14.

34. "Advertising Censorship Reaches Congress," *Printers' Ink,* June 8, 1933, 82.

35. G. A. Nichols, "Beat the Tugwell Bill," *Printers' Ink,* November 2, 1933, 11. See also "Tugwell Bill Called Start of Regulation," *Advertising Age,* November 11, 1933, 1; and Calkins, "Another Look at the Pure Food Bill," 90.

36. Editorial, *Nation,* December 27, 1933, 719–20.

37. John Benson, statement in Senate Subcommittee on Commerce, *Food, Drugs, and Cosmetics Hearing before a Subcommittee on Commerce on S 1944,* 73rd Cong., 2nd sess., 1934 (hereafter referred to as *S 1944 Hearing*), 330–31.

38. "Drug Bill Will Aid Advertising, Tugwell Asserts," *Advertising Age,* September 16, 1933, 18.

39. Henry Wallace, "Why Advertising Must Have a New Food and Drugs Law," *Advertising and Selling,* November 22, 1934, 19–20.

40. "Drug Bill Will Aid"; "Here Is the Administration's Position on Copeland Bill," *Printers' Ink,* November 30, 1933, 6.

41. "The Tugwell Bill Becomes an Issue," *Advertising Age,* October 14, 1933, 4.

42. Paul W. West quoted in "Advertisers Fear Abuse of Food Law," *New York Times,* September 27, 1933, 37.

43. "Why All Advertisers Are Interested in the Tugwell Bill," *Advertising Age,* October 21, 1933, 4.

44. See, for example, "Copy Regulation and Costs Head NPA Discussion," *Advertising Age,* September 6, 1934, 1.

45. For the full wording of the Printers' Ink Model Statute, see "U.S. Law Regulating Advertising Is Under Way," *Printers' Ink,* May 4, 1933, 10–11.

46. Gordon E. Miracle and Terence Nevett, "A Comparative History of Advertising Self-Regulation in the UK and the US," *European Journal of Marketing* 2, no. 4 (1988): 7–23.

47. Daniel Pope, "Advertising as a Consumer Issue: An Historical View," *Journal of Social Issues* 47, no. 1 (1991): 41–56.

48. The local advertising clubs first entrusted with imposing the Printers' Ink Model Statute eventually evolved into local better business bureaus; see Daniel Pope, "Advertising as a Consumer Issue: A Historical View," *Journal of Social Issues* 47, no. 1 (1991): 41–56.

49. "A Master Code for Advertising," *Printers' Ink,* June 23, 1932, 33. See also "Federation Adopts New Declaration of Ideals, Principles," *Advertising Age,* June 25, 1932, 1.

50. "Advertisers Would Have Team Work with the Politicians," *Printers' Ink,* June 30, 1932, 61.

51. "The Truth about Advertising," *Advertising Age,* December 6, 1930, 4.

52. Arthur Capper, "Truthful Advertising Is Essential to Business Recovery," *Printers' Ink,* June 29, 1933, 52; John Benson, "Needed: Closer Working Plan in Advertising as a Whole," *Printers' Ink,* July 6, 1933, 88; "Ad Reforms Urged to Avoid Censor," *New York Times,* April 12, 1933, 22.

53. Ibid. The codes were based on the 1911 truth-in-advertising movement's definition of advertising's "seven sins": false statements or misleading exaggerations; indirect misrepresentation of a product or service through distortion of details, either editorially or pictorially; statements or suggestions offensive to public decency; statements that tended to undermine an industry by attributing to its products faults and

weaknesses true only of a few; misleading price claims; pseudoscientific advertising, including claims that were insufficiently supported by accepted authority or that distorted the true meaning or application of a statement made by a professional or scientific authority; and advertising testimonials that did not reflect the real choice of a competent witness; see Frederic R. Gamble to Roy C. Witmer, memo, August 15, 1932, box 5, folder 103, National Broadcasting Company Papers, Wisconsin Center for Historical Research, State Historical Society of Wisconsin, Madison (hereafter referred to as NBC Papers).

54. Report from the National Better Business Bureau, March 30, 1933, box 20, folder 5, NBC Papers. See also Pease, *Responsibilities of American Advertising,* 46–49; "Advertisers Would Have Team Work with the Politicians," 60–64; "Advertising Sets Up Code, 'Supreme Court,'" *Business Week,* June 6, 1932, 11; "Advertising Field to Have 'High Court,'" *New York Times,* December 11, 1932, 29; "Ad Regulation Group to Put Plan in Force," *New York Times,* July 14, 1933, 24; "Committee Completed to Review Questionable Advertising," *Printers' Ink,* February 9, 1933, 77; "Advertising 'Reform' Movement Gains Momentum," *Advertising and Selling,* April 27, 1933, 28; "Acts to Enforce Advertising Code," *New York Times,* April 13, 1933, 31; and "Act to Preserve Confidence in the Printed Word," *Advertising Age,* February 6, 1932, 1.

55. Lawrence Valenstein quoted in Pease, *Responsibilities of American Advertising,* 71.

56. "Advertising: Federation Maps Code by Recovery Act," *Newsweek,* July 15, 1933, 25; "AFA Commends Advertising Code to Government," *Printers' Ink,* July 6, 1933, 25; "Advertising and the New Economics," *Printers' Ink,* July 6, 1933, 3; "Agency NRA Code Would Enforce Honesty in Advertising," *Printers' Ink,* August 31, 1933, 25; "Advertising Sets Up Code."

57. Pease, *Responsibilities of American Advertising,* 71.

58. "Administration Dodges Tugwell Bill Defense," *Printers' Ink,* November 16, 1933, 44; C. B. Larrabee, "Advertising and the Recovery Act," *Printers' Ink Monthly,* August 1933, 19.

59. See, for example, "Let's Save the NRA," *Printers' Ink,* July 5, 1934, 88; and "All Must Aid in Self-Regulation, Gardner Asserts," *Advertising Age,* September 8, 1934, 1.

60. Executive quoted in "Four A Convention Draws Record Group to Nation's Capital," *Advertising Age,* May 13, 1933, 15.

61. "Urges Informative Ads," *New York Times,* June 2, 1934, 3.

62. Frederic R. Gamble quoted in "Advertising Is 95% Pure, Coast Group Is Told," *Advertising Age,* July 1, 1935, 6. Advertising expenditures dropped from $2 billion to well below $1 billion between 1929 and 1933. Therefore, using the industry's own estimates, even during the most economically depressed years in the early 1930s, advertisers spent approximately $50 million each year on advertising that even the industry itself found to be of questionable value; see, for example, "Advertising Must Fight as Well as Clean Up," *Printers' Ink,* April 19, 1934, 33–34.

63. "Advertising Copy Must Be Cleaned Up, Four A's Told," *Advertising Age,* May 26, 1934, 1; "To Clean Up Advertising," *Printers' Ink,* October 25, 1934, 86.

64. "A National Advertiser Asks Media Owners for a Czar," *Advertising and Selling,* August 16, 1934, 23 (emphasis in the original), clipping in box 23, folder 62, NBC Papers.

65. "Self-Regulation of Advertising—Now," *Advertising Age,* April 14, 1934, 4.

66. C. B. Larrabee quoted in "Warns of Abuses of Advertising," *New York Times,* November 11, 1934, 39.

67. "Advertising Needs Cleaning from Within," *Printers' Ink,* April 5, 1934, 8.

68. Bernhard A. Grimes, "Ready to Clean House," *Printers' Ink,* June 28, 1934, 41–46; "A.F.A. on Advertising," *Advertising Age,* June 21, 1934, 12. The AFA's 1934 spring convention was broadcast over the Columbia radio network; see "Advertising Talks on Air," *New York Times,* May 31, 1934, 6; and "Advertising on Trial," *Printers' Ink,* June 21, 1934, 37.

69. "Advertising Needs Cleaning," 10.

70. "Current Public Relations Problems of Advertising," *Advertising Age,* December 1, 1934, 10; "The A.N.A. on Self-Regulation," *Advertising Age,* January 5, 1935, 10; "Is Advertising Now Ready for Self-Regulation?" *Advertising Age,* June 2, 1934, 4; "A Czar Maybe?" *Printers' Ink,* June 21, 1934, 122–23.

71. "Is Advertising Now Ready?" 4.

72. "Self-Regulation of Advertising—Now," 4.

73. Roy S. Durstine, "Why Advertising Really Is an Economic Tool," *Printers' Ink,* November 29, 1934, 93.

74. "A National Advertiser Asks Media Owners."

75. Alfred H. Haase and I. W. Digges, "How Media Owners Can Curb False Advertising," *Printers' Ink,* September 27, 1934, 7.

76. C. B. Larrabee, "Guinea Pig Books," *Printers' Ink,* April 16, 1936, 76.

77. "A Czar Maybe?" 123.

78. "A National Advertiser Asks Media Owners"; Paul W. West, "How Advertisers Can Help Censor Advertising," *Printers' Ink,* October 4, 1934, 17.

79 "A National Advertiser Asks Media Owners." *Printers' Ink* asked for "an unapproachable, impeccable czar who would be paid a salary large enough to keep him that way"; "A Czar Maybe?" 123.

80. Dexter Masters, "An Advertising Critic Speaks Up," *Advertising and Selling,* February 1938, 29.

81. Robert S. Lynd, statement in *S 1944 Hearing,* 329.

82. Advertising Review Committee quoted in "Federal Regulation of Advertising," 4.

83. Calkins, "Another Look at the Pure Food Bill," 152.

84. Elisha Hanson's statement in *S 1944 Hearing,* 456–58; "The Tugwell Bill: In the Matter of S 1944 and HR 6110, 73rd Congress," *American Newspaper Publishers Association Bulletin,* no. 6218 (December 27, 1933): 730. See also C. Ellesworth Wylie

to Franklin D. Roosevelt, telegram, December 28, 1933, box 375, Tugwell PFA 1933–35 folder, President's Official Files, Franklin D. Roosevelt Library, Hyde Park, N.Y. (hereafter referred to as FDR Official Files).

85. "Advertiser Censorship Reaches Congress," *Printers' Ink*, June 8, 1933, 83.

86. *National Association of Broadcasters Reports*, May 21, 1936, 1331. See also *Evening Tribune* publishers to Franklin D. Roosevelt, telegram, December 28, 1933, box 375, Tugwell PFA 1933–35 folder, FDR Official Files.

87. James W. Baldwin's statement in *S 1944 Hearing*, 120; "Tugwell Bill Is Target of Bitter Attack," *Advertising Age*, October 14, 1933, 1; "Tug-o-War," *Tide*, October 1933, 20–21. These sentiments were shared by the Institute of Medicine Manufacturers as well; see, for example, "Ambiguity of Tugwell Bill Is Criticized," *Advertising Age*, October 28, 1933, 8; "Drug Act Revision Backed by Women," *New York Times*, November 17, 1933, 40; and "Proprietary Association President Answers Tugwell on New Drug Bill," *Oil, Paint, and Drug Reporter*, October 9, 1933, 15.

88. "The Tugwell Bill S 1944—A JACK S.," *Spectro-Chrome*, Orange 1934, 1057, clipping in box 375, Tugwell PFA 1933–35 folder, FDR Official Files. A hearing on S 2800 (a rewritten version of S 1944) gave the organization's president and treasurer a chance to publicly express his anger about the measure; see Dinshah Ghadiali's statement in Senate Committee on Commerce, *Food, Drugs, and Cosmetics Hearing before the Committee on Commerce on S 2800*, 73rd Cong., 2nd sess., 1934, 58–62 (hereafter referred to as *S 2800 Hearing*).

89. "The Tugwell Bill S 1944," 1057.

90. James Rorty, *Our Master's Voice: Advertising* (1934; repr., New York: Arno Press, 1976), chap. 23.

91. "Jersey Health Officers O.K. Tugwell Bill," *Advertising Age*, December 2, 1933, 6. The National Association of Manufacturers launched a strong attack on the Tugwell bill; see, for example, "Food and Drug Act, Resolution No. 9," n.d., box 8246, National Association of Manufacturers folder, President's Personal Files, Franklin D. Roosevelt Library, Hyde Park, N.Y. (hereafter referred to as FDR Personal Files).

92. For an excellent account of how advertisers in general, and drug manufacturers in particular, pressured newspapers to ignore or criticize the Tugwell bill, see George Seldes, *Freedom of the Press* (Indianapolis, Ind.: Bobbs-Merrill, 1935), 56–61. See also George Seldes, *Lords of the Press* (New York: Julian Messner, 1938), 212, 300; statement of Elisha Hanson in *S 1944 Hearing*, 456–67; statement of Charles Coolidge Parlin in *S 1944 Hearing*, 312–28; and "Last Roundup," *Tide*, November 1933, 44.

93. Although bill opponents held a clear advantage in regard to media access, some trade journals provided bill proponents with a chance to be heard as well. *Printers' Ink* was a leader in this respect; see, for example, "Call for Mr. Rorty," *Printers' Ink*, January 1934, 29.

94. Frederick J. Schlink to Rexford G. Tugwell, May 26, 1933, box 6, Consumers' Research folder, Tugwell Papers.

95. "The American System," n.d., box 3, folder 9, Kallet Papers.

96. Ibid. See also Frederick J. Schlink to U. Kellogg, August 7, 1934, box 3, folder 9, Kallet Papers.

97. "Last Roundup."

98. Seldes, *Freedom of the Press*, 56.

99. Rorty, *Our Master's Voice*, 379.

100. See William Jacobs to Mr. Aylesworth, November 17, 1933, box 22, folder 37, NBC Papers. The exhibit inspired a book by Ruth DeForest Lamb entitled *American Chamber of Horrors* (New York: Farrar and Rinehart, 1936). See also Rorty, *Our Master's Voice*, 360.

101. Pease, *Responsibilities of American Advertising*, 118; "Last Roundup."

102. Jacobs to Aylesworth.

103. Ibid.

104. William Hedges to John F. Royal, November 6, 1933, box 22, folder 37, NBC Papers. "The Tugwell bill," telegraphed a representative from the broadcasting industry to Roosevelt, "is decisively inimical to legitimate advertising and should not be adopted in its present form." From C. Ellsworth Wylie to Franklin D. Roosevelt, December 28, 1933.

105. See Joint Committee for Sound and Democratic Consumer Legislation, radio script, January or February 1934, box 32, folder 70, NBC Papers. It cannot be determined, however, if these scripts resulted in actual broadcasts.

106. *Nation*, March 14, 1934, 296, excerpt in box 367, folder 29, CR Papers.

107. A. B. Walton to Frederick J. Schlink, July 16, 1934, excerpt in box 367, folder 29, CR Papers.

108. E. J. Adams, address delivered at the Annual Meeting of Broadcasters, Advertisers, and Agency Men, Chicago, June 11, 1935, box 36, folder 41, NBC Papers, 4.

109. "N.P.A. 'Tugwell Committee' Lays Down Platform," *Advertising Age*, December 9, 1933, 9; "Tugwell Bill Center of Attention as Hearings Open," *Advertising and Selling*, December 7, 1933, 18; "Tugwell Bill to Be Entirely Rewritten, Is Current Opinion," *Advertising Age*, December 16, 1933, 1. The U.S. Chamber of Commerce supported the Proprietary Association in stating that it believed no new law was necessary and that the Federal Food and Drugs Act of 1906 offered sufficient consumer protection; see "No Demand Seen for Changes in Food, Drug Bill," *Advertising Age*, December 9, 1933, 6.

110. Statement of Arthur Kallet in *S 1944 Hearing*, 355–56.

111. Frederick J. Schlink to Benjamin Marsh, December 4, 1933, box 352, folder 20, CR Papers; Arthur Kallet to Frederick J. Schlink, memo, November 11, 1933, box 352, folder 20, CR Papers.

112. "Fakers and Adulterators Win First Round," *Consumers' Research Bulletin*, January 1934, 20–23.

113. *Dictionary of American Biography*, s.v. "Copeland, Royal Samuel (November 7, 1868–June 17, 1938)."

114. "A Little Fellow in a Big Post," editorial from an unnamed Poughkeepsie, N.Y.,

newspaper, spring 1934, clipping in box 651, Royal S. Copeland folder, FDR Personal Files. The columnist refers to a syndicated newspaper column that Copeland wrote for the Hearst newspaper chain.

115. Paul Dwyer, "The Radio Robot—Or Unadulterated Music," *Consumers' Research Bulletin,* October 1937, 9–10. See also Roland Marchand, *Advertising the American Dream: Making Way for Modernity, 1920–1940* (Berkeley: University of California Press, 1985).

116. Arthur Kallet, statement in *S 1944 Hearing,* 355–56. Concerns about Copeland's commercial endorsements were not limited to the floor of Congress; see "Drugs and Yeast," *Tide,* December 1933, 36.

117. O. S. Cox to Arthur Kallet, December 16, 1933, box 3, folder 9, Kallet Papers.

118. Emergency Conference of Consumer Organizations, "Consumers Charge Copeland Oversteps Law in Wrecking Tugwell Bill," n.d., box 352, folder 23, CR Papers.

119. Arthur Kallet to D. F. Cavers, December 29, 1933, box 356, folder 11, CR Papers.

120. Statement of Arthur Kallet in *S 1944 Hearing,* 355–56; "Drugs and Yeast." Copeland's commercial endorsements worried others as well. Both Arthur S. Morton from Tacoma, Washington, and Warren Munsell from New York City wrote letters to Roosevelt and expressed their concerns regarding this matter; see Arthur S. Morton to Franklin D. Roosevelt, January 11, 1934, box 375, Tugwell PFA 1933–35 folder, FDR Official Files; and Warren Munsell to Franklin D. Roosevelt, January 8, 1934, box 375, Tugwell PFA 1933–35 folder, FDR Official Files.

121. "Drugs and Yeast." Drug interests claimed that the American Medical Association opposed certain forms of self-medication on the ground that it would translate into less business for its members. Not surprisingly, the association vehemently denied the charge; see "A.M.A. Endorses Principles of Tugwell Bill," *Advertising Age,* December 9, 1933, 10. To further their agenda, the proprietary interests created an industry front operation called the Women's Health Foundation of America, which claimed the pending bill was an invasion of American wives' and mothers' right to select the remedies they believed would best treat their families and themselves. This strategy severely upset writers at *Printers' Ink,* who denounced the foundation's claim as a pathetic attempt at "dragging wifehood and motherhood into the controversy"; see "Mother, Home, and Tugwell," *Printers' Ink,* December 28, 1933, 87.

122. "Is the Tugwell Bill an Administrative Measure?" *Advertising Age,* December 30, 1933, 4.

123. Arthur Kallet to Frederick J. Schlink, January 10, 1934, box 183, folder 12, CR Papers; Arthur Kallet, "No 'New Deal' on Food, Drugs, and Cosmetics," *Consumers' Research General Bulletin,* October 1934, 1–3.

124. G. A. Nichols, "It's the Copeland Bill, Now," *Printers' Ink,* January 11, 1934, 69; *National Association of Broadcasters Reports,* January 6, 1934, 267; *National Association of Broadcasters Reports,* February 19, 1934, 299; "Self Regulation under the Tugwell

Bill?" *Advertising Age,* January 6, 1934, 4; "Drastic Revisions Made in New Draft of Tugwell Bill," *Advertising Age,* January 8, 1934, 1.

125. "Four Food Bills and All Good," *Printers' Ink,* February 1, 1934, 69.

126. M. C. Phillips to James Campbell, January 16, 1934, box 356, folder 10, CR Papers.

127. Arthur Kallet to Frederick Russell Bassin, January 17, 1934, box 3, folder 9, Kallet Papers.

128. "Copeland Bill Unsatisfactory to Dr. Tugwell," *Advertising Age,* January 13, 1934, 1.

129. Rexford G. Tugwell to Franklin D. Roosevelt, February 21, 1934, box 375, Tugwell PFA 1933–35 folder, FDR Official Files.

130. Emergency Conference of Consumer Organizations, "Consumers Charge Copeland Oversteps Law."

131. Kallet to Bassin, January 17, 1924. See also Louis Filler, "Marsh, Benjamin C. (1877–1952)," *Dictionary of American Social Reform* (New York: Philosophical Library, 1963), 480; Richard L. D. Morse, ed., *The Consumer Movement: Lectures by Colston E. Warne* (Manhattan, Kans.: Family Economics Trust Press, 1993), xiv.

132. "Is U.S. Against Advertising?" *Printers' Ink,* November 2, 1933, 100.

133. "Backs Food and Drug Bill," *New York Times,* November 16, 1933, 6; "Advertising and the U.S.," *Printers' Ink,* November 30, 1933, 84.

134. Bernhard Sternsher argues that Tugwell was largely unprepared for his whipping-boy role in connection with the amended Food and Drugs Act but that he endured the ordeal without complaining; see Bernhard Sternsher, *Rexford Tugwell,* chap. 19.

135. "Professor Tugwell's Political Influence Is Waning," *Advertising Age,* April 7, 1934, 4; "Copeland Bill Slated for Quick Passage," *Printers' Ink,* February 15, 1934, 21. See also "Priming the Pump," *Printers' Ink,* January 18, 1934, 92; and "President to Aid Copeland Bill, Report," *Advertising Age,* February 10, 1934, 2.

136. "Copeland Bill Slated."

137. "Form Group to Fight Proposed Food, Drug Bill," *Advertising Age,* February 10, 1934, 1; "Copeland Bill Revised Once More," *Printers' Ink,* February 8, 1934, 18.

138. "Four Food Bills"; "Battered Bill," *Tide,* March 1934, 26.

139. A. L. Ashby, "The Tugwell Bill," January 9, 1934, box 42, folder 18, NBC Papers.

140. "A.N.P.A. Asks Copeland Bill Revisions," *Printers' Ink,* May 3, 1934, 77; "Constructive Revision of Food, Drug Bill Is Approved by A.N.P.A.," *Advertising Age,* April 28, 1934, 1; "A.N.A Withholds Approval of Food, Drug Legislation," *Advertising Age,* February 2, 1935, 30; "Battered Bill."

141. M. C. Phillips to James Campbell, February 16, 1934, box 356, folder 10, CR Papers.

142. Statement of Arthur Kallet in *S 2800 Hearing,* 278.

143. Statement of James R. Rorty, in *S 2800 Hearing,* 410.

144. Statement of Arthur Kallet in *S 2800 Hearing,* 299–300; "Six Bills: Take Your Choice," *Printers' Ink,* March 8, 1934, 33–34.

145. Statement of John A. Benson in *S 2800 Hearing,* 194–96.

146. "A.F.A. Not to Fight Newest Copeland Bill," *Advertising Age,* March 17, 1934, 16.

147. "A.N.A. Calls for Fight on Copeland Bill," *Printers' Ink,* February 22, 1934, 21. For the view of the National Publishers' Association, see statement of Charles Coolidge Parlin in *S 2800 Hearing,* 30–34, 175–77.

148. Arthur Kallet to Franklin D. Roosevelt, telegram, March 4, 1934, box 355, folder 3, CR Papers.

149. Unsigned and undated memo, box 3, folder 9, Kallet Papers; Arthur Kallet to Frederick J. Schlink, memo, March 3, 1934, box 335, folder 3, CR Papers, copy in box 3, folder 9, Kallet Papers.

150. Kallet memo to Schlink, March 3, 1934. For a copy of the speech not allowed into the *Congressional Record,* see unsigned and undated memo marked "Consumers' Research, Inc., Washington, N.J.," box 356, folder 10, CR Papers.

151. Kallet memo to Schlink, March 3, 1934.

152. Royal S. Copeland, "The Proposed Food, Drug, and Cosmetic Law," script of radio talk, March 9, 1934, box 25, Food and Drug Legislation folder, Copeland Papers.

153. Ibid.

154. Rachel Palmer to O. S. Cox, September 14, 1934, box 356, folder 10, CR Papers; Frederick J. Schlink to Roger M. Pfitzenmeyer, April 12, 1934, box 22, folder 7, CR Papers; Schlink to Kellogg, August 7, 1934.

155. Schlink to Pfitzenmeyer, April 12, 1934; "Consumers and the New Deal," n.d., box 328, folder 9, CR Papers; Kallet, "No 'New Deal,'" 1–3.

156. Schlink to Kellogg, August 7, 1934.

157. "Consumers and the New Deal."

158. Kallet, "No 'New Deal,'" 2.

159. Ibid., 2.

160. Ibid.

161. "Copeland Bill Debated," *National Association of Broadcasters Reports,* May 19, 1934, 414; "Copeland Bill Hits Snag," *Printers' Ink,* May 24, 1934, 65; "Latest Changes in Food, Drug Bill Detailed," *Advertising Age,* March 24, 1934, 8; "Dog Days," *Tide,* May 1934, 10–11; "Copeland Bill Called Up Suddenly; Hope for Its Passage Dwindles," *Advertising Age,* May 19, 1934, 1; "Copeland Staff Can See Little Hope for Bill," *Advertising Age,* June 9, 1934, 15.

Chapter 4: A Consumer Movement Divided

1. The best term for this approach, according to Lawrence B. Glickman, is *technocratic individualist consumerism;* see Lawrence B. Glickman, "The Strike in the

Temple of Consumption: Consumer Activism and Twentieth-Century American Political Culture," *Journal of American History* 88, no. 1 (June 2001): 99.

2. Richard L. D. Morse, ed., *The Consumer Movement: Lectures by Colston E. Warne* (Manhattan, Kans.: Family Economics Trust Press, 1983), 51.

3. Norman Isaac Silber, *Test and Protest: The Influence of Consumers Union* (New York: Holmes and Meier, 1983), 19.

4. "Facts in Brief of the Strike at Consumers' Research," September 5, 1935, box 4, folder 4, Arthur Kallet Papers, Consumers Union Archives, Yonkers, N.Y. (hereafter referred to as Kallet Papers); "M. C. Phillips," in *A Guide to the Records of Consumers' Research Inc.: Biographies, Bibliographies, and Further Reading*, http://www.libraries. rutgers.edu/rul/libs/scua/consumers_research/consumers_research_menu_4.shtml (accessed May 17, 2003). In spite of having been removed from the board, Kallet stayed on as CR's secretary.

5. Norman D. Katz, "Consumers Union: The Movement and the Magazine" (Ph.D. diss., Rutgers University, 1977), 48, 70.

6. Morse, *Consumer Movement*, 45; "Speakers Available," *Consumers' Research General Bulletin*, September 1932, 12.

7. Morse, *Consumer Movement*, 50–51.

8. Ibid., 48. In 1932 Schlink earned an annual salary of $7,000 whereas the next highest-ranking person in the organization was paid $2,080. By 1936 Schlink was reported to be earning between $9,000 and $10,000 annually. Katz, "Consumers Union, " 69; "Consumers Union Reports," *Printers' Ink,* May 1936, 64.

9. Katz, "Consumers Union," 70.

10. Ibid.

11. "Facts in Brief"; Katz, "Consumers Union," 74–75.

12. "Report of the Director of Research, J. B. Matthews, to the Special Committee on Un-American Activities on Communist Work in Consumer Organizations," December 11, 1939, box 2, folder 5, Consumers Union Papers, Consumers Union Archives, Yonkers, N.Y. (hereafter referred to as CU Papers); Frederick J. Schlink, "The Communists and Their Fellow Travelers," November 16, 1940, box 92, folder 20, Consumers' Research Papers, Special Collections and University Archives, Rutgers University, New Brunswick, N.J. (hereafter referred to as CR Papers).

13. M. C. Phillips, "Communists and the High Cost of Living," *Consumers' Digest,* February 1940, 33–38; M. C. Phillips, "Communists and the Milk Strike," *Consumers' Digest,* March 1940, 49–54.

14. J. B. Matthews to Ingram Bander, July 29, 1935, box 8, folder 21, CR papers; Ingram Bander to Consumers' Research, July 6, 1935, box 8, folder 21, CU Papers; J. B. Matthews to Ingram Bander, July 12, 1935, box 8, folder 21, CR Papers; J. B. Matthews to Ingram Bander, July 29, 1935, box 8, folder 21, CU Papers.

15. Matthews to Bander, July 12, 1935.

16. Technical, Editorial, and Office Assistants' Union Local 20055, "Digest of National Labor Relations Board Report on Consumers' Research Strike," n.d., box

4, folder 2, Kallet Papers; "Thunder on the Left," *Tide,* September 1935, 22, clipping in box 4, folder 2, CU Papers.

17. [Arthur Kallet] to [Charles S.] Wyand, September 1, 1935, box 4, folder 4, Kallet Papers.

18. "Minutes of the Special Meeting of the Board of Directors of Consumers' Research Inc.," August 28, 1935, box 41, folder 31, CR Papers.

19. Ibid.; "Minutes of the Special Meeting of the Board of Directors of Consumers' Research Inc.," September 4, 1935, box 41, folder 31, CR Papers; Kallet to Wyand, September 1, 1935; Morse, *Consumer Movement,* 52. Not surprisingly, the union account of the events leading up to the strike differed quite a bit from the CR management's version. For a union account, see Technical, Editorial, and Office Assistants' Union Local 20055, "The Strike at Consumers' Research: The Union's Reply to the Management's Statement," September 16, 1935, box 4, folder 8, Kallet Papers; and Consumers' Research Strike Aid Committee, "Text of Final Strike Ultimatum; Addressed to the Board of Directors; Dated 9/3/35," November 3, 1935, box 4, folder 8, Kallet Papers. For CR's account, see "The Strike at Consumers' Research," September 10, 1935, box 28, folder 21, CR Papers.

20. Kallet to Wyand, September 1, 1935.

21. Ibid.

22. Technical, Editorial, and Office Assistants' Union Local 20055 to J. B. Matthews, September 6, 1935, box 4, folder 3, Kallet Papers; Shop Committee to J. B. Matthews for the Board of Directors, August 31, 1935, box 4, folder 3, Kallet Papers.

23. Technical, Editorial, and Office Assistants' Union Local 20055 to Consumers' Research Board, September 4, 1935, box 4, folder 3, Kallet Papers; "Facts in Brief." The use of the term *consumer-worker* was a subtle way of getting back at Matthews, who had used the term in his prolabor book *Partners in Plunder;* see J. B. Matthews and Ruth Shallcross, *Partners in Plunder: The Cost of Business Dictatorship* (New York: Convici-Friede, 1935), 30–31.

24. Shop Committee to Frederick J. Schlink, September 9, 1935, box 4, folder 3, Kallet Papers. A draft of a letter containing more modest demands was composed three days earlier, but there is no evidence that the first version was ever sent; see Technical, Editorial, and Office Assistants' Union Local 20055 to Consumers' Research Board, September 6, 1935, box 4, folder 3, Kallet Papers; and "Facts in Brief."

25. "Later Strike Developments at CR," *Consumers' Research Bulletin,* October 1935, 18.

26. Ibid.

27. Susan Jenkins to William Hayes, November 6, 1935, box 4, folder 4, Kallet Papers; Silber, *Test and Protest,* 20–21.

28. Technical, Editorial, and Office Assistants' Union Local 20055, "Questions for J. B. Matthews to Answer," September 18, 1935, box 4, folder 3, Kallet Papers.

29. Jenkins to Hayes, November 6, 1935.

30. Arthur Kallet to Elizabeth Wickenden, October 19, 1935, box 4, folder 4, Kallet Papers.

31. M. C. Hade to Frederick J. Schlink, September 10, 1935, box 4, folder 3, Kallet Papers.

32. Arthur Kallet to Consumers' Research members ("Dear Friend" form letter), October 13, 1935, box 4, folder 4, Kallet Papers.

33. Kallet to Wickenden; undated and unsigned memo pleading for financial support for CR strikers, box 4, folder 4, Kallet Papers; Technical, Editorial, and Office Assistants' Union Local 20055, *CR Board Refuses Government Arbitration,* October 17, 1935, box 4, folder 2, Kallet Papers.

34. Technical, Editorial, and Office Assistants' Union Local 20055 to American Federation of Labor National Executive Committee, October 9, 1935, box 4, folder 1, Kallet Papers.

35. J. B. Matthews, affidavit subscribed and sworn before Alvin Sloan, October 10, 1935, 4, box 43, folder 4, CR Papers. See also "Later Strike Developments at CR," 18.

36. Matthews affidavit, 2.

37. Norman Thomas to Technical, Editorial, and Office Assistants' Union Local 20055, October 9, 1935, box 4, folder 2, Kallet Papers; Technical, Editorial, and Office Assistants' Union, *CR Board Refuses.*

38. Technical, Editorial, and Office Assistants' Union Local 20055, "Digest of National Labor Relations Board Report."

39. "Thunder on the Left."

40. Glickman, "Strike in the Temple of Consumption," 99–100.

41. Ibid., 109.

42. "F. J. Schlink," in *A Guide to the Records of Consumers' Research Inc.*

43. "New Organization to Rate Labor Conditions," *Consumers' Research General Bulletin,* January 1933, 9 (emphasis in the original); Frederick J. Schlink to Bradford Young, May 3, 1932, box 8, folder 21, CR Papers; Bradford Young to Frederick J. Schlink, May 6, 1932, box 8, folder 21, CR Papers.

44. L. B. Young to Jerome Davis, May 25, 1932, box 8, folder 21, CR Papers.

45. Frederick J. Schlink to Bradford Young, May 13, 1932, box 8, folder 21, CR Papers.

46. Frederick J. Schlink to Francis A. Henson, October 14, 1932, box 8, folder 21, CR Papers.

47. Jerome Davis to L. B. Young, May 30, 1932, box 8, folder 21, CR Papers; M. C. Phillips to Hugh Kirkland, November 6, 1933, box 8, folder 21, CR Papers; M. C. Phillips to Joseph K. Howard, November 12, 1934, box 8, folder 21, CR Papers.

48. Frederick J. Schlink to Mark Starr, October 26, 1933, box 414, folder 3, CR Papers.

49. Frederick J. Schlink to John M. Gaston Jr., February 8, 1935, box 8, folder 21, CR Papers.

50. M. C. Phillips to John M. Gaston Jr., December 6, 1934, box 8, folder 21, CR Papers.

51. Ibid.

52. M. C. Phillips to Charles S. Wyand, April 18, 1935, box 183, folder 16, CR Papers.

53. Ibid. See also Frederick J. Schlink to Howard Hare, December 6, 1938, box 8, folder 20, CR Papers.

54. Matthews and Shallcross, *Partners in Plunder.* For a discussion of Matthews's political views, see George Seldes, *Witch Hunt: The Technique and Profits of Redbaiting* (New York: Modern Age Books, 1940), chap. 12.

55. Matthews and Shallcross, *Partners in Plunder,* 4–5. See also "The Consumer Sees Red," *American Mercury,* November 16, 1936, 313–20, clipping in box 21, folder 15, CR Papers.

56. "Thunder on the Left."

57. Ibid.

58. Dewey H. Palmer to Colston E. Warne, January 29, 1936, box 5, folder 1, Kallet Papers.

59. Arthur Kallet to Colston E. Warne, February 4, 1936, box 5, folder 1, Kallet Papers; "Sponsors of Consumers Union of United States (as of February 13, 1936)," n.d., box 5, folder 1, Kallet Papers.

60. "By-Laws of the Consumers Union Inc.," n.d., box 5, folder 1, Kallet Papers; Morse, *Consumer Movement,* 64; Silber, *Test and Protest,* 24.

61. In 1942 CU changed the name of *Consumers Union Reports* (hereafter referred to as CUR) to *Consumer Reports,* which it is still called today; see "Minutes of the Board of Directors of Consumers Union of the United States Inc.," June 3, 1942, box 1, Minutes 1942–49 folder, Board of Directors Minutes, Group 1B, Series 1936–65, CU Papers.

62. "Consumers' Goods Makers Unfair to Labor," *CUR,* May 1936, 20–21.

63. "Consumers and Labor," *CUR,* October 1936, 1.

64. Ibid.

65. "Minutes of Executive Committee Meeting," July 8, 1936, box 1, Minutes 1936–38 folder, Board of Directors Minutes, Group 1B, Series 1936–65, CU Papers. For a critical response to CU from a CR subscriber, see Pamela Redfield to Arthur Kallet, April 4, 1936, box 201, folder 11, CR Papers.

66. Frederick J. Schlink to William A. Consodine, November 25, 1936, box 204, folder 7, CR Papers.

67. C. P Cheney to Nelson J. Molter, April 1, 1938, box 204, folder 6, CR papers. See also C. P. Cheney to Robert W. Duncan, November 10, 1937, box 204, folder 6, CR Papers.

68. Frederick J. Schlink to Don Wharton, August 24, 1937, box 204, folder 13, CR Papers; Frederick J. Schlink to C. W. Schwartz, June 17, 1937, box 204, folder 13, CR Papers.

69. Silber, *Test and Protest,* 24, 27.

70. "The Attacking Stage," *CUR,* December 1937, 1; "Consumer Movement," *Advertising and Selling,* December 2, 1937, clipping in box 204, folder 12, CR Papers; "Not Acceptable," *American Consumer,* September 1939, 4–8, clipping in box 204, folder 13, CR Papers.

71. "The Good Housekeeping Institute," *CUR,* July 1936, 1.

72. Hearst Corporation quoted in Silber, *Test and Protest,* 28.

73. Publications that by mid-1937 rejected CU's ads included the *New York Times,* the *New York Herald Tribune,* the *New York Post,* the *Philadelphia Record,* the *New York Sunday News,* the *Christian Science Monitor, News-Week, American Home, Letters, Literary Digest,* the *New Yorker, Review of Reviews, This Week, Science,* the *Grade Teacher,* the *Rural New Yorker, Popular Science Monthly, Popular Mechanics,* the *Journal of Home Economics, Esquire,* and the *Sunday Evening Post;* see Arthur Kallet to Mark Starr, June 29, 1937, box 7, folder 7, Colston E. Warne Papers, Consumers Union Archives, Yonkers, N.Y. (hereafter referred to as Warne Papers); and George Seldes, "Do Advertisers Dominate the Press?" *CUR,* January 1939, 9.

74. Arthur Kallet to Jacob Baker, January 29, 1937, box 2, folder 1, CU Papers. Further complicating the matter was that CU's lack of testing facilities and experts. Much of its work was conducted in outside labs by sympathetic scientists who, for various reasons, did not want their names to be known.

75. Cheney to Molter, April 1, 1938; Cheney to Duncan, November 10, 1937. See also "Minutes of the Meeting of the Board of Directors of Consumers Union of the United States Inc.," March 5, 1938, box 1, Minutes 1936–38 folder, Board of Directors Minutes, Group 1B, Series 1936–65, CU Papers.

76. "Minutes of the Meeting of the Board of Directors of Consumers Union of the United States Inc.," May 8, 1937, box 1, Minutes 1936–38 folder, Board of Directors Minutes, Group 1B, Series 1936–65, CU Papers; "Minutes of the Meeting of the Board of Directors of Consumers Union of the United States Inc.," May 16, 1938, box 1, Minutes 1936–38 folder, Board of Directors Minutes, Group 1B, Series 1936–65, CU Papers. The boycott continued into the 1940s; see Bernard R. Kaplan to Arthur Kallet, December 28, 1939, box 99, folder 6, Warne Papers; Arthur Kallet to Joseph W. Gannon, February 5, 1940, box 99, folder 6, Warne Papers; and Colston E. Warne to Arthur Kallet, November 25, 1938, box 7, folder 7, Warne Papers.

77. Douglas Taylor to Colston E. Warne, April 19, 1940, box 99, folder 6, Warne Papers; "Our Chuckle Producing Department," *Linotype's Shining Lines,* January 1939, clipping in box 204, folder 13, CR Papers.

78. Silber, *Test and Protest,* 27.

79. Lizabeth Cohen, *A Consumers' Republic: The Politics of Mass Consumption in Postwar America* (New York: Alfred A. Knopf, 2003), 60–61.

80. Colston E. Warne to Arthur Kallet, January 29, 1937, box 7, folder 7, Warne Papers.

81. Colston E. Warne to Arthur Kallet, n.d., box 7, folder 7, Warne Papers.

82. "Minutes of the Meeting of the Board of Directors of Consumers Union of the United States Inc.," December 18, 1937, 5, box 1, Minutes 1936–38 folder, Board of Directors Minutes, Group 1B, Series 1936–65, CU Papers.

83. "Minutes of the Meeting of the Board of Directors of Consumers Union of the United States Inc.," September 27, 1937, box 1, Minutes 1936–38 folder, Board of Directors Minutes, Group 1B, Series 1936–65, CU Papers; Cohen, *Consumers' Republic,* 61; "Using Consumers," *Consumer Education Service,* February 1939, 35, clipping in box 84, folder 13, Richard L. D. Morse Papers, Consumer Movement Archives, Kansas State University, Manhattan.

84. "Consumers Union at the World's Fair," *CUR,* March 1939, 2; "Consumers Union at the New York World's Fair," *CUR,* April 1939, 15; "Consumers Union's Exhibit at the New York World's Fair," *CUR,* May 1939, 15. For a general discussion of the fair, see David Gellernter, *1939: The Lost World of the Fair* (New York: Avon Books, 1995); and William L. Bird Jr., *Better Living: Advertising, Media, and the New Vocabulary of Business Leadership, 1935–1955* (Evanston, Ill.: Northwestern University Press, 1999), 133–38.

85. "Advertising Is Exhibition Theme," *New York Times,* March 18, 1939, 22. See also "World's Fair Film to Refute Attacks on Advertising," *Advertising Age,* February 6, 1939, 4; Cohen, *Consumers' Republic,* 61.

86. Arthur Kallet to Consumers' Research members ("Dear Friend" form letter), April 14, 1937, box 26, folder 7, Warne Papers. See also "CU's First Annual Meeting," *CUR,* June 1937, 8–10.

87. Kallet to Starr, June 29, 1937; "Minutes of the Meeting of the Board of Directors of Consumers Union of the United States Inc.," December 18, 1937; Cheney to Duncan, November 10, 1937.

88. "Minutes of the Meeting of the Board of Directors of Consumers Union of the United States Inc.," September 14, 1937, box 1, Minutes 1936–38 folder, Board of Directors Minutes, Group 1B, Series 1936–65, CU Papers.

89. "Minutes of the Meeting of the Board of Directors of Consumers Union of the United States Inc.," September 27, 1937.

90. "Consumers National Council," *CUR,* April 1937, 1.

91. "A Federal Department of the Consumer," *Consumers' Digest,* January 1937, 52–54; see also "Mr. Schlink's New Paper," *Printers' Ink,* January 14, 1937, 49; "New Consumers' Digest Focuses Group's Strife," *Advertising Age,* February 3, 1937, 41.

92. "What Advertising Does and Does Not Do," *Consumers' Digest,* January 1937, 8 (emphasis in the original).

93. "Mr. Schlink's New Paper"; "Those Guinea Pig Engineers," *Printers' Ink,* February 1, 1934, 37.

94. "Mr. Schlink's New Paper."

95. Allyn B. McIntyre, "Fight Back," *Printers' Ink,* May 31, 1934, 64.

96. S. H. Walker and Paul Sklar, *Business Finds Its Voice* (New York: Harper and Brothers, 1938), 59–63. See also Edward L. Bernays, *Public Relations* (Norman: Uni-

versity of Oklahoma Press, 1952), 101; Donald D. Davis, "Public Must Be Given Facts about Business," *Printers' Ink,* October 31, 1935, 29; and "Urges Institutional Ads," *New York Times,* September 25, 1936, 32. Those who have studied business's opposition to the New Deal generally agree that 1936–37 represented the major turning point in business's propaganda strategies. This period witnessed a shift from propaganda that blatantly attacked the New Deal and the consumer movement toward propaganda that operated on a more subtle and sophisticated level; see Richard S. Tedlow, *Keeping the Corporate Image: Public Relations and Business, 1900–1950* (Greenwich, Conn.: JAI Press, 1979), 65; and "The American Way," *Time,* September 28, 1936, 61.

97. "Calls on Business to Rebuild Faith," *New York Times,* April 29, 1937, 30.

98. "Urges 'Selling' of Business," *New York Times,* December 4, 1936, 47.

99. Edgar Kobak quoted in Walker and Sklar, *Business Finds Its Voice,* 61–62.

100. Tedlow, *Keeping the Corporate Image,* 62. See also Roland Marchand, *Creating the Corporate Soul: The Rise of Public Relations and Corporate Imagery in American Big Business* (Berkeley: University of California Press, 1998), 202–4; Walker and Sklar, *Business Finds Its Voice,* chap. 8; and Stuart Ewen, *PR! The Social History of Spin* (New York: Basic Books, 1996). For excellent examples of radio's use for corporate propaganda in the 1930s, see Elizabeth Fones-Wolf, "Creating a Favorable Business Climate: Corporations and Radio Broadcasting, 1934 to 1954," *Business History Review* 73, no. 2 (Summer 1999): 221–55; and Bird, *Better Living,* chaps. 3–6.

101. Lawrence M. Hughes, "Industry Starts to Show How 'Enterprise' Pays the Nation," *Sales Management,* September 1, 1936, 329–31. The National Association of Manufacturers also produced newsreels on the subject of taxation and unemployment.

102. Ewen, *PR!* 298–99.

103. "News and Notes of the Advertising World," *New York Times,* May 17, 1937, 36J. See also Livingston, "Recovery (in Advertising) Can't Be Stopped," *Advertising and Selling,* January 14, 1937, 74. See also "Advertising Can Soften Taxes," *Business Week,* July 4, 1936, 32–33. For information about Hill and Knowlton's use of PR in the 1930s, see Karen S. Miller, *The Voice of Business: Hill & Knowlton and Postwar Public Relations* (Chapel Hill: University of North Carolina Press, 1999), chap. 1.

104. This is not to say that all manufacturers were fully convinced. In 1939, for example, *Printers' Ink* reminded American manufacturers of advertising's important role in a successful business enterprise and warned them not to cut advertising budgets with the excuse of financial hardship; see "What Advertising Is, What It Has Done, What It Can Do Now," *Printers' Ink,* January 12, 1939, 11–20.

105. Arthur H. Little, "Industry Writes Its Story," *Printers' Ink,* December 19, 1935, 10.

106. Bruce Barton quoted in ibid., 10.

107. "Advertising as Interpreter," *Printers' Ink,* November 5, 1936, 44.

108. "Advise Ad Leaders to 'Sell' Industry," *New York Times,* July 4, 1936, sec. 3; "Urges 'Selling' of Business."

109. Chester H. Lang quoted in "Advertising Held Better-Living Aid," *New York Times,* June 30, 1936, 36. See also Frank F. Brooks, "Seeks Advertising Drive on Economic Literacy," *Printers' Ink,* September 12, 1935, 78–80; and "Ad Agencies Urged to Take New Tasks," *New York Times,* May 1, 1937, 22.

110. "What Advertising Is," 17.

111. "Broader Policies Urged on Business," *New York Times,* April 23, 1938, 20.

112. Ibid.

113. Walker and Sklar, *Business Finds Its Voice,* 5.

114. "Advertising's Public Relations," *Advertising Age,* May 26, 1934, 4.

115. "Self-Regulation Is Endorsed by A.F.A.," *Advertising Age,* June 23, 1934, 34; "A.F.A. to Continue Fight on Objectionable Advertising," *Advertising Age,* June 17, 1935, 1.

116. "Correct Evils and Refute Falsehood, Kobak Tells A.F.A," *Advertising Age,* June 23, 1934, 2.

117. H. H. Kynett, "Advertising's Contribution," *Printers' Ink Monthly,* August 1936, 30.

118. Roy S. Durstine, "How Advertising Can End Depression," *Nation's Business,* June 1935, 24–26; James W. Young, "The Professor Looks at Advertising," *Good Housekeeping,* May 1935, 86–87; Charles Coolidge Parlin, "Advertising—Master Builder," *Nation's Business,* September 1938, 54; Ralph Starr Butler, "The Place of Advertising in the American Scheme," *Advertising and Selling,* February 15, 1940, 88.

119. Walker and Sklar, *Business Finds Its Voice,* chap. 9.

120. John Benson quoted in "Coast Agencies Meet," *Printers' Ink,* October 31, 1935, 59.

121. Malcolm P. McNair, "The Right to Advertise," n.d., box 118, Advertising Federation of America folder, Bruce Barton Papers, Wisconsin Center for Historical Research, State Historical Society of Wisconsin, Madison.

122. Young, "The Professor Looks," 150. The advertising industry also claimed that its products were agents in the democratizing process; see Roland Marchand, *Advertising the American Dream: Making Way for Modernity, 1920–1940* (Berkeley: University of California Press, 1985), 217–22.

123. Young, "The Professor Looks," 153.

124. "What Is Advertising," *Advertising Age,* July 25, 1938, 12.

125. Don Francisco, "The Stanleys and the Livingstones," *Banking,* December 1939, 84.

126. Marchand, *Advertising the American Dream,* 89–94.

127. Edgar Kobak to John Royal, April 7, 1936, box 43, folder 17, National Broadcasting Company Papers, Wisconsin Center for Historical Research, State Historical Society of Wisconsin, Madison; "Truth on the Air," *Printers' Ink,* May 28, 1936, 86. A few weeks prior to the convention NBC aired a program that celebrated the advertising industry's progress in "cleaning up advertising"; see Edgar Kobak to

Marvin McIntyre, May 28, 1936, box 602, Advertising Federation of America folder, the President's Personal Files, Franklin D. Roosevelt Library, Hyde Park, N.Y.

128. "Frontal Attack on Advertising," *Business Week,* February 8, 1936, 12.

129. "The Consumer Menace," *Printers' Ink,* January 4, 1937, 96. Some government programs, designed with consumers' interest in mind, were salvaged from the debris after the NRA was dissolved in July 1935. The CAB continued in a severely weakened form as the Consumers' Project. The latter continued the CAB's efforts to educate consumers on labeling and specifications and conducted research on a wide variety of consumer issues. The Agricultural Adjustment Administration's consumer councils did not work out as well as consumer advocates had hoped. Although a large number of councils conducted excellent work, many had faded away by 1936. Prospects for a Department of the Consumer, supported by many CAB members, were uncertain as well; see "Orphans of the NRA," *Printers' Ink,* January 28, 1937, 33; and "Major Consumer Role Seen for Federal Government," *Advertising Age,* November 6, 1939, 31.

130. "The 'Consumer Movement:' Who's Behind It and What It's Doing," *Sales Management,* June 15, 1937, 1141.

131. "Trends and Perspectives," *Advertising and Selling,* January 1938, 40. See also Dexter Masters, "An Advertising Critic Speaks Up," *Advertising and Selling,* February 1938, 35–38; "Advertising Is Exhibit Theme," *New York Times,* March 18, 1939, 22; and Little, "Industry Writes Its Story."

132. "The Attacking Stage," *CUR,* December 1937, 1.

Chapter 5: Defining the Consumer Agenda

1. See, for example, "Frontal Attack on Advertising," *Business Week,* February 8, 1936, 10; "Trends and Perspectives," *Advertising and Selling,* January 1938, 35–38; Dexter Masters, "An Advertising Critic Speaks Up," *Advertising and Selling,* February 1938, 28–30; "Advertising Is Exhibit Theme," *New York Times,* March 18, 1939, 22.

2. Edward Reich, "Consumer Education Problem and What It Means to Today's Merchandiser," *Printers' Ink,* February 10, 1938, 1–13; "Educating the Consumer," *Advertising Age,* July 29, 1935, 10; "Consumer Groups Harass Advertising, Bristol Declares," *Advertising Age,* June 12, 1939, 1; R. I. Elliot, "Spokesmen and Their Audience in the Consumer Movement Today," *Advertising and Selling,* November 18, 1937, 29–30.

3. Henry Link quoted in Stuart Ewen, *PR! The Social History of Spin* (New York: Basic Books, 1996), 186.

4. Robert S. Lynd quoted in Ewen, *PR!* 189.

5. For a discussion of 1930s public opinion polling, see Ewen, *PR!* 188–89; and J. Michael Sproule, *Propaganda and Democracy: The American Experience of Media and Mass Persuasion* (Cambridge: Cambridge University Press, 1997), chap. 3.

6. The National Industrial Information Committee, "The Public Looks at You," n.d., 3, box 845, Misc. NIIC material 1938–40 folder, Series 3, Accession (hereaf-

ter referred to as Acc.) 1411, National Association of Manufacturers Papers, Hagley Library, Wilmington, Del. (hereafter referred to as NAM Papers).

7. "Advertising Stride Told," *Los Angeles Times,* January 30, 1935, clipping in box 22, folder 9, Consumers' Research Papers, Special Collections and University Archives, Rutgers University, New Brunswick, N.J. (hereafter referred to as CR Papers); "Check on Impure Goods at Source Urged in Speech," *New Orleans Times-Picayune,* January 19, 1935, clipping in box 22, folder 9, CR Papers.

8. Anna Steese Richardson quoted in "Faith in Ads Urged on Women," clipping from unidentified newspaper, n.d., box 22, folder 3, CR Papers.

9. Anna Steese Richardson, "An Advertising Odyssey," *Advertising and Selling,* April 11, 1935, 40, clipping in box 22, folder 9, CR Papers; "Signs and Portents," *Consumers' Research Bulletin,* July 1935, 24, clipping in box 22, folder 9, CR Papers. See also "Types of Advertising for Women," *Electric Refrigeration News,* July 17, 1935, clipping in box 30, folder 3, CR Papers.

10. "Types of Advertising for Women." For CR's denial of these charges, see correspondence in box 30, folder 3, CR Papers.

11. Robert S. Lynd quoted in "Consumer Group Asks More Laws to Curb Prices," *Advertising Age,* December 20, 1937, 23. For more information on Collier's strategy see "New Consumer Council Ready to Start Work," *Advertising Age,* June 20, 1938, 19; and "Advertising's Counter-Attack Gets Under Way," *Advertising Age,* February 21, 1938, 23.

12. Crowell Publishing Company, *Advertising and the Consumer Movement: Digest of a Survey on Consumer Activities,* November 1, 1937, 5, box 181, folder 15, CR Papers.

13. Ibid., 25.

14. J. A. Welch to W. C. Laros, December 2, 1937, box 181, folder 15, CR Papers.

15. Margaret Cuthbert to John F. Royal, December 30, 1937, box 56, folder 47, National Broadcasting Company Papers, Wisconsin Center for Historical Research, State Historical Society of Wisconsin, Madison (hereafter referred to as NBC Papers).

16. Anna Steese Richardson quoted in "Consumer Groups Harass Advertising," 26.

17. Anna Steese Richardson quoted in "Ask Business to Rebut Lies Spread by 'Consumer Agitators,'" *Sales Management,* May 15, 1939, 55.

18. Anna Steese Richardson, "Who Is Fighting the Consumer Movement?" *Advertising and Selling,* October 1940, 38; Elliot, "Spokesmen and Their Audience," 29–30; J. A. Welch to W. Laros, May 31, 1939, box 181, folder 14, CR Papers.

19. T. L. Brantly to W. Laros, December 1, 1939, box 181, folder 14, CR Papers. For examples of individual advertisements, see box 181, folder 14, CR Papers.

20. "What Has Advertising Ever Done for Me?" (advertisement), *Women's Home Companion,* September 1939, 92.

21. E. R. Reynolds, "President's Annual Report," June 23, 1937, 4, box 51, folder 38, NBC papers. Margaret Cuthbert, NBC's director of women's activities, referred to

Crowell's Consumer Division as "the Consumer Movement"; see Cuthbert to Royal, December 30, 1937.

22. Anna Steese Richardson to Margaret Cuthbert, November 19, 1937, box 56, folder 47, NBC Papers; Margaret Cuthbert to Anna Steese Richardson, November 22, 1937, box 56, folder 47, NBC Papers; Anna Steese Richardson to Margaret Cuthbert, December 27, 1937, box 56, folder 47, NBC Papers; Cuthbert to Royal, December 30, 1937.

23. Anna Steese Richardson, "Does the Consumer Know What She Wants?" 7–8, speech delivered at the Third Annual Editorial Conference, Cleveland, Ohio, January 27, 1939, box 157, folder 42, Richard L. D. Morse Papers, Consumer Movement Archives, Kansas State University, Manhattan (hereafter referred to as Morse Papers). For more information on Richardson's opinions of the consumer movement, see Anna Steese Richardson, "The Consumer Movement and You," report to the Fourth Annual Convention of the National Federation of Sales Executives, Philadelphia, June 5–7, 1939, box 181, folder 14, CR Papers.

24. Anna Steese Richardson quoted in "Consumer Relations," *Consumer Education Services,* October 6, 1938, 32, typewritten copy in box 148, folder 8, CR Papers.

25. "Brand B Doesn't Like It," *Consumers Union Reports* (hereafter referred to as *CUR*), December 1939, 16.

26. Edward Reich, "In Honest Advertising Is Logical and Best Means of Educating Consumer," *Printers' Ink,* April 7, 1938, 21.

27. Alice L. Edwards, "Consumer Interest Groups," *Public Opinion Quarterly* 1, no. 3 (July 1937): 104–11. See also "What about the Consumer Movement?" *Advertising Age,* January 6, 1940, 23–29.

28. John Benson, "Trends in Consumer Advertising," 331, on sheet marked "U.S. Dept. of Commerce Domestic Commerce," March 30, 1938, box 122, folder 3, CR Papers.

29. "New Council of Education," *Advertising Age,* May 9, 1938, 1; "Ad Council to Meet Consumer Charges," *New York Times,* April 30, 1938, 20; "New Consumer Council Ready to Start," *Advertising Age,* June 20, 1938, 19.

30. "Trends and Perspectives," 40.

31. "Macy's Woos Club Women with New 'Consumer Clinics,'" *Advertising Age,* March 18, 1940, 17. See also "More Information for Consumers," *Advertising Age,* June 1, 1936, 12.

32. "The Consumer Movement: A Pain in the Neck—Or a Sales Opportunity?" *Sales Management,* March 15, 1939, 18.

33. "Awakened Consumers Hold Retail Spotlight," *Advertising Age,* June 28, 1937, 28; "More Information for Consumers," 12.

34. "Trends and Perspectives," 40; "Report on Publisher Smith," *CUR,* October 1937, 16.

35. Crump Smith quoted in "Trends," *Advertising and Selling,* August 12, 1937, 26, clipping in box 181, folder 16, CR Papers.

36. "A Bad Start," *CUR*, November 1937, 16.

37. M. C. Phillips to Francis T. Barnes, January 4, 1938, box 181, folder 16, CR Papers.

38. "Crump Smith," *Tide*, December 15, 1939, 36, clipping in box 148, folder 8, CR Papers.

39. "The National Consumer-Retailer Council: A Non-Profit Organization Promoting Cooperation between Consumers and Retailers," n.d., box 181, folder 17, CR Papers.

40. "Three Groups Act to Push Ad Truth," *New York Times*, December 12, 1939, 42. See also "Public Held Ready to Aid Advertising," *New York Times*, October 25, 1939, 33; and "Consumers Advise Business of Needs," *New York Times*, May 14, 1940, 34.

41. "Consumer Groups Ask More Laws to Curb Prices," *Advertising Age*, December 20, 1937, 37; Mark S. Smith, "Robert Lynd and Consumerism in the 1930s," *Journal of the History of Sociology* 2, no. 1 (Fall-Winter 1979–80): 99–119.

42. Mabel Crews Ringwald, "On Knowing the Consumer," *Printers' Ink*, September 23, 1937, 64, 68. The AAAA preferred a female manager for the Consumer-Advertising Council, a public relations group started by the association in 1938; see "New Council of Education AAAA Project," *Advertising Age*, May 9, 1938, 1.

43. Ringwald, "On Knowing the Consumer," 64.

44. "Realistic Attitude Urged towards Growth of Consumer Movement," *Advertising Age*, June 12, 1939, 1.

45. "Consumer Relations Program," *Printers' Ink*, September 23, 1937, 12.

46. Ringwald, "On Knowing the Consumer," 63–64.

47. "Consumer Groups Harass Advertising," 26; Elliot, "Spokesmen and Their Audience," 29–30.

48. C. B. Larrabee, "National Advertising Needs Sharper Consumer Angle," *Printers' Ink*, May 13, 1937, 16.

49. "New Council of Education," *Advertising Age*, May 9, 1938, 1; "New Consumer Council Ready to Start Work," *Advertising Age*, June 20, 1938, 19; "Four A's Revives Plan for Consumer Relations Council," *Advertising Age*, December 25, 1939, 1; "Dameron Named Head of Consumer Relations Group," *Advertising Age*, January 15, 1940, 4; "The Committee on Consumer Relations in Advertising Inc.," *New York Times*, April 16, 1941, 42; "Reaching the Teacher," *Business Week*, October 5, 1940, 40–41.

50. Margaret Cuthbert to John F. Royal, memo, July 12, 1938, box 62, folder 69, NBC Papers; William B. Warner to Lammont Du Pont, June 10, 1938, box 52, NAM June 1938–October 1938 folder, Office of the President, Administrative Papers, Accession 1662, Records of E. I. Du Pont de Nemours and Co., Hagley Library, Wilmington, Del. (hereafter referred to as OP, AP, Acc. 1662, Du Pont Papers).

51. Lammont Du Pont to George H. Davis, November 9, 1937, box 13, Chamber of Commerce March 1937–December 1938 folder, OP, AP, Acc. 1662, Du Pont Papers.

52. "The American Family Robinson," *National Association of Broadcasters Reports* 7, no. 32 (August 11, 1939), clipping in box 111, Public Relations—Radio Report folder,

Series 1, Accession 1411, NAM Papers. See also Elizabeth Fones-Wolf, "Creating a Favorable Business Climate: Corporations and Radio Broadcasting, 1934 to 1954," *Business History Review* 73, no. 2 (Summer 1999): 221–55; and William L. Bird Jr., *Better Living: Advertising, Media, and the New Vocabulary of Business Leadership, 1935–1955* (Evanston, Ill.: Northwestern University Press, 1999), 53–59. For an excellent discussion of the NAM's use of public relations in the postwar era, see Elizabeth A. Fones-Wolf, *Selling Free Enterprise: The Business Assault on Labor and Liberalism, 1945–60* (Urbana: University of Illinois Press, 1994).

53. "Consumers and the Campus," *Printers' Ink,* February 10, 1938, 108; W. G. Preston to Ken R. Dyke, April 12, 1940, box 76, folder 65, NBC Papers. See also James E. Mendenhall, "The Institute for Consumer Education: A Report of Work in Progress," January 1942, box 172, folder 3, CR Papers.

54. Helen Sorenson, *The Consumer Movement: What It Is and What It Means* (New York: Harper and Brothers, 1941), 76–79. For information on activities to thwart the consumer movement, see John M. Cassels to Colston E. Warne, March 5, 1940, box 26, folder 7, Colston E. Warne Papers, Consumers Union Archives, Yonkers, N.Y. (hereafter referred to as Warne Papers); Grace S. M. Zorbaugh, "The Consumer Movement and Business," address delivered to the Consumer Conference of Greater Cincinnati, Ohio, October 1940, box 148, folder 6, CR Papers.

55. Consumers' National Federation, "The Consumer Movement: An Informal Symposium," rev. ed., January 1940, box 181, folder 12, CR Papers.

56. Henry Harap, "What Is the Consumer Movement?" *Frontier Democracy,* November 15, 1904, 48–50, clipping in box 148, folder 7, CR Papers. The Consumers' National Federation did not completely fade from view. In 1939, and then again in 1940, it published a useful overview of the groups in the general consumer movement. These included the General Federation of Women's Clubs, the American Home Economics Association, the American Association of University Women, the National League of Women Voters, the National League of Business and Professional Women's Clubs, the National Public Housing Conference, the National Council of Jewish Women, the National Council of Catholic Women, the national board of the Young Women's Christian Association, the Federal Council of the Churches of Christ in America, the Colorado Division of the Farmers Educational and Cooperative Union, the Cooperative League of the U.S., the Rochdale Institute; the Cooperative Book Club Inc., the Credit Union National Association, the Intermountain Consumers' Service Inc., the Institute for Consumer Education, the Consumer Education Association; the National Federation of Settlements, the National Consumers' League, and CU. Conspicuously absent from the list was CR, which by this time was pursuing a largely separatist path. For a description of the groups, their funding, and their goals, see Consumers' National Federation, "Consumer Movement." *Advertising Age,* not surprisingly, held a slightly different view of what the consumer movement entailed. A detailed article outlining the different organizations included the many business-backed consumer organizations as well as

the more grassroots ones; see "What about the Consumer Movement?" *Advertising Age,* January 6, 1940, 23–29.

57. "Experts Study Approach to Consumer Education," *Advertising Age,* April 10, 1939, 1. Emotional appeals versus factual information was a major issue at the Business Consumer Relations Conference sponsored by the NBBB in 1940 as well; see Irwin Robinson, "Consumer Problem Monopolizes Attention at Admen's Meeting," *Advertising Age,* May 20, 1940, 1. See also "The Consumer Reporter," *CUR,* April 1939, 1; and Zorbaugh, "The Consumer Movement and Business."

58. "Urges Advertisers Bow to Consumers," *New York Times,* October 27, 1939, 32. For more information about advertisers' assessment of consumers' attitudes toward advertising see D. E. Robinson, "172 Advertisers Give 8 Main Reasons for Consumer Movement," *Printers' Ink,* June 14, 1940, 12.

59. John M. Cassels to Colston E. Warne, May 27, 1939, box 26, folder 7, Warne Papers.

60. "Consumer Education Meeting Shows Distrust of Advertising," *Broadcasting,* April 15, 1940, 20.

61. "Advertising and Business Put on Grill at Consumer Meet," *Advertising Age,* April 8, 1940, 1.

62. Frederick J. Schlink to James M. Matthews, March 24, 1939, box 172, folder 4, CR Papers.

63. Ibid.

64. C. B. Larrabee, "Teachers Grab Show at Stephens College Consumer Conference," *Printers' Ink,* April 12, 1940, 72. See also C. B. Larrabee, "Consumer Groups Gain as Advertisers Beat Bushes for Witches," *Printers' Ink,* November 24, 1939, 11–12, clipping in box 22, folder 13, CR Papers; Wallace Warble, "Consumer Movements and Advertising: Rational Approach Suggested as One Way to Reach Agreement," *Broadcasting,* January 1, 1940, 15, clipping in box 22, folder 13, CR Papers.

65. C. B. Larrabee quoted in "Consumer Year," *Food Field Reporter,* January 8, 1940, 14, clipping in box 22, folder 13, CR Papers.

66. Unsigned memo, May 27, 1940, box 204, folder 13, CR Papers; unsigned memo, May 29, 1940, box 204, folder 13, CR Papers.

67. Preston to Dyke, April 12, 1940.

68. Ibid.

69. "Realistic Attitude Urged," 27. See also "A Message to Business, Consumers, Education, and Government from the National Better Business Bureaus, Inc.," n.d., box 602, National Association of Better Business Bureaus folder, President's Personal Files, Franklin D. Roosevelt Library, Hyde Park, N.Y.

70. Loda Mae Davis to Lydia Altschuler, April 18, 1939, box 2, folder 1, Consumers Union Papers, Consumers Union Archives, Yonkers, N.Y. (hereafter referred to as CU Papers).

71. Harold F. Clark to Lydia Altschuler, April 17, 1939, box 2, folder 1, CU Papers.

72. Margaret G. Reid to Lydia Altschuler, April 17, 1939, box 2, folder 1, CU Papers.

73. "A Message to Business"; "Realistic Attitude Urged," 1.

74. Donald E. Montgomery to Lydia Altschuler, April 19, 1939, box 2, folder 1, CU Papers.

75. "Consumer Problem Monopolizes Attention," 1.

76. "Ad Men Support Consumer Groups," *New York Times,* June 22, 1940, 32.

77. In 1937, just two years earlier, the AFA had made few efforts at cooperation with consumer groups. At the 1937 convention, however, the AFA pledged to devote more attention to consumer groups and their opinions and sponsor an "impartial" study on advertising's economic value to serve as a prelude to a consumer education campaign; see "Resolved by the A.F.A.," *Printers' Ink,* July 1, 1937, 66.

78. Norman S. Ross to John O. Boyd, May 13, 1940, box 181, folder 14, CR Papers.

79. Ibid.; Advertising Federation of America, *A Public Relations Program for Advertising Clubs Affiliated with the Advertising Federation of America* (New York: Advertising Federation of America, n.d.), box 11, Public Relations Program of Advertising Clubs folder, Series 1, Acc. 1411, NAM Papers. See also "Outline of Organization and Operation of a Public Information Program for Members of the Advertising Federation of America," n.d., box 111, Public Relations Committee Program—Outline of Organization and Operation of a Public Information Program folder, Series 1, Acc. 1411, NAM Papers. Far from all efforts were one-sided, however. In 1940, for example, the Advertising Club of St. Louis invited Colston E. Warne to give a paid talk to its members; see Robert A. Willier to Colston E. Warne, June 20, 1940, box 62, folder 1, Warne Papers.

80. "Eye Consumer Views," *Business Week,* June 24, 1939, 37; "Ad Men Support Consumer Groups."

81. Allen Rose quoted in "AFA Head Demands Energetic Defense of Advertising," *Advertising Age,* September 25, 1939, 20.

82. See, for example, "The Consumer Movement Today," *Advertising and Selling,* November 18, 1937, 29; "Fight Consumer Propaganda," *Printers' Ink,* August 4, 1938, 63; "Truth about Advertising," *Business Week,* June 17, 1939, 51; "Consumer Relations Problems," *Advertising Age,* October 23, 1939, 12; and "Advertising Must Attack Defamers, Coast Admen Told," *Advertising Age,* July 15, 1940, 1.

83. "Searching Analysis of Consumer Needs Made by Four A's," *Advertising Age,* May 20, 1940, 4.

84. "Consumer Activity Faces Scrutiny by ANA Microscope," *Advertising Age,* October 16, 1939; "Urges Advertisers Bow," 32. The Advertising Research Foundation was first established as a special unit within the Association of National Advertisers in 1934. Its purpose was to conduct marketing and advertising research. The AAAA recognized that it sought the same information, so the foundation became a joint venture in 1936; see "ANA Discusses Agency Compensation; Announces Ad

Research Foundation," *Sales Management,* December 1, 1934, 558–59; "Cooperation in Research," *Advertising Age,* November 24, 1934, 10; and Advertising Research Foundation, *The First Fifty Years* (New York: Advertising Research Foundation, 1986).

85. Andrew M. Howe, "With War an Uninvited Guest A.F.A. Hails Advertising as Aid to 'American Way,'" *Printers' Ink,* July 5, 1940, 23–24. See also "AGM Members Adopt Five Point Program for Consumer Education," *Food Field Reporter,* November 13, 1939, 3, clipping in box 22, folder 13, CR Papers.

86. "Advertising and Business Put on Grill," 1.

87. "Consumer Education Meeting Shows Distrust," 20.

88. Ibid.; "Advertisers Get Complete Picture of Consumer Activity," *Advertising Age,* October 30, 1939, 25.

89. John M. Cassels quoted in "Realistic Attitude Urged," 27. Transcripts and recordings from the 1940 conference were made available to schools, clubs, and radio stations; see "Memorandum on Playback Equipment," n.d., box 5, Institute for Consumer Education 1939–40 folder, Charles H. Sandage Papers, 1930–63, University of Illinois Archives, Urbana.

90. Colston E. Warne to Arthur Kallet, October 24, 1939, box 7, folder 7, Warne Papers. See also Sorenson, *Consumer Movement,* chap. 7.

91. Zorbaugh, "The Consumer Movement and Business."

92. "Conference on Consumer Education, Institute for Consumer Education, Stephens College, Columbia, Missouri, April 7th, 8th, and 9th, 1941," n.d., 2–3, box 172, folder 3, CR Papers.

93. "Consumer Institute Folds at Stephens; Leaders Join OPA," *Advertising Age,* February 9, 1942, 1; "The Consumer Movement *Is Not Dead!" Printers' Ink,* May 14, 1943, 15–16.

94. George Gallup, "An Analysis of the 'Study of Consumer Agitation,'" February 9, 1940, 2, 3, 8, box 76, folder 11, NBC Papers.

95. "Propaganda over the Schools," *Propaganda Analysis,* February 25, 1941, 12.

96. Robert S. Lynd and Helen Merrell Lynd, *Middletown* (1929; repr., New York: Harcourt, Brace, and World, 1967), 195–96. James Rorty pointed to the same tendencies in *Our Master's Voice: Advertising* (1934; repr., New York: Arno Press, 1976), 150–52.

97. Frederick J. Schlink, "Shall the Consumer Have Rights in School?" *Progressive Education,* May 1932, 1–6, clipping in box 93, folder 20, CR Papers. For a copy of the originally submitted manuscript, see Frederick J. Schlink, "The Consumer . . . Shall He Have Rights in the Schools?" n.d., box 93, folder 20, CR Papers.

98. Dewey H. Palmer to John F. Brougher, May 11, 1932, box 16, folder 9, CR Papers. For the Department of Public Instruction's request for help, see John F. Brougher to Consumers' Research, April 27, 1932, box 16, folder 9, CR Papers. For a similar request, see Jerry Vinyard to Consumers' Research, June 23, 1932, box 16, folder 9, CR Papers.

99. John F. Brougher to Dewey H. Palmer, May 14, 1932, box 16, folder 9, CR Papers.

100. Proctor W. Maynard, "Outline for a Practical Unit in Consumption Economics," *Historical Outlook* 24, no. 8 (December 1933): 457, clipping in box 16, folder 8, CR Papers.

101. "When Teachers Tell Pupils How to Buy," *Consumers' Research General Bulletin,* January 1933, 10–11.

102. For 1932 fall semester the material consisted of four handbooks: *Food, Medicine, and Hygiene and Cosmetics* (vol. 6, part 1); *Radio Sets and Musical Instruments, Household Supplies, Appliances, Utensils, and Miscellaneous Instruments* (vol. 8, part 1); *Heating and Ventilating, Lighting, Fire Extinguishers, Building Materials* (vol. 7, part 2); and *Introduction to Consumers' Research;* see "Using CR Material in College and High School Classes," *Consumers' Research General Bulletin,* September 1932, 5. A few months later more handbooks covering a wider variety of products were added to the school offerings; see "Use of CR Material in School and College Classes," *Consumers' Research General Bulletin,* October 1933, 17–18.

103. "Using CR Material in College and High School Classes," *Consumers' Research General Bulletin,* January 1933, 11. CU considered outreach activities to schools of utmost importance. The organization offered greatly reduced subscriptions to groups of fifteen or more students and provided help and advice to teachers. CU also offered to read teachers' course outlines and provide feedback; see "Consumer Courses in Schools," *CUR,* September 1936, 1.

104. "Campus Critics of Advertising to Hear Reply," *Advertising Age,* March 15, 1937, 32.

105. "Advertising is 95% Pure, Coast Group Is Told," *Advertising Age,* July 1, 1935, 6.

106. Herbert L. Stephen, "Startling Facts in re Consumer Attitudes Are Brought Out in A.N.A. Convention," *Printers' Ink,* November 3, 1939, 25–26.

107. John Benson, "Why Worry the Cow That Gives the Milk?" *Dun's Review,* September 1938, 5, 7.

108. "BBB Urges Need of New Defense of Advertising," *Advertising Age,* November 16, 1936, 11.

109. "Pink-Cheeked Professors," *Printers' Ink,* June 6, 1935, 47–48; "Professors and Advertising," *Printers' Ink,* June 20, 1935, 68–69; John K. Massey, "College View of Advertising Not Moscow Tainted Say Comrade Professors," *Printers' Ink,* October 20, 1938, 11–13; "What Economists Say about Advertising," *Printers' Ink,* June 1, 1934, 33–34; "Skeptical Students," *Printers' Ink,* June 30, 1938, 69–70. Other educators defended advertising as well; see, for example, Grace Morrison Poole, "She Believes in Advertising," *Printers' Ink,* July 2, 1936, 72–74.

110. "Shots Fired at Advertising at the University of Chicago," *Advertising Age,* March 3, 1937, 6.

111. "This Is Not a Crusade," *Advertising Age,* March 29, 1937, 12.

112. G. D. Crain quoted in "Urges Action on Ad Criticism," *New York Times,* May 20, 1937, 30.

113. "Student Told Advertising Is 'Racket,'" *Advertising Age,* March 1, 1937, 1; "Shots Fired at Advertising," 6; "Students Told Testimonials Are a 'Racket,'" *Advertising Age,* March 10, 1937, 10; "Librarian at Denver U. 'Directs' New Students to '100,000,000 Guinea Pigs,'" *Advertising Age,* March 15, 1937, 10; "Skepticism of Advertising Is Columbia Tenet," *Advertising Age,* March 22, 1937, 24.

114. "Students Told Testimonials," 10. For more information on "business-friendly" professors, see "Suggest Ad Groups Keep Eye on Critics," *New York Times,* October 1, 1937, 30. Neil H. Borden went on to publish an influential book called *The Economic Effects of Advertising* (Chicago: Richard D. Irwin, 1942). This book was funded by a $30,000 memorial grant from the widow of A. W. Erickson, a high-profile contributor to the New York Economic Council, which attempted to censor school material it deemed unfriendly to business interests; see "Propaganda over the Schools"; and "Harvard Study Urges New Program to Guide Consumers," *Advertising Age,* December 5, 1938, 8. For a treatment of the rise of business schools in America, see William Leach, *Land of Desire: Merchants, Power, and the Rise of a New American Culture* (New York: Pantheon Books, 1993), 158–63.

115. Edward J. Storey, "Effective Advertising to School Markets," *Advertising and Selling,* November 1939, 44. See also "For Educational Purposes," *Printers' Ink Monthly,* February 1938, 17–19.

116. Storey, "Effective Advertising."

117. "School Promotion Opportunity," *New York Times,* November 27, 1939, 21; Alfred E. Bray, "Consumer Teacher Tells School Needs," *Printers' Ink,* June 6, 1941, 25; "Reaching the Teacher," *Business Week,* October 5, 1940, 40–41.

118. Storey, "Effective Advertising"; "Schoolroom Farm," *Printers' Ink,* March 10, 1938, 96.

119. See L. P. Fisher, "Reaching the Child through the Teacher: How Advertisers are Using Educational Material in the Classroom," *Printers' Ink Monthly,* August 1933, 34–35, clipping in box 247, folder 15, CR Papers.

120. Ibid.

121. "The Need for Discrimination," *American Journal of Public Health* 27 (November 1937): 1125, copy dated November 23, 1937, box 249, folder 9, CR Papers.

122. Carolyn M. Goldstein, "Part of the Package: Home Economics Moves into the Twenty-First Century," in *Rethinking Home Economics: Women and the History of a Profession,* ed. Sarah Stage and Virginia B. Vincenti (Ithaca, N.Y.: Cornell University Press, 1997), 276.

123. Ibid., 271–96.

124. Dewey H. Palmer to Alice Edwards, July 5, 1934, box 174, folder 26, CR Papers.

125. Frederick J. Schlink to Margaret Choate, January 28, 1933, box 247, folder 15,

CR Papers; Dewey H. Palmer to C. C. Burns, March 12, 1933, box 174, folder 19, CR Papers.

126. "School Use of Advertising Material," *Journal of Home Economics* 26, no. 10 (December 1934): 633–34.

127. Gerald B. Wadsworth to Dip-It Incorporated, November 10, 1930, box 175, folder 1, CR Papers.

128. "A Clean Clear Skin," *Home-Makers Bulletin,* February 1931, 14, clipping in box 175, folder 1, CR Papers.

129. "What They Say," *Home-Makers Bulletin,* September 1932, 23, clipping in box 175, folder 1, CR Papers.

130. Gerald B. Wadsworth to Dip-It Incorporated, April 25, 1931, box 175, folder 1, CR Papers (emphasis in the original).

131. "Home Economist— Powerful Friend of the Consumer," *Glass Packer,* October 1937, 646, clipping in box 249, folder 9, CR Papers.

132. California Fruit Growers Exchange, "Educational Work," clipping received December 2, 1935, box 247, folder 9, CR Papers.

133. M. Elizabeth Winkelhake quoted in "Commercial Propaganda in Schools," *Consumers' Digest,* April 1937, 15, clipping in box 249, folder 9, CR Papers.

134. Marion F. Breck to Dewey H. Palmer, April 14, 1934, box 175, folder 1, CR Papers.

135. "Survey of Use of Home Makers Educational Bulletin Service, Delaware—April 1934," box 175, folder 1, CR Papers.

136. "Buy a New Jersey School Teacher," 1938, box 247, folder 13, CR Papers.

137. Frederick J. Schlink to Rebecca Gibbons, January 31, 1938, box 249, folder 9, CR Papers.

138. "The Public Relations Counsel and Propaganda," *Propaganda Analysis* 1, no. 11 (August 1938): 2, clipping in box 84, folder 13, Morse Papers.

139. Frederick J. Schlink to Colston Leigh, September 1936, box 249, folder 9, CR Papers. For suggestions on how to present a sales talk to a Parent-Teacher Association, see Lee Floyd, "Sunlamp Talk," *House Furnishing Review,* September 1936, clipping in box 249, folder 9, CR Papers. See also "Home Economist Promotes G-E Sales in Schools," *Electric Refrigeration News,* February 12, 1936, 8, clipping in box 249, folder 9, CR Papers.

140. Evelyn E. Grumbine, "Reaching Children through Schools—Part 2," *Printers' Ink Monthly,* April 1937, 22–23. See also Evelyn E. Grumbine, "Reaching Children through Schools—Part 1," *Printers' Ink Monthly,* March 1937, 16–17.

141. "Youngsters to Learn Benefits of Advertising," *Advertising Age,* February 24, 1936, 1.

142. "Educators Hail Essay Contest on Advertising," *Advertising Age,* March 2, 1936, 18.

143. "Educating the Public," *Advertising Age,* February 24, 1936, 12; "Organize Facts to Meet Attack on Advertising," *Advertising Age,* May 24, 1937, 25; "1936 Witnessed

Growing Demand for Regulation," *Advertising Age,* January 4, 1937. For additional details on *Advertising Age*'s 1937 essay contest, including the journal's efforts to get students interested, see various brochures and letters in box 122, folder 22, CR Papers.

144. "Why the Students' Essay Contest?" *Advertising Age,* June 12, 1939, 12; "$1,000,000 Offered for Consumer Education Plan," *Advertising Age,* February 26, 1940, 6. In 1940 *Advertising Age* altered the contest to include entries from the general public as well. Entrants were asked to devise a program to improve the relationship between advertisers and consumers. *Advertising Age* ended the contest in the early 1940s.

145. "Student Copy Test Is Staged by Pall Mall," *Advertising Age,* February 22, 1937, 1.

146. E. H. McReynolds, "President's Annual Report," American Federation of Advertisers, June 23, 1937, 10, box 51, folder 38, NBC Papers.

147. Charles Bellatty and Ruth Bellatty, "Learning from the Advertisements in the *Saturday Evening Post* of February 17, 1940," *Criticism, Suggestions, and Advice* 10, no. 11 (February 17, 1940): 4, clipping in box 247, folder 12, CR Papers.

148. Ibid., 6. Contests for the college crowd consisted of creating marketing ideas for Fortuna Foundation Garments (with a Fortuna girdle offered as a prize for the best result) and a competition to devise the best advertising campaign for Gruen watches. The latter contest tried to enlist teachers' cooperation by offering prizes to the winning students as well as their teachers. Wolfe and Lang Inc. to Charles S. Wyand, February 16, 1940, box 247, folder 12, CR Papers; Gruen Watch Company to Charles S. Wyand, September 20, 1940, box 247, folder 12, CR Papers.

149. *History in This Hour: The Cavalcade of America Presented by Du Pont* 1940 or 1941, box 75, folder 41, NBC papers. For more on *Cavalcade of America,* see Bird, *Better Living,* chaps. 4–5; and Fones-Wolf, "Creating a Favorite Business Climate." For a general discussion of Du Pont's use of PR, see Robert F. Burke, *The Corporate State and the Broker State* (Cambridge, Mass.: Harvard University Press, 1990). *Cavalcade of America* is mentioned on page 204 in the book. The trend toward using radio for PR purposes was spurred by promotional specialists who believed that traditional probusiness editorial policy spread by groups such as the NAM and the U.S. Chamber of Commerce no longer moved the public. With business's need to find new ways to create social and political leadership, many PR experts urged their corporate clients to use radio as a PR vehicle; see William L. Bird, "Order, Efficiency, and Control: The Evolution of the Political Spot Advertisement, 1936–1956" (Ph.D. diss., Georgetown University, 1985), 118–19.

150. Gerhardt Jacob Horton, "Radio Goes to War: The Cultural Politics of Propaganda during World War II" (Ph.D. diss., University of California at Berkeley, 1994), 51–52. See also Bird, *Better Living,* chap. 5.

151. "Information on *Cavalcade of America,*" n.d., 2, box 75, folder 41, NBC Papers; "Cavalcade Begins Sixth Season on NBC," clipping from unidentified newsletter, September 17, 1940, box 75, folder 41, NBC Papers. In 1935 the NAM considered *The*

American Cavalcade as a potential title for a radio series. Lammont Du Pont, the NAM president at the time, rejected the title for use by the association but chose a nearly identical title (*Cavalcade of America*) for his own company's radio show later that year; see Lammont Du Pont to Edgar Kobak, April 9, 1935, box 39, folder 40, NBC Papers.

152. *History in This Hour.*

153. "Pyroxylin Coated Fabrics for CAVALCADE Broadcast of September 15, 1937" (commercial announcement), box 4, Advertising Department January 1937–December 1937 folder (c-24), OP, AP, Acc. 1662, Du Pont Papers. See also "Old Hickory" (commercial announcement), September 22, 1937, box 4, Advertising Department January 1937–December 1937 folder (c-24), OP, AP, Acc. 1662, Du Pont Papers.

154. "Du Pont Air Show Wins Favor as School Material," *Advertising Age,* March 25, 1940, 14; Lawrence M. Hughes, "Industry Starts to Show How 'Enterprise' Pays the Nation," *Sales Management,* September 1, 1936, 229–31.

155. "Selling Industry to America," *Advertising Age,* October 19, 1936, 12.

156. "Information on *Cavalcade of America,*" 5.

157. Paul Sampson to W. G. Preston Jr., December 20, 1939, box 67, folder 81, NBC Papers.

158. "Du Pont Air Show Wins," 14.

159. Dixon Ryan Fox to Roy S. Durstine, n.d., box 4, Advertising Department January 1937–December 1937 folder, OP, AP, Acc. 1662, Du Pont Papers.

160. Lynd and Lynd, *Middletown;* Robert S. Lynd and Helen Merrell Lynd, *Middletown in Transition* (1937; repr., New York: Harcourt, Brace, Jovanovich, 1965).

161. Colston E. Warne quoted in "Federal Help for Consumer Asked by Colston Warne," *Advertising Age,* April 14, 1941, 37.

162. "Propaganda in Schools?" (excerpt from *Advertising and Selling,* November 1939), *Consumer Education* 2, no. 3 (1939): 1, clipping in box 247, folder 13, CR Papers.

Chapter 6: Legislative Closure

1. "A.N.A. Withholds Approval of Food, Drug Legislation," *Advertising Age,* February 2, 1935, 1.

2. Otis Pease, *The Responsibilities of American Advertising: Private Control and Public Influence, 1920–1940* (New Haven, Conn.: Yale University Press, 1958), 119.

3. "Composite Foods Bill," *Printers' Ink,* January 17, 1935, 109. See also "Re S 5 and S 580," *Printers' Ink,* January 17, 1935, 25–26; "New Copeland Bill Would Govern Food, Drug Copy," *Advertising Age,* January 12, 1935, 1; Charles M. Wright, "As Congress Opens," *Printers' Ink,* January 10, 1935, 7; "Copeland Bill Is Introduced: Its Full Text," *Printers' Ink,* January 10, 1935, 12–14; "What Is False Advertising?" *Advertising Age,* February 2, 1935, 10.

4. "Too Many Bills," *Printers' Ink,* November 8, 1934, 105.

5. Edgar Kobak to Frank M. Russell, March 13, 1935, box 35, folder 47, National Broadcasting Company Papers, Wisconsin Center for Historical Research, State Historical Society of Wisconsin, Madison (hereafter referred to as NBC Papers).

6. "Self-Regulation under U.S. Auspices?" *Advertising Age,* January 26, 1935, 10. This plan complemented the advertising industry's self-regulatory efforts.

7. "Gardner Tells Federation of New Mead Bill," *Advertising Age,* February 16, 1935, 1. See also "A.N.A. Withholds Approval," 1.

8. Copeland quoted in "Copeland Exhibits Drug Law 'Horrors,'" *New York Times,* April 2, 1935, 7. See also "Discuss Food, Drug Bill on Senate Floor," *Advertising Age,* April 6, 1935, 4; and "Senate Votes on S 5," *Printers' Ink,* April 4, 1935, 10–12.

9. "Revised S 5 as Seen by One Who Helped Make It," *Printers' Ink,* February 21, 1935, 32–33; "Bureaucracy Defeated," *Printers' Ink,* February 14, 1935, 120; "Copeland Bill News," *Printers' Ink,* February 7, 1935, 106; "Copeland Bill Sidetracked," *Printers' Ink,* February 14, 1935, 12; "S 5's Advertising Section," *Printers' Ink,* March 7, 1935, 48–49; "A Fairly Good Bill," *Printers' Ink,* March 7, 1935, 114–15.

10. "Copeland Bill Sidetracked; Hope for Passage Fading," *Advertising Age,* April 13, 1935, 2. Otis Pease writes that the players in the legislative struggle knew that Bailey was alert to the interests of Vick Chemical Company in Greensboro, North Carolina, and that Clark was partial to the interests of the Lambert Company, manufacturer of Listerine, in St. Louis; see Otis Pease, *The Responsibilities of American Advertising,* 122n15. Even prior to the first hearing on the Tugwell bill back in 1933, Clark had expressed his intention to fight the measure tooth and nail; see Bennett Champ Clark to James Henkle, December 18, 1933, box 3, folder 9, Arthur Kallet Papers, Consumers Union Archives, Yonkers, N.Y. (hereafter referred to as Kallet Papers).

11. Joshua W. Bailey quoted in "Copeland Bill Sidetracked; Hope for Passage Fading," 2.

12. "S 5 Rests Comfortably," *Printers' Ink,* April 18, 1935, 12.

13. Copeland quoted in "Food Bill Passage Expected," *Printers' Ink,* June 6, 1935, 69.

14. "Hearings Scheduled March 2 on Food and Drug Legislation," *Broadcasting,* March 1, 1935, 8.

15. For Bristol's statement before the committee, see Senate Subcommittee on Commerce, *Food, Drugs, and Cosmetics Hearings before a Subcommittee of the Committee on Commerce on S 5, 1935,* 74th Cong., 1st sess., 30–33 (hereafter referred to as *S 5 Senate Hearing*). Bristol did not oppose multiple government seizures in cases where products were adulterated, however; see "Paucity of Objection Makes 'Love Feast' of Copeland Hearing," *Advertising Age,* March 9, 1935, 20–21.

16. "S 5 Evidence Is In," *Printers' Ink,* March 14, 1935, 28; "Advertising Supervision Asked by F.T.C. in Hearing on Copeland Food-Drug Bill," *Oil, Paint, and Drug Reporter,* March 18, 1935, 25. See also James F. Hoge's statement on behalf of the Proprietary Association of New York in *S 5 Senate Hearing,* 125–42.

17. "Paucity of Objection"; statement of Lee Bristol of Bristol-Myers Co. in *S 5 Senate Hearing,* 30–33.

18. Statement of Alice L. Edwards on behalf of the American Home Economics Association in *S 5 Senate Hearing,* 33–43; "S 5 Rests Comfortably," 12.

19. Statement of Arthur Kallet, testifying on behalf of Consumers' Research, quoted in *S 5 Senate Hearing,* 64.

20. Senator Joel Bennet Clark quoted in *S 5 Senate Hearing,* 65.

21. Frederick J. Schlink to Franklin D. Roosevelt, telegram, March 5, 1935, 2, box 3323, Consumers folder, President's Official Files, Franklin D. Roosevelt Library, Hyde Park, N.Y. (hereafter referred to as FDR Official Files).

22. *S 5 Senate Hearing,* 143; "S 5 Evidence Is In," 32.

23. Franklin D. Roosevelt to M. H. McIntyre, memo, March 7, 1935, box 3323, Consumers folder, FDR Official Files.

24. "Pure Foods Can Wait," *New Republic,* May 1, 1935, 329.

25. House Subcommittee on Interstate and Foreign Commerce, *Hearing before a Subcommittee of the Committee on Interstate and Foreign Commerce of the House of Representatives on HR 6906, HR 8805, HR 8941, and S 5,* 74th Cong., 1st sess., 506. (hereafter referred to as *House Hearing*). HR 8941, introduced by Virginia Ellis Jenckes, was a revised version of the Mead bill (HR 3972). HR 8805 (mainly concerned with labeling and shipping of foods, drugs, nonalcoholic beverages, and cosmetics) and HR 8941 (a bill to prevent the adulteration, misbranding, and false advertising of food, drugs, and cosmetics) were debated during the same hearing. The latter two bills, however, did not receive much attention in advertising circles.

26. "Sixty Advertising Bills," *Printers' Ink,* September 12, 1935, 7; "Walsh Bill," *Printers' Ink,* June 6, 1935, 25–26.

27. Frederick J. Schlink to Arthur Kallet, July 19, 1935, box 356, folder 10, Consumers' Research Papers, Special Collections and University Archives, Rutgers University, New Brunswick, N.J. (hereafter referred to as CR Papers); Arthur Kallet to David K. Niles, July 5, 1935, box 356, folder 19, CR Papers.

28. Arthur Kallet, "Copeland Drug Bill Hit as Adulterated Product," Federated Press Washington Bureau, August 9, 1935, 2, clipping in box 3, folder 9, Kallet Papers.

29. For Matthews's statement on behalf of CR, see *House Hearing,* 505–21; for Kallet's, see 532–36; for Josephine Junkin Dogget's statement on behalf of the General Federation of Women's Clubs, see 386–90; for Mrs. Harvey W. Wiley's statement on behalf of the American Pure Food League and the District of Columbia Federation of Women's Clubs, see 163–72; for Paul E. Hodge's statement on behalf of the American Home Economics Association, see 380–83; for Mrs. Harris T. Baldwin's statement on behalf of the National League of Women Voters, see 369–77; for Alfred T. Falk's statement on behalf of the AFA, see 251–53; for John Benson's statement on behalf of the AAAA, see 145–52; for Charles Coolidge Parlin's statement on behalf of the National Publishers Association, see 137–45; for William Woodward's statement on behalf of the American Medical Association, see 298–321; for William Jacobs's state-

ment on behalf of the Institute of Medicine Manufacturers, see 189–206; for James F. Hoge's statement on behalf of the Proprietary Association, see 694–707; and for Horace Bigelow's statement on behalf of the American Drug Manufacturers' Association, see 585–95.

30. C. B. Larrabee, "Reasonable and Fair," *Printers' Ink,* December 19, 1935, 100. See also "Hearings on Copeland Bill Continue; Varied Views Are Considered," *Advertising Age,* August 5, 1935, 1; "Copeland Bill Hearings Go On; Changes Offered," *Advertising Age,* August 12, 1935, 1; "Opposition to Copeland Bill Still Fighting," *Advertising Age,* October 28, 1935, 24; and "Business on Guard," *Advertising Age,* August 26, 1935, 18. *Printers' Ink* accused the Institute of Medicine Manufacturers of being the major obstacle to S 5's passage; see "A United House," *Printers' Ink,* September 5, 1935, 102.

31. Arthur Kallet, "Copeland Bill Seen as Brain Child of Patent Medicine People," *Upton Sinclair's National Epic News,* August 5, 1935, clipping in box 3, folder 9, Kallet Papers.

32. "Food Bill Passage Expected," *Printers' Ink,* June 6, 1935, 69.

33. Edward R. Keyes, "Federal Trade Commission's Police Record," *Advertising and Selling,* February 11, 1937, 25.

34. Rexford G. Tugwell to Donald R. Richberg, January 24, 1935, box 375, Tugwell PFA 1933–35 folder, FDR Official Files; Erwin L. Davis to Marvin McIntyre, August 8, 1935, box 375, Tugwell PFA 1933–35 folder, FDR Official Files.

35. "S 5 Evidence Is In," 27–28; Richard S. Tedlow, "From Competitor to Consumer: The Changing Focus of Federal Regulation of Advertising, 1914–1938," *Business History Review* 55, no. 1 (Spring 1981): 35–38.

36. Tedlow, "From Competitor to Consumer," 35–38. Gabriel Kolko argues that by 1914 big business had acquired the most essential legislation it sought from the federal government. The resulting laws complemented business's general conduct and gave it considerable power over the government's regulatory bodies. The FDA was a notable exception in this respect; see Gabriel Kolko, *Main Currents in Modern American History* (New York: Harper and Row, 1976), 16.

37. Tugwell to Richberg, January 24, 1935. See also Richard A. Harris and Sidney M. Milkis, *The Politics of Regulatory Change: A Tale of Two Agencies* (New York: Oxford University Press, 1996), chap. 5.

38. Pease, *Responsibilities of American Advertising,* 122.

39. "Bureaucracy Defeated," *Printers' Ink,* February 14, 1935, 120.

40. Joshua W. Bailey quoted in "S 5 Rests Comfortably," 16.

41. Rexford G. Tugwell to Joshua W. Bailey, April 26, 1935, box 375, Tugwell PFA 1933–35 folder, FDR Official Files. See also Keyes, "Federal Trade Commission's Police Record," 25.

42. "Drug Bill [Friends] Shift Tactics," *Business Week,* November 28, 1936, 19; "New Pure Food Bill Will Omit FTC: Copeland," *Advertising Age,* November 16, 1936, 30; "Dove of Peace Attending New Food, Drug Bill," *Advertising Age,* November 2, 1936,

20; James F. Hoge, "A Law and a Bill," *Printers' Ink,* October 29, 1936, 25; "Senate Has S 5," *Printers' Ink,* February 18, 1937, 12.

43. "Benson Offers Amendment to Copeland Bill," *Advertising Age,* January 25, 1937, 27.

44. "Congressional Fight on Advertising Regulation Starts at First Gong," *Advertising Age,* January 11, 1937, 1.

45. "Fourth Food and Drug Fight," *Business Week,* January 16, 1937, 38. See also Charles Wesley Dunn, "The Food and Drug Bills," *Printers' Ink,* January 14, 1937, 12.

46. "Legislative Flood," *Printers' Ink,* February 4, 1937, 79–80; "Noisy and Troublesome," *Printers' Ink,* January 21, 1937, 124–25.

47. "Resent White House S 5 Stand," *Printers' Ink,* March 4, 1937, 12; "Drug Bill Weak, President Fears," *New York Times,* February 24, 1937, 3. For a discussion of some of the major objections to the bill, see "The Copeland Bill," *Consumers Union Reports* (hereafter referred to as *CUR*), April 1937, 15–16.

48. "Resent White House S 5 Stand."

49. "Broadening of FTC's Power over Competition Is Sought," *Broadcasting,* December 15, 1936, 24; "Trade Commission Will Seek Direct Advertising Control," *Advertising Age,* November 30, 1936, 1.

50. Jay Franklin quoted in "Noisy and Troublesome," 124. The bills Franklin referred to were the O'Mahoney bill (S 10) to establish a federal licensing system for corporations engaging in interstate commerce, the Tydings bill (S 100) to amend the Federal Trade Commission Act, and the Lea bill (HR 3143) to give administrative power over the food and drugs bill to the FTC. Others stressed the FTC's quest for power as well; see, for example, Keyes, "Federal Trade Commission's Police Record."

51. "Pressure Groups Revive," *Printers' Ink,* January 21, 1937, 12.

52. "Quick Thinking," *Printers' Ink,* February 18, 1937, 118; "Copeland Bill Passes Senate," *Printers' Ink,* March 11, 1937, 12; "S 5 Is Passed; Rep. Lea Sees Rocky Road in House," *Advertising Age,* March 15, 1937, 1.

53. "Legislative Pink Elephants," *Printers' Ink,* March 11, 1937, 104; "Arthur Kallet: His Bill," *Printers' Ink,* March 11, 1937, 14; "The Coffee Bill," *CUR,* April 1937, 16. It should be noted that even Consumers Union did not claim that the Coffee bill was perfect and eagerly sought other consumer organizations' help in rewriting the bill or drafting an entirely new one; see "The Old Question," *CUR,* January 1938, 15.

54. "Minutes of the Meeting of the Board of Directors of Consumers Union Inc.," April 29, 1937, 2, box 1, Minutes 1936–38 folder, Board of Directors Minutes, Group 1B, Series 1936–65, Consumers Union Papers, Consumers Union Archives, Yonkers, N.Y.

55. Clarence F. Lea, "Would the FTC's 'Purge' of Advertising Cure the Patient or Kill It?" *Sales Management,* August 15, 1937, 62–64. For the full text of the Lea bill (HR 3143), see "F.T.C. to Rule Advertising," *Printers' Ink,* July 15, 1937, 29.

56. Lea, "Would the FTC's Purge of Advertising," 62–63.

57. Ibid., 62–64.

58. "F.T.C. to Rule Advertising."

59. "Noisy and Troublesome," 124–25.

60. "Ready for Drug Bill 'Solution,'" *Business Week,* June 20, 1937, 25–26; "Mr. Dunn Writes to Mr. Lea," *Printers' Ink,* May 27, 1937, 64; "Predict Early Action on Remodeled Lea Bill," *Advertising Age,* July 12, 1937, 1.

61. Lea, "Would the FTC's 'Purge' of Advertising," 62–64; "Bill Helps FTC," *Business Week,* July 17, 1937, 16; "Lea Bill Passes House," *Printers' Ink,* January 20, 1938, 24–26; "FTC Gets New Power," *Business Week,* March 19, 1938, 41–42.

62. "New Food and Drug Bill," *Printers' Ink,* March 25, 1937, 14; "Combine against S 5," *Printers' Ink,* March 18, 1937, 12; "Copeland Bill Is Shelved for Lea Substitute," *Advertising Age,* March 29, 1937, 2; "Who Shall Control Advertising?" *Business Week,* April 3, 1937, 42.

63. "Women's Demands Delay Lea Bill," *Printers' Ink,* June 3, 1937, 14. See also A. J. Carlson, "Food and Drug Legislation," *Consumers' Digest,* July 1937, 67.

64. Samuel D. McReynolds quoted in Tedlow, "From Competitor to Consumer," 52.

65. The Federal Trade Act of 1914 contained specific procedures for the FTC's dealings with advertisers suspected of using unfair business methods. The accused was to be warned to cease and desist; on compliance with such warnings, charges were dropped. If the accused refused to comply with the FTC's orders, no penalty would be given until the unlawfulness of the actions had been established by the court. Only after a court order was violated could the FTC use penalizing measures; see Lea, "Would the FTC's 'Purge' of Advertising," 62–64.

66. "Wheeler-Lea Bill Broadening Powers of the FTC over Advertising Is Now Law," *Broadcasting,* April 1, 1938, 18; "Lea Bill Passes House," 24–25.

67. George S. McMillan, "Much Advertising 'Regulation' in Prospect; Sixty Bills Now before Congress," *Printers' Ink,* December 16, 1937, 11–13; "Lea Bill Passes House," 24–26.

68. "New Advertising Bill Passed by House," *Broadcasting,* January 15, 1938, 17.

69. "Wheeler-Lea Bill Broadening Powers"; "Advertising Control Here as Senate Passes Lea Bill," *Advertising Age,* March 21, 1938, 1; Clarence F. Lea, "Congressman Lea Reviews His Law," *Advertising and Selling,* May 1938, 21; "FTC Launches First Wheeler-Lea Action in Court," *Advertising Age,* September 19, 1938, 4.

70. James Harvey Young, *The Medical Messiahs: A Social History of Health Quackery in Twentieth-Century America* (1967; repr., Princeton, N.J.: Princeton University Press, 1992); E. M. Witherspoon, "Courage of Conviction: The *St. Louis Post-Dispatch,* the *New York Times,* and Reform of the Pure Food and Drug Act, 1933–1937," *Journalism and Mass Communication Quarterly* 75, no. 4 (Winter 1998): 776–88. See also "Amendment to Food and Drug Act Is Sought," *Advertising Age,* November 22, 1937, 1; "Let's Have S 5," *Printers' Ink,* January 20, 1938, 96; "Our Old Friend S 5,"

Printers' Ink, February 24, 1938, 94–95; "Substitute for S 5," *Printers' Ink,* March 10, 1938, 17–18; "Fourth Version of Food, Drugs Bill Reported," *Advertising Age,* March 14, 1938, 2; "New Food Bill Reported, but Road Is Rough," *Advertising Age,* March 21, 1938, 8; "Re Substitute S 5," *Printers' Ink,* March 24, 1938, 76–77; "Food Bill Passed at Last," *Printers' Ink,* June 16, 1938, 76; Charles Wesley Dunn, "How S 5 Will Work," *Printers' Ink,* July 7, 1938, 44; and "Food, Drug Act Will Dovetail with FTC Work," *Advertising Age,* July 18, 1938, 28.

71. Consumer Education Service, "Comments on the Federal Food, Drug, and Cosmetics Act," *C.E.S. Miscellaneous Publications,* ser. 3, no. 5 (Washington, D.C.: Consumer Education Service, 1938), 6, clipping in box 84, folder 13, Richard L. D. Morse Papers, Consumer Movement Archives, Kansas State University, Manhattan (hereafter referred to as Morse Papers).

72. "Important JWT Forum," May 9, 1938, J. Walter Thompson Company Staff Meeting Minutes, box 7, folder 4, J. Walter Thompson Company Archives, Hartman Center for Sales, Advertising, and Marketing History in the Rare Book, Manuscript, and Special Collections Library, Duke University, Durham, N.C. (hereafter referred to as JWT Papers); Frederick J. Schlink, "Off the Editor's Chest," *Consumers' Research Bulletin,* June 1938, 1.

73. Henry Miller, "A New and Stronger Advertising Statute," *Broadcasting,* April 1, 1938, 19.

74. Tedlow, "From Competitor to Consumer," 53.

75. "New Advertising Bill Passed by House," 17–18.

76. George Gallup, "An Analysis of the Study of Consumer Agitation," box 76, folder 11, NBC Papers.

77. "Wheeler-Lea Bill Broadening Powers," 18.

78. Ibid.

79. "New Advertising Bill Passed by House," 17. For an excellent discussion regarding "trade puffing" under the Wheeler-Lea Amendment, see Ivan L. Preston, *The Great American Blowup* (Madison: University of Wisconsin Press, 1996).

80. Pease, *Responsibilities of American Advertising,* 131.

81. "The Food Bill Situation," *Printers' Ink,* July 15, 1937, 95; "Lea Bill Passes House," 24–26; "Why Hysterics over the FTC?" *Advertising and Selling,* March 1940, 36.

82. John Benson quoted in "Coast Council Hears Benson Applaud Wheeler-Lea Act," *Advertising Age,* October 31, 1938, 19; "Cosmetic Ad Plan Urged on Industry," *New York Times,* May 27, 1938, 33.

83. "Unfair to the Consumer," *CUR,* March 1938, 1.

84. Wilbur Van Sant, *The Wheeler-Lea Law and What to Do about It,* April 25, 1938, excerpts in box 345, folder 11, CR Papers.

85. John A. Killan, "The Wheeler Lea Bill," 4, J. Walter Thompson Forum, May 10, 1938, J. Walter Thompson Company Staff Meeting Minutes, box 7, folder 4, JWT Papers.

86. M. C. Phillips to the FTC, May 3, 1938, box 345, folder 11, CR Papers; Schlink,

"Off the Editor's Chest," 1; Consumer Education Service, "Advertising and Trade Promotion," *C.E.S. Miscellaneous Publications,* ser. 3, no. 2 (Washington, D.C.: Consumer Education Service, 1938), 27, box 84, folder 12, Morse Papers.

87. "The Great American Cure-All," *CUR,* October 1938, 14–15; "Advertising and Trade Promotion," 27.

88. "Truth in Advertising," *New Republic,* September 16, 1940, clipping in box 99, folder 6, Colston E. Warne Papers, Consumers Union Archives, Yonkers, N.Y. (hereafter referred to as Warne Papers); see also "$250 Isn't Enough," *CUR,* June 1939, 15.

89. Pease, *Responsibilities of American Advertising,* 132. The FTC soon realized that not holding advertising agencies directly responsible for false and misleading advertising presented a potential loophole. Agencies could use their immunity as a means to shield clients from the law. Soon the FTC demanded that agencies could be held liable for false and misleading advertising along with their clients; see "Agencies to Be Held Liable for Copy under New FTC Policy," *Advertising Age,* February 20, 1939, 1.

90. "Wheeler-Lea Act," n.d., box 63, folder 3, Warne Papers.

91. John Benson quoted in "Advertising Claims Found 'Cleaned Up' during First Year Under Wheeler-Lea Act," *New York Times,* March 26, 1939, 9.

92. Pgad Bryan Morehouse, "After Two Years of Wheeler-Lea," *Advertising and Selling,* May 1940, 23.

93. Stephens Rippey, "The FTC in Unofficial Profile," *Advertising and Selling,* February 1940, 20.

94. *Valentine v. Chrestensen,* 316 U.S. 52 (1942).

Chapter 7: Red-Baiting the Consumer Movement

1. See, for example, "Frontal Attack on Advertising," *Business Week,* February 8, 1936, 10; "Trends and Perspectives," *Advertising and Selling,* January 1938, 35–38; Dexter Masters, "An Advertising Critic Speaks Up," *Advertising and Selling,* February 1938, 28–30; and "Advertising Is Exhibit Theme," *New York Times,* March 18, 1939, 22.

2. "Business Week Reports to Executives on the Consumer Movement," *Business Week,* April 22, 1939, 40, clipping in box 148, folder 8, Consumers' Research Papers, Special Collection and University Archives, Rutgers University, New Brunswick, N.J. (hereafter referred to as CR Papers). CU operated with even higher numbers. At its third annual membership meeting in June 1939 the consumer organization assessed its total membership to be around eighty-five thousand. Of these, seventy-one thousand were full members whereas fourteen thousand subscribed on a limited basis. Although CU was pleased that it had attracted twenty-nine thousand members through its group membership program, it still stressed the need to attract more people from the lower income brackets; see "CU Members Meet," *Consumers Union Reports* (hereafter referred to as *CUR*), June 1939, 14–15. For more on the plan to attract members through labor unions, see "Minutes of the Meeting of the Board of

Directors of Consumers Union of the United States Inc.," June 21, 1938, box 1, Minutes 1936–38 folder, Board of Directors Minutes, Group 1B, Series 1936–65, Consumers Union Papers, Consumers Union Archives, Yonkers, N.Y. (hereafter referred to as CU Papers).

3. Chester Leasure, "Measures of Subversive Activities," memo to secretaries, chairs, and members of legislative committees of member organizations, September 14, 1936, box 13, Chamber of Commerce June 1936–February 1937 folder (c-43–k), Office of the President, Administrative Papers, Accession 1662, Records of E. I. Du Pont de Nemours and Co., Hagley Library, Wilmington, Del. (hereafter referred to as OP, AP, Acc. 1662, Du Pont Papers).

4. "Communist Activities throughout the World, January–June, 1938," *Safeguards against Subversive Activities* 22 (October 1938), clipping in box 13, Chamber of Commerce March 1937–December 1938 folder (c-43–k), OP, AP, Acc. 1662, Du Pont Papers; Thomas Watson to Lammont Du Pont, February 11, 1937, box 13, Chamber of Commerce June 1936–February 1937 folder (c-43–k), OP, AP, Acc. 1662, Du Pont Papers; "Ninth General Meeting International Chamber of Commerce, Berlin June 28th to July 3rd, 1937," box 13, Chamber of Commerce June 1936–February 1937 folder (c-43–k), OP, AP, Acc. 1662, Du Pont Papers.

5. "Dictatorship and Democracy," *Safeguards against Subversive Activities* 15 (December 1936): 8, clipping in box 13, Chamber of Commerce June 1936–February 1937 folder (c-43–k), OP, AP, Acc. 1662, Du Pont Papers.

6. "Mr. Dies Goes to Town," *Propaganda Analysis,* January 15, 1940, 2.

7. For excellent discussions of Martin Dies and his committee, see Walter Goodman, *The Committee* (New York: Farrar, Straus, and Giroux, 1938), chaps. 1–3; Richard M. Fried, *Nightmare in Red* (New York: Oxford University Press, 1990), 47–49; and George Seldes, *Witch Hunt: The Technique and Profits of Redbaiting* (New York: Modern Age Books, 1940), chap. 12.

8. "Dies Committee Investigation," *Safeguarding against Subversive Activities* 22 (October 1938): 1, clipping in box 13, Chamber of Commerce March 1937–December 1938 folder (c-43–k), OP, AP, Acc. 1662, Du Pont Papers.

9. "Dies Committee Investigation," 1.

10. "The Mysterious Mr. Matthews: Man Who Formed Twenty Red Fronts Now Masterminds U.S. Fascists!" *Expose* 1, no. 3 (January 1952), clipping in box 2, folder 5, CU Papers.

11. Ibid.; Seldes, *Witch Hunt,* chap. 12.

12. Frederick J. Schlink to Martin Dies, January 19, 1940, 5, box 505, folder 14, CR Papers; Frederick J. Schlink to Kenneth Haas, March 4, 1938, box 181, folder 15, CR Papers. For more on CU's boycott of German and Japanese goods, see "The State of the Union," *CUR,* July 1938, 11.

13. Schlink to Dies, January 19, 1940.

14. Ibid., 9.

15. Schlink to Haas, March 4, 1938.

16. Frederick J. Schlink to J. Parnell Thomas, October 14, 1939, box 181, folder 13, CR Papers; "The *Readers' Digest* Gets a Muddled Appraisal of the Consumer Movement," *Consumers' Research Bulletin,* October 1939, 1. See also "Dies Investigator Says Reds Utilize Consumer Groups," *New York Times,* December 11, 1939, 1; and "Dies Report Stirs Indignation of Consumer Leaders," *Advertising Age,* December 18, 1939, 31.

17. "A Trojan Horse at Stephens College?" *Consumers' Research Bulletin,* November 1939, clipping in box 148, folder 6, CR Papers. For CR's criticism of the Institute for Propaganda Analysis, see various correspondence and clippings in box 532, folders 21 and 22, CR Papers.

18. Clyde R. Miller to Martin L. Dies, May 25, 1939, box 82, Dies Committee 1939–49 folder, Alfred McClung Lee Papers, Brooklyn College Archives and Special Collections, Brooklyn, N.Y. (hereafter referred to as Lee Papers); Frederick J. Schlink to Bernhard DeVito, November 19, 1937, box 532, folder 22, CR Papers; Frederick J. Schlink to Bernard DeVito, July 17, 1939, box 532, folder 21, CR Papers; George E. Sokolsky, manuscript marked "Confidential," June 13, 1939, box 532, folder 21, CR Papers. For more information about the Institute for Propaganda Analysis, see J. Michael Sproule, *Propaganda and Democracy: The American Experience of Media and Mass Persuasion* (Cambridge: Cambridge University Press, 1997), chap. 5; and "Dies vs. Consumers," *Business Week,* November 11, 1939, clipping in box 2, folder 4, CU Papers.

19. Frederick J. Schlink, "The Communists and Their Fellow Travelers," November 16, 1940, 6, box 92, folder 20, CR Papers.

20. "Sticks and Stones," *CUR,* October 1939, 15; "Sounds Plea for FTC Investigation of Consumers' Research," *Advertising Age,* November 27, 1939, clipping in box 22, folder 13, CR Papers; "Debate Merits of Consumer Move in U.S.," *Des Moines Register,* November 17, 1939, clipping in box 22, folder 13, CR Papers.

21. Frederick J. Schlink, "Off the Editor's Chest," *Consumers' Research Bulletin,* December 1939, 1, clipping in box 22, folder 13, CR Papers.

22. "Collier's Defense of Advertising," *Consumers' Digest,* September 1939, 28–29.

23. "The *Reader's Digest* Gets a Muddled Appraisal," 26.

24. "Dies vs. Consumers," 4. For another critical industry perspective on the Dies committee's decision to investigate the consumer movement, see "Baiting the Consumers?" *Glass Packer,* November 1939, 652, clipping in box 22, folder 13, CR Papers.

25. Seldes, *Witch Hunt,* 144, chap. 12; Otis Pease, *The Responsibilities of American Advertising: Private Control and Public Influence, 1920–1940* (New Haven, Conn.: Yale University Press, 1958), 128–31. The FTC's decision was met with industry resistance not only from *Good Housekeeping* but also from the advertising community in general. The final decision in 1941 supported the original charges that a number of advertisements that had appeared in *Good Housekeeping* were false or misleading and that the various seals and warranties of the magazine tended to make the public think that all products were guaranteed when such was not the case. The FTC ordered *Good*

Housekeeping to change its seal of approval. For more detailed information about this case, see correspondence in box 286, Docket 3872–1, Docket Section, Records of the Federal Trade Commission, Record Group 122, National Archives II, College Park, Md. (hereafter referred to as FTC Records); and box 2863, Docket 1–1/3872–1, Files 1915–43, Docketed Case, FTC Records. See also "Good Housekeeping Stands Indicted," *CUR*, September 1939, 2–4; "The Case against Good Housekeeping," *CUR*, January 1940, 26; "End of an Advertising Era?" *CUR*, September 1940, 14; "FTC Docket No. 3872," *CUR*, April 1941, 103–5; "FTC Orders 'Good House' to Change Testings, Seals," *Advertising Age*, May 26, 1941, 1; "'Good House' Changes Seals, Guaranty Emblem," *Advertising Age*, June 16, 1941, 1; and "'Good House' Restricts Seals to Own Advertisers," *Advertising Age*, August 25, 1941, 1.

26. The telegram's message was later sent by Richard E. Berlin in a memo to "Advertisers and manufacturers," December 9, 1939, box 4, folder 4, CU Papers. See also "Mr. Berlin's Telegram," *Printers' Ink*, December 12, 1939, clipping in box 2, folder 4, CU Papers.

27. "Defense," *Tide*, November 1, 1938, 26, clipping in box 122, folder 22, CR Papers.

28. Ibid. For more information about George E. Sokolsky, see George Seldes, *Lords of the Press* (New York: Julian Messner, 1938), 319–30; Seldes, *Witch Hunt*, chap. 11; and Stuart Ewen, *PR! The Social History of Spin* (New York: Basic Books, 1996), 305–6. For Sokolsky's attack on the consumer movement, see "Views Consumer Groups as Threat to Merchandising," Advertising Age, June 19, 1939, 32; "Advertising's Basic Sales Function Is Stressed by AFA," *Advertising Age*, June 26, 1939, 25; and "President Greets A.F.A.," *Printers' Ink*, June 29, 1939, 67–68.

29. Drew Pearson and Robert S. Allen, "Consumer Groups Irate over Red Charge, Plan to Ask Probe of Dies," *St. Louis Star-Times*, December 22, 1939, clipping in box 2, folder 4, CU Papers.

30. Untitled and undated report citing evidence against the Matthews report, box 4, folder 4, CU Papers. See also Harold Lavine to George E. Sokolsky, December 18, 1939, box 87, Dies Committee 1939–40 folder, Lee Papers. Contacted by the Institute for Propaganda Analysis, several of the individuals that had been present at the Sokolsky dinner denied that the report had been discussed; see Paul West to Harold Lavine, December 28, 1939, box 87, Dies Committee 1939–40 folder, Lee Papers; Anne Simmons to Donald E. Montgomery, January 2, 1940, box 87, Dies Committee 1939–40 folder, Lee Papers; and J. B. Matthews to Institute for Propaganda Analysis, January 11, 1940, box 87, Dies Committee 1939–40 folder, Lee Papers.

31. Pease, *Responsibilities of American Advertising*, 155–56; House Subcommittee to Investigate Un-American Activities, "For Release, Monday, December 11, 1939," December 3, 1939, box 2, folder 5, CU Papers, copy in box 4, folder 4, CU Papers.

32. J. B. Matthews, "Report of the Director of Research to the Special Committee on Un-American Activities on Communist Work in Consumer Organizations," December 11, 1939, 11, box 2, folder 5, CU Papers.

33. Ibid.

34. Seldes, *Witch Hunt,* 139. Walter Trumbull (the lawyer representing the striking CR workers in 1935) and Susan Jenkins (a CR strike organizer) were framed as Communists in the report; see Matthews, "Report of the Director of Research." See also "'Consumer' Movement Revealed as Red Tactic," *Daily Mirror,* December 11, 1939, 2, clipping in box 22, folder 13, CR Papers; House Subcommittee to Investigate Un-American Activities, "For Release, Monday, December 11, 1939"; and "Dies Investigator," 1; Goodman, *The Committee,* 83.

35. Kallet quoted in "Dies Report Stirs Indignation," 31.

36. Susan Jenkins quoted in "Matthews Meets Denials, Attacks," *New York Times,* December 12, 1939, clipping in box 2, folder 4, CU Papers.

37. Helen Hall and Robert S. Lynd quoted in "Red Charges Denied by Consumer Groups," *New York Times,* December 13, 1939, clipping in box 2, folder 4, CU Papers.

38. Donald E. Montgomery quoted in "Montgomery Sees No Anti-Advertising Drive," *Editor and Publisher,* December 21, 1939, clipping in box 2, folder 4, CU Papers.

39. "Attack from the Die-Hards," *CUR,* January 1940, 32.

40. Ibid. (emphasis in the original).

41. Frank J. Cogan, "Reply to Washington," memo to Stephen Rippey, February 19, 1940, 18, clipping in box 22, folder 13, CR Papers. Similar opinions were expressed in other publications as well; see, for example, "Ad Men Told to Face Test of Consumers," *Boston Transcript,* June 4, 1940, clipping in box 22, folder 13, CR Papers; "Consumer Year," *Food Field Reporter,* January 8, 1940, 14, clipping in box 22, folder 13, CR Papers; "Dies Pay Dirt," *New York World-Telegram,* December 29, 1939, 13, clipping in box 22, folder 13, CR Papers; "Horsefeathers!" *Bridgeport (Conn.) Herald,* November 26, 1939, clipping in box 2, folder 4, CU Papers; "Smearing the Consumer Movement," *St. Louis Post-Dispatch,* December 11, 1939, clipping in box 2, folder 4, CU Papers; and "The Dies Committee," *New York Times,* December 16, 1939, 16, clipping in box 22, folder 13, CR Papers.

42. One of the few major newspapers to carry the report in full was the *New York Herald,* which was owned by the Hearst corporation; see Frederick J. Schlink, "Off the Editor's Chest," *Consumers' Research Bulletin,* January 1940, clipping in box 22, folder 13, CR Papers.

43. "The Bungled Red Exposure," *Advertising and Selling,* January 1940, 34. Others concurred; see, for example, Wallace Warble, "Consumer Movements and Advertising: Rational Approach Suggested as One Way to Reach Agreement," *Broadcasting,* January 1, 1940, 15, clipping in box 22, folder 13, CR Papers.

44. "Matthews Lifts a Lid," *Printers' Ink,* December 15, 1939, 102, clipping in box 22, folder 13, CR Papers.

45. "The Dies Report on Consumers," *Advertising Age,* December 18, 1939, 12.

46. Kenneth G. Crawford quoted in "Mr. Dies Goes to Town," 44.

47. Pearson and Allen, "Consumer Groups Irate"; Dorothy Dunbar Bromley,

"Strike a Balance," *New York Post,* January 12, 1940, clipping in box 22, folder 13, CR Papers.

48. Colston E. Warne to John Cassels, December 1, 1939, box 26, folder 7, Colston E. Warne Papers, Consumers Union Archives, Yonkers, N.Y. (hereafter referred to as Warne Papers). Most major newspapers, with the clear exception of the Hearst chain, considered the Matthews report to be a serious mistake; see unsigned and undated memo beginning "Exhibit A—A statement detailing conspiracy between at least one member of the committee's staff and anti-consumer interests, and suggesting possible lines of inquiry," 1, box 4, folder 4, CU Papers; *New York Times,* untitled and undated clipping in box 2, folder 2, CU Papers.

49. Reginald Joyce to George Laros, January 31, 1940, box 22, folder 13, CR Papers.

50. For examples of the tendency to lump CU and CR together and CR's rebuttal of these charges, see Frederick J. Schlink, "Off the Editor's Chest," *Consumers' Research Bulletin,* January 1940, 1; Schlink to Dies, January 19, 1940; Fredrick J. Schlink to Warner K. Gabler, January 30, 1940, box 148, folder 7, CR Papers; *Wenatchee (Wash.) Daily World,* December 6, 1939, clipping in box 22, folder 13, CR Papers; "Sounds Pleas for FTC Investigation of Consumers' Research," *Advertising Age,* November 27, 1939, clipping in box 22, folder 13, CR Papers; and "Sticks and Stones," *CUR,* October 1939, 15. Schlink and CR were also up in arms whenever someone mentioned CR and CU as competitors and thus ignored the distinction between the groups that Schlink so carefully protected. Reginald Joyce to George Laros, January 21, 1940, box 22, folder 13, CR Papers; Frederick J. Schlink to William A. Consodine, March 26, 1940, box 22, folder 13, CR Papers.

51. Frederick J. Schlink, "Off the Editor's Chest," *Consumers' Research Bulletin,* December 1939, 1, clipping in box 22, folder 13, CR Papers.

52. Ibid., 26.

53. Schlink to Dies, January 19, 1940.

54. Ibid.

55. Unsigned memo beginning "Exhibit A," 1.

56. Abraham J. Isserman to Jerry Voorhis, December 15, 1939, box 1, Dies Committee Un-American Activities folder, Abraham J. Isserman Papers, Consumers Union Archives, Yonkers, N.Y. (hereafter referred to as Isserman Papers); Abraham J. Isserman to David A. Pine, December 19, 1939, box 1, Dies Committee Un-American Activities folder, Isserman Papers; Seldes, *Witch Hunt,* 141.

57. Pease, *Responsibilities of American Advertising,* 155.

58. Untitled and undated report citing evidence against the Matthews report; Bromley, "Strike a Balance," 9.

59. Pease, *Responsibilities of American Advertising,* 156.

60. Untitled and undated report citing evidence against the Matthews report; J. Howard Haring to Consumers Union, April 9, 1940, box 4, folder 4, CU Papers; Colston E. Warne to Martin Dies, April 17, 1940, box 4, folder 4, CU Papers.

61. Statement of Jerry Voorhis, December 11, 1939, 1, box 3, folder 2, CU Papers.

62. Ibid., 1–2.

63. Stanley High to Mr. Bell, memo, n.d., box 39, folder 40, National Broadcasting Company Papers, Wisconsin Center for Historical Research, State Historical Society of Wisconsin, Madison (hereafter referred to as NBC Papers); Stanley High, "General Objections of *American Cavalcade,*" n.d., box 39, folder 40, NBC Papers.

64. Paul S. Willis quoted in "Willis Defends Consumer," *Printers' Ink,* December 22, 1939; "Backs Consumer Groups," *New York Times,* n.d., clipping in box 22, folder 13, CR Papers; "P. S. Willis Deplores Dies Consumer Attack," *Food Field Reporter,* December 25, 1939, 1, clipping in box 22, folder 13, CR Papers; "Trojan Horse," *Food Field Reporter,* December 25, 1939, 14, clipping in box 22, folder 13, CR Papers.

65. For a discussion of the relationship between business and labor during this period, see Elizabeth A. Fones-Wolf, *Selling Free Enterprise: The Business Assault on Labor and Liberalism, 1945–1960* (Urbana: University of Illinois Press, 1994).

66. "Evaluation of the Consumer Movement," n.d., box 76, folder 11, NBC Papers; C. B. Larrabee, "Guinea Pig Books," *Printers' Ink,* April 16, 1936, 71–73; "Business Week Reports to Executives," 40. In 1939 Schlink denied that 250 million copies of *100,000,000 Guinea Pigs* had been sold. It is unknown, however, if this was true or if it was yet another attempt at downplaying the contributions Kallet, his coauthor and by now his archenemy, had made to the consumer movement; see Frederick J. Schlink to *Business Week,* April 25, 1939, box 148, CR Papers.

67. "Crowell Organizes Movement to Educate Consumers on Services and Benefits of Advertising," *Sales Management,* November 15, 1937, 36.

68. James Henle, "Who Hurts Advertising?" *Printers' Ink,* October 22, 1936, 33.

69. "The Consumer Menace," *Printers' Ink,* January 4, 1937, 96.

70. "The Consumer Reporter," *CUR,* November 1939, 1; "ANA Analyst Finds Consumer Movement Had Nine Objectives," *Food Field Reporter,* November 15, 1939, 3, clipping in box 22, folder 13, CR Papers.

71. "ANA Analyst," 3.

72. For a discussion of consumer education in schools, see Helen Sorenson, *The Consumer Movement: What It Is and What It Means* (New York: Harper and Brothers, 1941), chap. 3.

73. Anna Steese Richardson quoted in "Anti-Business Rumors Found Rife in Schools," *New York Herald Tribune,* June 8, 1939, 37, clipping in box 181, folder 14, CR Papers.

74. "Report of Activities: The Speakers' Bureau—National Association of Manufacturers," n.d., 1, box 110, Speakers' Bureau Report Activities 1937 folder, Series 1, Accession (hereafter referred to as Acc.) 1411, National Association of Manufacturers' Papers, Hagley Library, Wilmington, Del. (hereafter referred to as NAM Papers). See also *N.A.M. Speakers Bureau* (New York: National Association of Manufacturers, n.d.), box 110, Questionnaire 1936 folder, Series 1, Acc. 1411, NAM Papers.

75. National Association of Manufacturers, *Speaking for American Industry* (New York: National Association of Manufacturers, n.d.), box 110, Speakers' Bureau Pro-

motional Material 1938–39 folder, Series 1, Accession 1411, NAM Papers. See also *Dr. Allen Stockdale Presented under the Auspices of the Speakers' Bureau of the National Association of Manufacturers* (New York: National Association of Manufacturers, n.d.), box 110, Speakers' Bureau Promotional Material 1938–39 folder, Series 1, Accession 1411, NAM Papers.

76. Lammont Du Pont to Members of the Committee on Educational Cooperation, April 10, 1940, box 54, NAM Educational Co-op June 1940–November 1940 folder, OP, AP, Acc. 1662, Du Pont Papers.

77. "History of the Activities of the National Association of Manufacturers Committee on Educational Cooperation," n.d., box 54, NAM Educational Co-op June 1940–November 1940 folder, OP, AP, Acc. 1662, Du Pont Papers.

78. Du Pont to Members of the Committee on Educational Cooperation, April 10, 1940 [emphasis in original].

79. "N.A.M. Educational Cooperation Meeting," April 22, 1940, 4, box 54, NAM Educational Co-op June 1940–November 1940 folder, OP, AP, Acc. 1662, Du Pont Papers.

80. Committee on Educational Cooperation, "Not for Publication: Official Draft of a Memorandum of Industry's Recommendations for the Improvement of American Educational Methods in the Preparing of Students of a Republic," June 28, 1939, 2, box 54, NAM Educational Co-op June 1940–November 1940 folder, OP, AP, Acc. 1662, Du Pont Papers.

81. "Propaganda over the Schools," *Propaganda Analysis,* February 25, 1941, 8.

82. Ibid., 3.

83. Ibid., 4.

84. "How Can Economic Illiteracy Be Reduced?" was the theme of an extremely well-attended meeting organized by the Committee on Educational Cooperation during spring 1940; see Howard Coonley to Lammont Du Pont, February 8, 1940, 2, box 54, NAM Educational Co-op June 1940–November 1940 folder, OP, AP, Acc. 1662, Du Pont Papers; Lammont Du Pont, "The Need for Leadership," speech delivered at the Eighth Conference on Educational Policies, Teachers College, Columbia University, April 4, 1940, box 54, NAM Educational Co-op June 1940–November 1940 folder, OP, AP, Acc. 1662, Du Pont Papers.

85. National Education Association of the United States, "Principles of Academic Freedom," June 1940, 1, box 54, NAM Educational Co-op December 1939–May 1940 folder, OP, AP, Acc. 1662, Du Pont Papers.

86. Lammont Du Pont to D. W. Hoppock, June 20, 1940, 2, box 54, NAM Educational Co-op June 1940–November 1940 folder, OP, AP, Acc. 1662, Du Pont Papers.

87. Lammont Du Pont to William S. Taylor, June 9, 1940, box 54, NAM Educational Co-op December 1939–May 1940 folder, OP, AP, Acc. 1662, Du Pont Papers.

88. Alfred T. Falk, *Does Advertising Harm or Benefit Consumers?* (New York: Advertising Federation of America, n.d.), box 63, folder 3, Warne Papers.

89. William K. Deggert to Lammont Du Pont, April 25, 1940, box 54, NAM Edu-

cational Co-op June 1940–November 1940 folder, OP, AP, Acc. 1662, Du Pont Papers; "Teachers College," undated memo, box 54, NAM Educational Co-op June 1940–November 1940 folder, OP, AP, Acc. 1662, Du Pont Papers; "History of the Activities of the National Association of Manufacturers Committee on Educational Cooperation," box 54, NAM Educational Co-op June 1940–November 1940 folder, OP, AP, Acc. 1662, Du Pont Papers. For a general outline of the plan by the National Federation of Sales Executives for the educational sector, see National Federation of Sales Executives, *General Outline of 1940–41 Program of National Economic Educational Committee* (New York: National Federation of Sales Executives, n.d.), box 54, NAM Educational Co-op December 1939–May 1940 folder, OP, AP, Acc. 1622, Du Pont Papers.

90. National Federation of Sales Executives, *General Outline* (emphasis in the original).

91. "Report of Findings: Survey of N.A.M. School Services—Conducted by Henry E. Abt," January 15–29, 1941, 2, box 846, Report of Findings—Survey of NAM School Service folder, Series 3, Acc. 1411, NAM Papers.

92. Ibid., 4.

93. Ibid., 11.

94. Ibid.

95. "Outline of Organization and Operation of a Public Information Program for Members of the Advertising Federation of America," n.d., 9, box 111, Public Relations Committee Program—Outline of Organization and Operation of a Public Information Program folder, Series 1, Acc. 1411, NAM Papers. See also Advertising Federation of America, *A Public Relations Program for Advertising Clubs Affiliated with the Advertising Federation of America* (New York: Advertising Federation of America, n.d.), box 111, Public Relations Program of Advertising Clubs folder, Series 1, Acc. 1411, NAM Papers.

96. Advertising Federation of America, *A Public Relations Program for Advertising Clubs*, 12.

97. "Teachers College (Affiliated with Columbia University)," n.d., 1, box 54, NAM Educational Co-op June 1940–November 1940 folder, OP, AP, Acc. 1662, Du Pont Papers.

98. "Proceedings Luncheon Meeting—National Industrial Unity Committee of the National Association of Manufacturers," March 28, 1940, box 846, series I, Proceedings—Luncheon Meeting National Industrial Unity Committee of the NAM, Series 3, Acc. 1411, NAM Papers. See also "Too Many Things Attempted," *Economic Council Letter*, January 1, 1940, clipping in box 63, folder 3, Warne Papers; "Teachers College," *Economic Council Letter*, January 1, 1940, clipping in box 63, folder 3, Warne Papers.

99. Harold Rugg, *An Introduction to Problems of American Culture* (Boston: Ginn and Company, 1931), 459–65.

100. Augustin G. Rudd, "The Rugg Social Science Books and What They Mean," in *Revolution through "Social Science" in the School: Three Addresses by Augustin G. Rudd, Archibald E. Stevenson, and Mervin K. Hart Broadcast by Courtesy of WIBX,*

Utica, N.Y., on May 7, 8, and 10, 1940, Respectively by American Parents Committee on Education (New York: American Parent Committee on Education, n.d.), 7, box 54, NAM Educational Co-op June 1940–November 1940 folder, OP, AP, Acc. 1662, Du Pont Papers. See also "Think This Over," *Economic Council Letter,* January 1, 1940, clipping in box 63, folder 3, Warne Papers.

101. "Propaganda over the Schools," 1–12.

102. Arthur T. Falk quoted in "News and Notes of the Advertising Field," *New York Times,* June 12, 1939, 26. See also "Propaganda Purge," *Time,* July 10, 1939, 42.

103. Norman S. Rose quoted in "Defense of Advertising Voiced by Rose at Fair," *New York Herald,* June 22, 1940, 6, clipping in box 22, folder 13, CR Papers.

104. Archibald E. Stevenson, "The Rugg Social Science Books and What They Mean," in *Revolution through "Social Science" in the School,* 10.

105. "Propaganda over the Schools," 1; "Consumers on Campus," *Printers' Ink,* February 10, 1938, 108.

106. Melvin K. Hart, "The Rugg Social Science Books and What They Mean," in *Revolution through "Social Science" in the School,* 11–14. See also "Consumers on Campus," 108.

107. It did not take long, however, before critics of the New York State Economic Council pointed to the organization's close links with Dies as well as with several Fascist and anti-Semitic groups; see Roger N. Baldwin, "Gilt-Edged Patriots: Presenting the New York State Economic Council and Its Presiding Genius," *Frontiers of Democracy,* November 15, 1940, 45–47, clipping in box 519, folder 15, CR Papers. For Mervin Hart's (largely unconvincing) attempt at denying these charges, see "Let's Discuss This on the Merits," *Frontiers of Democracy,* December 15, 1940, 82–87, clipping in box 519, folder 15, CR Papers. See also "Roger N. Baldwin Replies," *Frontiers of Democracy,* December 15, 1940, 87–88, clipping in box 519, folder 15, CR Papers.

108. "Advertising Groups Pursuing Professor Rugg's Books," *Publishers Weekly,* September 28, 1940, 1323. Interestingly enough, when advertisers were given the chance to debate Rugg in public, they elected, at least on one occasion, not to do so; see "Washington Letter," *Space and Time,* April 10, 1940, 3, clipping in box 172, folder 4, CR Papers.

109. "Warning of Communist Infiltration in Schools and Colleges Sounded," *Newark Star-Ledger,* November 17, 1940, 12, clipping in box 92, folder 20, CR Papers; "Dies Committee," *Economic Council Newsletter,* January 1, 1940, clipping in box 63, folder 3, Warne Papers.

110. "Report on Proposed Text-Book Project, Submitted to the N.A.M. Board, September 27, 1940," box 54, NAM Educational Co-op December 1939–May 1940 folder, OP, AP, Acc. 1662, Du Pont Papers.

111. H. W. Prentis Jr. to Lammont Du Pont, October 31, 1940, box 54, NAM Educational Co-op December 1939–May 1940 folder, OP, AP, Acc. 1662, Du Pont Papers.

112. Lammont Du Pont to H. W. Prentis Jr., November 7, 1940, box 54, NAM Educational Co-op December 1939–May 1940 folder, OP, AP, Acc. 1662, Du Pont Papers.

113. H. W. Prentis Jr. to Lammont Du Pont, November 9, 1940, 2, box 54, NAM

Educational Co-op December 1939–May 1940 folder, OP, AP, Acc. 1662, Du Pont Papers (emphasis in the original).

114. "N.A.M. Educational Cooperation Meeting," April 22, 1940, box 54, NAM Educational Co-op June 1940–November 1940 folder, OP, AP, Acc. 1662, Du Pont Papers.

115. "For Inclusion in Mr. Fuller's Remarks for the Board Meeting, Friday, January 24th," January 21, 1941, box 846, Principles Campaign 1941 folder, Series 3, Accession 1411, NAM Papers.

116. "Letter from the N.A.M.," *CUR,* March 1941, 59.

117. "Fireworks Missing at Conference of Consumer Educators," *Advertising Age,* April 14, 1941, 1–2; "Consumers Union to Fight Attacks on School Material," *Advertising Age,* April 14, 1941, 22; "Propaganda over the Schools," 8; "Letters from the N.A.M.," 59; "The NAM and School Books," *Advertising and Selling,* January 1941, 34.

118. "Mr. Schlink Pipes Down," *Printers' Ink,* November 15, 1940, 87.

Epilogue

1. Frank W. Fox, *Madison Avenue Goes to War* (Provo, Utah: Brigham Young University Press, 1975), chap. 5; Inger L. Stole, "The Salesmanship of Sacrifice: The Advertising Industry's Use of Public Relations during the Second World War," *Advertising and Society Review* 2, no. 2 (2001), http://muse.jhu.edu/journals/asr/v002/2.2stole.html (accessed June 1, 2004); Mark Leff, "The Politics of Sacrifice on the American Home Front in World War II," *Journal of American History* 77, no. 4 (March 1991): 1296–1318.

2. Richard L. D. Morse, ed., *The Consumer Movement: Lectures by Colston E. Warne* (Manhattan, Kans.: Family Economics Trust Press, 1993), 106–7. See also Blake Clark, *The Advertising Smokescreen* (New York: Harper and Brothers, 1943), chap. 12.

3. Norman I. Silber, *Test and Protest: The Influence of Consumers Union* (New York: Holmes and Meier, 1983), 29; Morse, *Consumer Movement,* 108.

4. C. Wright Mills, *The Power Elite* (New York: Oxford University Press, 1956).

5. Eric Johnston, the president of the U.S. Chamber of Commerce, coined the term *People's Capitalism* in the 1940s; see *America Unlimited* (Garden City, N.Y.: Doubleday, Doran, 1944), chap. 8.

6. Robert Griffith, "The Selling of America: The Advertising Council and American Politics, 1942–1960," *Business History Review* 58, no. 1 (Autumn 1983): 388. For an interesting discussion of the Advertising Council's agenda in the postwar era, see Robert Ziegler, "The Paradox of Plenty: The Advertising Council and the Post-Sputnik Crisis," *Advertising and Society Review* 4, no. 1 (2003), http://muse.jhu.edu/journals/asr/v004/4.1ziegler.html (accessed June 1, 2004).

7. See, for example, Stephen J. Whitfield, *The Culture of the Cold War* (Baltimore: Johns Hopkins University Press, 1992); Douglas Miller and Marion Novak, *The Fif-*

ties: *The Way We Really Were* (Garden City, N.Y.: Doubleday, 1977); Richard H. Pells, *The Liberal Mind in a Conservative Age: American Intellectuals in the 1940s and 1950s* (Middletown, Conn.: Wesleyan University Press, 1989); William Graebner, *The Engineering of Consent: Democracy and Authority in Twentieth-Century America* (Madison: University of Wisconsin Press, 1987), chap. 6; Elaine Tyler May, *Homeward Bound: American Families in the Cold War* (New York: Basic Books, 1988); and George Lipsitz, *Time Passages: Collective Memory and American Popular Culture* (Minneapolis: University of Minnesota Press, 1990).

8. *Valentine v. Chrestensen,* 316 U.S. 52 (1942).

9. Lizabeth Cohen, *A Consumer's Republic: The Politics of Mass Consumption in Postwar America* (New York: Alfred A. Knopf, 2003), 274–78.

10. The most recent U. S. Supreme Court case dealing with the issue of First Amendment protection for advertisers left the issue in a legislative limbo; see *Nike v. Kasky,* 123 S. Ct. 225 (2003); 156 L. Ed. 2d 580; 2003 U.S. LEXIS 5015; 71 U.S.L.W. 4602; 67 U.S. Q.2D (BNA) 1262; 2002 Cal. Daily O Service 3790; 2000 Daily Journal DAR 3007.

11. Ivan Preston, *The Great American Blowup* (Madison: University of Wisconsin Press, 1996); Ivan Preston, *The Tangled Web They Weave: Truth, Falsity, and Advertising* (Madison: University of Wisconsin Press, 1996).

12. Susan M. Hartmann, *The Homefront and Beyond: American Women in the 1940s* (Boston: Twayne, 1982), 8.

13. Lawrence R. Samuel, introduction to *Brought to You By: Postwar Television Advertising and the American Dream* (Austin: University of Texas Press, 2001); Lipsitz, *Time Passages,* chap. 1. For an excellent treatment of television's early years, see James L. Baughman, *The Republic of Mass Culture: Journalism, Filmmaking, and Broadcasting in America since 1941* (Baltimore: Johns Hopkins University Press, 1992), chap. 3. See also William Boddy, *Fifties Television: The Industry and Its Critics* (Urbana: University of Illinois Press, 1990); and Lynn Spigel, *Making Room for TV: Television and the Family Ideal in Postwar America* (Chicago: University of Chicago Press, 1992).

14. For the public's reaction to commercial radio, see Roland Marchand, *Advertising the American Dream: Making Way for Modernity, 1920–1940* (Berkeley: University of California Press, 1985), 88–94; Boddy, *Fifties Television,* 22.

15. See, for example, Lipsitz, *Time Passages,* 44–46.

16. For contemporary critiques of consumer society, see John Kenneth Galbraith, *The Affluent Society* (Boston: Houghton Mifflin, 1958); and David Riesman, *The Lonely Crowd: A Study of the Changing American Character* (New Haven, Conn.: Yale University Press, 1953).

17. Griffith, "Selling of America," 412. See also T. J. Jackson Lears, "A Matter of Taste: Corporate Cultural Hegemony in a Mass-Consumption Society," in *Recasting America,* ed. Lary May (Chicago: University of Chicago Press, 1989), 38–57; Warren Susman with the assistance of Edwin Griffin, "Did Success Spoil the United States? Dual Representation in Postwar America," in *Recasting America,* 19–37; and Stepha-

nie Koontz, *The Way We Never Were: American Families and the Nostalgia Trap* (New York: Basic Books, 1992).

18. Norman D. Katz, "Consumers Union: The Movement and the Magazine" (Ph.D. diss., Rutgers University, 1977), 239–40. A survey conducted in late 1945 or early 1946 found CU members to have a median income in the $3,000–$3,999 bracket. Letter to Arthur Kallet from unknown sender, January 18, 1946, box 7, folder 8, Colston E. Warne Papers, Consumers Union Archives, Yonkers, N.Y. (hereafter referred to as Warne Papers).

19. Katz, "Consumers Union," 239–64; Silber, *Test and Protest,* 30–31. For a chart of CR's growth between 1936 and 1961, see Morse, *Consumer Movement,* 150; for information about Consumers Union's return to consumer activism, see the organization's Web site at www.consumersunion.org (accessed May 30, 2005).

20. Peter L. Spencer, "Consumers' Research," in *Encyclopedia of the Consumer Movement,* ed. Stephen Brobeck (Santa Barbara, Calif.: ABC-CLIO, 1997), 179–82.

21. Stephen Brobeck, "Consumer Federation of America," in *Encyclopedia of the Consumer Movement,* 146–51.

22. Ralph Nader, *Unsafe at Any Speed* (New York: Harcourt, Brace, Jovanovich, 1973).

23. David Bollier, "Ralph Nader," in *Encyclopedia of the Consumer Movement,* 383; Morse, *Consumer Movement,* 234–37.

24. Michael Pertschuk, *Revolt against Regulation: The Rise and Fall of the Consumer Movement* (Berkeley: University of California Press, 1982).

25. Hayagreeva Roa, "Caveat Emptor: The Construction of Nonprofit Consumer Watchdog Organizations," *American Journal of Sociology* 103, no. 4 (January 1998): 946–47.

26. Ralph Nader to Colston E. Warne, July 7, 1975, box 12, folder 5, Warne Papers.

27. "Draft of Reply to Ralph Nader's Letter of Resignation," n.d., box 12, folder 5, Warne Papers.

28. Nader to Warne, July 7, 1975. For a discussion of the relationship between Nader, the movement he helped create, and CU, see Morse, *Consumer Movement,* 243–46.

29. Robert O. Herrmann and Robert N. Mayer, "U.S. Consumer Movement: History and Dynamics," in *Encyclopedia of the Consumer Movement,* 593.

30. Morse, *Consumer Movement,* 30.

31. Pertschuk, *Revolt against Regulation,* 50, 58–59; David Vogel, "The Power of Business in America: A Re-appraisal," *British Journal of Political Science* 13, no. 1 (January 1983): 19–43.

32. Pertschuk, *Revolt against Regulation,* 57–58.

33. Patrick J. Akard, "Corporate Mobilization and Political Power: The Transformation of U.S. Economic Policy in the 1970s," *American Sociological Review* 57, no. 5 (October 1992): 602.

34. Vogel, "Power of Business," 31.

35. Pertschuk, *Revolt against Regulation,* 32–33; Vogel, "Power of Business," 30.

36. Vogel, "Power of Business," 37.

37. Ibid., 37–38.

38. For an excellent discussion of the 1996 Telecommunications Act, including some of its social, cultural, and economic implications, see Robert W. McChesney, *Rich Media, Poor Democracy: Communication Politics in Dubious Times* (Urbana: University of Illinois Press, 1999), 73–76.

39. See, for example, Michael Gartner, *Advertising and the First Amendment* (New York: Priority Press Publications, 1989). For a discussion of how expanded First Amendment protection for free speech has affected society, see Matthew McAllister, *The Commercialization of American Culture: New Advertising Control and Democratic Media* (Thousand Oaks, Calif.: Sage Publications, 1996); David Bollier, *Silent Theft: The Private Plunder of Our Common Wealth* (New York: Routledge, 2002); Herbert I. Schiller, *Culture Inc.: The Corporate Takeover of Public Expression* (New York: Oxford University Press, 1989); and Naomi Klein, *No Logo: Taking Aim at the Brand Bullies* (New York: Picador, 2000).

40. Vance Packard, *The Hidden Persuaders* (New York: David McKay, 1958). After only one year this book was in its thirteenth printing, suggesting a strong curiosity about advertising among the American public.

41. Betty Friedan, *The Feminine Mystique* (1963; repr., New York: W. W. Norton, 1974).

42. See, for example, Erving Goffman, *Gender Advertisements* (New York: Harper and Row, 1976); Alice E. Courtney, *Sex Stereotyping in Advertising: An Annotated Bibliography* (Cambridge, Mass.: Marketing Science Institute, 1980); Susan Faludi, *Backlash: The Undeclared War Against American Women* (1991; repr., New York: Doubleday, 1994); Naomi Wolf, *The Beauty Myth: How Images of Beauty Are Used Against Women* (1991; repr., New York: Doubleday, 1994); and Jean Kilbourne, *Deadly Persuasion: Why Women and Girls Must Fight the Addictive Power of Advertising* (New York: Free Press, 1999).

43. For a discussion of advertisers' influence on the educational system, see Alex Molnar, *Giving Kids the Business* (Boulder, Colo.: Westview Press, 1996). For an excellent account of advertising's influences on the mass media, see McChesney, *Rich Media*.

44. Klein, *No Logo,* chaps. 6–8.

Index

AAAA. *See* American Association of Advertising Agencies

academic freedom, 176–77, 181. *See also under* education; schools

Adams, Samuel Hopkins, 9

advertising, vii–x, 14, 166; boycott, 95; capitalism and, 159; Communist plot against, 167; consumer confidence in, 150; corporate, ix–x, 2, 10, 99; educational, 106, 108; feminist critique of, 196; gender-specific, 17–18; illustrations in, 18, 155; image-driven, 22; institutional, 98–99; legitimacy of, ix, 182–83, 187; oligopolistic markets and, x, xiii, xiv, 29, 32, 103, 106; parity in, 4, 102–3; public antipathy for, vii, 29, 138, 158; second wave of consumer activism and, 22–32; testimonials in, 29; women and, 17–18. *See also* advertising industry; false advertising

advertising, regulation of. *See* federal regulation; self-regulation

Advertising Age (trade publication), 20, 33, 102, 169; on advertising in schools, 126–27, 133, 135; consumer movement and, 118, 121, 122; on product information, 31, 103; regulation and, 57, 59, 62, 74

Advertising and Selling (trade publication), 35, 68, 105, 127, 156, 168, 181

Advertising and the Consumer Movement (pamphlet), 108

advertising clubs, 114–15, 178

advertising codes, 59–60, 229n53

Advertising Council, 185–87, 199

"advertising czar," 64

Advertising Federation of America (AFA), xiii, 15, 33, 47, 199; Advertising Research Foundation and, 121, 123, 174, 251n84; Bureau of Research and Education, 176; consumer education and, 120–21, 122; fair trade codes and, 41; fear of Communism and, 159, 172–73, 179, 180, 182; public relations and, 100, 102, 104; regulation and, 59, 62–64, 68–69, 76, 139–40, 141

advertising industry, 30–32, 189; commercialism in schools and, 125–26, 127, 129, 131, 133–34, 136; consumer movement and, 32–36, 101, 102, 103–5, 118, 121–24, 133; Copeland bill (S 5) and, 144, 146; CR strike and, 89; grading controversy and, 45–47; lobbying by, 138, 157; NRA and, 40–42; post–World War I, 15–20; product information and, 27; public relations and, viii–ix, xi, xiii, 2, 19–20, 101–5, 106, 139, 185, 189; reaction to Tugwell bill, 54–55, 56–58, 72, 78–79; self-regulation by, xiv, 55, 58, 64; Wheeler-Lea amendment and, 137, 150, 153, 158; World War I and, 13–14, 214n56

Advertising Research Foundation, 121, 123, 174, 251n84

Advertising Review Committee, 54–55, 62, 65

Advisory Committee on Consumer Interests, 96–97
Advisory Committee on Ultimate Consumer Goods, 112
AFA. *See* Advertising Federation of America
Agricultural Adjustment Act (1933), 37
Agricultural Adjustment Administration, 39, 40, 120, 167, 245n129
Agriculture, Department of. *See* Department of Agriculture
American Association of Advertising Agencies (AAAA), xiii, 15, 100, 121, 199; Committee on Consumer Relations in Advertising, 115; Consumer's Advertising Council and, 111; on emotional appeals, 31; public dissatisfaction and, vii; regulation and, 57, 59, 76, 147, 156. *See also* Benson, John
American Association of University Women, 97, 108, 113
American Can Company (Canco), 127, 128
American Civil Liberties Union, 43
The American Economic System, 160–61
American Family Robinson (radio program), 116
American Federation of Labor (AFL), 83, 92
American Home Economics Association, 75, 76, 97, 108, 113; commercial sponsorship and, 129, 131
Americanism, xiii, 177, 179. *See also* American way
American Legion, 180
American Medical Association, 10, 66, 68, 69, 144, 234n121
American Newspaper Publishers Association, 65
American Parents Committee on Education, 180
American Standards Association, 23, 24, 26, 45, 112, 162
American way, 7, 99, 159, 173; advertising and, 187; Red scare in schools and, 175–78, 180–81
anti-Communism, xv, 122, 190; of Schlink, 35, 83, 98, 118, 160, 162–63. *See also* Dies Committee; Red-scare campaigns
antiglobalization movement, 196–97
Associated Grocery Manufacturers, 97, 164, 172
Association Advertising Clubs of the World (AACW), 15, 58

Association of National Advertisers, xiii, 15, 76, 100, 121, 200, 251n84; regulation and, 57, 59, 138–39
Association of School Film Libraries, 135
Atlantic Monthly (magazine), 6
AT&T, 99, 100

Bailey, Joshua W., 140, 141
Ballyhoo (magazine), 29–30
Bankers Association, 177
Banking (trade publication), 103
Barton, Bruce, 100, 153
Benson, John, 31, 57, 61, 103, 200; on consumer education, 111, 117, 126; on Wheeler-Lea amendment, 147, 154, 156
Berlin, Richard E., 165, 171
Bernays, Edward L., xi, 13, 215n63
Black Bill (HR 6376), 75, 205
Blue Eagle program (NRA), 41–42, 44
Bok, Edward, 8
Boland bill (HR 8316), 76, 206
Borah, William E., 149
Borden, Neil, 127, 254n114
Boren, Wallace, 18–19
brand loyalty, 6, 22, 48, 53, 101
brand-name products, 14, 16, 32, 108; in schools, 124, 125
Breck, Marion F., 132
Brightman, Harold, 112
Bristol, Henry P., 165
Bristol, Lee, 56, 57, 67, 141
Bristol-Myers Company, 56, 141
British Broadcasting Corporation, 30
Broadcasting (trade publication), 122
Bureau of Research and Education (NRA), 41
Bureau of Standards, 44, 45
business: consumer movement and, 80, 105, 109, 112, 117, 182; New Deal and, 40, 99, 243n96; propaganda by, 181; public relations and, 193
business-backed institutes, 133, 194
business-consumer conferences, 116–21, 122–23
business groups, conservative, 172–73, 194
business leaders, 9, 95; fair competition codes and, 38; public relations and, 99–100, 101
business schools, 127
Business Week (magazine), 56, 104, 121, 164
"buy now" campaign, 41–42

CAB. *See* Consumers' Advisory Board (CAB)
Campbell, Walter G., 53, 78
canned goods, labeling of, 45–46
capitalism, viii, 26, 35, 53, 159
Capper bill (S 1592), 55–57, 57, 205
Carey, Alex, 11
Carnegie Institution, 135
Carter administration, 192
Carver, David F., 52
Cassels, John M., 122, 123
Cavalcade of America (radio program), 134–36
Cavers, 78
CBS (radio network), 134, 135
cease and desist orders, 152–53, 154, 155, 262n66
censorship, 63, 64, 141, 153, 181
Center for the Study of Responsive Law, 191
Chamber of Commerce. *See* U.S. Chamber of Commerce
Chapman, Virgil, 143–44
Chapman bill (HR 300), 147, 149, 207
Chase, Stuart, 23–24, 26, 33, 81, 125, 200
Chemistry and Wheels (textbook), 127
Chicago World's Fair (1933), 68, 140
children. *See* education; schools
Circuit Court of Appeals, U.S., 154
Citizens' Union, 12
Clapp, E. W., 128
Clark, Joel Bennett "Champ," 140, 141, 142
Clinton, Bill, 195
Code of Ethics and Practice (AAAA), 59
Coffee bill (HR 5286), 149, 207
Cohen, Lizabeth, 37
Colgate, S. B., 67
Colgate-Palmolive-Peet Company, 5, 67, 129
colleges and universities, 125–27, 134, 136, 194; Red scare in, 174–75, 178. *See also* education
Collier's (magazine), 8, 109
Columbia University Teachers College, 175, 178–79, 200
commercialism, ix, 1, 20, 188, 197. *See also* schools, commercialism in
commercial speech, 157, 187, 195, 197
Committee on Educational Cooperation (CEC), 175–78, 200
Committee on Planning and Fair Practice, 60
Committee on Public Information (CPI), 13–14, 200

Committees, Congressional: *See* Dies Committee; House of Representatives; Senate
Communications Act of 1934, ix, 30
Communism, fear of, xv, 35, 83, 98, 122, 126, 159. *See also* Red-scare campaigns
Communist International, 82
Communist party, 62, 82–83, 87–88, 118, 123
competitive markets, 3, 22, 61, 103, 152–53. *See also* fair competition codes
Congress, U.S., 149, 150, 151, 160, 191, 192; Agricultural Adjustment Act (1933) and, 37; Copeland bill and, 139, 145, 146–47; Tugwell bill and, 49, 52–53, 66, 78. *See also under* House of Representatives, U.S.; Senate, U.S.
Congressional lobbies. *See* lobbying
consumer activism/advocates, 21, 131, 133, 138; Copeland bill and, 142, 144, 147; decline in, 188; federal regulation and, 55–56, 65, 67, 69, 72, 73, 151; global focus of, 196–97; history of, 196; Nader, 191–92; Progressive Era, xiv, 7–11; second wave of, 22–32. *See also* consumer movement; Consumers' Research Inc. (CR)
consumer cooperatives, 11, 44
consumer councils, 39–40, 245n129
consumer culture, advertising and, 2–7
Consumer Division of Crowell Publishing, 107–10, 200
consumer education. *See* education
Consumer Federation of America, 190–91, 192, 195
consumer groups, industry-fronted. *See* industry front groups
consumer movement, viii, ix, 20, 61, 136–37; advertising industry response to, 32–36, 101, 102, 103–5, 118, 121–24, 133; anti-Communism and, 158, 159, 160, 162, 172–73, 183; business and, 80, 105, 109, 117, 182; consumer education and, 106; history of, x–xi; neoliberalism and, 195; propaganda of, 108, 109; schools and, 126, 174; split in, 80, 138. *See also* consumer activism
Consumer Movement Trends (newsletter), 113
consumer protection legislation, 52, 148, 151, 153–54, 157. *See also* federal regulation; Tugwell bill; Wheeler-Lea amendment
Consumer Quiz Club (radio program), 112
Consumer Reports (newsletter), 189, 190, 191, 192

Consumer-Retailer Dry Goods Association, 112
consumers: fears and insecurities of, 16, 17, 19, 22, 29; irrationality of, 16, 17, 48; manufacturers and, 6–7, 21, 32; sovereignty of, 45–46; spending by, 41; taste of, 47
Consumer's Advertising Council, 111
Consumers' Advisory Board (CAB), 22, 38–39, 42–43, 44, 200, 245n129; mandatory grading controversy and, 45–48; Tugwell bill and, 65, 75, 77–78, 79
Consumers' Bill of Rights, 190
Consumers' Club (White Plains, N.Y.), 24
Consumers' Digest (magazine/newsletter), 97–98
Consumers Foundation, 112
Consumers' Guide (NRA), 40
Consumers in Wonderland (play), 30
Consumers' National Council, 97
Consumers' National Federation, 116, 163, 167–68
Consumers' Research (General) Bulletin (newsletter), 24, 44, 85, 91, 94, 98, 112, 200
Consumers' Research Inc. (CR), xiv, 42–45, 48, 119, 136, 186, 200; advertising industry attack on, 33–34, 36; beginnings of, 22, 24–27, 30; Copeland bill (S 5) and, 142, 143–44; Council of Advisors, 81; federal regulation and, 50, 52, 54, 68, 69, 72, 75–79; leadership of, 93; Matthews report and, 164, 167, 169–70; propaganda of, 108; publications of, 24, 44, 85, 91, 94, 97–98, 200; rivalry with CU, 95, 97, 160, 162–63, 169, 190; schools and, 125; subscribers of, 87, 92, 97, 142. See also Schlink, Frederick J.; strike at Consumers' Research Inc.
Consumers Union of the United States Inc. (CU), 108, 119, 174, 182, 195, 201, 264n2; beginnings of, 92–97; business-consumer conferences and, 120, 121, 123; CR strike and, xii, xiv, 80; Dies Committee and, xv, 160, 162–63, 167, 168–70, 171; links to organized labor, 80, 93, 94, 105; Nader and, 191–92; product testing by, 94, 95, 96, 188, 189–90; rivalry with CU, 95, 97, 160, 162–63, 169, 190; tax breaks for advertisers and, 186; Wheeler-Lea amendment and, 149, 156; World's Fair exhibit and, 96–97
Consumers Union Reports (CUR) (newsletter), 93, 94, 96, 105, 110, 112, 168, 201

Cooperative Distributors, 35, 108
Cooperative League of the United States, 11
cooperative movement, 11, 35, 39, 44
Copeland, Royal S., 49, 53, 70–74, 77, 201; Fleischmann's Yeast and, 70–72, 141, 155; legislation sponsored by (See specific bill); Wheeler-Lea amendment and, 152, 153
Copeland bill (S 5), 138–44, 145, 206; revised version, 146–49, 152, 207
Copeland bill (S 2000), 73–74, 206
Copeland bill (S 2800), 74–75, 78, 145, 206
corporate advertising, ix–x, 2, 10. See also advertising industry
corporate culture, xiii, 1–20; consumer culture and, 2–7; mergers and consolidations, 3–4; post–World War I, 15–20; Progressive era consumer activism, 7–11; propaganda and PR, 11–15
corporate power, 11, 34, 78, 194
cosmetics industry exposé, 27. See also Skin Deep (Phillips)
Cosmopolitan (magazine), 5, 8
Coughlin, Charles, 142
Counterfeit (Kallet), 202
Counts, George S., 178
court injunctions, 147, 154
Cox, Oscar S., 83
CR. See Consumers' Research Inc. (CR)
Crain, G. D., 126–27
Creel, George, 13–14, 200
Creel Commission, 13–14, 200
Criticism, Suggestions, and Advice (textbook), 134
Crowell-Collier Publishing Company, 107–10, 121, 174, 200
CU. See Consumers' Union of the United States Inc.
CUR. See Consumers Union Reports
Curtis, Cyrus H. K., 8
Curtis Publishing Company, 134
Cuthbert, Margaret, 110

D'Arcy, William C., 61
Davis, Ewin L., 144–45, 151
Delineator (magazine), 27, 35
Del Monte, 113
democracy, 7, 48, 106, 116; academic freedom and, 176–77; corporate power and, 11
Democratic Party, 37, 40, 142

Dempsey, John, 161
Department of Agriculture, 54, 57, 67, 73, 146; consumer protection and, 52, 53, 68; proposed legislation and, 139, 141, 144, 148
Department of Justice, 156, 160
Department of Labor, 88–89, 214n56
Department of the Consumer, 44, 90, 98, 117, 123, 192
Depression. *See* Great Depression
Dewey, John, 178
Dickinson, Roy, 35
Dies, Martin, 161, 201, 202
Dies Committee, 159–72, 182, 189, 201; CU and, xv, 160, 162–63, 167, 168–70, 171; Matthews report to, 164–72
district courts, U.S., 147, 154
Douglas, Paul H., 39–40
Drug Institute, 67
drug manufacturers, 34, 139, 150, 168; Copeland bill (S 5) and, 140, 141, 143, 144; FTC and, 145–46, 151; patent-medicine industry, 8–9, 55, 70, 141; Tugwell bill and, 66, 67, 72. *See also* specific manufacturer
Dunn, Charles Wesley, 140, 150, 154
Du Pont, Lammont, 115–16, 175, 177, 180, 181
Du Pont de Nemours and Company, 100, 115, 134–36
Durstine, Roy S., 31, 63, 136

economic recovery, 37. *See also* Great Depression; National Recovery Administration
economic system, 99, 103. *See also* capitalism; free enterprise
Edison Electric Institute, 133
education, xiv, 30, 98, 111–12, 119; advertising and, 101, 102, 106, 108; business agenda and, 105; business-consumer conferences, 116–21, 122–23; propaganda and, 100. *See also under* schools; teachers
educational materials, xii, 97; industry-sponsored, 124, 125, 126, 127–33, 134. *See also* textbooks
Edwards, Alice, 76, 119
Elmhirst, Dorothy, 24
Emergency Conference of Consumer Organizations (1934), 74
emotional appeals in ads, 4, 23, 48, 61, 117; branding and, 22; fears and insecuri-

ties, 16, 17, 19, 22, 29; public relations and, 102–3; women and, 18, 31
employment/unemployment, 33, 36–37
Enlightenment ideals, 13
Equitable Life (insurance company), 12–13
Erickson, A. W., 180
ethics code, 59–60. *See also* fair competition codes
Evans, M. Stanton, 190
Everybody's (magazine), 8
Ewen, Stuart, 13
excess-profits tax, 14, 214n56

fact and factoid, 13
factory inspections, 11
fair competition codes, 37–38, 40, 43–44, 60
Falk, Alfred T., 47, 176, 177, 179
false advertising, 27, 30, 94, 132, 149; Copeland bill (S 5) and, 139, 141, 143, 147, 206; criteria for, 55, 57, 140; Fleischmann's Yeast, 70–72, 141, 155; FTC and, 164–65, 264n90; self-regulation and, 60, 140; Tugwell bill and, 49, 54, 58, 73, 75–76, 79; Wheeler-Lea amendment and, 150, 151, 153, 154, 157
fascism, fear of, 161, 162, 163, 171
FDA. *See* Food and Drug Administration
fears and insecurities, 16, 17, 19, 22, 29. *See also* emotional appeal in ads
Federal Communications Commission, 30
Federal Food and Drug Act (1906), 8, 10, 21, 55, 201; attempts to amend, xiv, 49, 50–51, 53, 65, 75, 146–47; Mead bill (HR 3972) revision of, 139; Tugwell and, 146, 204; Wheeler-Lea amendment and, 79, 152, 157. *See also* Copeland bills
federal government, 47. *See also* specific branch of government
Federal Radio Commission, 30, 75
federal regulation, viii, xi, 9, 21, 49–79; banning false advertising, 49, 54, 58, 60, 73, 75–76, 79; CR and, 50, 52, 54; industry self-regulation and, xiv, 55, 58–65; legislative developments (1933–38), 205–7; *Printers' Ink* Model Statute, 55, 56, 58, 63. *See also* specific laws; Tugwell bill; Wheeler-Lea amendment
Federal Trade Commission Act (1914), 145, 207, 262n.66; Wheeler-Lea Amendment and, xv, 149, 150, 152, 155, 187

Federal Trade Commission (FTC), 39, 49, 69, 95, 149–57, 201, 264n90; cease and desist orders, 153, 154, 155, 262n66; FDA and, 69, 143, 144–48; *Good Housekeeping* ads and, 164–65, 171, 266n25; Lea bill (HR 3143) and, 149–51; legislation and, 75, 139, 141; misbranding and, 50; Nader and, 191; Walsh bill and, 143, 207; Wheeler-Lea Amendment and, 152–57

Federation of Sales Executives, 177

The Feminine Mystique (Friedan), 195–96

Filler, Louis, 10

First Amendment, 157, 187, 195, 197

Fleischmann's Yeast ad, 70–72, 94, 140, 155, 165

Food, Drugs and Cosmetics Act, 153–54, 156; also Federal Food and Drug Act of 1906

Food and Drug Administration (FDA), 44, 45, 49, 143, 156, 201; FTC and, 69, 143, 144–48; Tugwell bill and, 67–68, 69, 78; Wheeler-Lea amendment and, 149, 150

food and drug manufacturers, 34, 75; consumer legislation and, 139, 140, 143, 150, 154

Fox, Dixon Ryan, 136

Fox, Frank W., 186

Franklin, Jay, 145, 148

free enterprise, 80, 103, 116, 173, 187; schools and, 175, 176, 177. *See also* capitalism

free speech, 176–77, 195. *See also* First Amendment

Freud, Sigmund, 16, 215n63

Friedan, Betty, 195

front groups. *See* industry front groups

FTC. *See* Federal Trade Commission

Gallup, George, 123–24, 165–66

gender-specific advertising, 17–18

General Motors, 100, 127, 191

Germany, Fascism in, 161, 162

Glickman, Lawrence B., 89

globalization, 196–97

Gold, Ben, 166

Golden Orange (film), 132

Goldstein, Carolyn M., 129

Good Housekeeping Institute, 94, 221n67

Good Housekeeping (magazine), 27, 68, 94–95, 167, 221n67; fraudulent advertising in, 164, 171, 266n25

government programs, 41. *See also specific program*

grade labeling, 45–48, 54, 112–13, 117, 123, 147

grassroots organizing, 193, 194

Grayban hair coloring, 94

Great Depression, 30, 41, 63, 81, 95, 96, 104; unemployment in, 33, 36–37. *See also* National Recovery Administration (NRA); New Deal

Griffith, Robert, 187, 189

Hall, Helen, 168

Handler, Milton, 51, 52, 53, 82

Harper's (magazine), 6, 36

Hart, Melvin K., 180

Harvard School of Business Administration, 127

Healy, Arthur D., 161

Hearst, William Randolph, 70, 168

Hearst Corporation, 95, 164, 165, 171, 269n48

Heasty, John, 83, 85

Heinze, Andrew, 7

Helena Rubenstein, 155

Hidden Persuaders (Packard), 195

High, Stanley, 172

Hires Root Beer, 131–32

Hitler dictatorship, 161

home economics teachers, 129–33

Home-Makers Bulletin (newsletter), 131, 132

Home Makers' Educational Service, 131–32

Hoover, Herbert, 36, 37

House of Representatives, U.S., 53; Committee on Interstate and Foreign Commerce, 143, 151, 152; Un-American Activities Committee, xv, 159–60. *See also* Congress, U.S.; Dies Committee

Howe, Frederick C., 39, 44

HR 8744 (Russell bill), 143, 207

HR 8941 (Jenckes bill), 206, 259n25

illustrations, in advertisements, 18, 155

immigrants, 7, 18

India Tea, 131

Industrial Advisory Board, 38, 39

industry codes, 45. *See also* advertising codes; fair competition codes

industry front groups, xi, xiv, 104–5, 107–16; consumer education and, 111–12; Crowell Publishing, 107–10; retailers and, 111–14, 115; women's clubs and, 111, 112, 113, 114–15

industry self-regulation. *See* self-regulation
Institute for Consumer Education, 116–17, 122–23, 201
Institute for Propaganda Analysis, 163
Institute of Distribution, 112
Institute of Medicine Manufacturers, 145
institutional advertising, 98–99
insurance companies, 12–13
interstate commerce, 144, 150, 152
An Introduction to Problems of American Culture (Rugg), 178–80
"irrational" consumer, 16, 17, 48
Isserman, Abraham J., 95
Ivory Soap, 6, 136

Jacobs, Meg, 39
Jantzen Knitting Mills, 109–10
Japan, Fascism in, 162, 166
Jenckes, Virginia Ellis, 205, 206, 259n25
Jenkins, Susan, 85–86, 87, 88, 166, 167
John Day Publishers, 35–36
Johnson, Hugh S., 38, 39, 42
Joint Committee for Sound and Democratic Consumer Legislation, 67, 68, 75
journalistic exposés, 8–9, 10, 12
The Jungle (Sinclair), 9
Justice Department, 156, 160

Kallet, Arthur, 33, 43, 44, 52, 104, 201; advertising industry and, 140; as author, 27, 34, 50, 69, 202; biographical sketch of, 202; Copeland bill (S 5) and, 142, 143–44; CR strike and, 81, 84, 86, 87–88; CU and, 92, 95, 96; Dies Committee and, 164, 169; photos of, 26, 28; product testing and, 189; Tugwell bill and, 69–70, 72–73, 76–77, 78. *See also* Consumers' Union of the United States Inc. (CU)
Kellogg Company, 129, 130, 136
Kilpatrick, John, 83, 85
Kilpatrick, William Heard, 178
Kobak, Edgar, 68–69, 99, 140

labeling practices, 8, 149, 152; grade labeling, 54, 112–13, 117, 123, 147; quality standards and, 45–48
Labor Advisory Board, 38, 39
Labor Department, 88–89, 214n56
labor movement, xi, 89, 90–91, 92, 193; CU links to, 80, 93, 94, 105, 162–63

labor standards, 21. *See also* minimum wage
labor unions, 39, 162, 190; CR strike and, 83–84, 85, 86, 87, 88–89
Ladies' Home Journal (magazine), 5, 8, 27
Lambert Pharmaceuticals, 129, 165
Lang, Chester H., 100–101
Larkin soap, 6
Larrabee, C. B., 33, 41, 61–62, 63, 202; on consumer movement, 115, 118–19. *See also Printers' Ink* (trade publication)
Lash, Joseph P., 166–67
Latshaw, Stanley, 35
Lea, Clarence F., 149
Lea bill (HR 3143), 149–52, 207
League of Women Shoppers, 163, 166, 167
League of Women Voters, 108, 115
Lears, T. J. Jackson, 18, 32
Lee, Ivy, 12, 13
legislative developments (1933–38), 205–7. *See also* federal regulation; specific laws
Liberty (magazine), 165
Lifebuoy soap, 129
Link, Henry, 107
Listerine antiseptic, 129, 155, 165
living standards, 31, 93, 98, 101
lobbying, xi, xiii, 110, 138, 190, 196; current expansion of, 193–94; by drug interests, 146, 151; patent-medicine lobby, 8–9, 55, 66, 68, 70, 141
Long, Huey, 142
Lord and Thomas (ad agency), 99
Lund, Robert, 99, 165
Lynd, Helen Merrell, 20, 124, 136, 202
Lynd, Robert S., 26, 39, 44, 107, 114, 202; as author, 20, 23, 202; on commercialism in schools, 124, 136; on grading controversy, 45, 46; Matthews report and, 168; on Tugwell bill, 65, 69

MacLellan, K. F., 67
McCarran bill (S 580), 139, 140, 206
McCarran-Jenckes bill (S 2858), 75, 150, 205
McChesney, Robert, ix
McClure's (magazine), 5, 8
McFadden Publishing Group, 97
McGovern, Charles, 7
McInerny, Kathleen, 167
McNair, Malcolm P., 103
McReynolds, Samuel D., 151
R. H. Macy and Co., 112

magazines, 10, 64, 66; advertising revenue for, x, 5–6. *See also* specific titles

Mann, Horace, 124

manufacturers, 3, 8, 23, 69, 214n56; brand-name goods and, 6, 32, 125; commercialism in schools and, 127–29, 131, 132; consumers and, 6–7, 21, 115; false claims by, x, 27, 54; food and drug, 34, 75, 139, 140, 143, 150, 154; labor policies of, 90, 93; misbranding by, 50; product testing by, 110; public relations and, 99–100; regulation and, 56, 78, 152, 157; World War II and, 185. *See also* drug manufacturers; National Association of Manufacturers (NAM); specific manufacturers

March, P. C., 142

Marchand, Roland, 7, 17, 30

marketing campaigns, 6

Marlies, Charles, 94

Marmola (diet product), 50, 51

Marsh, Benjamin, 74

Marxists, 35. *See also* Communism

Maslow, Will, 149

Mason, Noah M., 161

mass media, 65, 77, 107, 170, 194; advertising revenue for, x, xii, 34; boycott of CU by, 95, 168; national advertising and, 5, 155; patent-medicine advertising and, 8; public relations and, 12, 102; regulation of advertising by, 62–64, 139; Tugwell bill and, 67. *See also* newspapers; radio; television

mass production, 1, 7

Matthews, J. B., 160, 174, 190, 204; as author, 91–92, 169, 202; CR strike and, 83, 84–85, 86, 87–88; Dies Committee and, 164–72

Matthews report, 164–72

Maynard, Proctor W., 125

Mead bill (HR 3972), 139, 206

meatpacking industry, 9

media system, vii, 5. *See also* mass media

Meet the Consumer (play), 110

Men and Machines (Chase), 23

mergers and consolidations, 3–4

middle class, 10, 18, 112, 174, 189; consumer movement and, xi, 83, 92, 189; Progressives and, 2, 8, 12; women, 5, 33

Middletown (Lynd & Lynd), 20, 23, 202

Milk Consumers Protective League/Committee, 163, 167

Mills, C. Wright, 186

Milton Bradley Company, 135

minimum wage, 21, 36, 85

misbranding, 50, 54

modernity, advertisers and, 17, 101

Montgomery, Donald E., 120, 167, 168

Mosier, Harold G., 161

muckraking journalism, 8–9, 10, 12

Muncie, Indiana, 20

Nader, Ralph, 191–92, 194, 195

Nation (magazine), 36, 68, 84

national advertisers, 2–7, 15, 155. *See also* advertising industry

National Association of Broadcasters, 66

National Association of Manufacturers (NAM), 10, 99, 107, 115, 116, 194; anti-Communism in, 159, 162, 163, 168, 172, 173, 179, 180–81, 182; Committee on Educational Cooperation (CEC), 175–78, 200

National Association of Retail Druggists, 145

National Better Business Bureau (NBBB), 95, 115, 126, 202–3; Business-Consumer Conference and, 119, 122; fair trade codes and, 41; regulation and, 56, 59–60

National Canners Association, 132

National Conference on Consumer Education, 116–17, 201

National Consumer News (newsletter), 112–13

National Consumer-Retailer Council, 113–14

National Consumers' League (NCL), 10–11, 21, 90, 97, 203

National Council of Women, 113, 115

National Editorial Association, 76

National Education Association, 176

National Foundation of Religion and Labor, 90

National Industrial Information Committee, 107

National Industrial Recovery Act, 41

National Labor Relations Board, 89

National Publishers' Association, 76

National Recovery Administration (NRA), 22, 37–44, 77, 90–91, 203; advertising under, 40–42; Blue Eagle program, 41–42, 44; fair trade codes and, 37–38, 40–41, 43–44, 60. *See also* Consumers' Advisory Board (CAB)

National Wholesale Liquor Dealers Association, 9

NBBB. *See* National Better Business Bureau

NBC (radio network), 68, 104, 110, 119, 134, 135

neoliberalism, 195

New Deal, 37, 44, 58, 70, 161; business antipathy for, 99, 116, 142–43, 243n96. *See also* National Recovery Administration

New Republic (magazine), 14, 68, 84, 142–43

newspapers, 64, 77, 85, 120, 151; advertising revenue for, x, 5, 9; Tugwell bill and, 55, 65, 68

Newsweek (magazine), 36, 180

New York Board of Trade, 66

New York Herald Tribune (newspaper), 115

New York State Economic Council, 178, 180, 273n107

New York Times (newspaper), 36, 95

New York World's Fair (1939), 96–97

Nims, Harry D., 58

NRA. *See* National Recovery Administration (NRA)

oligopolistic markets, 3, 4–5, 106, 191; advertising and, x, xiii, xiv, 29, 32, 103

O'Mahoney bill (S 10), 150

100,000,000 Guinea Pigs (Kallet & Schlink), 27, 30, 34, 50, 69, 108, 174, 202

Our Master's Voice: Advertising (Rorty), 34, 35

Packard, Vance, 195

Pall Mall Cigarettes, 133–34

Palmer, Dewey H., 92, 94, 124–25, 131, 203; CR strike and, 83–84, 85, 87

Palmer, Frank L., 43

Parent-Teacher Association, 133

parity advertising, 4, 102–3

Parker, George F., 12

Partners in Plunder: The Cost of Business Dictatorship (Matthews & Shallcross), 91–92, 169, 202

patent-medicine lobby, 8–9, 55, 66, 68, 70, 141

patriotism, 17, 185, 186, 187

Pearl, Raymond, 34

Pease, Otis, 60, 155, 171

Peiss, Kathy, 7

People's Capitalism, 187

People's Lobby, 74, 142

Phillips, M. C., 82, 85, 113, 154, 160, 190; on labor groups and CR, 83, 84, 91, 92; marriage to Schlink, 81, 93, 203, 204; photo of, 28; *Skin Deep*, 27, 35–36, 164, 203

political action committees (PACs), 193, 194

political debate, viii, ix, 89–90, 187

political economy, xiii

political lobbying. *See* lobbying

political power, 21

Pond's Cold Cream, 155

Pouchet, Gabriel, 71

PR. *See* public relations (PR)

Prentis, H. W., Jr., 181

press, xii, 13, 66. *See also* newspapers

Preston, W. G., 119

Previews of Science (film show), 100

price competition, 3, 4, 32

Printers' Ink (trade publication), 39, 40, 104, 181, 182, 243n104; on Copeland bill (S 5), 139, 141, 144, 146, 148; on *CUR* stories, 96; on importance of advertising, 100, 101; Larabee and, 33, 41, 61–62, 63, 115, 118–19, 202; Matthews report and, 168–69; Model Statute, 55, 56, 58, 63; on radio advertising, 30; on regulation, 57, 59, 62, 64, 73, 74–75, 149, 154; Schlink and, 34–35, 98; on schools, 126

Procter and Gamble, 5, 6

product information, viii, xi, 32, 119, 156; advertising and, 21, 23–24; consumer demand for, 27, 48, 103, 106; oligopolistic markets and, xiii, xiv. *See also* grade labeling

product testing, 47, 89, 110, 162, 221n67; by Consumers Union, 94, 95, 96, 188, 189–90

profit motive, 3, 5, 11, 66, 75, 122. *See also* capitalism

Progressive Era, x–xi, 2, 12, 196; consumer activism in, xiv, 7–11, 21

propaganda, 11–15, 24, 78, 176; advertising as, viii, 15; anti-advertising, 34, 117, 125–26, 179; anti-business, 175; business, 181; Communist, 35, 163, 166, 167; consumer education and, 120; consumer movement, 108, 109; educational, 98; public relations and, 99; un-American, 161

Proprietary Association, 9, 66, 67, 139, 141

Psychological Corporation, 107

Psychological Sales Barometer (newsletter), 107

psychological testing, 16–17
Public Citizen (advocacy group), 195
public health, 77
public opinion, 107; of advertising, vii, 29, 138, 157–58; PR and, xiii, 65; of regulation, 58, 60, 69
Public Opinion Quarterly (academic publication), 111
public relations (PR), 33, 63, 98–105, 114, 119, 193; advertising industry and, viii–ix, xi, xiii, 2, 19–20, 101–5, 106, 139, 185, 189; business-backed "institutes," 133; commercial propaganda and, 11–15, 98; divide-and-conquer strategy, xi–xii. *See also* industrial front groups
publishing industry, 35–36, 42, 76, 150; regulation and, 56, 59, 62, 63, 64; Tugwell bill and, 65–66

quality standards, 45–48. *See also* grade labeling

radio programs, 64, 68, 104, 112, 116, 120, 134–36; advertising on, 30, 75, 141, 150
Raladam Company, 50
Reagan, Ronald, 195
Red-scare campaigns, 159–83; "American way" and, 175–78, 179, 180–81; conservative business groups, 172–73; Dies Committee and, 159–64, 166–72, 182, 189, 201; Matthews report, 164–72; in schools, 174–82; textbooks and, 178, 179–82
Reemployment Agreement, 36–37
regulation. *See* federal regulation; self-regulation; specific laws
Reid, Margaret G., 119–20
Republican Party, 37, 193
Resinol Chemical Company, 131
retailers, front groups and, 111–14, 115
Richardson, Anna Steese, 107–10, 174–75, 200
Ringwald, Mabel Crews, 114
Roby, Ralph W., 180–82
Rogers, Donald, 83, 85
Roosevelt, Eleanor, 67
Roosevelt, Franklin Delano, 22, 36–37, 49, 116; administration of, xiv, 90, 92; brain trust of, 53, 78; Copeland bill (S 5) and, 142, 145, 147–48; NRA and, 39, 41, 42, 44; Tugwell bill and, 74, 76, 79. *See also* New Deal

Roosevelt, Theodore, 9
"The Roots of Liberty" (school curriculum), 176
Rorty, James, 32, 34, 35, 44, 119, 203; regulation and, 62, 67, 75
Rose, Norman S., 179
Rubicam, Raymond, 14
Rugg, Harold, 178–80
Rumsey, Mary Harriman, 43
Russell, Richard B., Jr., 143
Russell, William F., 175
Russian Revolution (1917), 82

S 1944. *See* Tugwell bill (S 1944)
Safeguards against Subversive Activities (newsletter), 161
St. Louis Star-Times (newspaper), 169
Sales Management (trade publication), 47, 112
Samuel, Lawrence R., 188
Saturday Evening Post (newspaper), 134
Schlink, Frederick J., 33, 42–45, 46, 104, 178, 190; anti-Communism of, 35, 83, 98, 118, 160, 162–63, 180; as author, 23–24, 27, 34, 50, 69, 200, 204; beginnings of CR and, 24–27; biographical sketch of, 203–4; CAB and, 42–43, 44, 200; on commercialism in schools, 125, 131, 133; consumer legislation and, 51–52, 67, 68, 73, 78, 142; CR employees' strike and, 84, 87–88, 89–91, 160; leadership style of, 81, 82, 93, 137; marriage to Phillips, 81, 93, 203, 204; Matthews report and, 165, 167, 168, 169–70; on NRA strategy, 38; photo of, 25, 26; *Printer's Ink* and, 34–35. *See also* Consumers' Research Inc.
schools, commercialism in, xii, 124–36; advertisers and, 125–26, 127, 129, 131, 133–34, 136; home economics courses and, 129–33; industry-sponsored materials and, 124, 125, 126, 127–28, 129–33, 134; manufacturers and, 127–29, 131; radio programs, 134–36; universities and colleges, 125–27, 134, 136
schools, Red-scare campaign in, 174–82; American way of life and, 175–76, 177–78; NAM and, 175–78, 179, 180–81; Rugg and, 178–80; textbooks and, 178–82
Scott, Walter Dill, 16
The Secrets of Citrus (film), 132
The Seeing Eye (radio program), 134

self-regulation, xiv, 58–65, 101, 140; Advertising Review Committee and, 54–55, 62; mass media and, 62–64; truth-in-advertising movement and, 58–59, 65, 229n.53
Senate, U.S., 140, 142, 145; Commerce Committee, 75, 76–77, 148, 151, 152; Committee on Interstate Commerce, 56, 152; legislative development (1933–35), 205–7. *See also* Congress, U.S.
Shallcross, Ruth, 91–92, 202
Short Talks on Advertising (radio program), 120
Simplex Shoe Company, 129
Sinclair, Upton, 9
Sirovich, William I., 53, 72
Sirovich bill (HR 7426), 53, 72, 75, 206
Skin Deep (Phillips), 27, 35–36, 81, 164, 174, 203
Sklar, Kathryn Kish, 11
Sloan, Alfred P., 117, 180
Alfred P. Sloan Foundation, 116, 123, 201
Sloan, Harold S., 117, 122
Smith, Alfred E., 70
Smith, Crump, 112–13
social class. *See* middle class; working class
social influence, 34, 103
Socialism, fears of, 40, 90
Sokolsky, George E., 165, 172
Southern Pacific Railway, 128
speakers' bureaus, 120
Spectro-Chrome (trade publication), 66
Spool Cotton Company, 128
Standard Brands, 72, 155
standard of living, 31, 93, 98, 101, 188
Starnes, Joe, 161
Starr, Mark, 91
Stephens, Hubert D., 76–77
Stephens College, Missouri, 116, 123, 201
Strasser, Susan, 6
strike at Consumers' Research Inc., xii, xiv, 80, 81–92, 160, 162; events leading to, 81–84; labor unions and, 83–84, 85, 86, 87, 88–89, 162; photos of, 86, 88; Schlink's response to, 87–88, 89–91
Sunkist, 132
Supreme Court, U.S., 50, 154, 157, 187

tax breaks, for advertisers, 14, 185, 186, 214n56
teachers: academic freedom and, 176–77, 181; commercialism and, 124, 128, 129–33; consumer activism by, 174. *See also under* education; schools
Technical, Editorial and Officer Assistants' Union, 83–84
Telecommunications Act (1996), 195
television, 188
testing. *See* product testing
textbooks: academic freedom and, 176–77, 181; burning of, 179–80; commercialism in, 125, 126, 127, 134; Red scare and, 178, 179–82. *See also* educational materials
textile labeling, 45. *See also* grade labeling
third-party techniques, xi, xiv, 107. *See also* industry front groups
Thomas, J. Parnell, 161, 163
Thomas, Norman, 90
J. Walter Thompson (ad agency), 18–19, 22, 61, 154
Tide (trade publication), 35, 40, 89, 92, 165
Time (magazine), 36
toothpaste advertising, 103
trademark, 16, 131. *See also* brand names
Tragedy of Waste (Chase), 23
Transportation Progress (textbook), 127
Treason in the Textbooks (pamphlet), 180
Trumbull, Walter, 83
truth, public relations and, 13
truth in advertising, x, 156. *See also* false advertising
truth-in-advertising movement, 58–59, 65, 104, 229n53
Tugwell, Rexford G., 26, 44, 49, 53, 78; Copeland bill (S 5) and, 144, 145, 146; Food and Drugs Act and, 146, 204. *See also* Tugwell bill
Tugwell bill (S 1944), 49–58, 65–79, 80, 204; advertising industry reaction to, 54–55, 56–58, 72, 78–79; Capper bill (S 1592), 55–57, 205; Copeland revision of (S 5), 138–39, 141, 142, 144; Copeland revision of (S 2000), 73–75, 78, 206; hearings on, 69–73; Wheeler-Lea amendment and, 150, 156, 157
Tydings bill (S 100), 150

underconsumption, 36, 37
Uneeda Biscuit, 6
Union College, 136
United Fruit Company, 129

United Medicine Manufacturers of America, 67

U.S. Chamber of Commerce, 99, 160–61, 162, 177, 204; aggressive leadership of, 193

universities and colleges, 125–27, 134, 136, 174–75, 178, 194. *See also* education; specific institutions

University of Wisconsin, 125

Unsafe at Any Speed (Nader), 191

Valenstein, Lawrence, 60

Valentine v. Chrestensen, 157

Veblen, Thorstein, xiii

Vogel, David, 194

Voorhis, Jerry, 171–72

Wadsworth, Gerald B., 132

wages, 82; minimum, 36, 85, 93

Wallace, Henry A., 57, 140

Walsh, David I., 143

Walsh, Richard, 35–36

Walsh bill (S 2909), 143, 207

Warbasse, 104

Warne, Colston E., 27, 92, 118, 192, 201; as president of CU, 96, 117, 136, 186, 204

Washington Star (newspaper), 145, 148

Welch, J. A., 109

West, Paul W., 57–58

Wheatena Company, 129

Wheeler, Burton, 152, 153

Wheeler bill (S 1077), 151–57, 207

Wheeler-Lea Amendment (S 1077), 148–58, 183, 187–88, 207; advertising industry and, 137, 150, 153, 158; false advertising and, 150, 151, 153, 154, 157; Food and Drug Act of 1906 and, 79, 152, 157; FTC and, xv, 149–57; Lea bill (HR 3143) and, 149–52, 201; passage of, viii, 79, 152

Wiley, Harvey W., 8, 9

Willis, Paul S., 166, 172

The Willingness to Share (radio program), 134

Wilson, Woodrow, 13, 200

Wilson Company, 129

women: as consumers, 17–18, 31, 104, 108, 109; effect of advertising on, 196; emotional appeals and, 18, 31; as home economics teachers, 129, 132; middle class, 5, 33

women's groups, 10, 39, 107, 108, 119, 132; consumers, 163, 166, 167; Copeland bill (S 5) and, 140, 141–42, 144, 147, 148; CR and, 26, 123; Dies Committee and, 169; industry front groups and, 111, 112, 113, 114–15; regulation and, 68, 69, 75. *See also* specific group

Women's Home Companion, 27, 35, 107, 109, 115

women's magazines, 5, 10, 27, 35–36, 221n67. *See also* specific magazines

working class, xi, 7, 8. *See also under* labor

work week, 36, 85

World's Fair (Chicago, 1933), 68, 140

World's Fair (New York, 1939), 96–97

World War I, 13–14, 200; excess-profits tax in, 14, 214n56; psychological testing in, 16–17

World War II, 185–87

yellow-dog contract, 85

You and Industry (pamphlet), 175

Young, Bradford, 90

Young, James W., 103

Young America (newsletter), 177

Young Women's Christian Association, 113

Your Money's Worth: A Study in the Waste of the Consumer's Dollars (Schlink & Chase), 23–24, 174, 204

Zehntbauer, J. A., 109–10

INGER L. STOLE is an assistant professor at the Institute of Communications Research at the University of Illinois at Urbana-Champaign. Her work in the advertising and consumer studies fields has been published in *Advertising and Society Review;* the *Communications Review; Consumption, Markets, & Culture,* and *Historical Journal of Film, Radio and Television.* She lives in Urbana, Illinois, with her husband and two daughters.

THE HISTORY OF COMMUNICATION

Selling Free Enterprise: The Business Assault on Labor and Liberalism, 1945–60
   Elizabeth A. Fones-Wolf
Last Rights: Revisiting *Four Theories of the Press*   Edited by John C. Nerone
"We Called Each Other Comrade": Charles H. Kerr & Company, Radical Publishers
   Allen Ruff
WCFL, Chicago's Voice of Labor, 1926–78   Nathan Godfried
Taking the Risk Out of Democracy: Corporate Propaganda versus Freedom
   and Liberty   Alex Carey; edited by Andrew Lohrey
Media, Market, and Democracy in China: Between the Party Line and the
   Bottom Line   Yuezhi Zhao
Print Culture in a Diverse America   Edited by James P. Danky and Wayne A. Wiegand
The Newspaper Indian: Native American Identity in the Press, 1820–90
   John M. Coward
E. W. Scripps and the Business of Newspapers   Gerald J. Baldasty
Picturing the Past: Media, History, and Photography   Edited by Bonnie Brennen and
   Hanno Hardt
Rich Media, Poor Democracy: Communication Politics in Dubious Times
   Robert W. McChesney
Silencing the Opposition: Antinuclear Movements and the Media in the Cold War
   Andrew Rojecki
Citizen Critics: Literary Public Spheres   Rosa A. Eberly
Communities of Journalism: A History of American Newspapers and Their Readers
   David Paul Nord
From Yahweh to Yahoo!: The Religious Roots of the Secular Press   Doug Underwood
The Struggle for Control of Global Communication: The Formative Century
   Jill Hills
Fanatics and Fire-eaters: Newspapers and the Coming of the Civil War
   Lorman A. Ratner and Dwight L. Teeter Jr.
Media Power in Central America   Rick Rockwell and Noreene Janus
The Consumer Trap: Big Business Marketing in American Life   Michael Dawson
How Free Can the Press Be?   Randall P. Bezanson
Cultural Politics and the Mass Media: Alaska Native Voices   Patrick J. Daley and
   Beverly A. James
Journalism in the Movies   Matthew C. Ehrlich
Democracy, Inc.: The Press and Law in the Corporate Rationalization of the
   Public Sphere   David S. Allen
Investigated Reporting: Muckrakers, Regulators, and the Struggle over
   Television Documentary   Chad Raphael
Women Making News: Gender and Journalism in Modern Britain   Michelle Tusan
Advertising on Trial: Consumer Activism and Corporate Public Relations
   in the 1930s   Inger Stole

The University of Illinois Press
is a founding member of the
Association of American University Presses.

———————————————————————

Composed in 10.5/13 Adobe Minion
with Meta display
by Jim Proefrock
at the University of Illinois Press
Manufactured by Sheridan Books, Inc.

University of Illinois Press
1325 South Oak Street
Champaign, IL 61820-6903
www.press.uillinois.edu